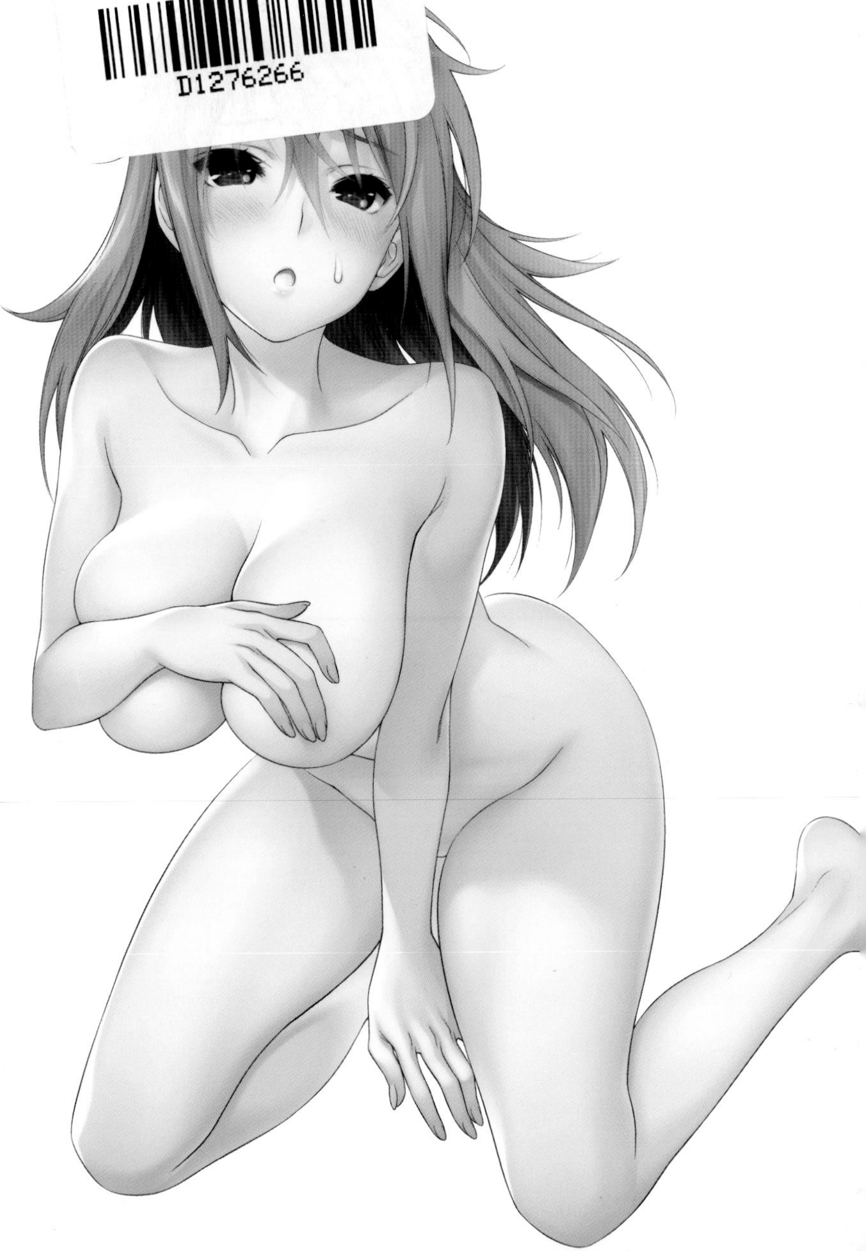

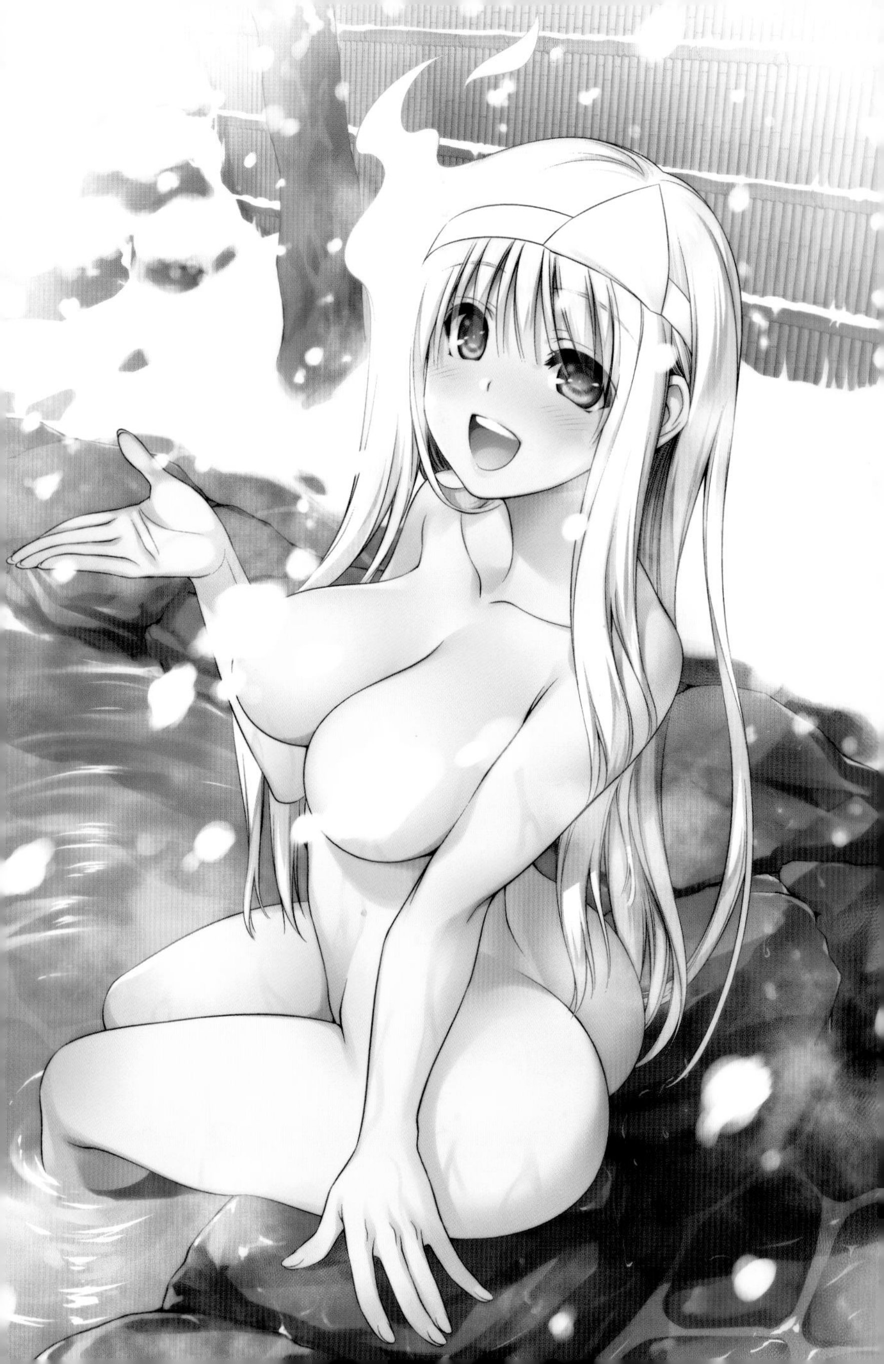

Yuuna and the Haunted Hot Springs

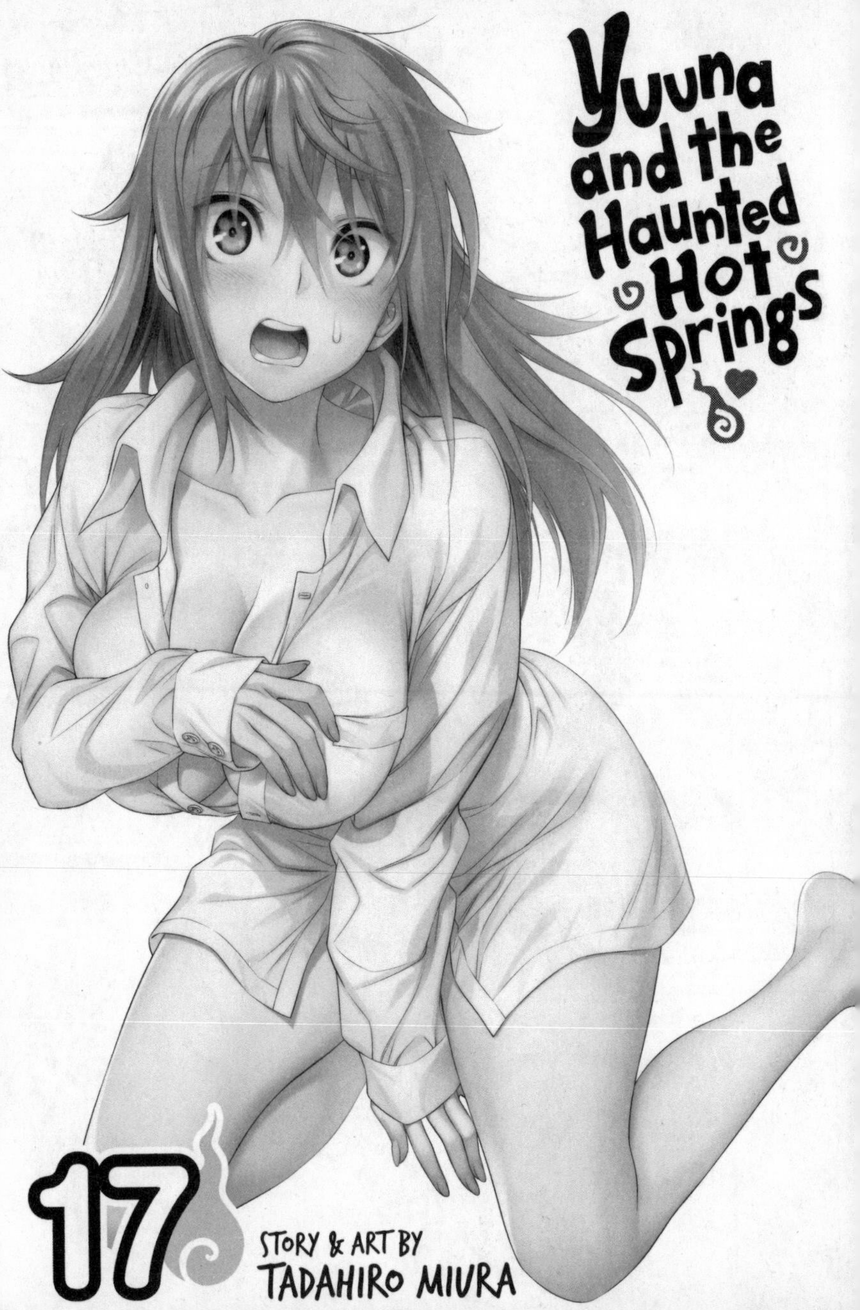

17

STORY & ART BY
TADAHIRO MIURA

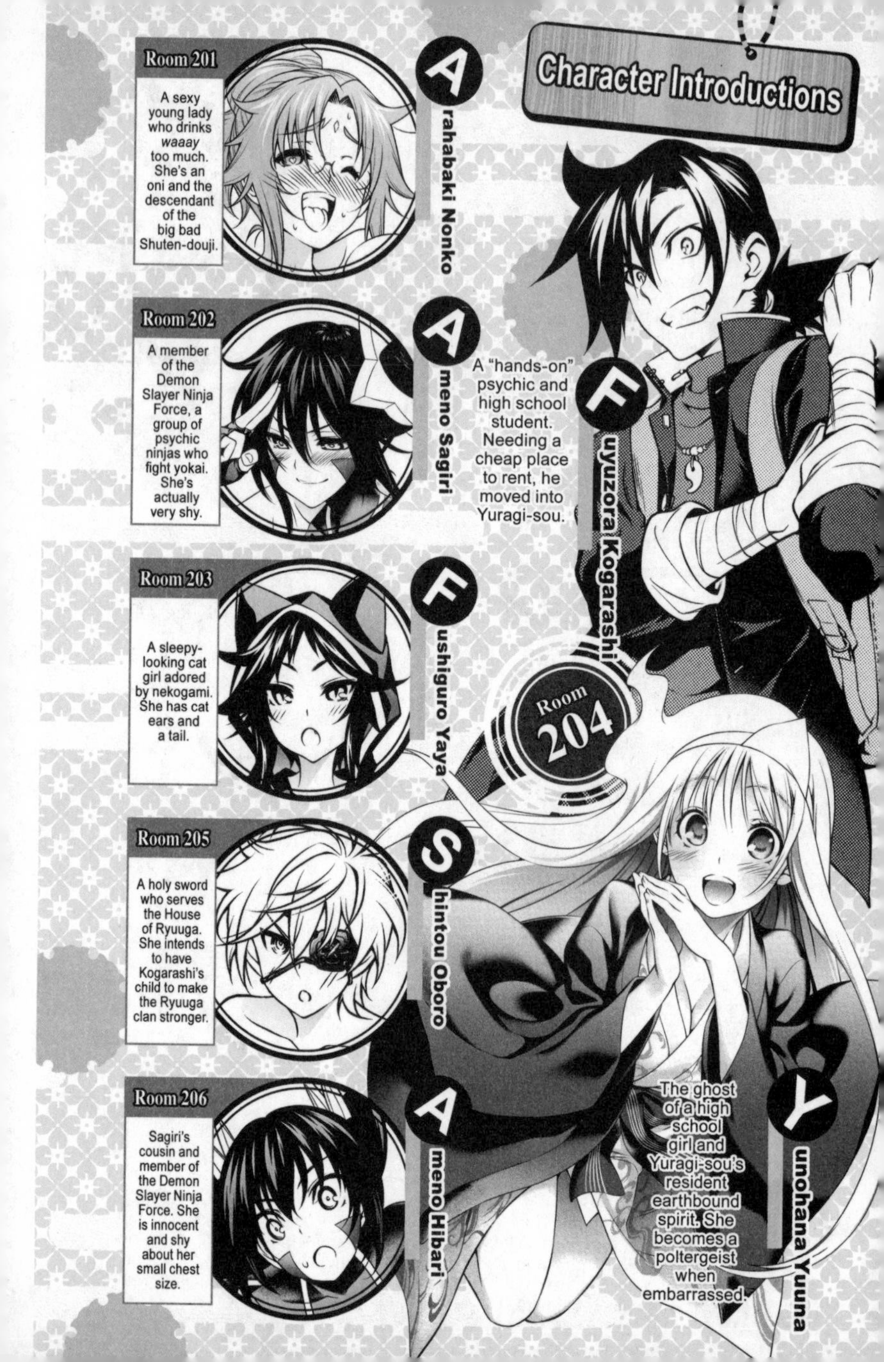
Character Introductions
Fuyuzora Kogarashi
A "hands-on" psychic and high school student. Needing a cheap place to rent, he moved into Yuragi-sou.
Room 204
Yunohana Yuuna
The ghost of a high school girl and Yuragi-sou's resident earthbound spirit. She becomes a poltergeist when embarrassed.
Room 201
Arahabaki Nonko
A sexy young lady who drinks *waaay* too much. She's an oni and the descendant of the big bad Shuten-douji.
Room 202
Ameno Sagiri
A member of the Demon Slayer Ninja Force, a group of psychic ninjas who fight yokai. She's actually very shy.
Room 203
Fushiguro Yaya
A sleepy-looking cat girl adored by nekogami. She has cat ears and a tail.
Room 205
Shintou Oboro
A holy sword who serves the House of Ryuuga. She intends to have Kogarashi's child to make the Ryuuga clan stronger.
Room 206
Ameno Hibari
Sagiri's cousin and member of the Demon Slayer Ninja Force. She is innocent and shy about her small chest size.

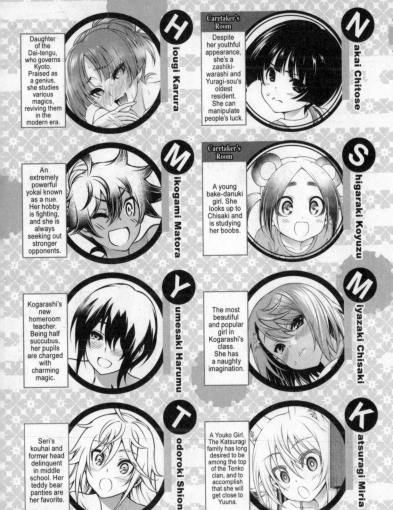

Nakai Chitose
Caretaker's Room
Despite her youthful appearance, she's a zashiki-warashi and Yuragi-sou's oldest resident. She can manipulate people's luck.
Hiougi Karura
Daughter of the Dai-tengu, who governs Kyoto. Praised as a genius, she studies various magics, reviving them in the modern era.
Shigaraki Koyuzu
Caretaker's Room
A young bake-danuki girl. She looks up to Chisaki and is studying her boobs.
Mikogami Matora
An extremely powerful yokai known as a nue. Her hobby is fighting, and she is always seeking out stronger opponents.
Miyazaki Chisaki
The most beautiful and popular girl in Kogarashi's class. She has a naughty imagination.
Yumesaki Harumu
Kogarashi's new homeroom teacher. Being half succubus, her pupils are charged with charming magic.
Katsuragi Miria
A Youko Girl. The Katsuragi family has long desired to be among the top of the Tenko clan, and to accomplish that she will get close to Yuuna.
Todoroki Shion
Seri's kouhai and former head delinquent in middle school. Her teddy bear panties are her favorite.

Summary

While living in Yuragi-sou, a hot spring inn-turned-boardinghouse with an unusual history, "hands-on" psychic Fuyuzora Kogarashi promised Yuuna, the earthbound spirit of a high school girl, that he would make her happy and help her pass on. Sagiri is forced into a political marriage with Shakuhito, the second son of the Yoinozakas, one of the three great families. However, the Yoinozaka patriarch planned the wedding to gather the Yuragi-sou residents together and wipe them out. Sagiri realizes her love for Kogarashi, and with his help, beats Shakuhito.

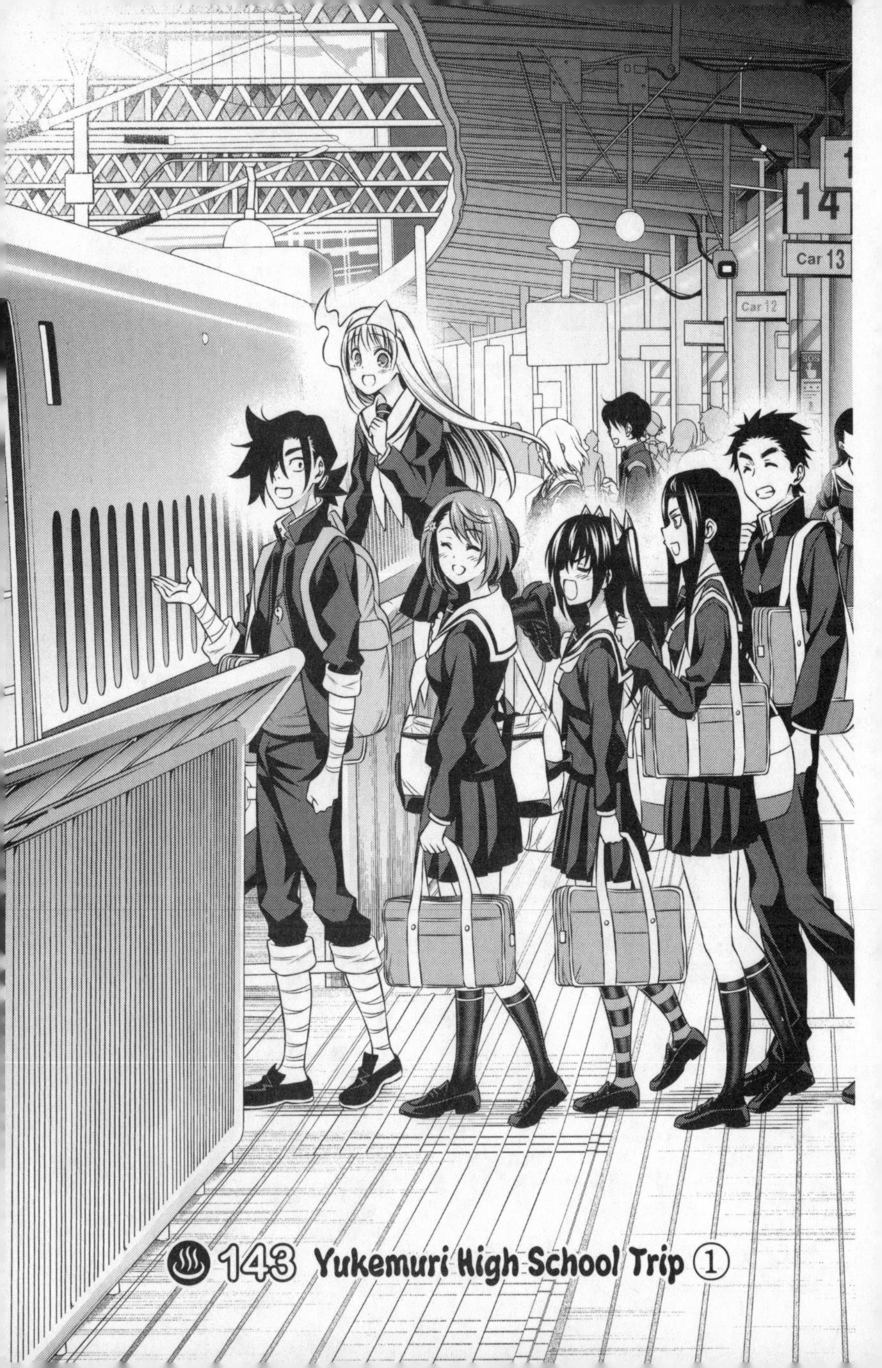
14
Car 13
Car 12

143 Yukemuri High School Trip ①

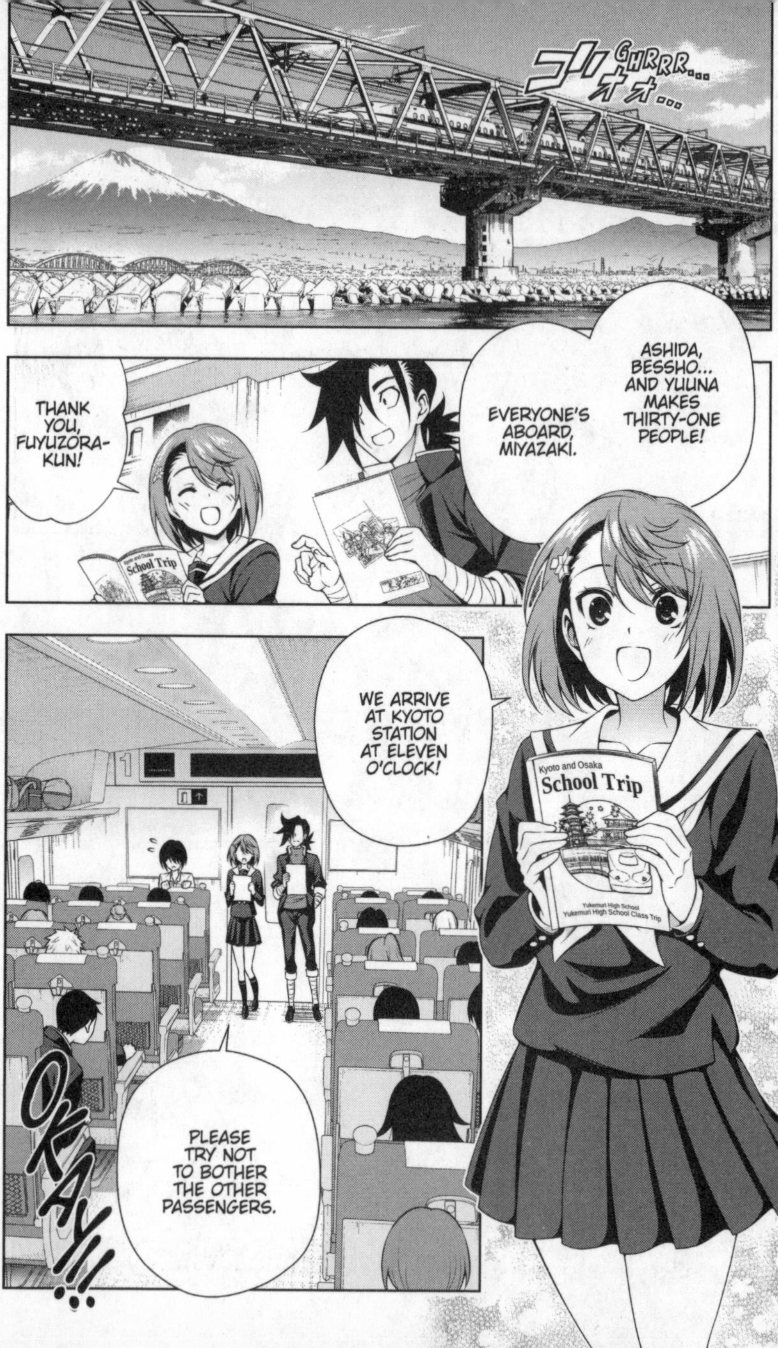
GHRRR...
ASHIDA, BESSHO... AND YUUNA MAKES THIRTY-ONE PEOPLE!
EVERYONE'S ABOARD, MIYAZAKI.
THANK YOU, FUYUZORA-KUN!
Kyoto and Osaka School Trip
WE ARRIVE AT KYOTO STATION AT ELEVEN O'CLOCK!
Kyoto and Osaka School Trip
Yukemuri High School
Yukemuri High School Class Trip
PLEASE TRY NOT TO BOTHER THE OTHER PASSENGERS.
OKAY!!!

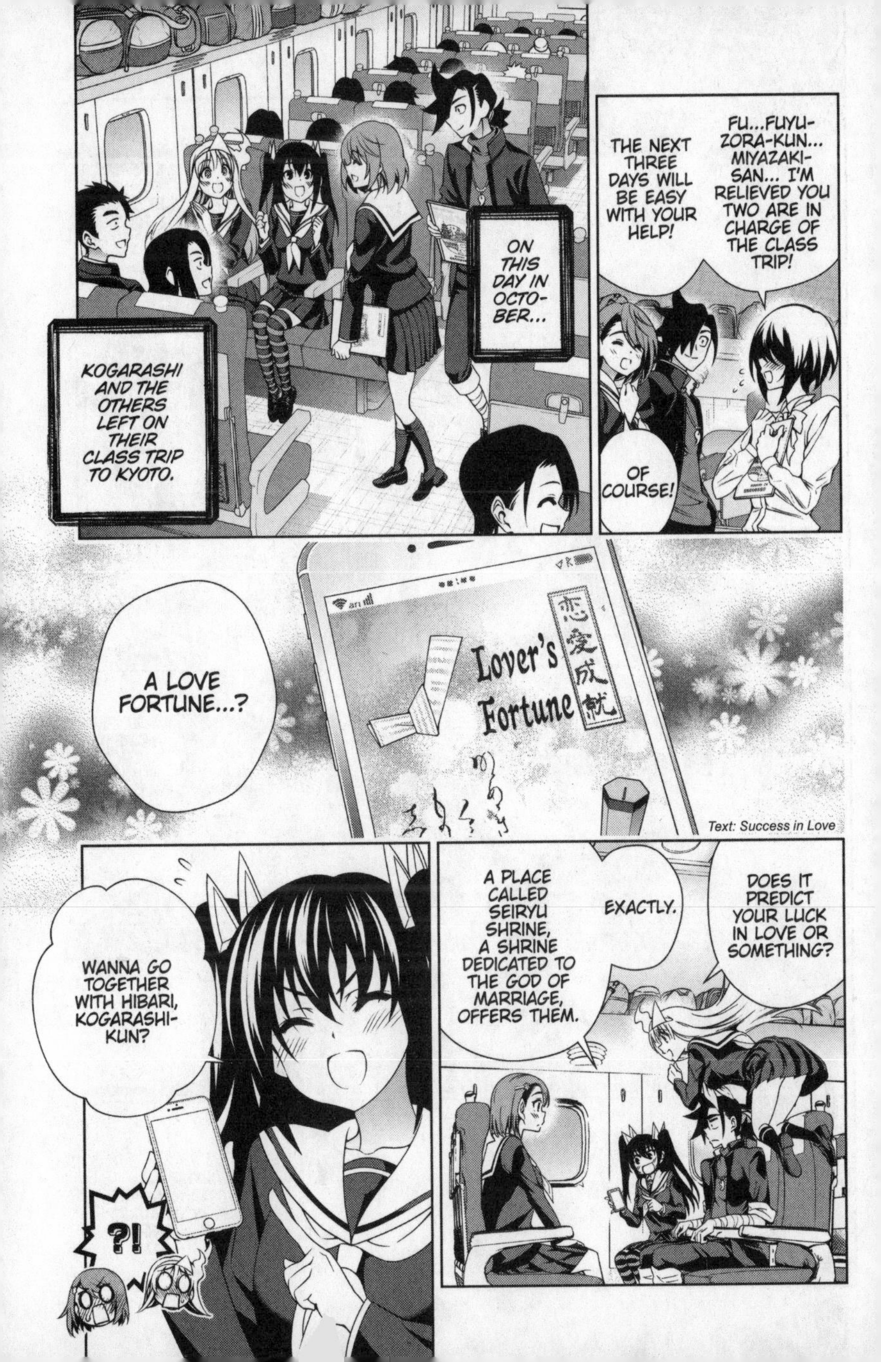
FU...FUYU-ZORA-KUN... MIYAZAKI-SAN... I'M RELIEVED YOU TWO ARE IN CHARGE OF THE CLASS TRIP!
THE NEXT THREE DAYS WILL BE EASY WITH YOUR HELP!
OF COURSE!
ON THIS DAY IN OCTOBER...
KOGARASHI AND THE OTHERS LEFT ON THEIR CLASS TRIP TO KYOTO.
恋愛成就
Lover's Fortune
A LOVE FORTUNE...?
Text: Success in Love
DOES IT PREDICT YOUR LUCK IN LOVE OR SOMETHING?
EXACTLY.
A PLACE CALLED SEIRYU SHRINE, A SHRINE DEDICATED TO THE GOD OF MARRIAGE, OFFERS THEM.
WANNA GO TOGETHER WITH HIBARI, KOGARASHI-KUN?
?!

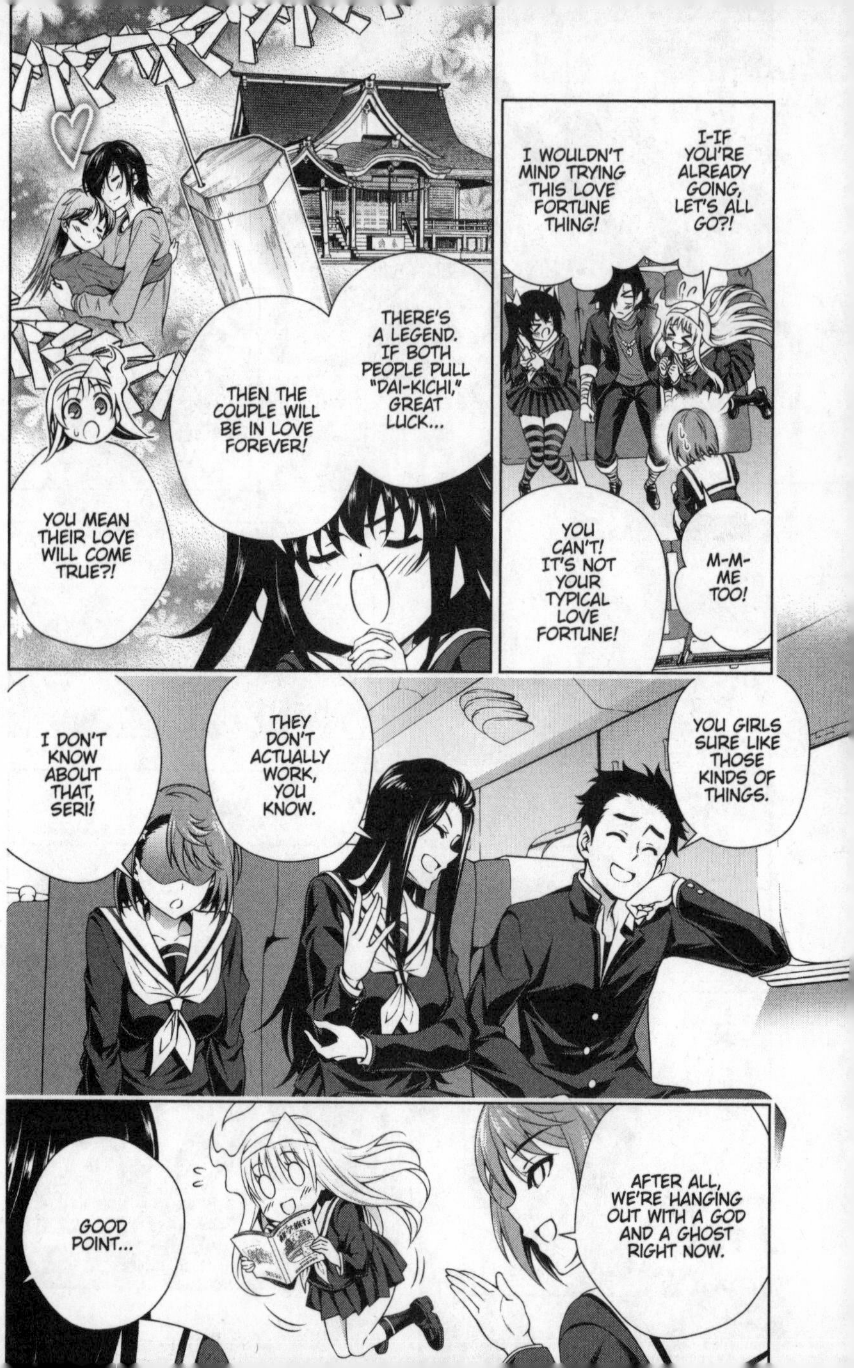
I-IF YOU'RE ALREADY GOING, LET'S ALL GO?!
I WOULDN'T MIND TRYING THIS LOVE FORTUNE THING!
M-M-ME TOO!
YOU CAN'T! IT'S NOT YOUR TYPICAL LOVE FORTUNE!
THERE'S A LEGEND. IF BOTH PEOPLE PULL "DAI-KICHI," GREAT LUCK...
THEN THE COUPLE WILL BE IN LOVE FOREVER!
YOU MEAN THEIR LOVE WILL COME TRUE?!
YOU GIRLS SURE LIKE THOSE KINDS OF THINGS.
THEY DON'T ACTUALLY WORK, YOU KNOW.
I DON'T KNOW ABOUT THAT, SERI!
AFTER ALL, WE'RE HANGING OUT WITH A GOD AND A GHOST RIGHT NOW.
GOOD POINT...

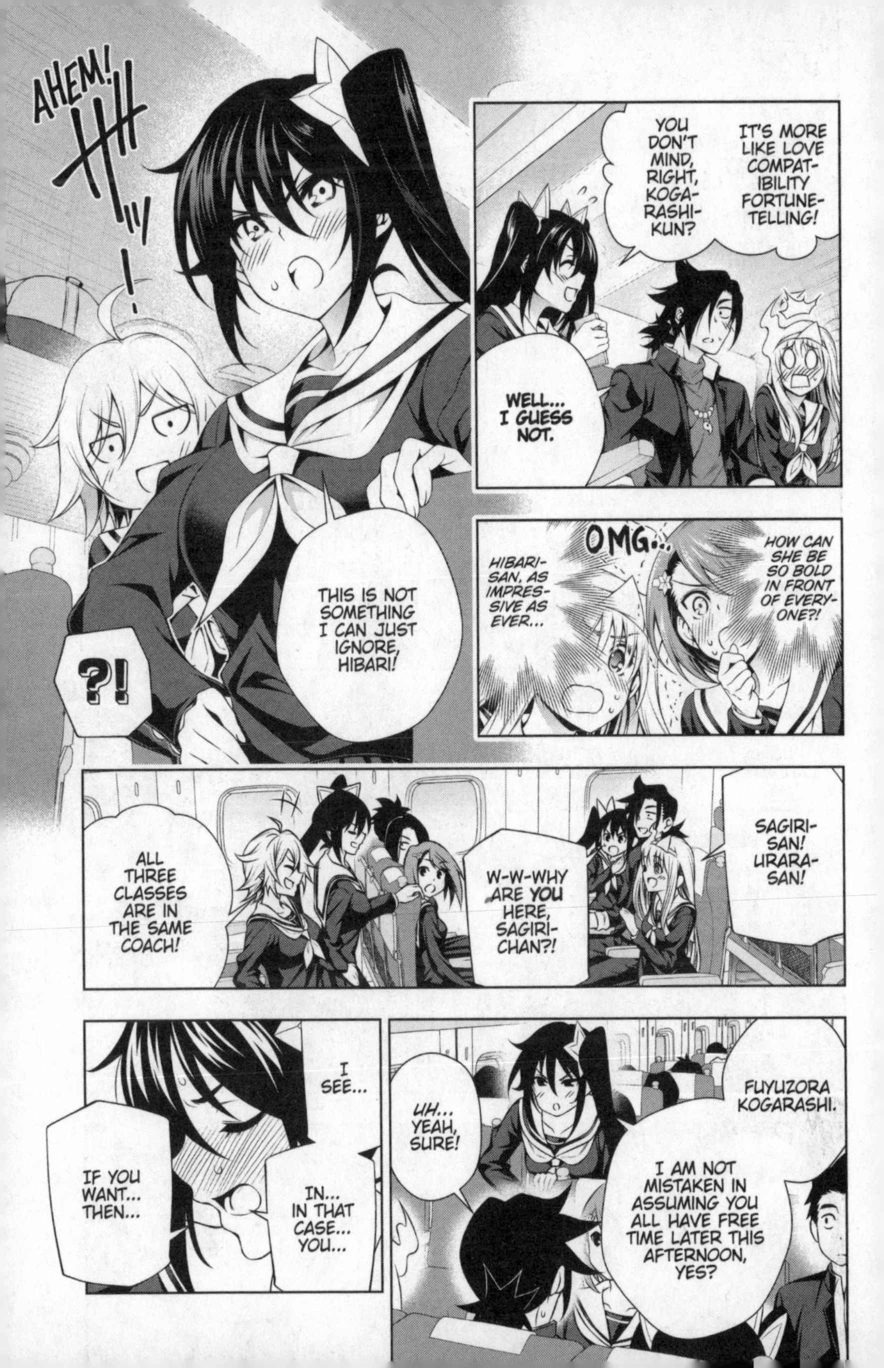
IT'S MORE LIKE LOVE COMPAT-IBILITY FORTUNE-TELLING!
YOU DON'T MIND, RIGHT, KOGA-RASHI-KUN?
WELL... I GUESS NOT.
HOW CAN SHE BE SO BOLD IN FRONT OF EVERY-ONE?!
OMG...
HIBARI-SAN, AS IMPRES-SIVE AS EVER...
AHEM!
THIS IS NOT SOMETHING I CAN JUST IGNORE, HIBARI!
?!
SAGIRI-SAN! URARA-SAN!
W-W-WHY ARE YOU HERE, SAGIRI-CHAN?!
ALL THREE CLASSES ARE IN THE SAME COACH!
FUYUZORA KOGARASHI.
I AM NOT MISTAKEN IN ASSUMING YOU ALL HAVE FREE TIME LATER THIS AFTERNOON, YES?
UH... YEAH, SURE!
I SEE...
IN... IN THAT CASE... YOU...
IF YOU WANT... THEN...

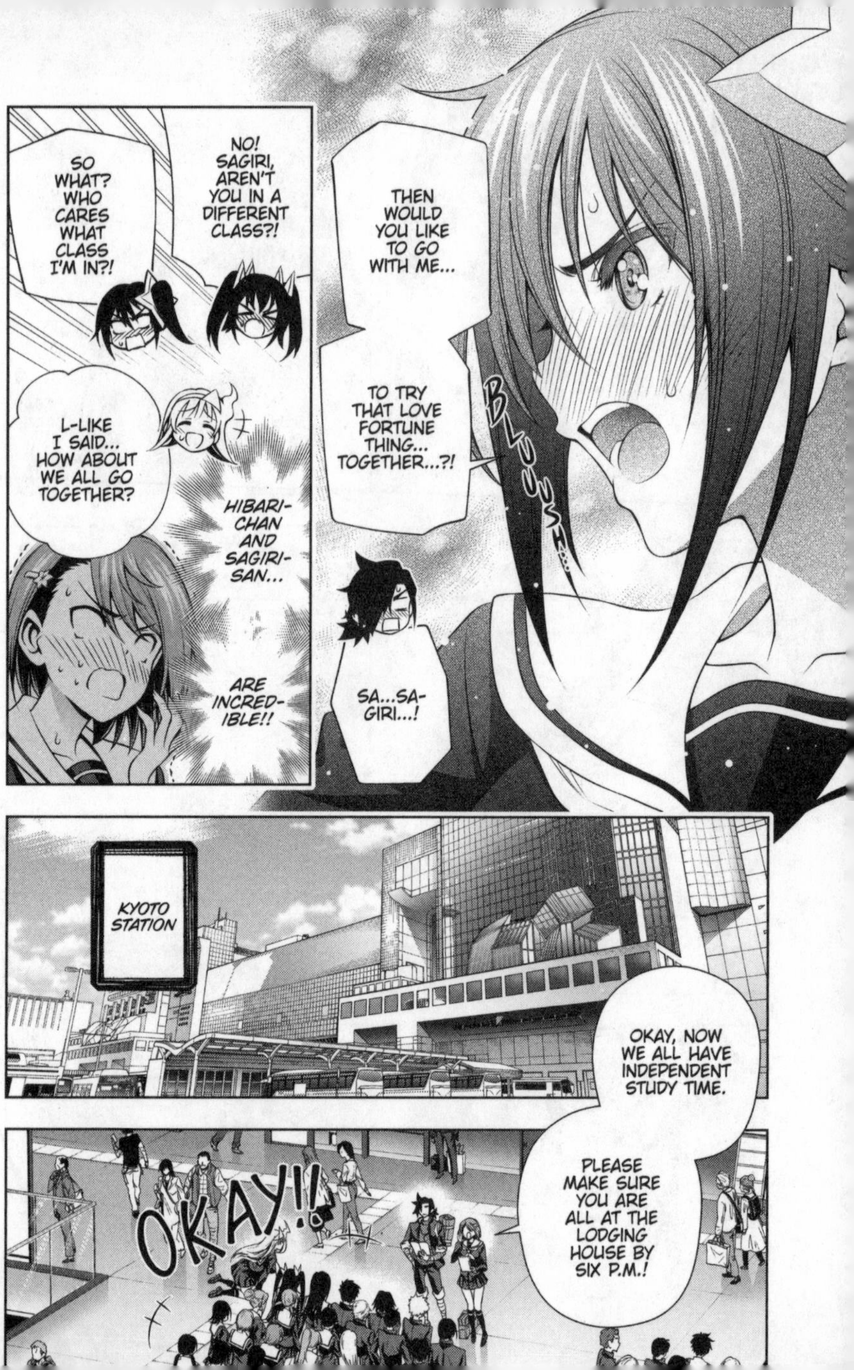
THEN WOULD YOU LIKE TO GO WITH ME...
TO TRY THAT LOVE FORTUNE THING... TOGETHER...?!
BLUUUSH
SA...SA-GIRI...!
NO! SAGIRI, AREN'T YOU IN A DIFFERENT CLASS?!
SO WHAT? WHO CARES WHAT CLASS I'M IN?!
L-LIKE I SAID... HOW ABOUT WE ALL GO TOGETHER?
HIBARI-CHAN AND SAGIRI-SAN...
ARE INCREDIBLE!!
KYOTO STATION
OKAY, NOW WE ALL HAVE INDEPENDENT STUDY TIME.
PLEASE MAKE SURE YOU ARE ALL AT THE LODGING HOUSE BY SIX P.M.!
OKAY!!

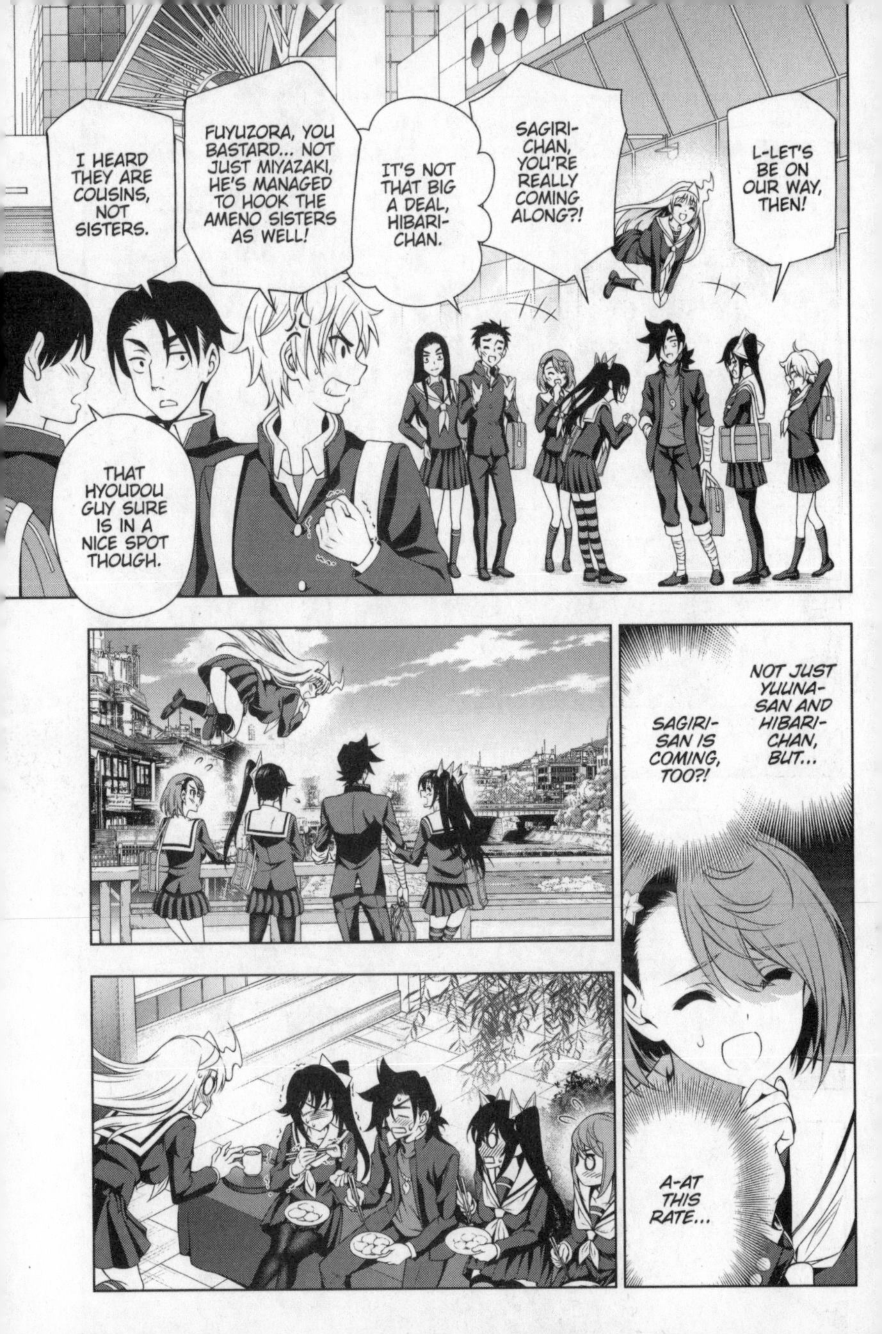
L-LET'S BE ON OUR WAY, THEN!
SAGIRI-CHAN, YOU'RE REALLY COMING ALONG?!
IT'S NOT THAT BIG A DEAL, HIBARI-CHAN.
FUYUZORA, YOU BASTARD... NOT JUST MIYAZAKI, HE'S MANAGED TO HOOK THE AMENO SISTERS AS WELL!
I HEARD THEY ARE COUSINS, NOT SISTERS.
THAT HYOUDOU GUY SURE IS IN A NICE SPOT THOUGH.
NOT JUST YUUNA-SAN AND HIBARI-CHAN, BUT...
SAGIRI-SAN IS COMING, TOO?!
A-AT THIS RATE...

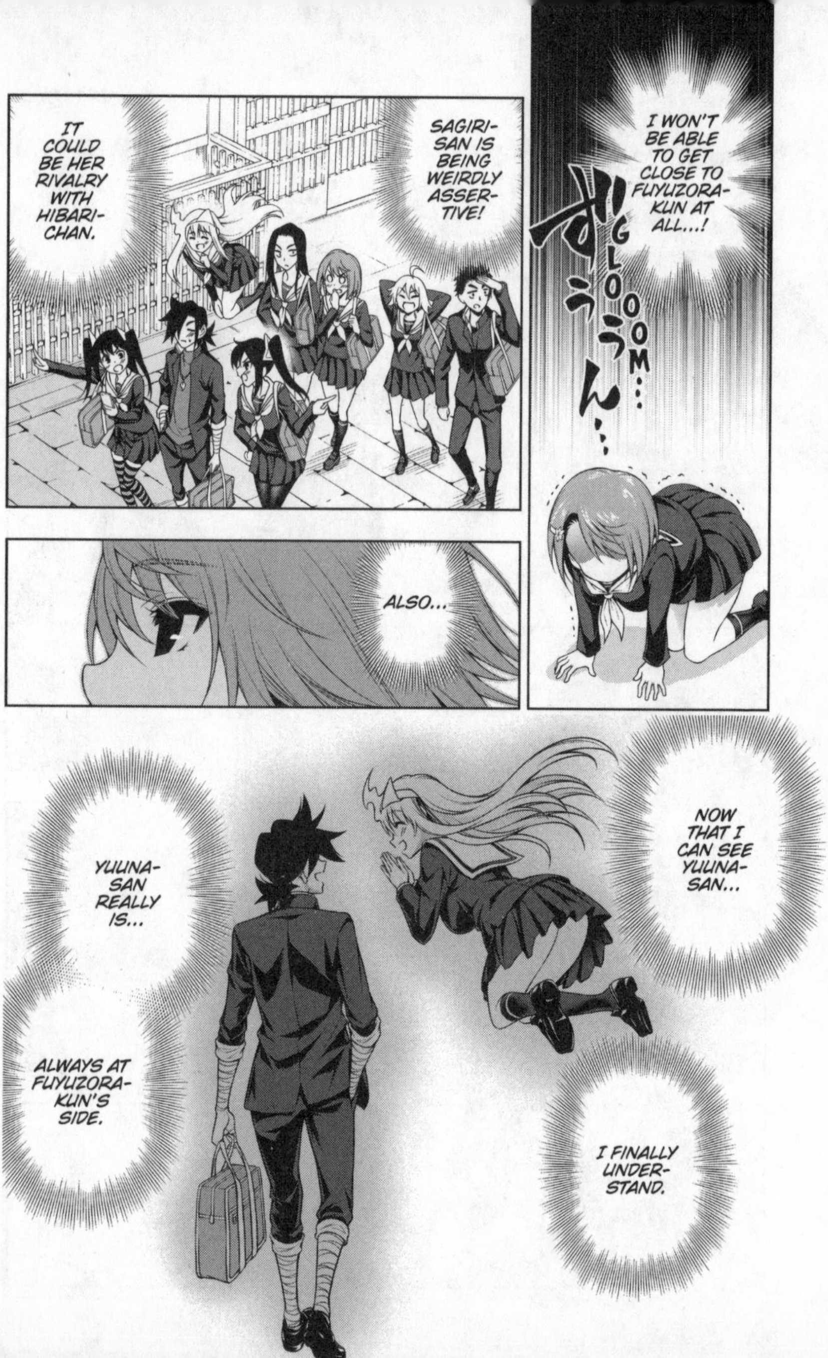
I WON'T BE ABLE TO GET CLOSE TO FUYUZORA-KUN AT ALL...!
GLOOOOM...
ずうぅん…
SAGIRI-SAN IS BEING WEIRDLY ASSERTIVE!
IT COULD BE HER RIVALRY WITH HIBARI-CHAN.
ALSO...
NOW THAT I CAN SEE YUUNA-SAN...
YUUNA-SAN REALLY IS...
I FINALLY UNDERSTAND.
ALWAYS AT FUYUZORA-KUN'S SIDE.

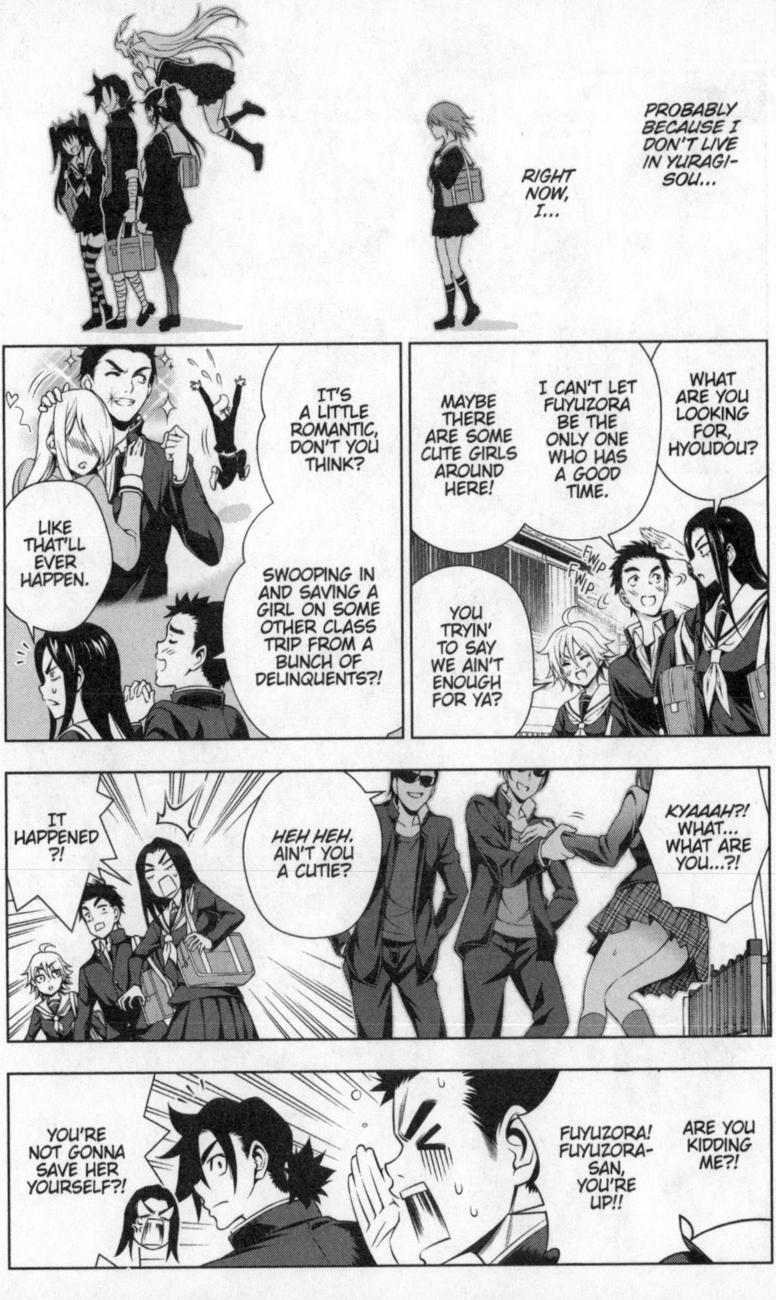
PROBABLY BECAUSE I DON'T LIVE IN YURAGI-SOU...
RIGHT NOW, I...
WHAT ARE YOU LOOKING FOR, HYOUDOU?
I CAN'T LET FUYUZORA BE THE ONLY ONE WHO HAS A GOOD TIME.
MAYBE THERE ARE SOME CUTE GIRLS AROUND HERE!
FWIP FWIP
YOU TRYIN' TO SAY WE AIN'T ENOUGH FOR YA?
IT'S A LITTLE ROMANTIC, DON'T YOU THINK?
SWOOPING IN AND SAVING A GIRL ON SOME OTHER CLASS TRIP FROM A BUNCH OF DELINQUENTS?!
LIKE THAT'LL EVER HAPPEN.
KYAAAH?! WHAT... WHAT ARE YOU...?!
HEH HEH. AIN'T YOU A CUTIE?
IT HAPPENED?!
ARE YOU KIDDING ME?!
FUYUZORA! FUYUZORA-SAN, YOU'RE UP!!
YOU'RE NOT GONNA SAVE HER YOURSELF?!

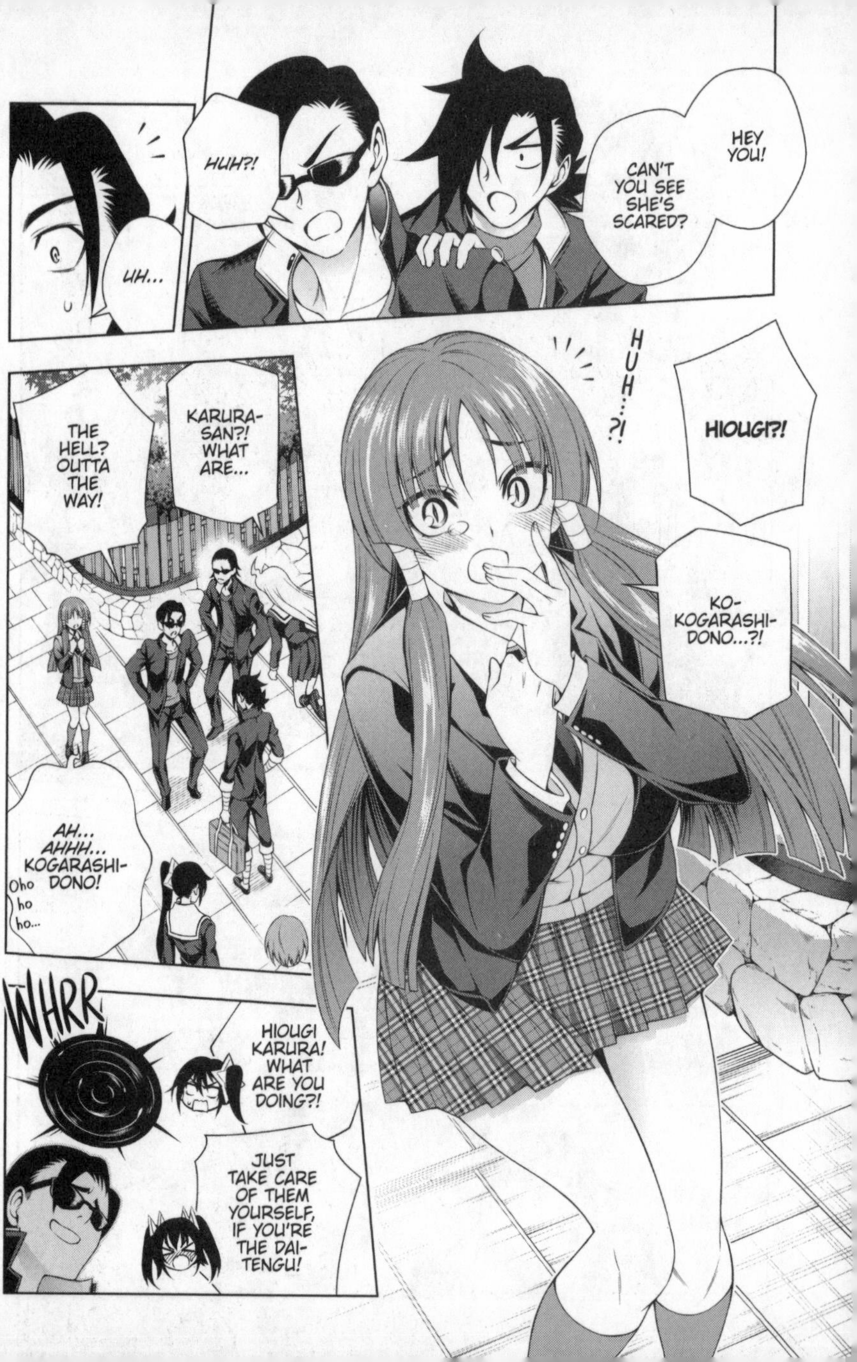
HEY YOU!
CAN'T YOU SEE SHE'S SCARED?
HUH?!
UH...
HUH...?!
HIOUGI?!
KO-KOGARASHI-DONO...?!
KARURA-SAN?! WHAT ARE...
THE HELL? OUTTA THE WAY!
AH... AHHH... KOGARASHI-DONO!
Oho ho ho...
WHRR
HIOUGI KARURA! WHAT ARE YOU DOING?!
JUST TAKE CARE OF THEM YOURSELF, IF YOU'RE THE DAI-TENGU!

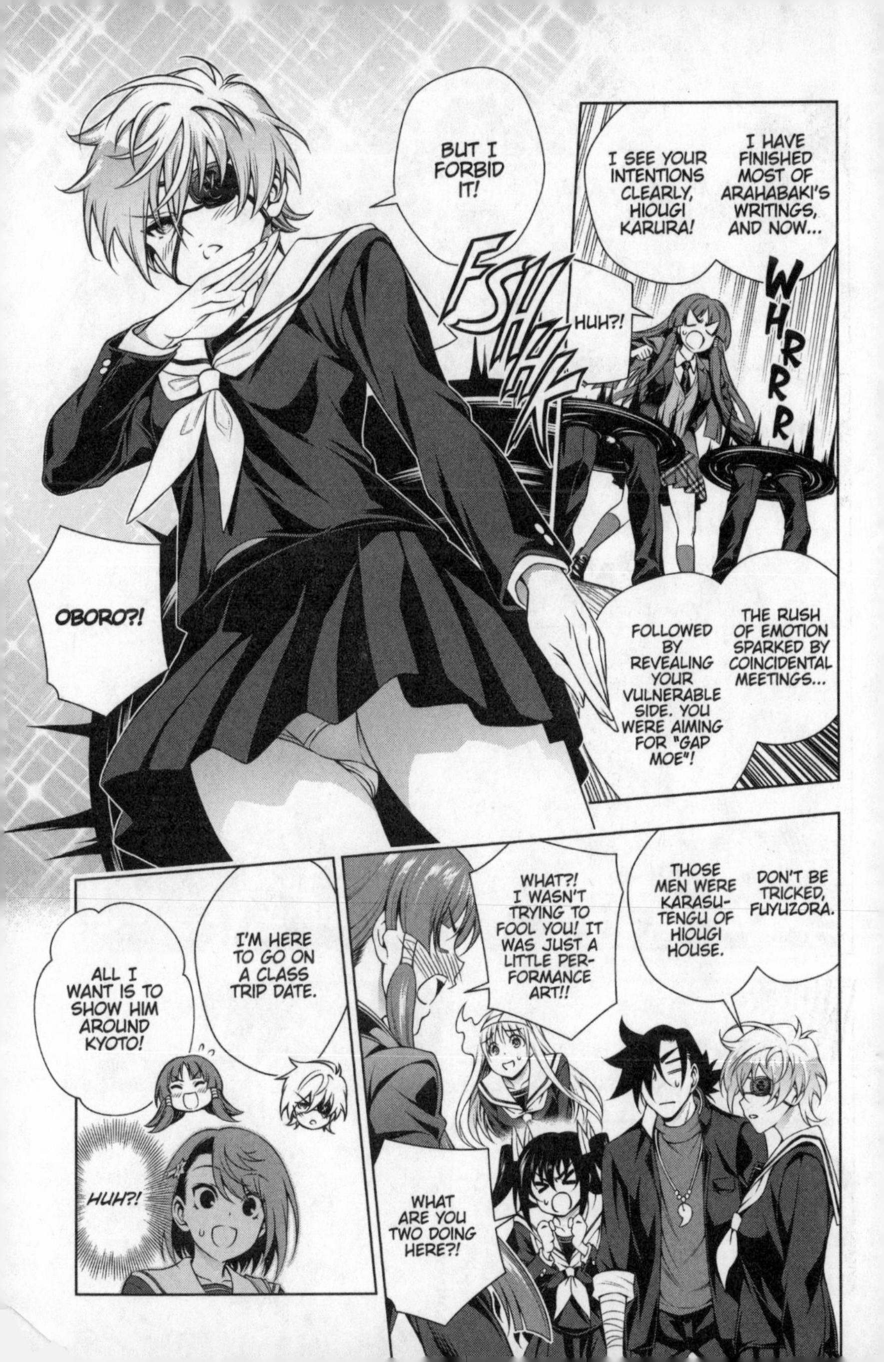
I HAVE FINISHED MOST OF ARAHABAKI'S WRITINGS, AND NOW...
I SEE YOUR INTENTIONS CLEARLY, HIOUGI KARURA!
WHRRR
THE RUSH OF EMOTION SPARKED BY COINCIDENTAL MEETINGS...
FOLLOWED BY REVEALING YOUR VULNERABLE SIDE. YOU WERE AIMING FOR "GAP MOE"!
HUH?!
FSHHK
BUT I FORBID IT!
OBORO?!
DON'T BE TRICKED, FUYUZORA.
THOSE MEN WERE KARASU-TENGU OF HIOUGI HOUSE.
WHAT?! I WASN'T TRYING TO FOOL YOU! IT WAS JUST A LITTLE PER-FORMANCE ART!!
WHAT ARE YOU TWO DOING HERE?!
I'M HERE TO GO ON A CLASS TRIP DATE.
ALL I WANT IS TO SHOW HIM AROUND KYOTO!
HUH?!

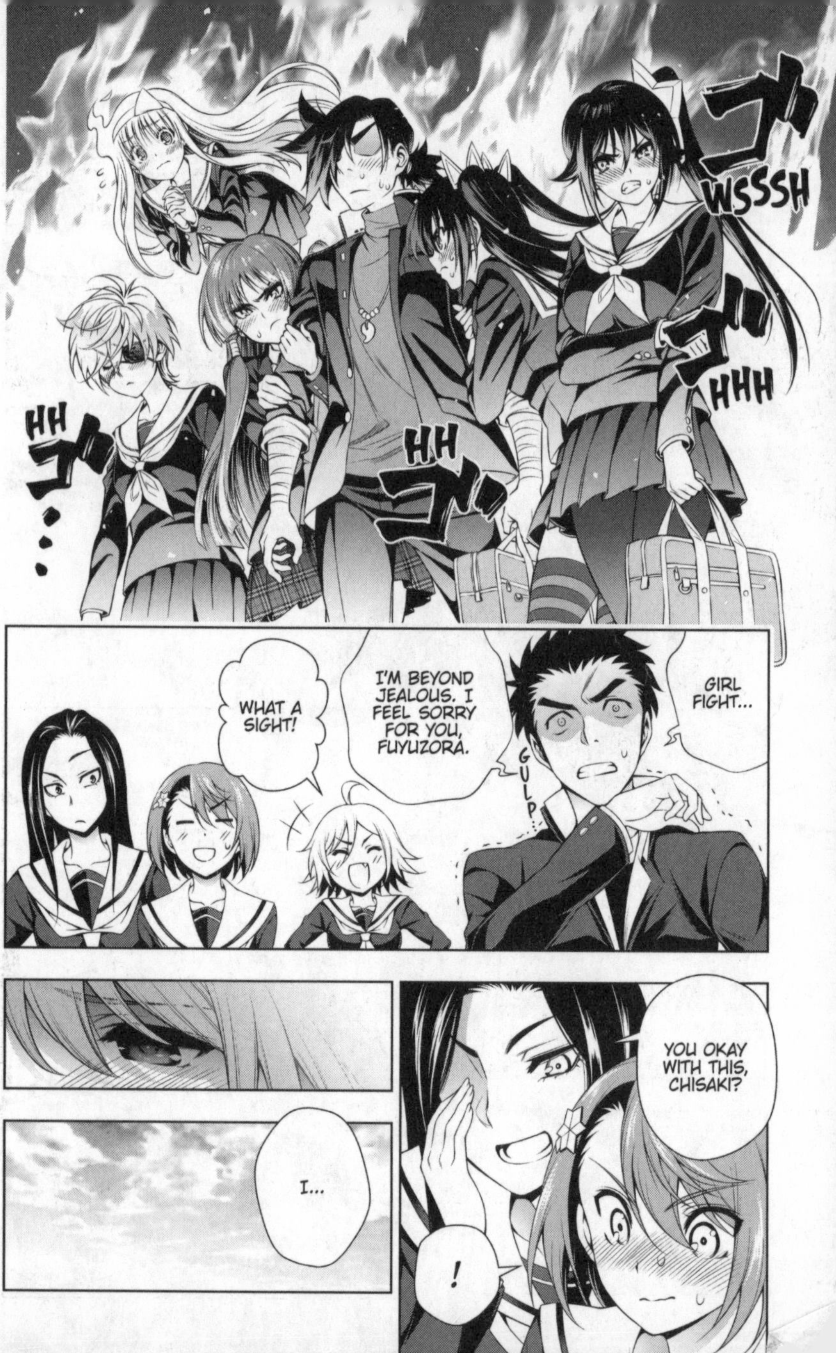
WSSSH
HHH
HH
HH
...
GIRL FIGHT...
GULP...
I'M BEYOND JEALOUS. I FEEL SORRY FOR YOU, FUYUZORA.
WHAT A SIGHT!
YOU OKAY WITH THIS, CHISAKI?
!
I...

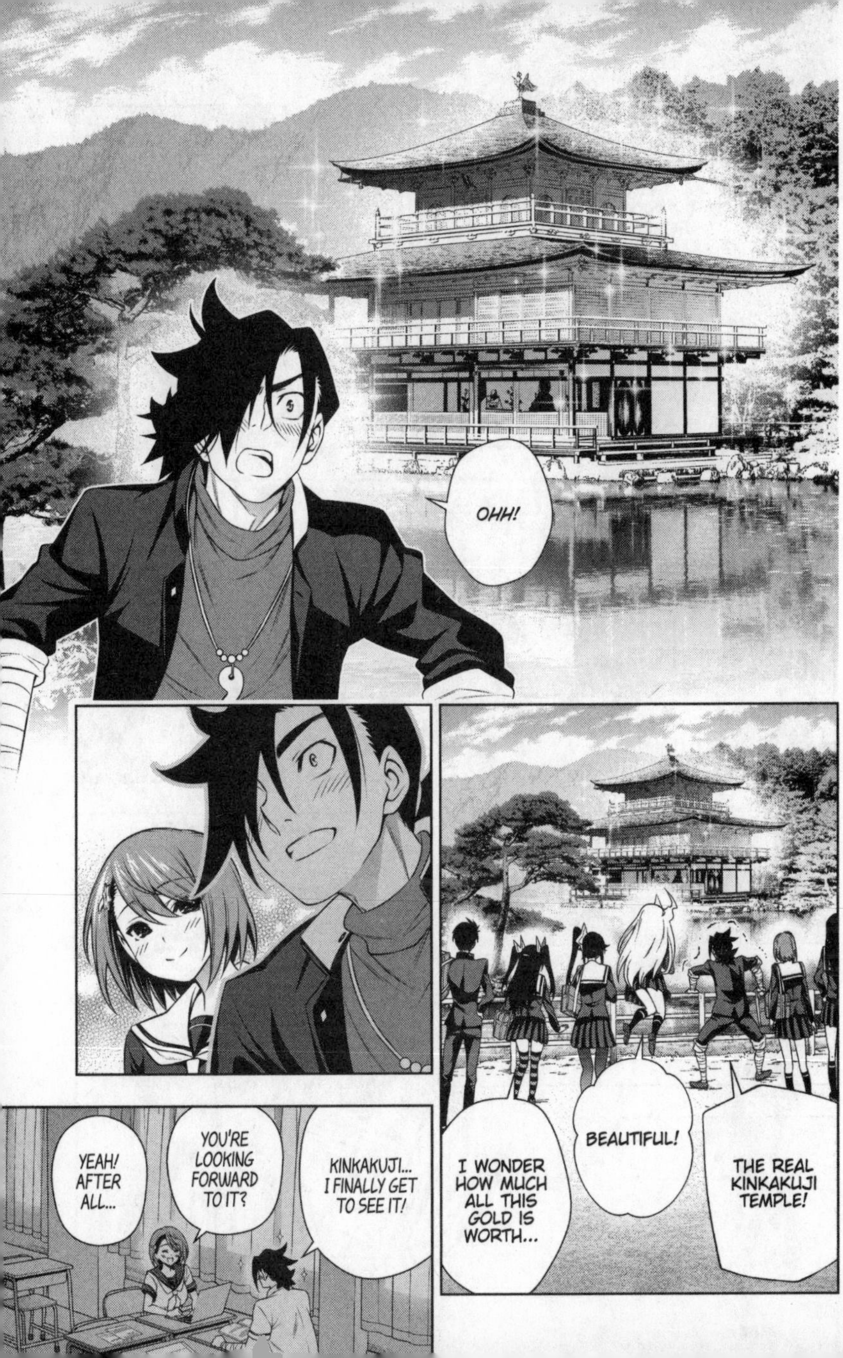
OHH!
THE REAL KINKAKUJI TEMPLE!
BEAUTIFUL!
I WONDER HOW MUCH ALL THIS GOLD IS WORTH...
KINKAKUJI... I FINALLY GET TO SEE IT!
YOU'RE LOOKING FORWARD TO IT?
YEAH! AFTER ALL...

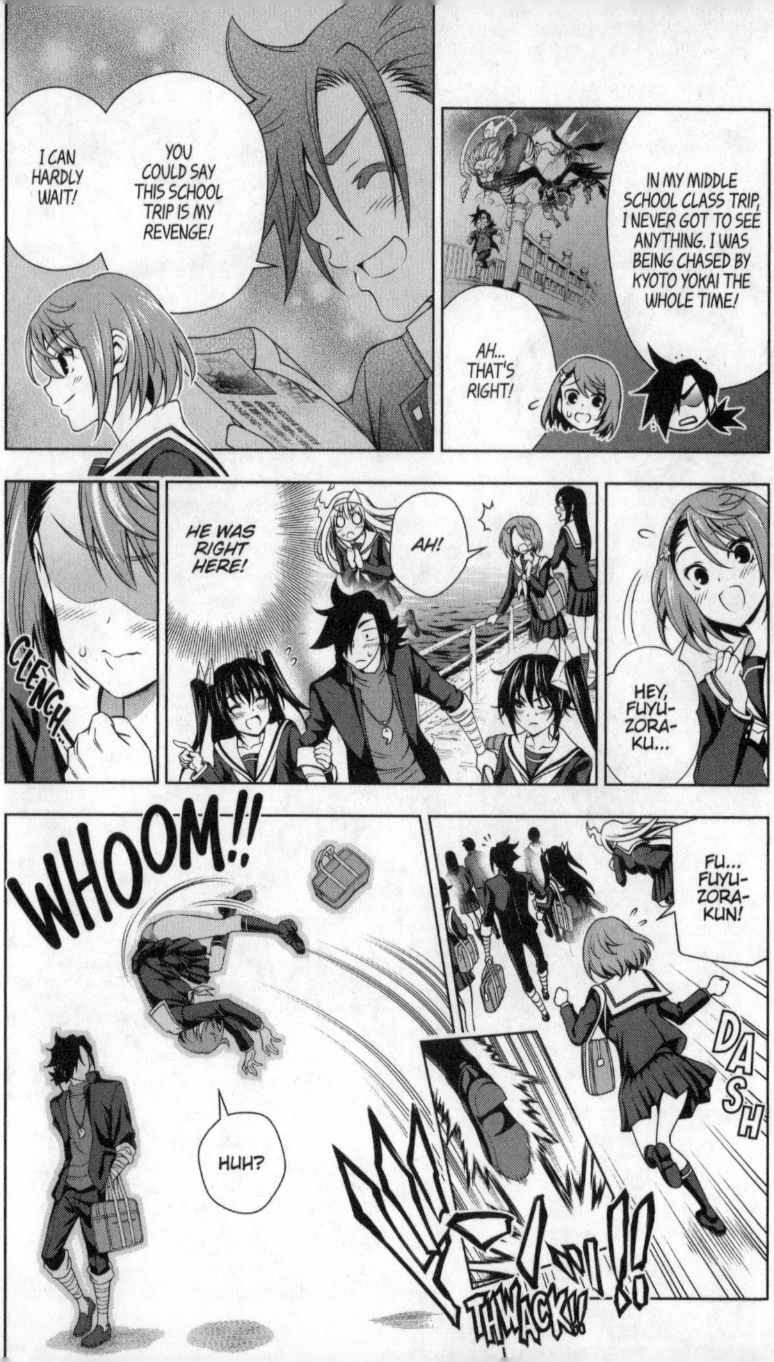
IN MY MIDDLE SCHOOL CLASS TRIP, I NEVER GOT TO SEE ANYTHING. I WAS BEING CHASED BY KYOTO YOKAI THE WHOLE TIME!
AH... THAT'S RIGHT!
YOU COULD SAY THIS SCHOOL TRIP IS MY REVENGE!
I CAN HARDLY WAIT!
HEY, FUYU-ZORA-KU...
AH!
HE WAS RIGHT HERE!
CLENCH...
FU... FUYU-ZORA-KUN!
DASH
WHOOM!!
HUH?
THWACK!!

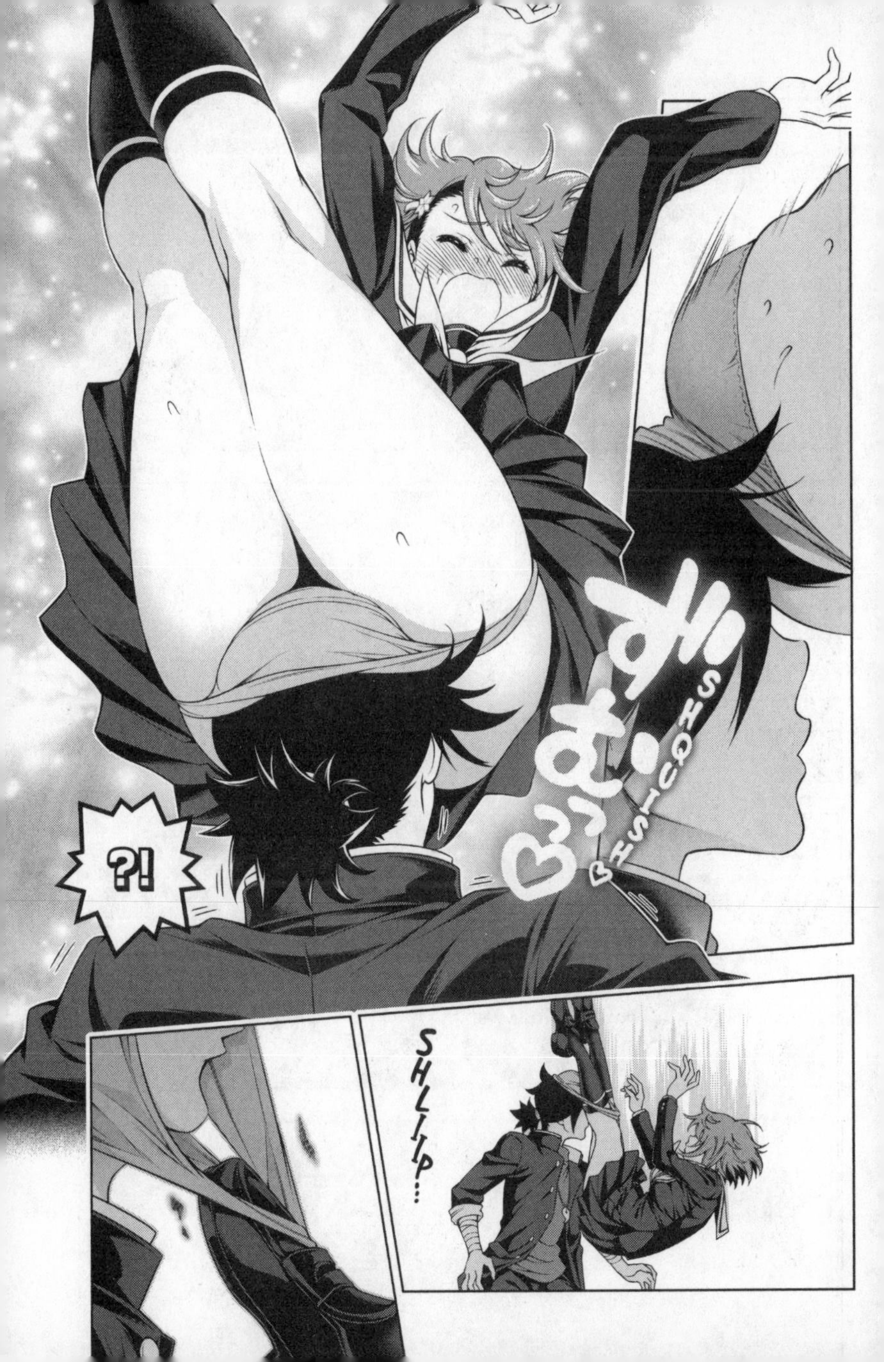
SHQUISH♡
?!
SHLIIP...

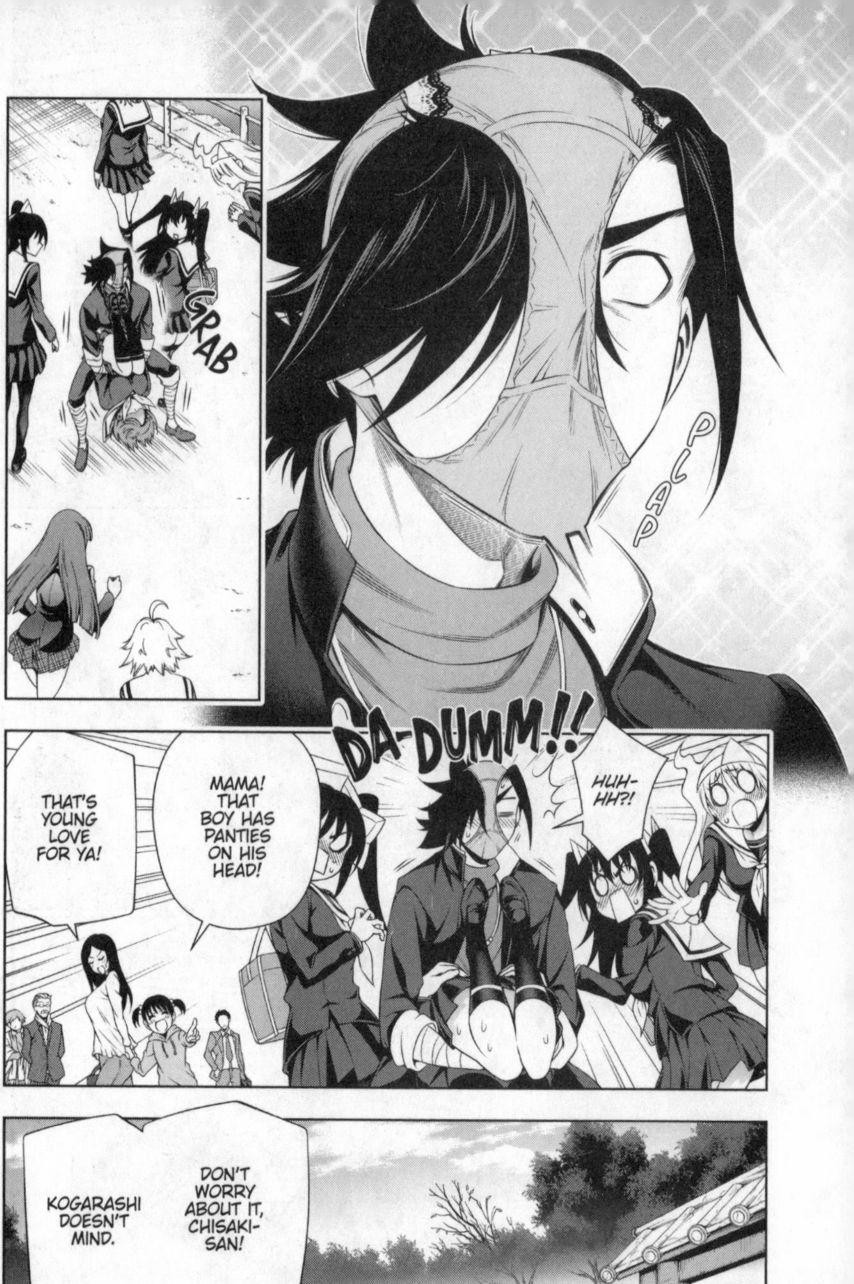
PLAP
DA-DUMM!!
GRAB
HUH-HH?!
MAMA! THAT BOY HAS PANTIES ON HIS HEAD!
THAT'S YOUNG LOVE FOR YA!
DON'T WORRY ABOUT IT, CHISAKI-SAN!
KOGARASHI DOESN'T MIND.

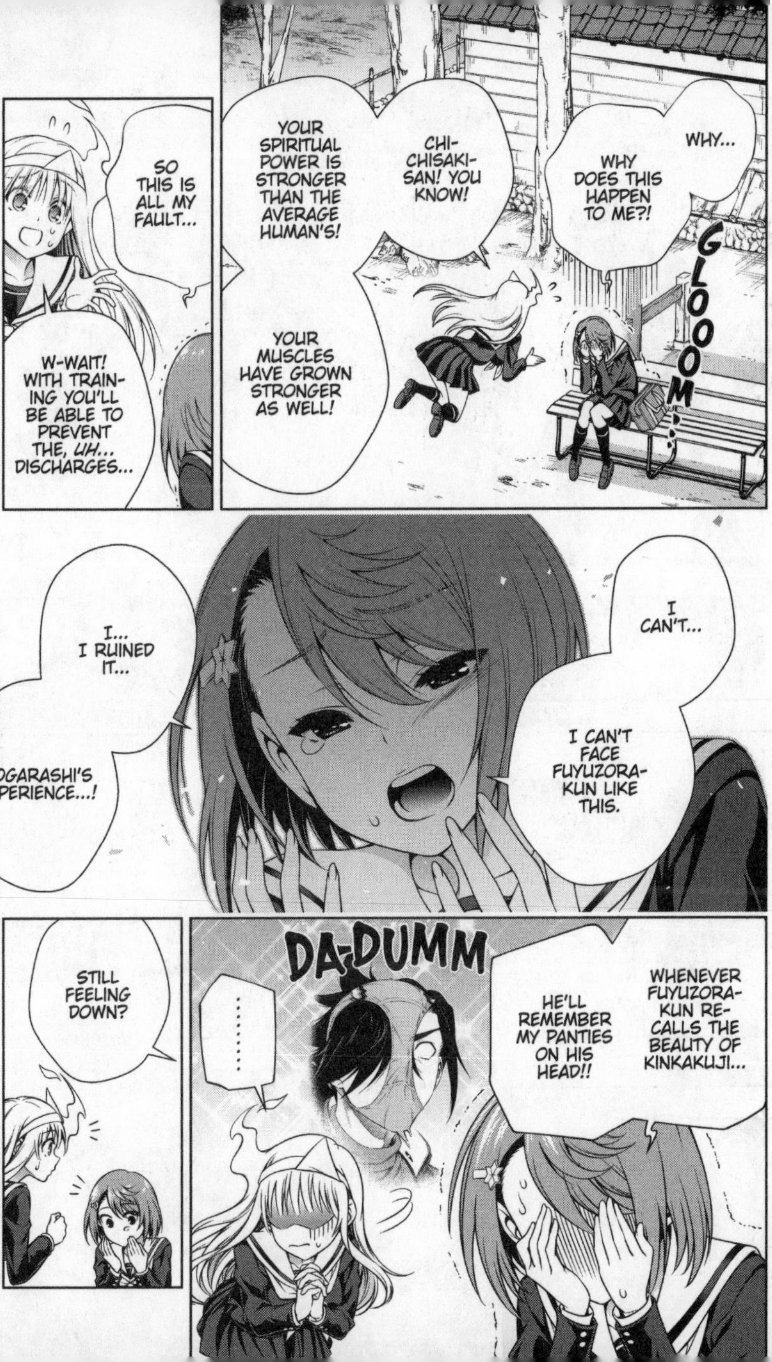
WHY...
WHY DOES THIS HAPPEN TO ME?!
GLOOOM...
CHI-CHISAKI-SAN! YOU KNOW!
YOUR SPIRITUAL POWER IS STRONGER THAN THE AVERAGE HUMAN'S!
YOUR MUSCLES HAVE GROWN STRONGER AS WELL!
SO THIS IS ALL MY FAULT...
W-WAIT! WITH TRAIN-ING YOU'LL BE ABLE TO PREVENT THE, *UH*... DISCHARGES...
I CAN'T...
I CAN'T FACE FUYUZORA-KUN LIKE THIS.
I... I RUINED IT...
KOGARASHI'S EXPERIENCE...!
WHENEVER FUYUZORA-KUN RE-CALLS THE BEAUTY OF KINKAKUJI...
HE'LL REMEMBER MY PANTIES ON HIS HEAD!!
DA-DUMM
......
STILL FEELING DOWN?

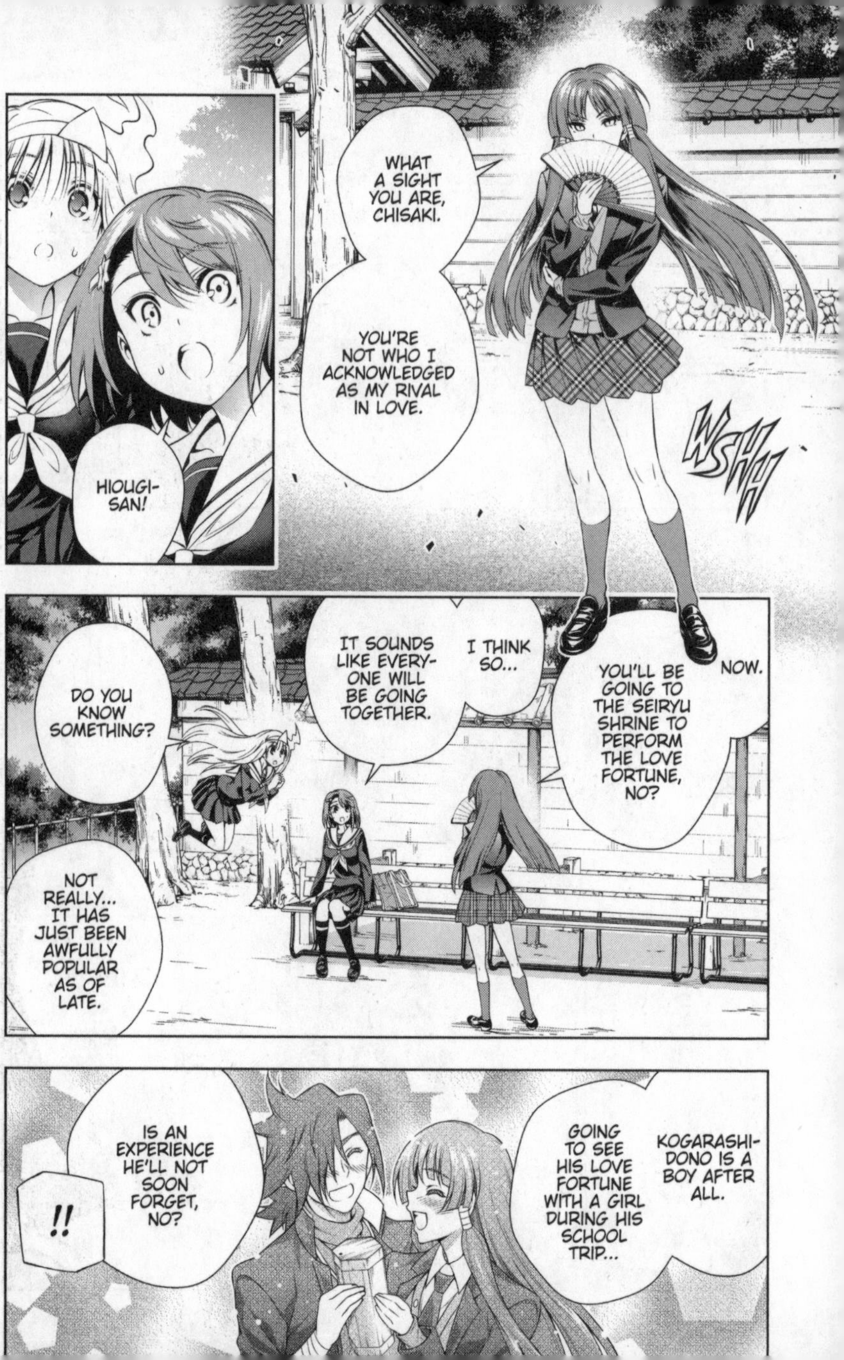
WHAT A SIGHT YOU ARE, CHISAKI.
YOU'RE NOT WHO I ACKNOWLEDGED AS MY RIVAL IN LOVE.
WSHH
HIOUGI-SAN!
NOW.
YOU'LL BE GOING TO THE SEIRYU SHRINE TO PERFORM THE LOVE FORTUNE, NO?
I THINK SO...
IT SOUNDS LIKE EVERY-ONE WILL BE GOING TOGETHER.
DO YOU KNOW SOMETHING?
NOT REALLY... IT HAS JUST BEEN AWFULLY POPULAR AS OF LATE.
KOGARASHI-DONO IS A BOY AFTER ALL.
GOING TO SEE HIS LOVE FORTUNE WITH A GIRL DURING HIS SCHOOL TRIP...
IS AN EXPERIENCE HE'LL NOT SOON FORGET, NO?
!!

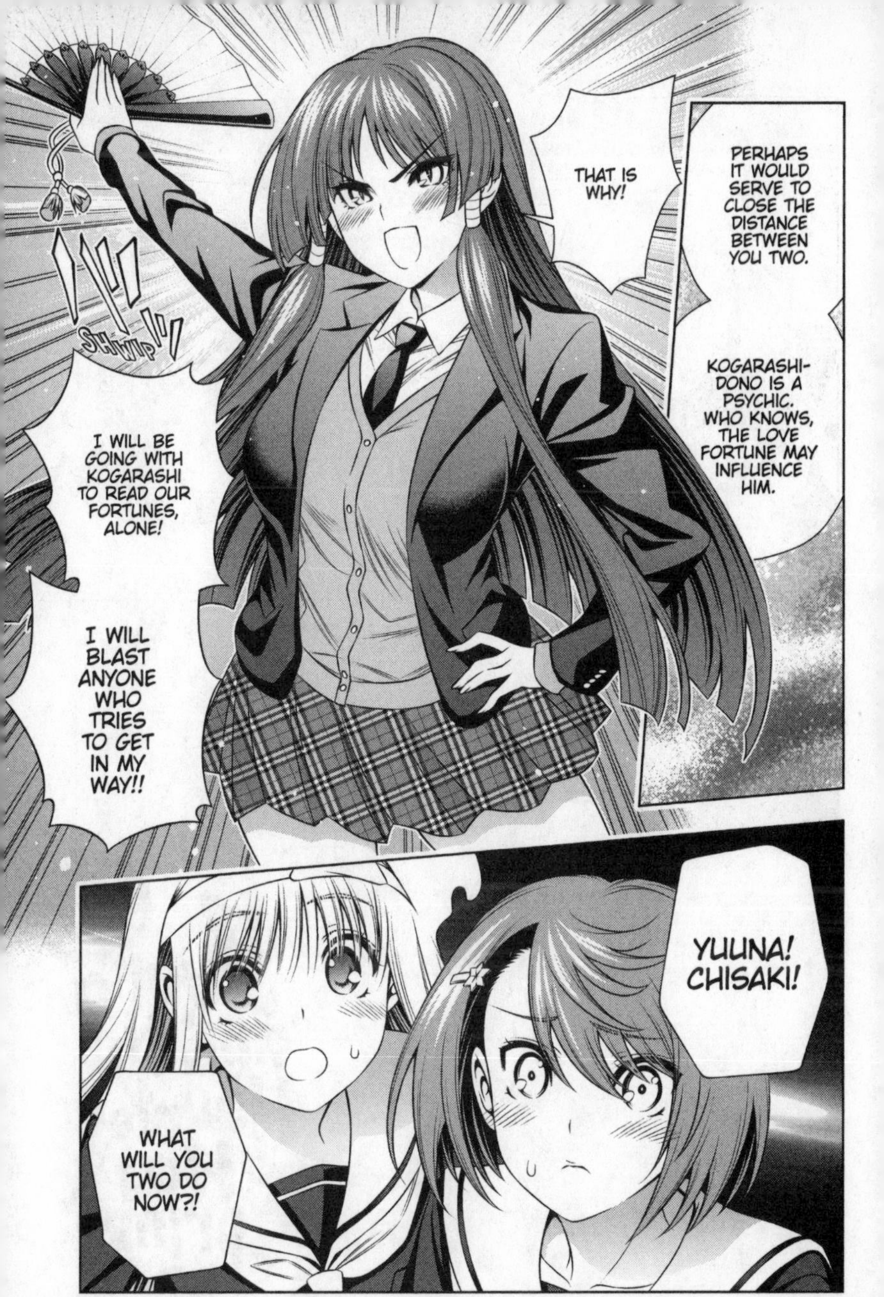
PERHAPS IT WOULD SERVE TO CLOSE THE DISTANCE BETWEEN YOU TWO.
KOGARASHI-DONO IS A PSYCHIC. WHO KNOWS, THE LOVE FORTUNE MAY INFLUENCE HIM.
THAT IS WHY!
SHWIP
I WILL BE GOING WITH KOGARASHI TO READ OUR FORTUNES, ALONE!
I WILL BLAST ANYONE WHO TRIES TO GET IN MY WAY!!
YUUNA! CHISAKI!
WHAT WILL YOU TWO DO NOW?!

Yuuna and the Haunted Hot Springs

♨ 144 Yukemuri High School Trip ②

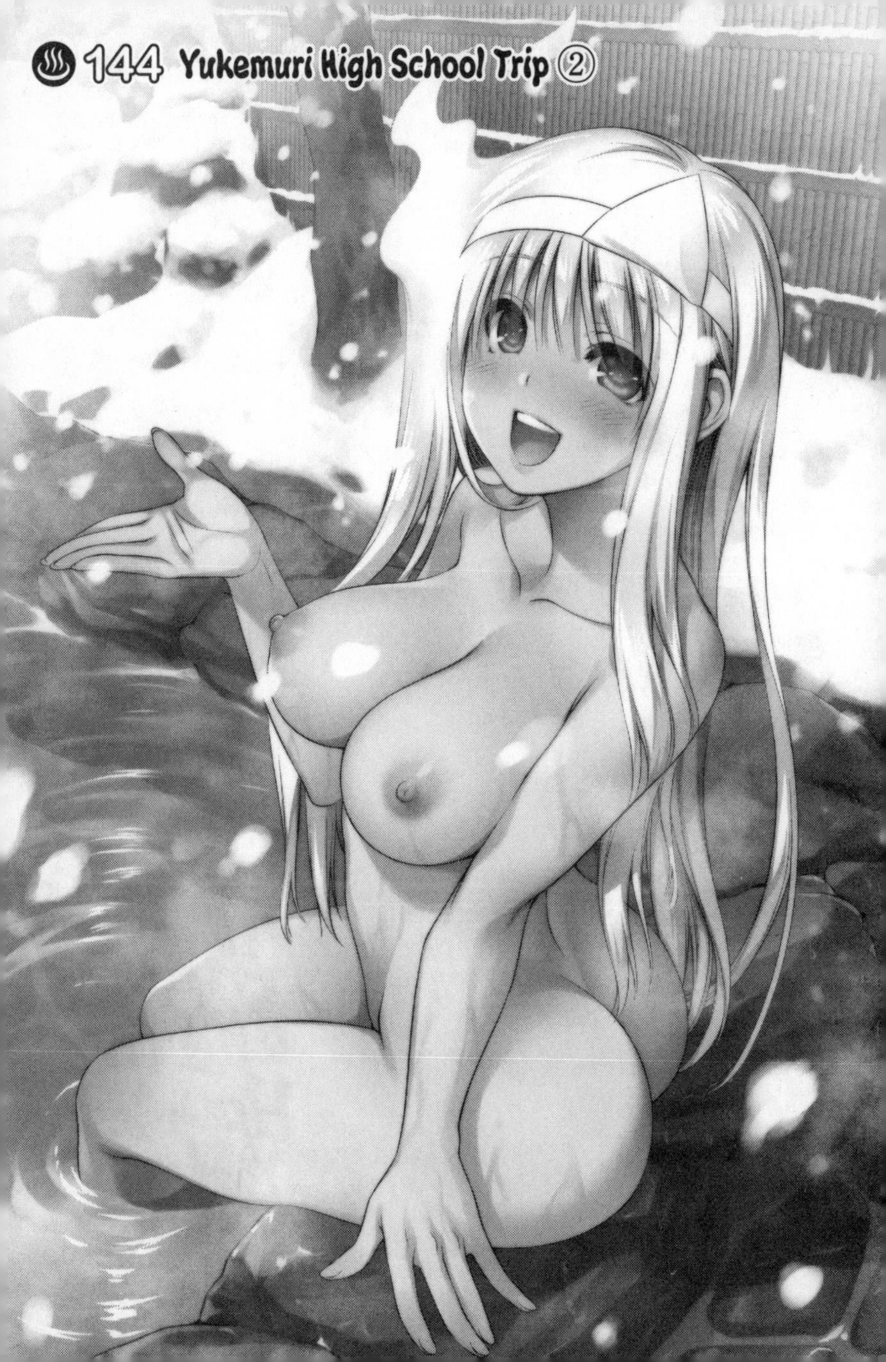

Yuuna
and the
Haunted
Hot
Springs

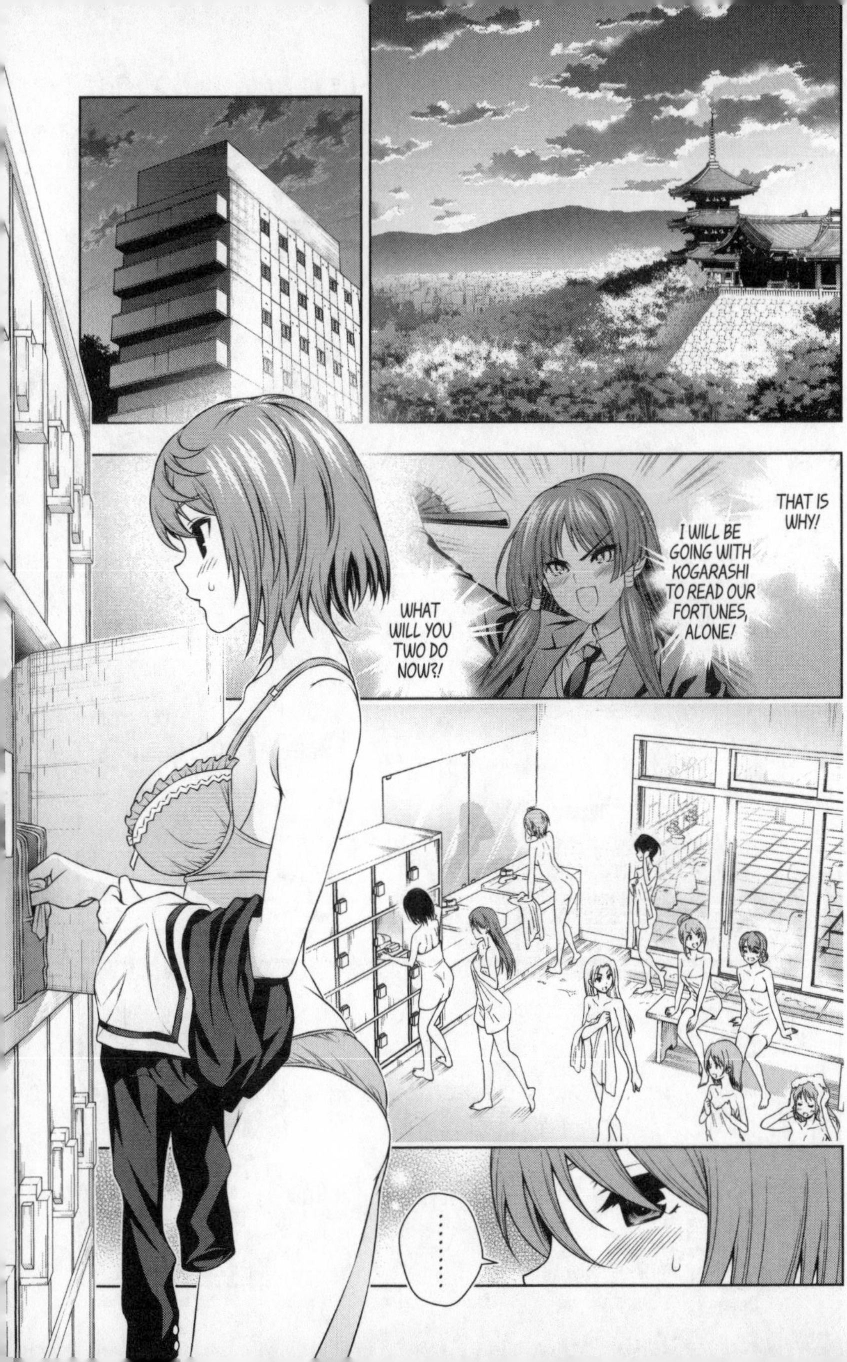
THAT IS WHY!
I WILL BE GOING WITH KOGARASHI TO READ OUR FORTUNES, ALONE!
WHAT WILL YOU TWO DO NOW?!
……

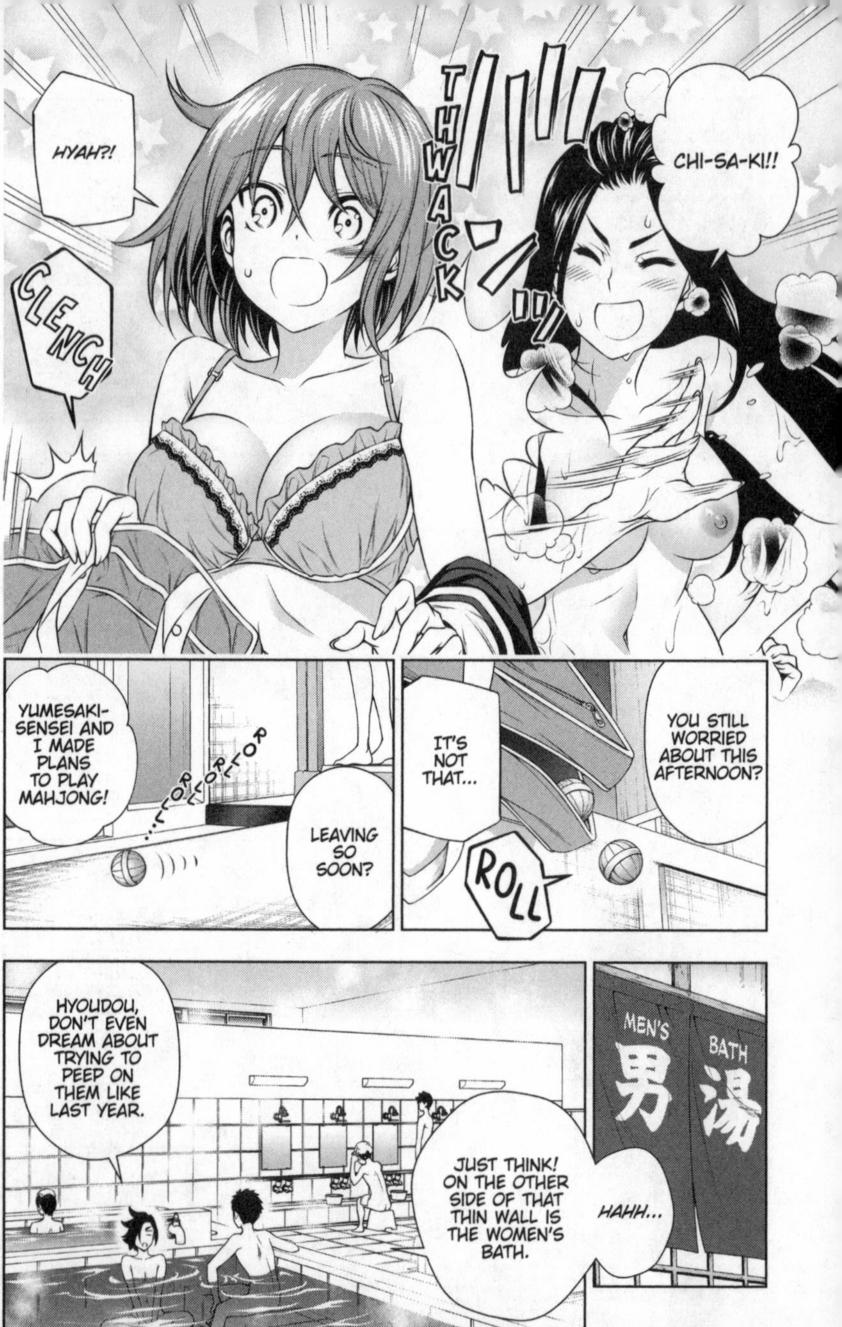
CHI-SA-KI!!
THWACK
HYAH?!
CLENCH
YOU STILL WORRIED ABOUT THIS AFTERNOON?
IT'S NOT THAT...
ROLL
LEAVING SO SOON?
YUMESAKI-SENSEI AND I MADE PLANS TO PLAY MAHJONG!
...ROLLROLLROLL
MEN'S
男
BATH
湯
JUST THINK! ON THE OTHER SIDE OF THAT THIN WALL IS THE WOMEN'S BATH.
HAHH...
HYOUDOU, DON'T EVEN DREAM ABOUT TRYING TO PEEP ON THEM LIKE LAST YEAR.

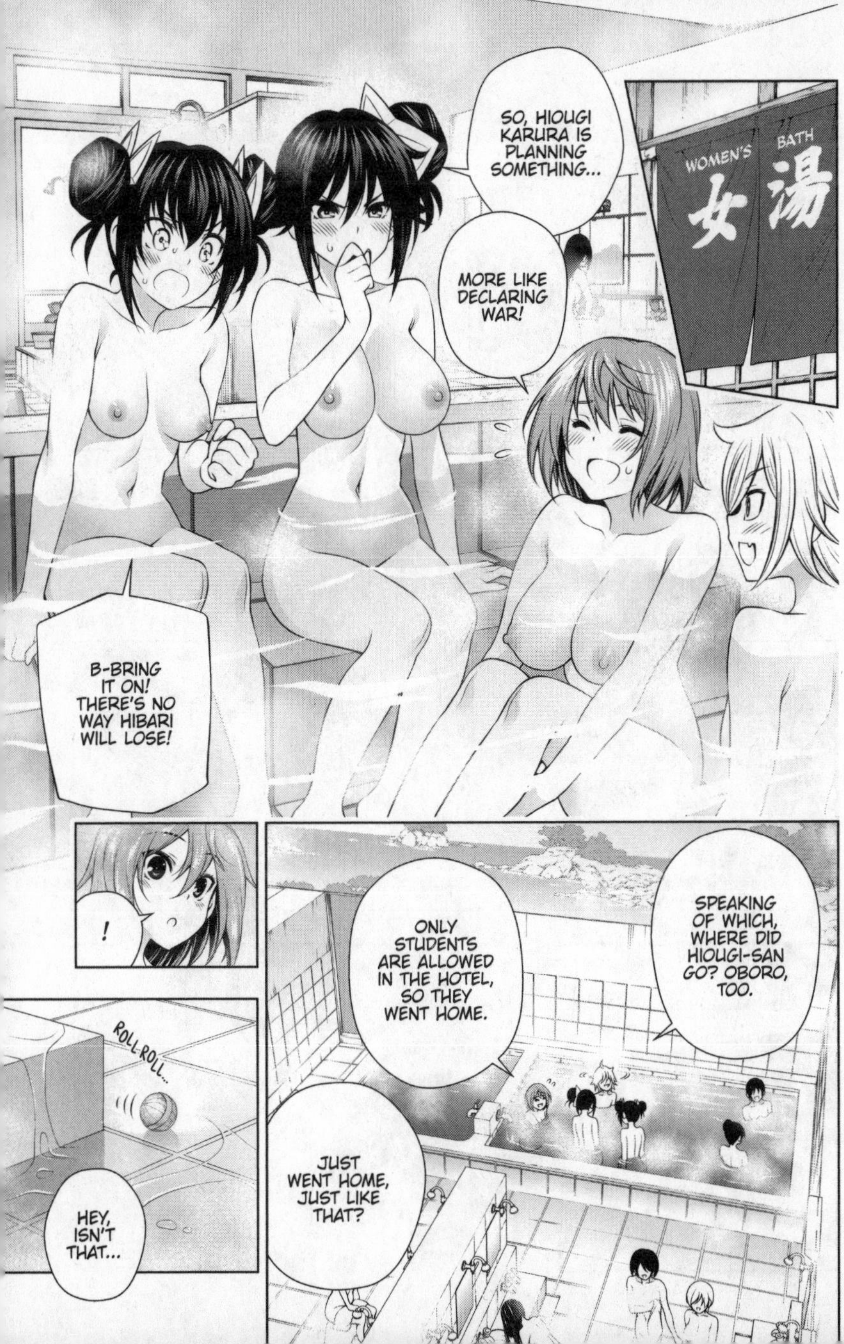
WOMEN'S BATH
女湯
SO, HIOUGI KARURA IS PLANNING SOMETHING...
MORE LIKE DECLARING WAR!
B-BRING IT ON! THERE'S NO WAY HIBARI WILL LOSE!
SPEAKING OF WHICH, WHERE DID HIOUGI-SAN GO? OBORO, TOO.
ONLY STUDENTS ARE ALLOWED IN THE HOTEL, SO THEY WENT HOME.
JUST WENT HOME, JUST LIKE THAT?
!
ROLL-ROLL...
HEY, ISN'T THAT...

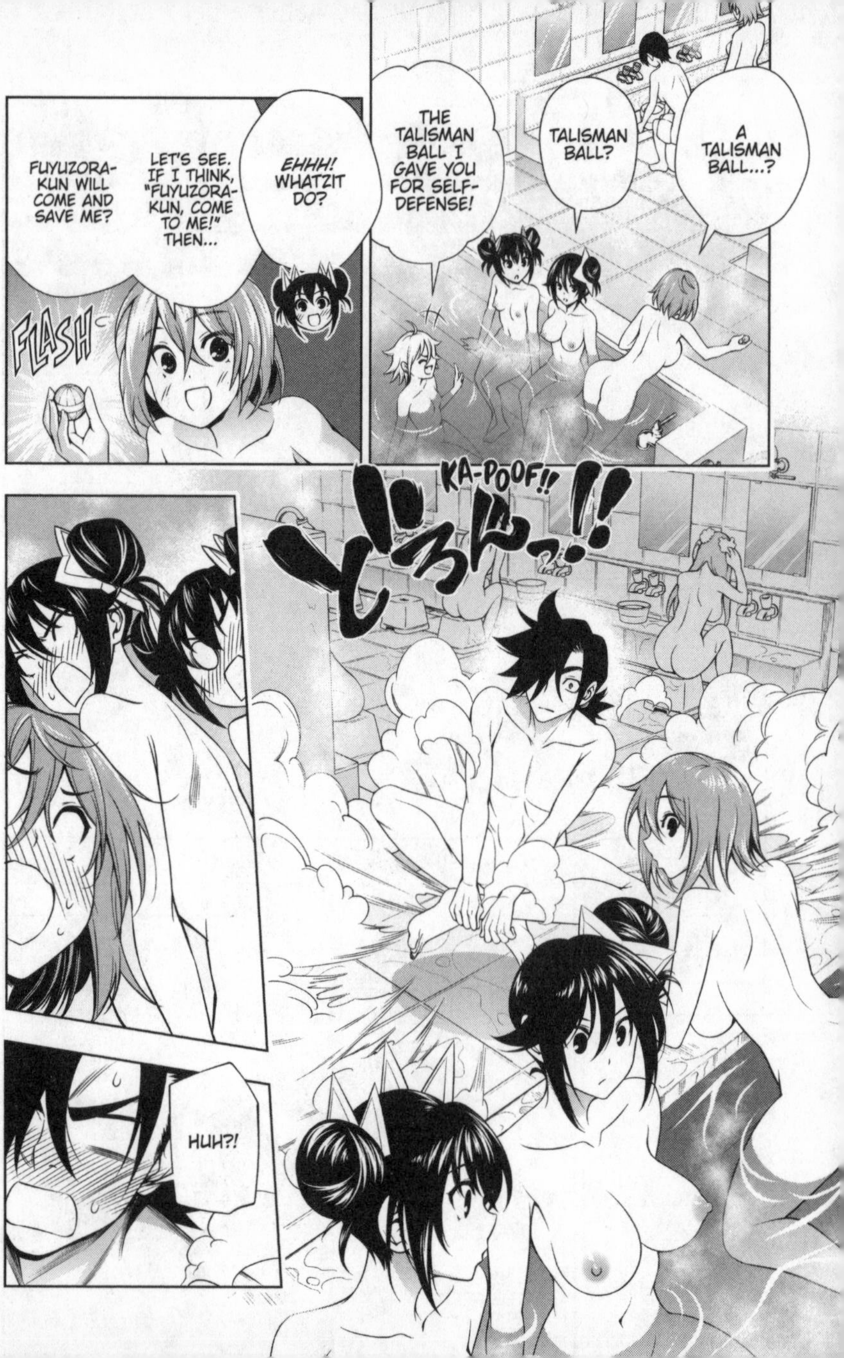
A TALISMAN BALL...?
TALISMAN BALL?
THE TALISMAN BALL I GAVE YOU FOR SELF-DEFENSE!
EHHH! WHATZIT DO?
LET'S SEE. IF I THINK, "FUYUZORA-KUN, COME TO ME!" THEN...
FUYUZORA-KUN WILL COME AND SAVE ME?
FLASH
KA-POOF!!
どろんっ!!
HUH?!

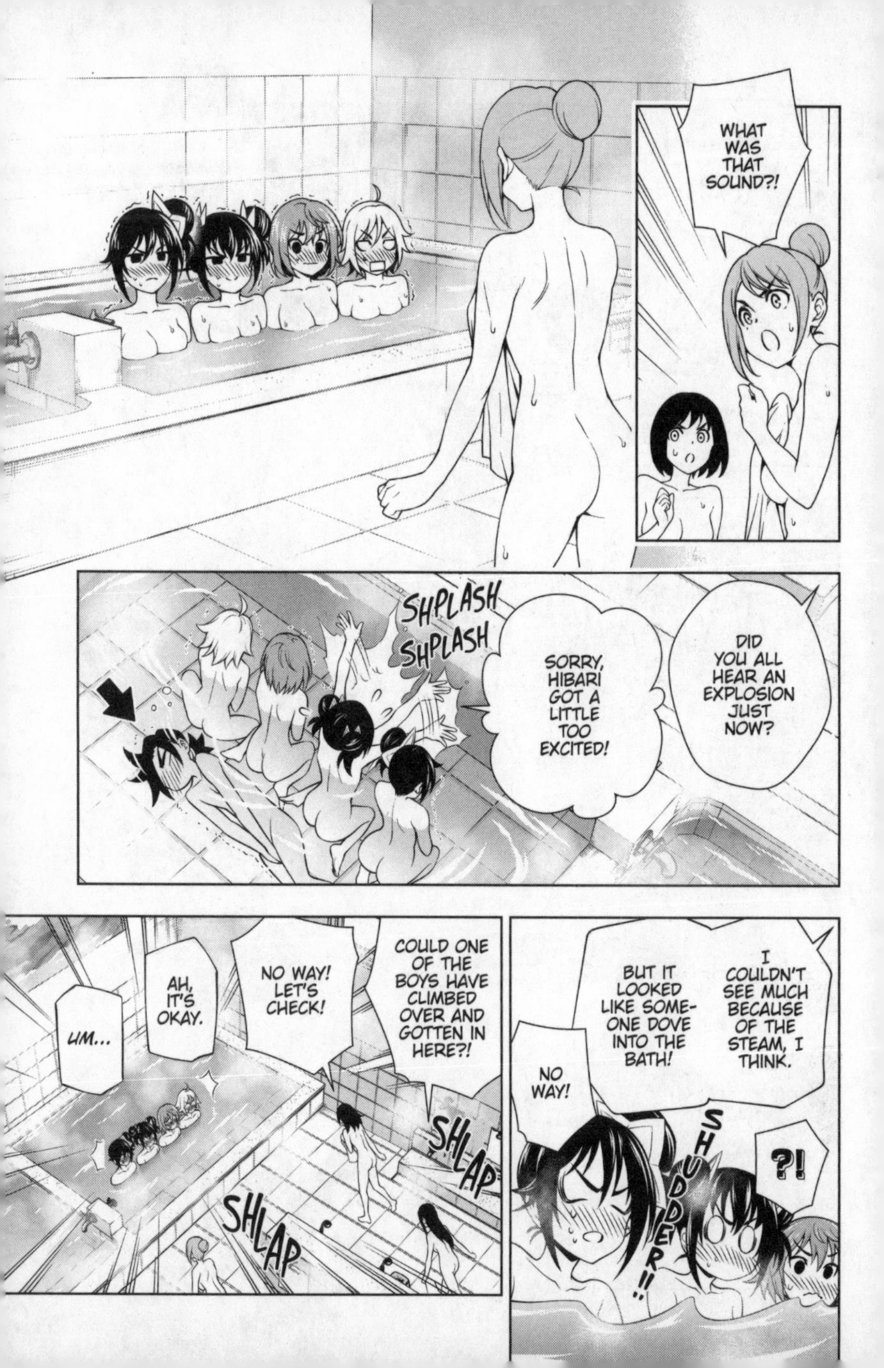
WHAT WAS THAT SOUND?!
DID YOU ALL HEAR AN EXPLOSION JUST NOW?
SORRY, HIBARI GOT A LITTLE TOO EXCITED!
SHPLASH
SHPLASH
I COULDN'T SEE MUCH BECAUSE OF THE STEAM, I THINK.
BUT IT LOOKED LIKE SOME-ONE DOVE INTO THE BATH!
NO WAY!
?!
SHUDDER!!
COULD ONE OF THE BOYS HAVE CLIMBED OVER AND GOTTEN IN HERE?!
NO WAY! LET'S CHECK!
AH, IT'S OKAY.
UM...
SHLAP
SHLAP

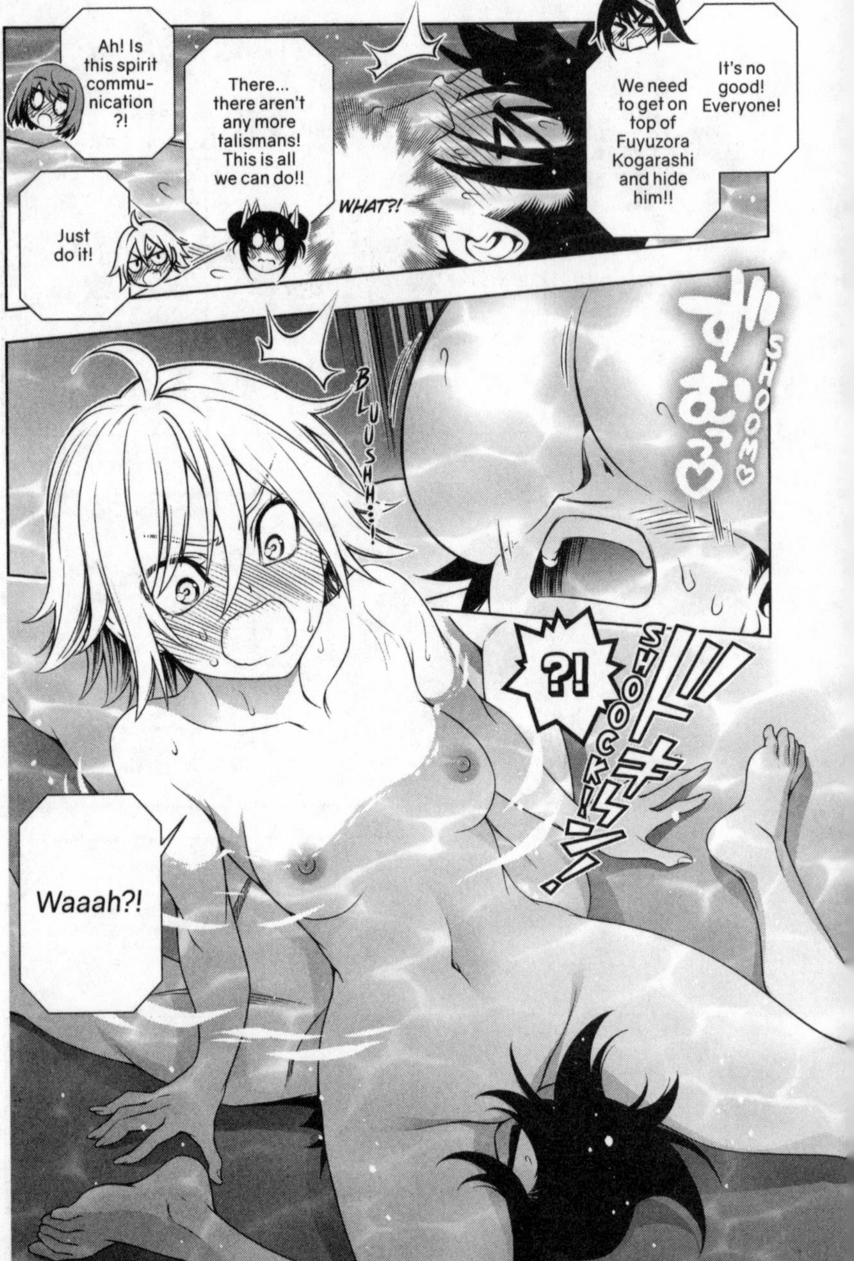
It's no good! Everyone!
We need to get on top of Fuyuzora Kogarashi and hide him!!
WHAT?!
There... there aren't any more talismans! This is all we can do!!
Ah! Is this spirit communication?!
Just do it!
SHOOOM♡
BLUUSHH...!
?!
SHOOOCK!!
Waaah?!

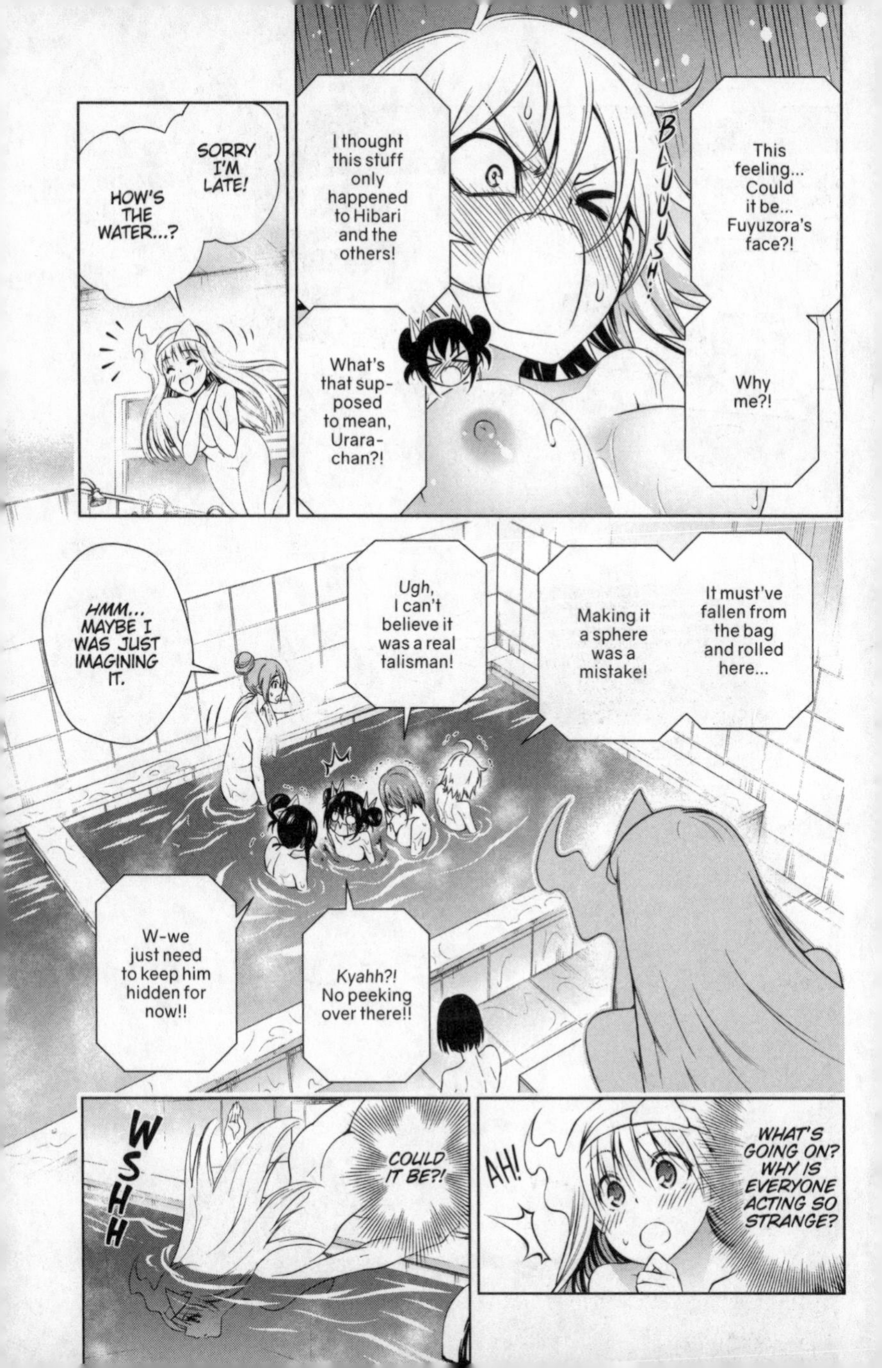
This feeling... Could it be... Fuyuzora's face?!
BLUUUSH!!
I thought this stuff only happened to Hibari and the others!
Why me?!
What's that sup-posed to mean, Urara-chan?!
SORRY I'M LATE!
HOW'S THE WATER...?
It must've fallen from the bag and rolled here...
Making it a sphere was a mistake!
Ugh, I can't believe it was a real talisman!
HMM... MAYBE I WAS JUST IMAGINING IT.
Kyahh?! No peeking over there!!
W-we just need to keep him hidden for now!!
WHAT'S GOING ON? WHY IS EVERYONE ACTING SO STRANGE?
AH!
COULD IT BE?!
WSHH

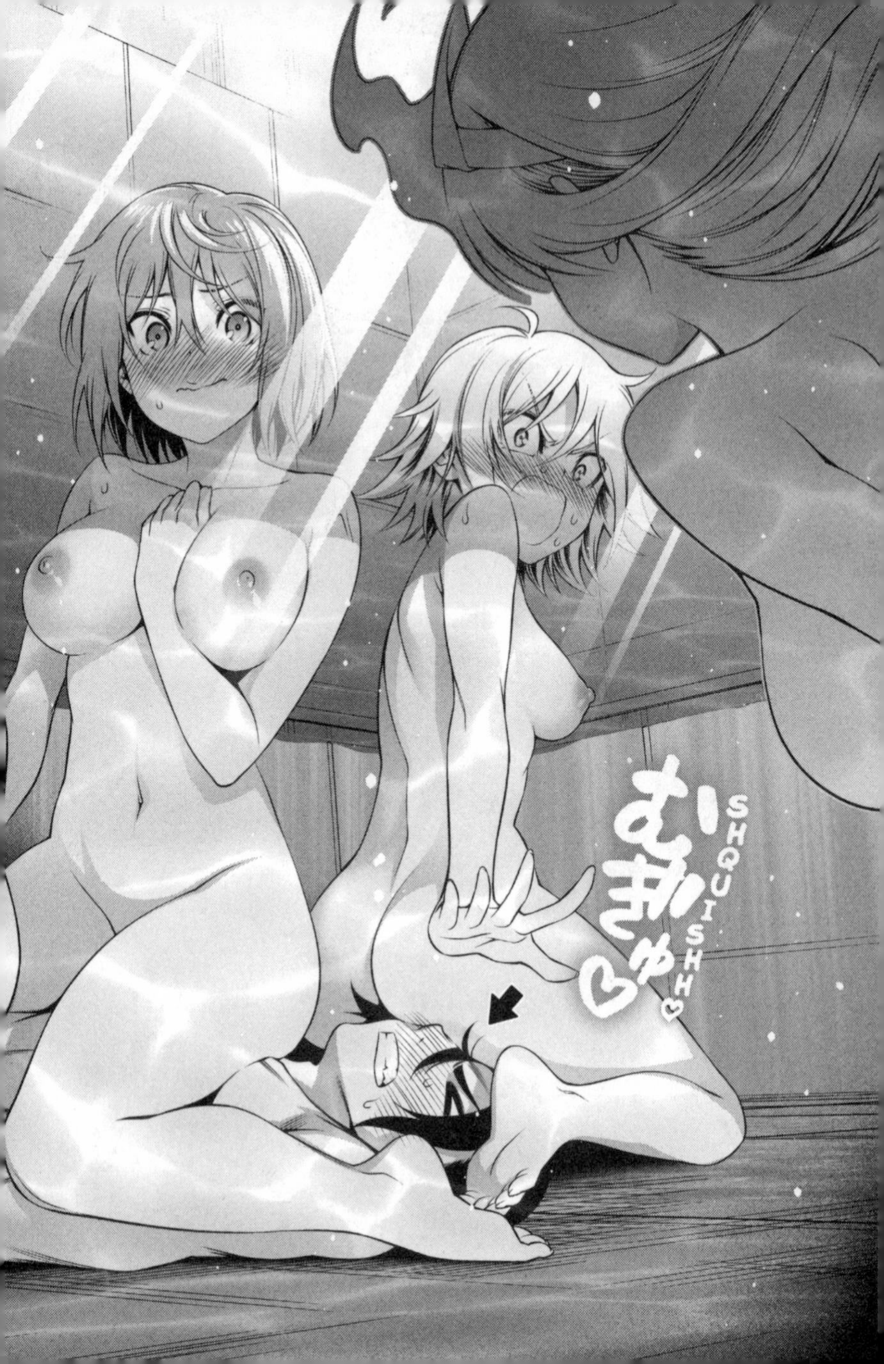
むぎゅ♡
SHQUISHH♡

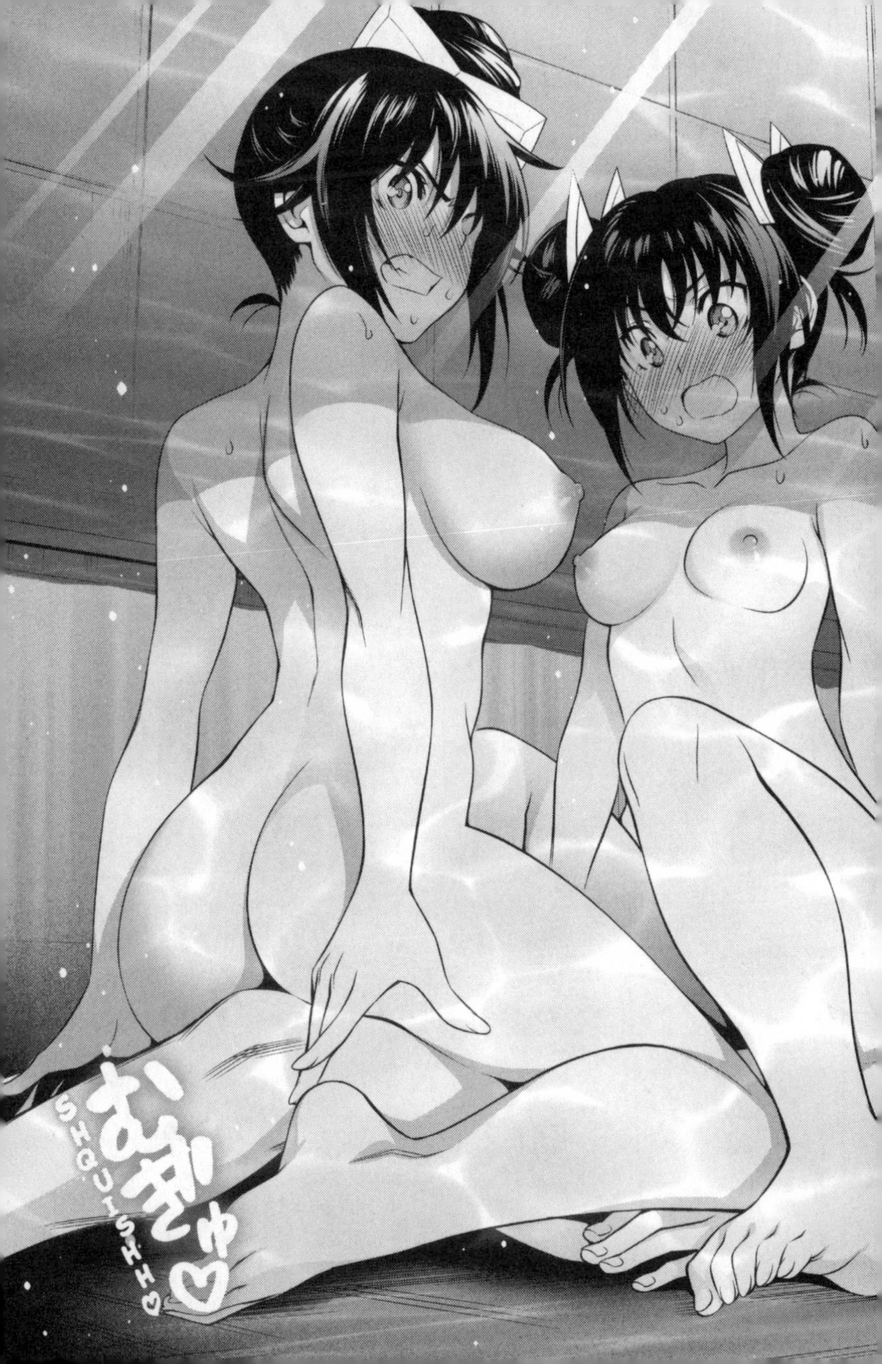
むぎゅ♡
SHQUISHH♡

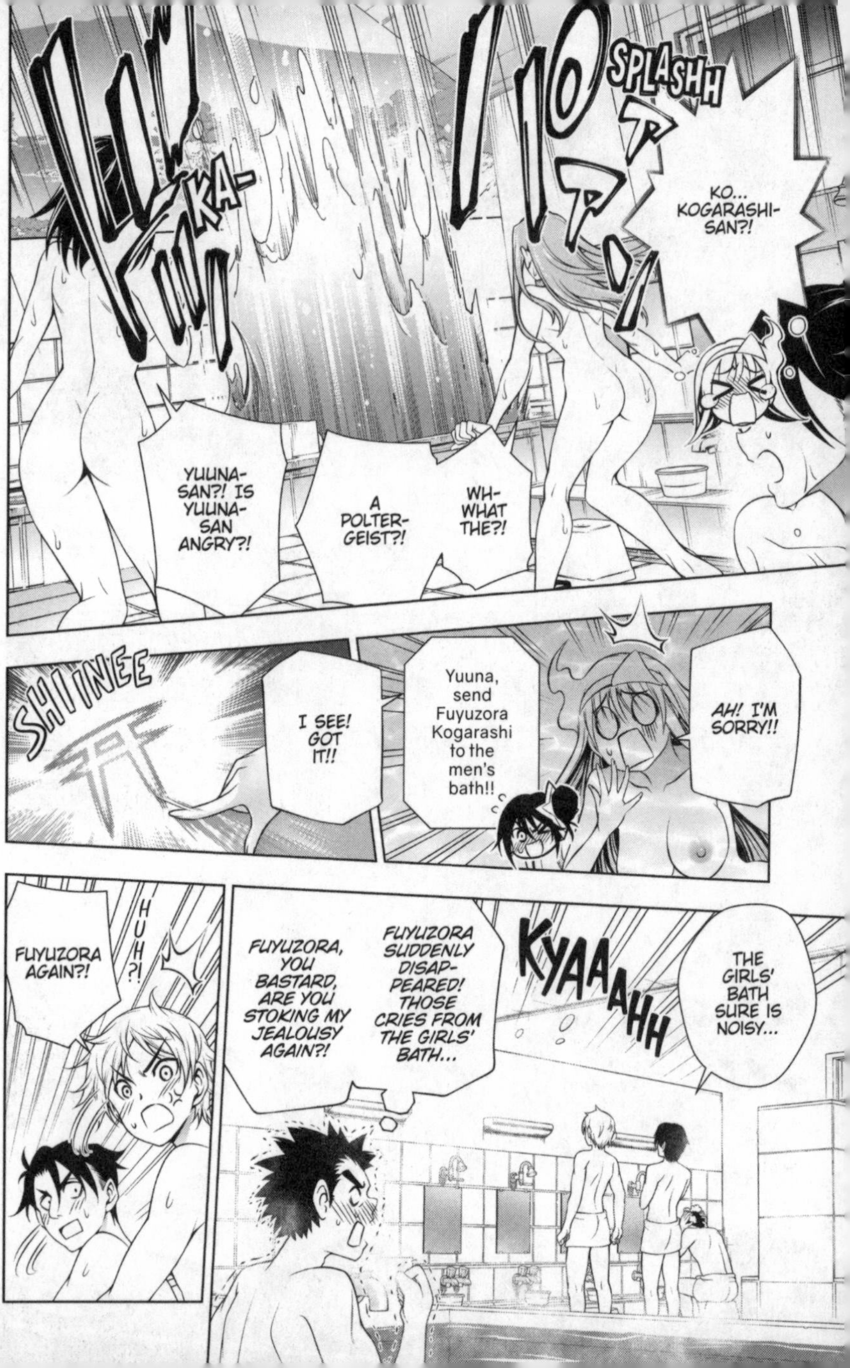
SPLASHH
KO... KOGARASHI-SAN?!
WH-WHAT THE?!
A POLTER-GEIST?!
KA-
YUUNA-SAN?! IS YUUNA-SAN ANGRY?!
AH! I'M SORRY!!
Yuuna, send Fuyuzora Kogarashi to the men's bath!!
I SEE! GOT IT!!
SHIINEE
THE GIRLS' BATH SURE IS NOISY...
KYAAAHH
FUYUZORA SUDDENLY DISAP-PEARED! THOSE CRIES FROM THE GIRLS' BATH...
FUYUZORA, YOU BASTARD, ARE YOU STOKING MY JEALOUSY AGAIN?!
HUH?!
FUYUZORA AGAIN?!

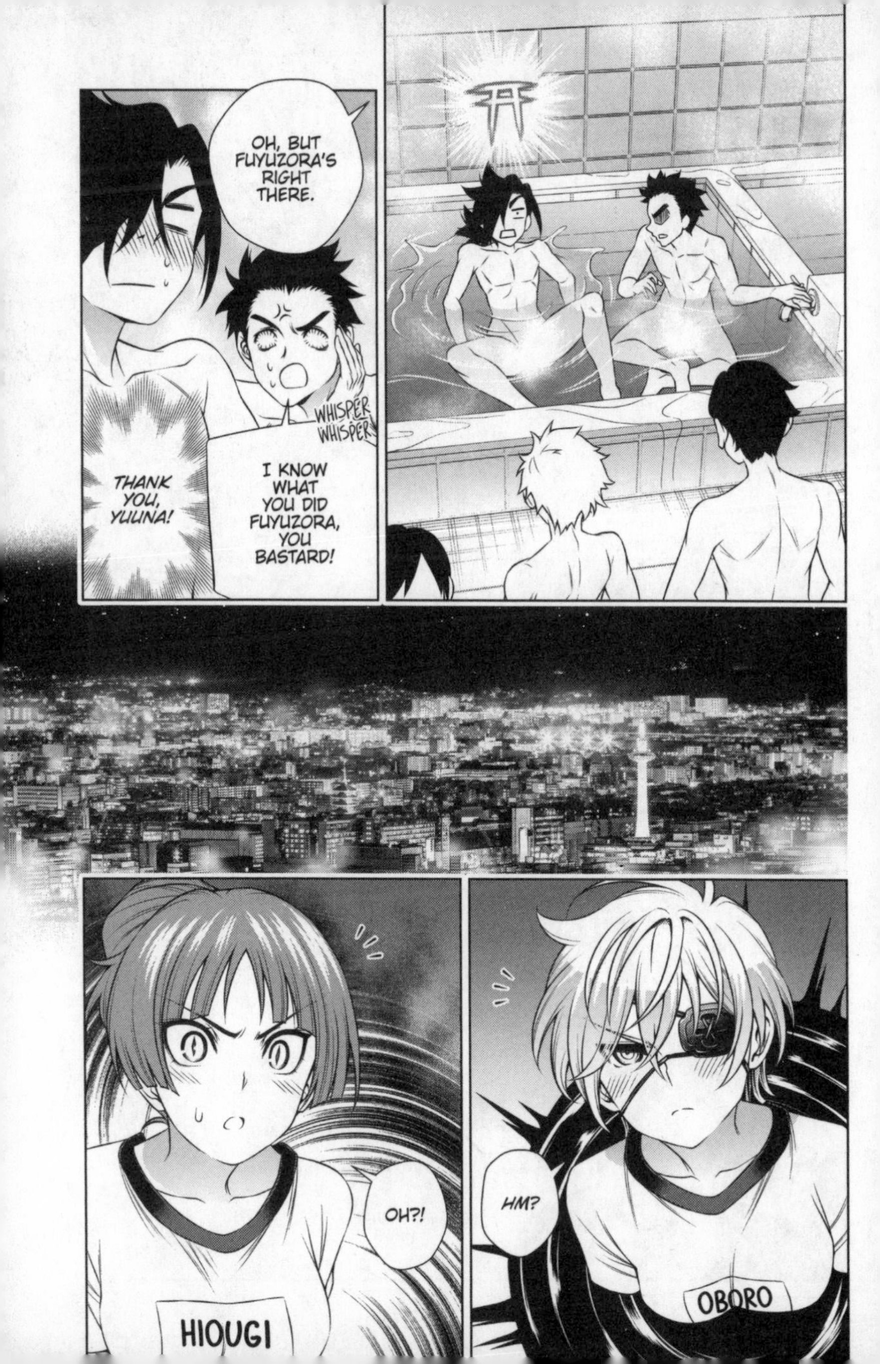
OH, BUT FUYUZORA'S RIGHT THERE.
WHISPER WHISPER
I KNOW WHAT YOU DID FUYUZORA, YOU BASTARD!
THANK YOU, YUUNA!
HM?
OBORO
OH?!
HIOUGI

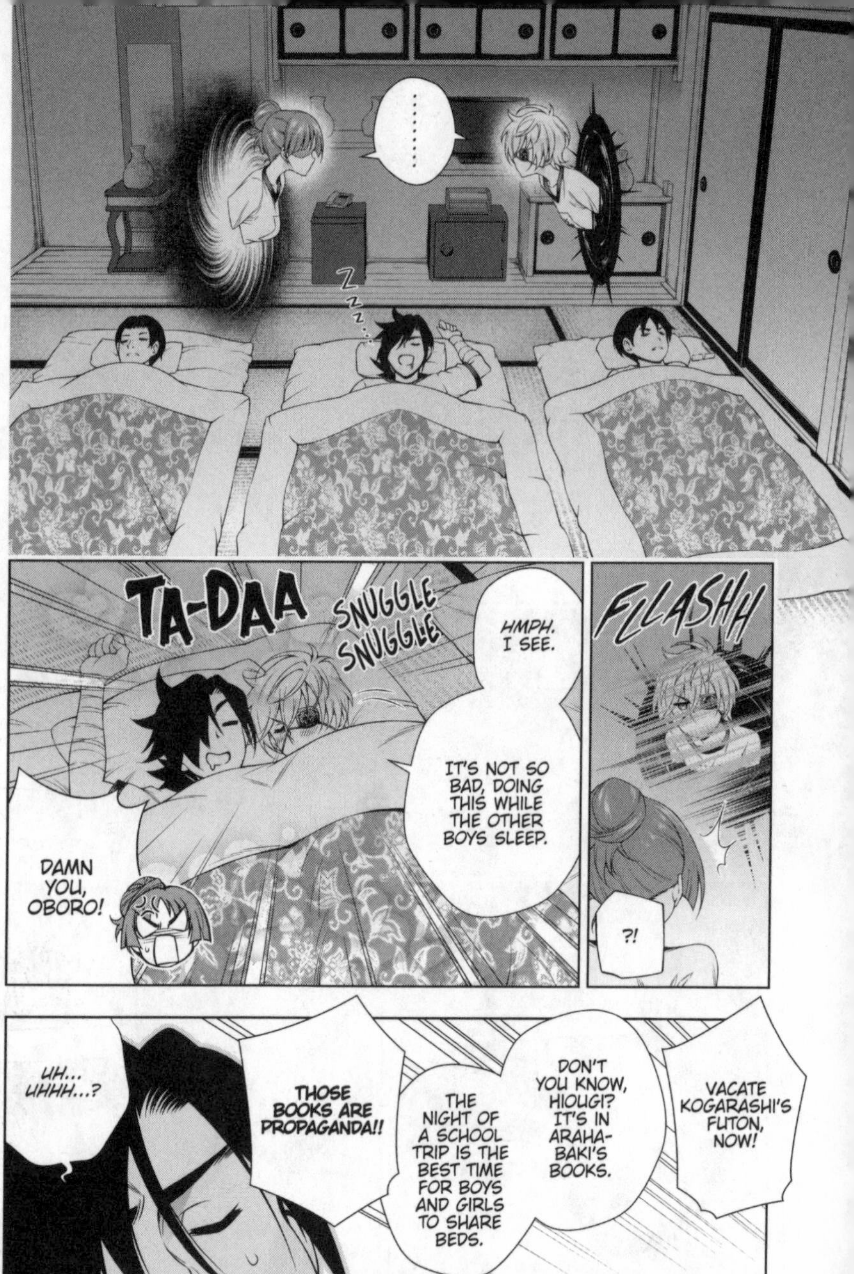
......
Z Z Z...
FLLASHH
?!
HMPH. I SEE.
SNUGGLE SNUGGLE
TA-DAA
IT'S NOT SO BAD, DOING THIS WHILE THE OTHER BOYS SLEEP.
DAMN YOU, OBORO!
VACATE KOGARASHI'S FUTON, NOW!
DON'T YOU KNOW, HIOUGI? IT'S IN ARAHA-BAKI'S BOOKS.
THE NIGHT OF A SCHOOL TRIP IS THE BEST TIME FOR BOYS AND GIRLS TO SHARE BEDS.
THOSE BOOKS ARE PROPAGANDA!!
UH... UHHH...?

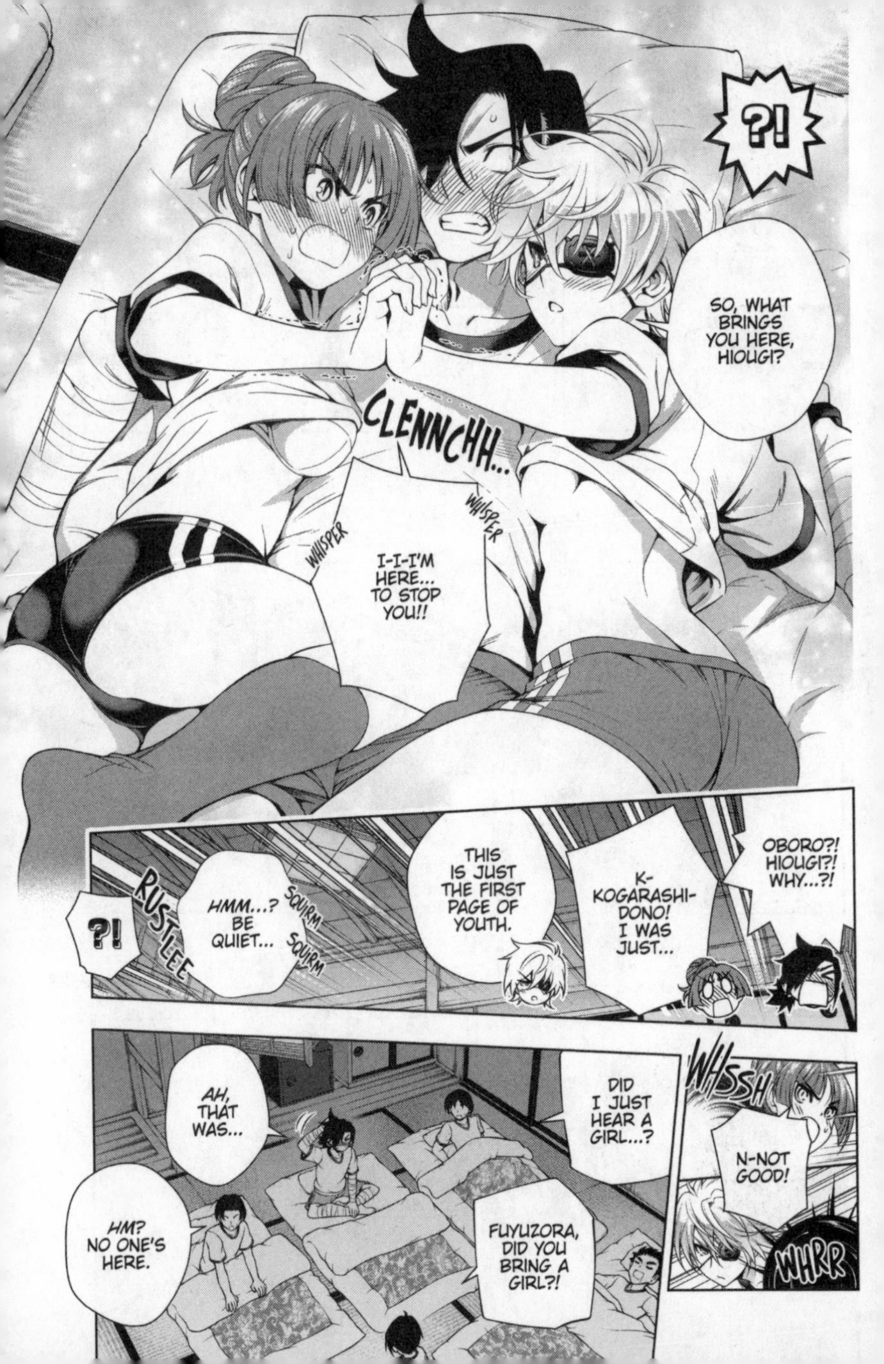
?!
SO, WHAT BRINGS YOU HERE, HIOUGI?
CLENNCHH...
WHISPER
WHISPER
I-I-I'M HERE... TO STOP YOU!!
OBORO?! HIOUGI?! WHY...?!
K-KOGARASHI-DONO! I WAS JUST...
THIS IS JUST THE FIRST PAGE OF YOUTH.
SQUIRM
SQUIRM
HMM...? BE QUIET...
RUSTLEE
?!
WHSSH
N-NOT GOOD!
WHRR
DID I JUST HEAR A GIRL...?
AH, THAT WAS...
FUYUZORA, DID YOU BRING A GIRL?!
HM? NO ONE'S HERE.

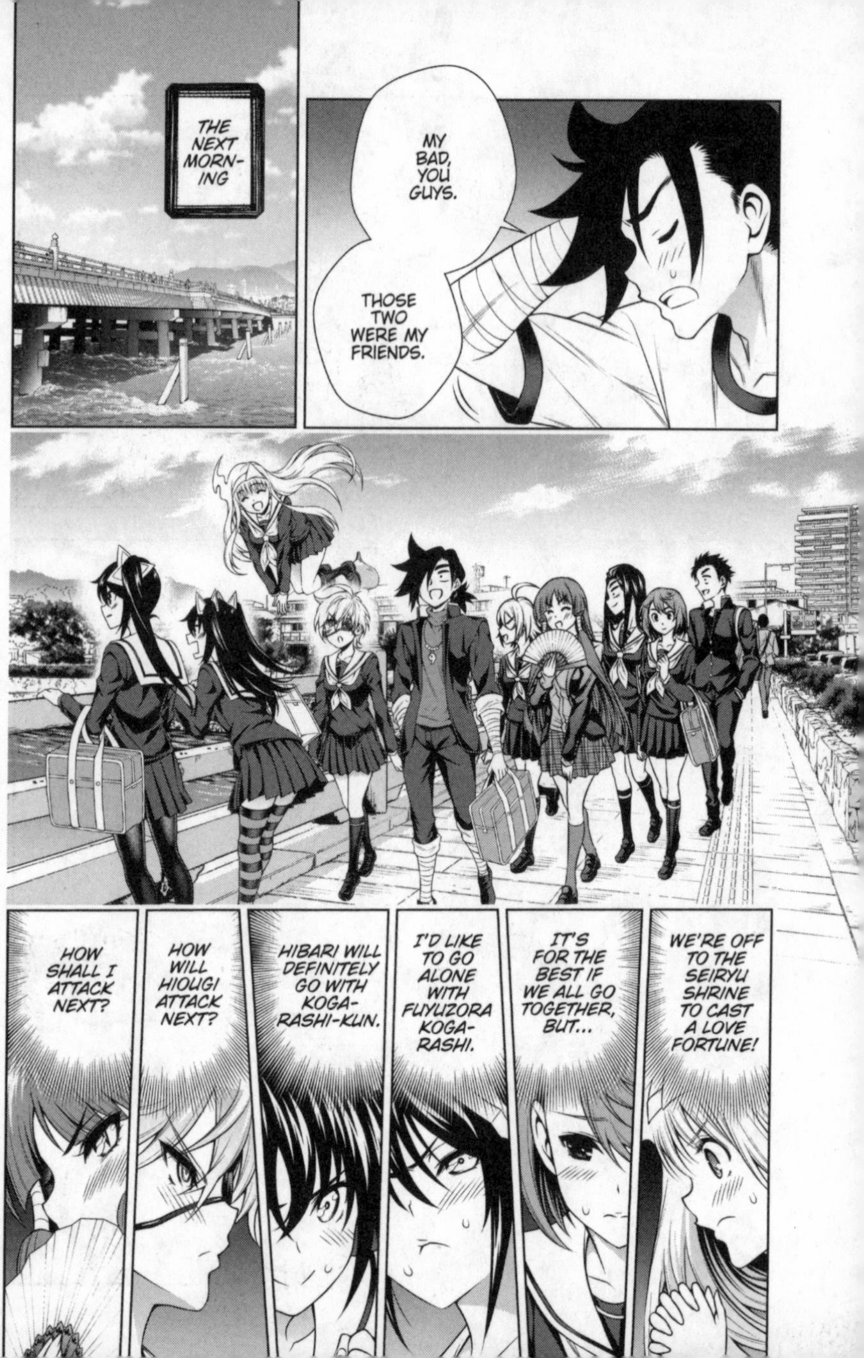
MY BAD, YOU GUYS.
THOSE TWO WERE MY FRIENDS.
THE NEXT MORNING
WE'RE OFF TO THE SEIRYU SHRINE TO CAST A LOVE FORTUNE!
IT'S FOR THE BEST IF WE ALL GO TOGETHER, BUT...
I'D LIKE TO GO ALONE WITH FUYUZORA KOGARASHI.
HIBARI WILL DEFINITELY GO WITH KOGARASHI-KUN.
HOW WILL HIOUGI ATTACK NEXT?
HOW SHALL I ATTACK NEXT?

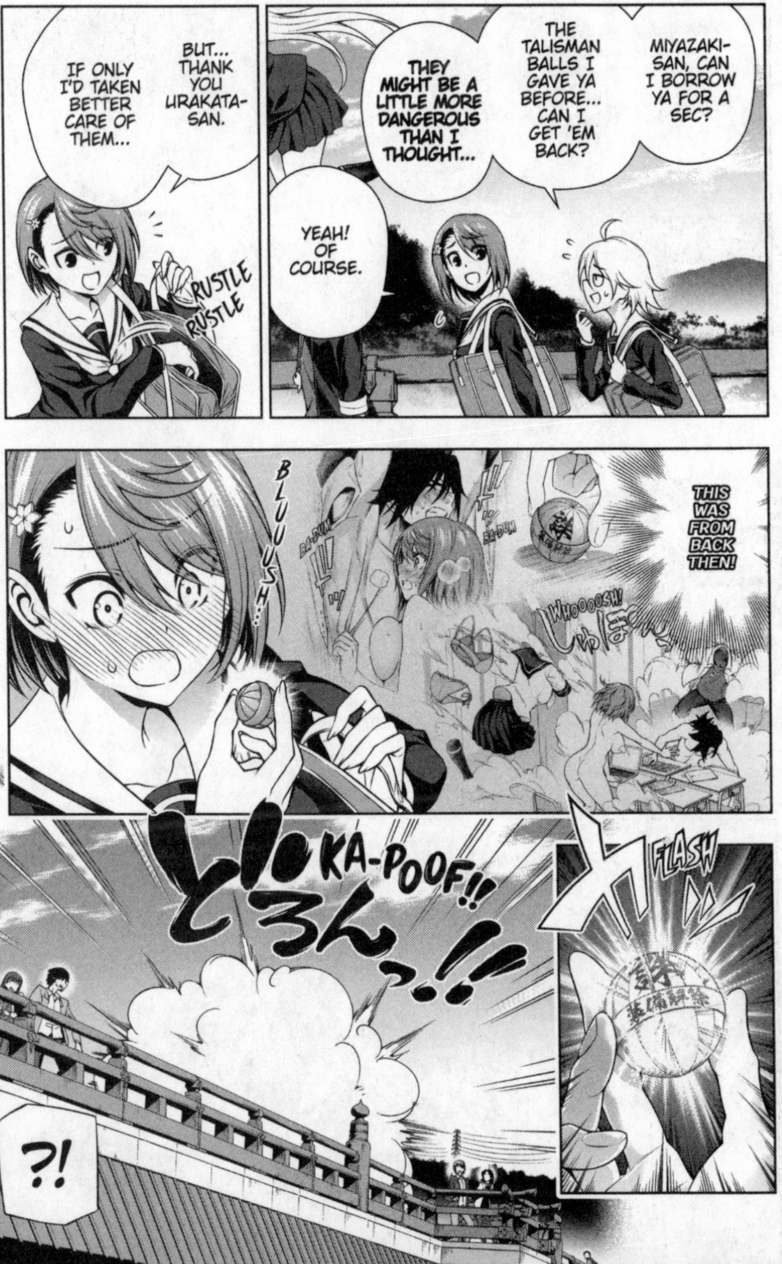
MIYAZAKI-SAN, CAN I BORROW YA FOR A SEC?
THE TALISMAN BALLS I GAVE YA BEFORE... CAN I GET 'EM BACK?
THEY MIGHT BE A LITTLE MORE DANGEROUS THAN I THOUGHT...
YEAH! OF COURSE.
BUT... THANK YOU URAKATA-SAN.
IF ONLY I'D TAKEN BETTER CARE OF THEM...
RUSTLE RUSTLE
THIS WAS FROM BACK THEN!
BA-DUM BA-DUM
WHOOOOSH!
BLUUUSH...
FLASH
KA-POOF!!
?!

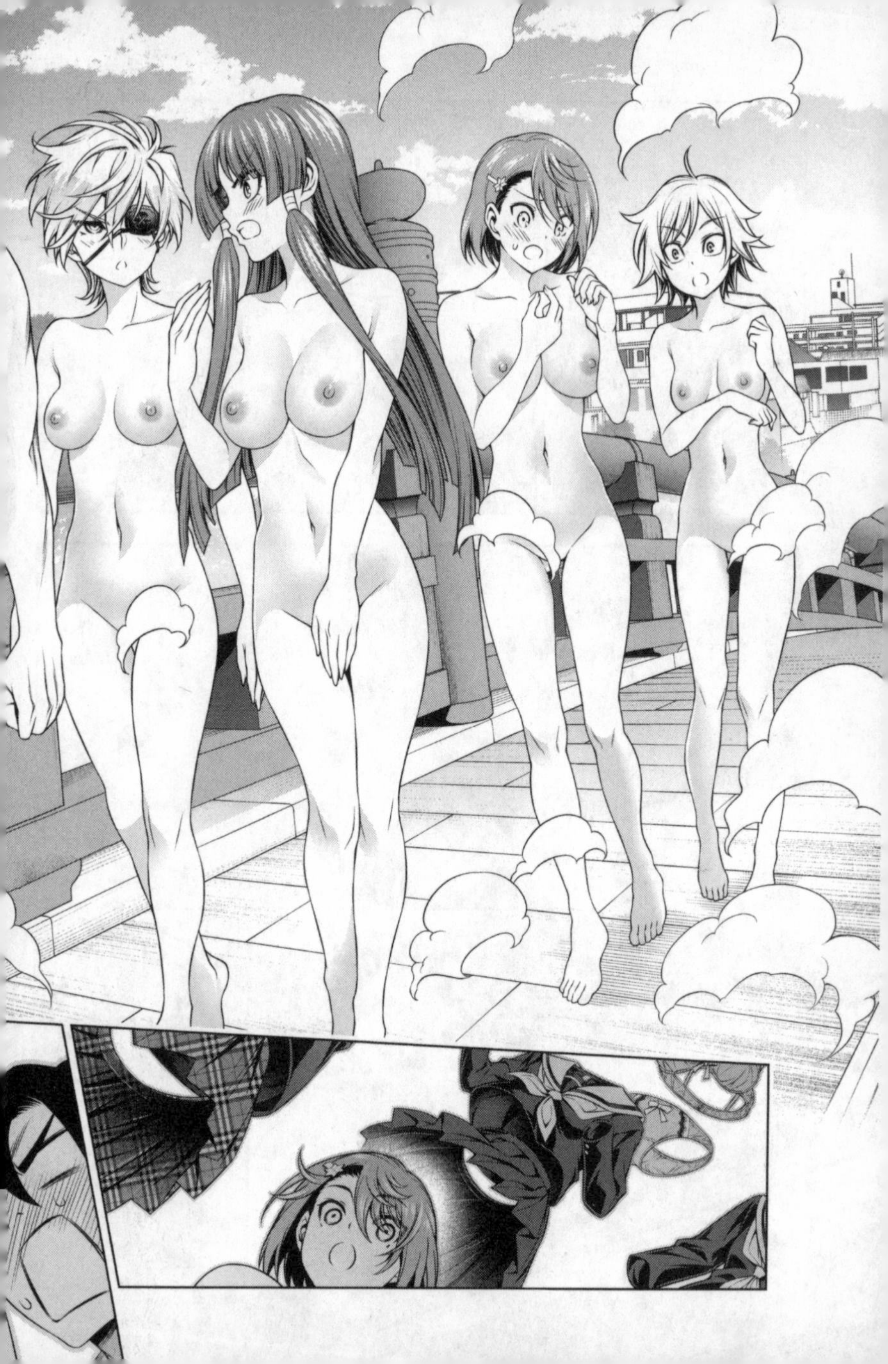

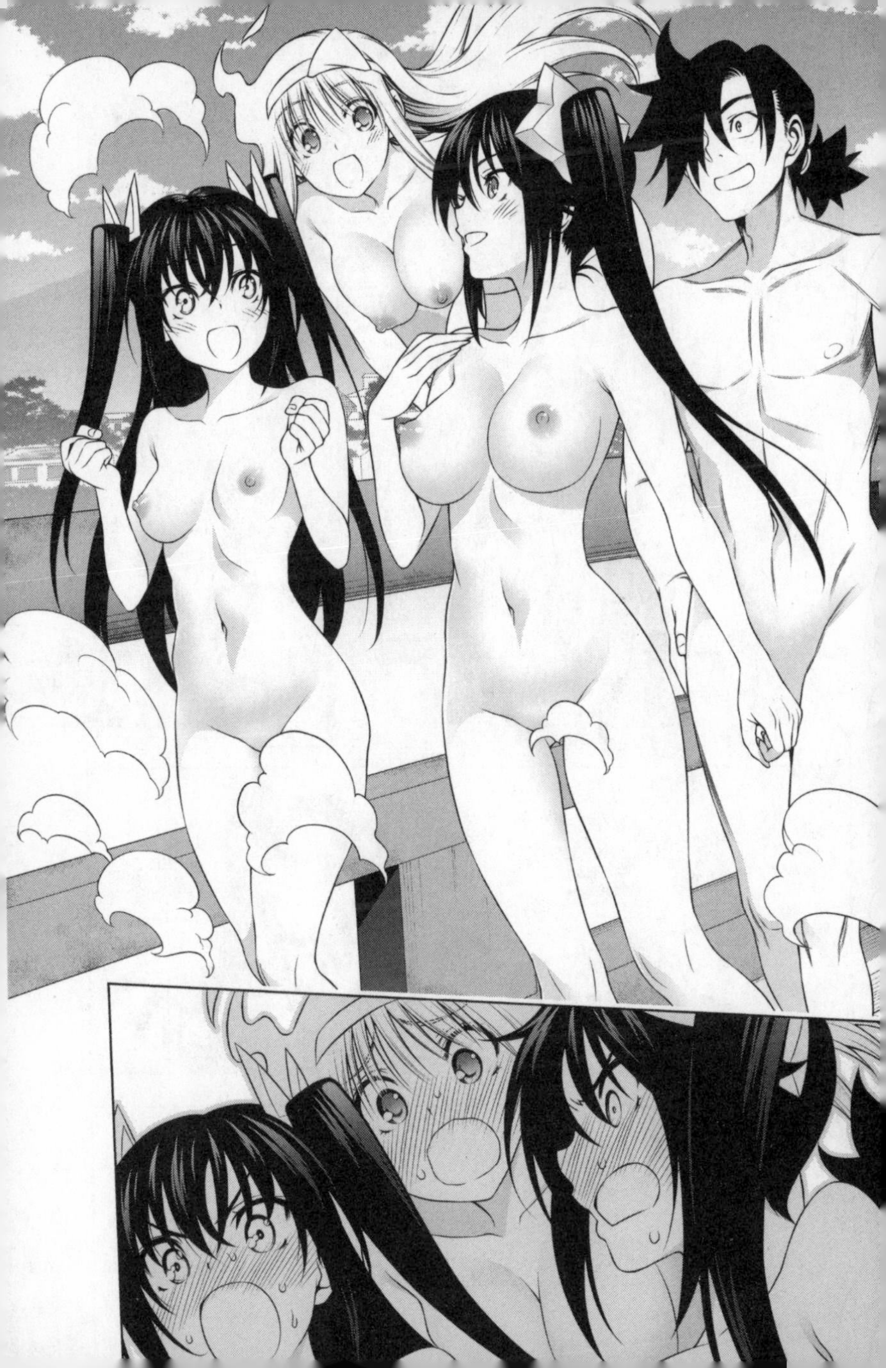

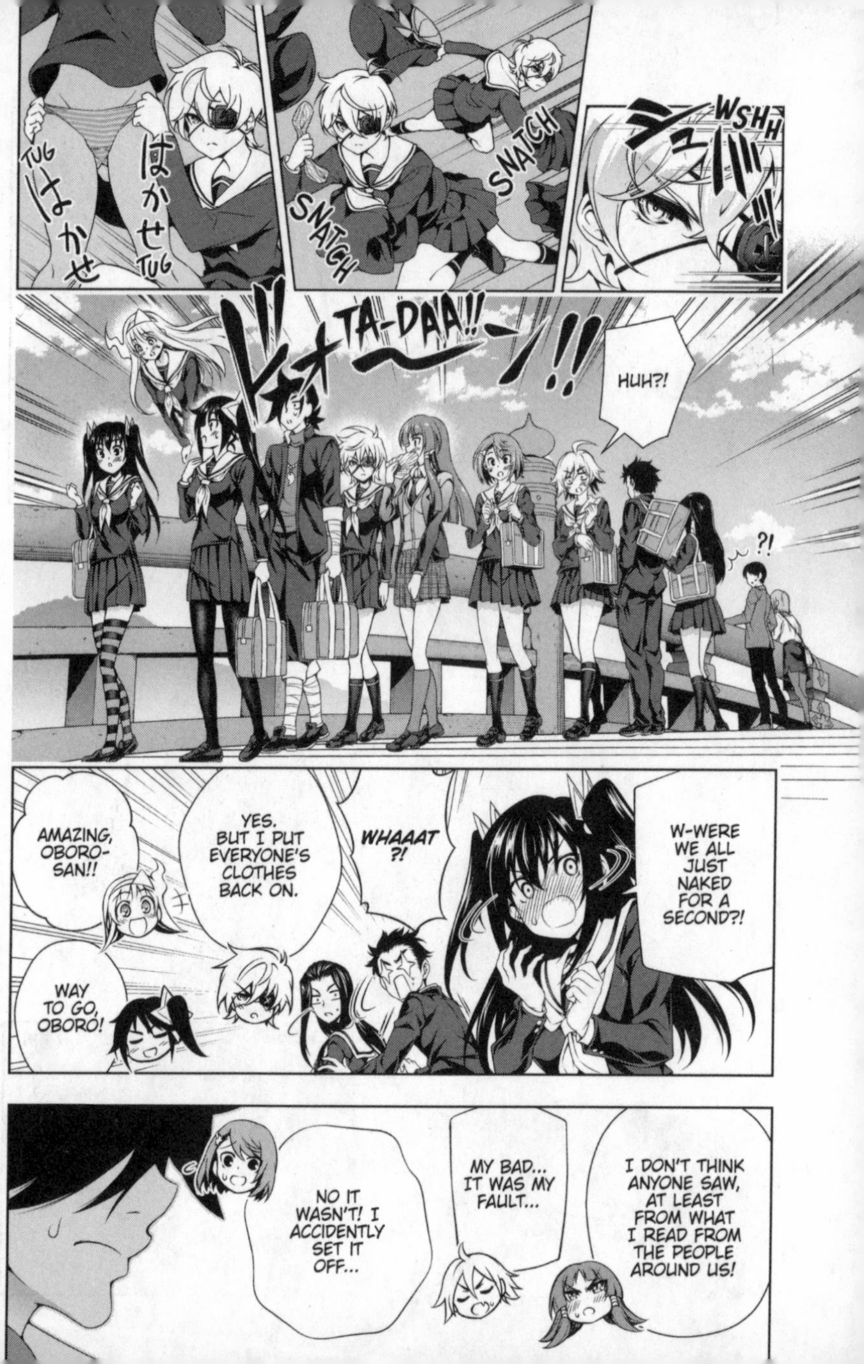

WSHH
SNATCH
SNATCH
はかせ
TUG
はかせ
TUG
TA-DAA!!
HUH?!
?!
W-WERE WE ALL JUST NAKED FOR A SECOND?!
WHAAAT?!
YES. BUT I PUT EVERYONE'S CLOTHES BACK ON.
AMAZING, OBORO-SAN!!
WAY TO GO, OBORO!
I DON'T THINK ANYONE SAW, AT LEAST FROM WHAT I READ FROM THE PEOPLE AROUND US!
MY BAD... IT WAS MY FAULT...
NO IT WASN'T! I ACCIDENTLY SET IT OFF...

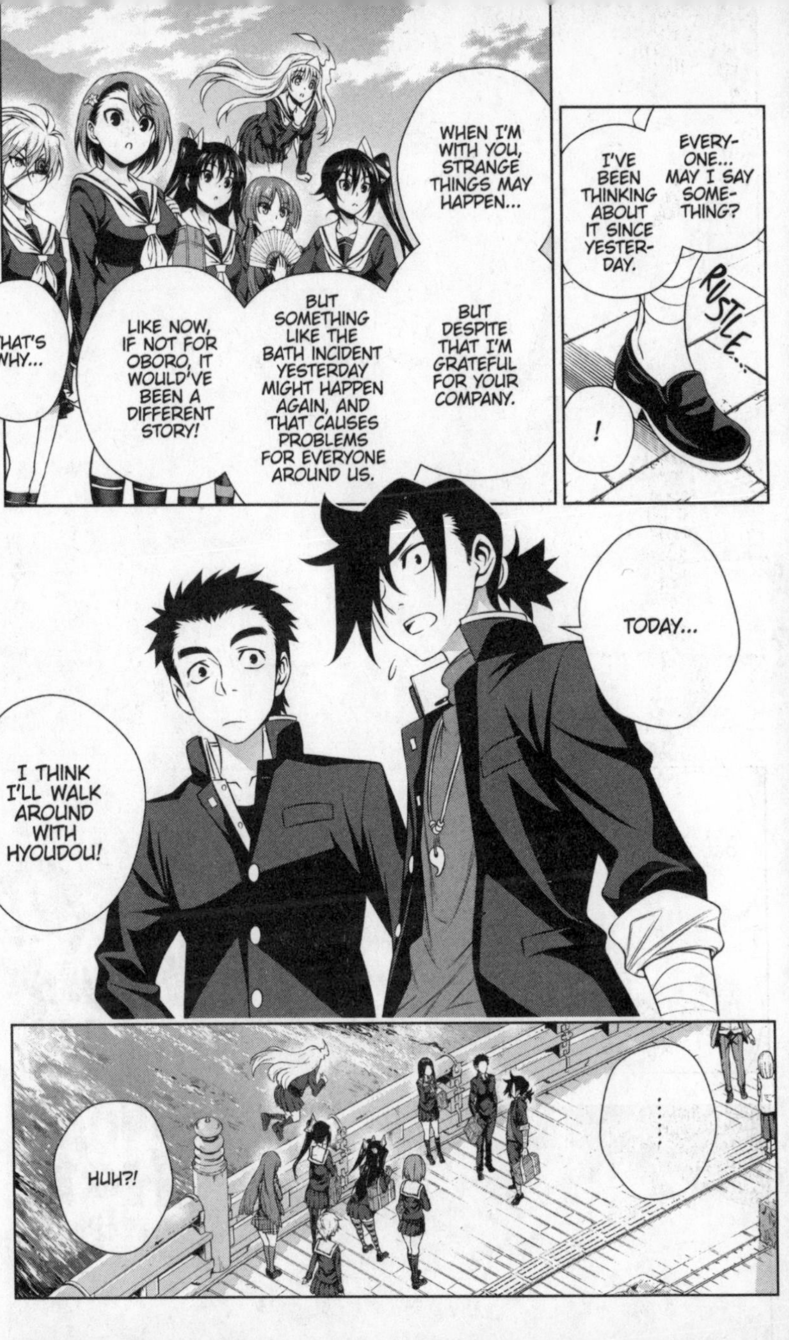
EVERY-ONE... MAY I SAY SOME-THING?
I'VE BEEN THINKING ABOUT IT SINCE YESTER-DAY.
RUSTLE...
!
WHEN I'M WITH YOU, STRANGE THINGS MAY HAPPEN...
BUT DESPITE THAT I'M GRATEFUL FOR YOUR COMPANY.
BUT SOMETHING LIKE THE BATH INCIDENT YESTERDAY MIGHT HAPPEN AGAIN, AND THAT CAUSES PROBLEMS FOR EVERYONE AROUND US.
LIKE NOW, IF NOT FOR OBORO, IT WOULD'VE BEEN A DIFFERENT STORY!
THAT'S WHY...
TODAY...
I THINK I'LL WALK AROUND WITH HYOUDOU!
......
HUH?!

Yuuna and the Haunted Hot Springs

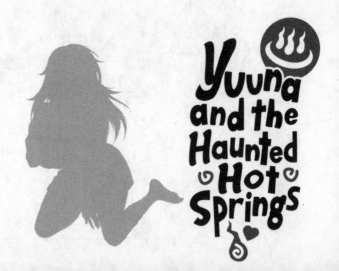

145 Chisaki-san and a White T-shirt

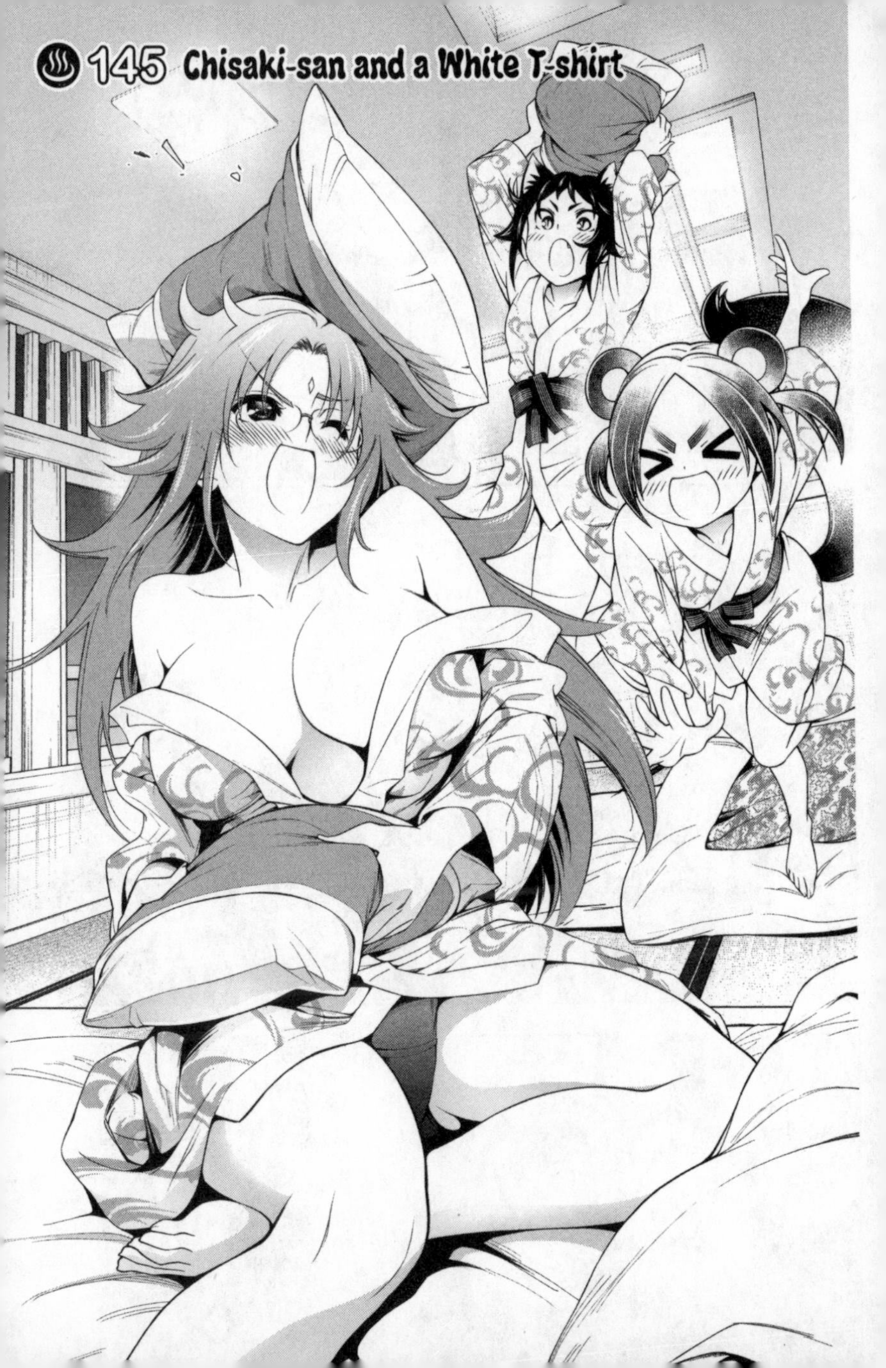

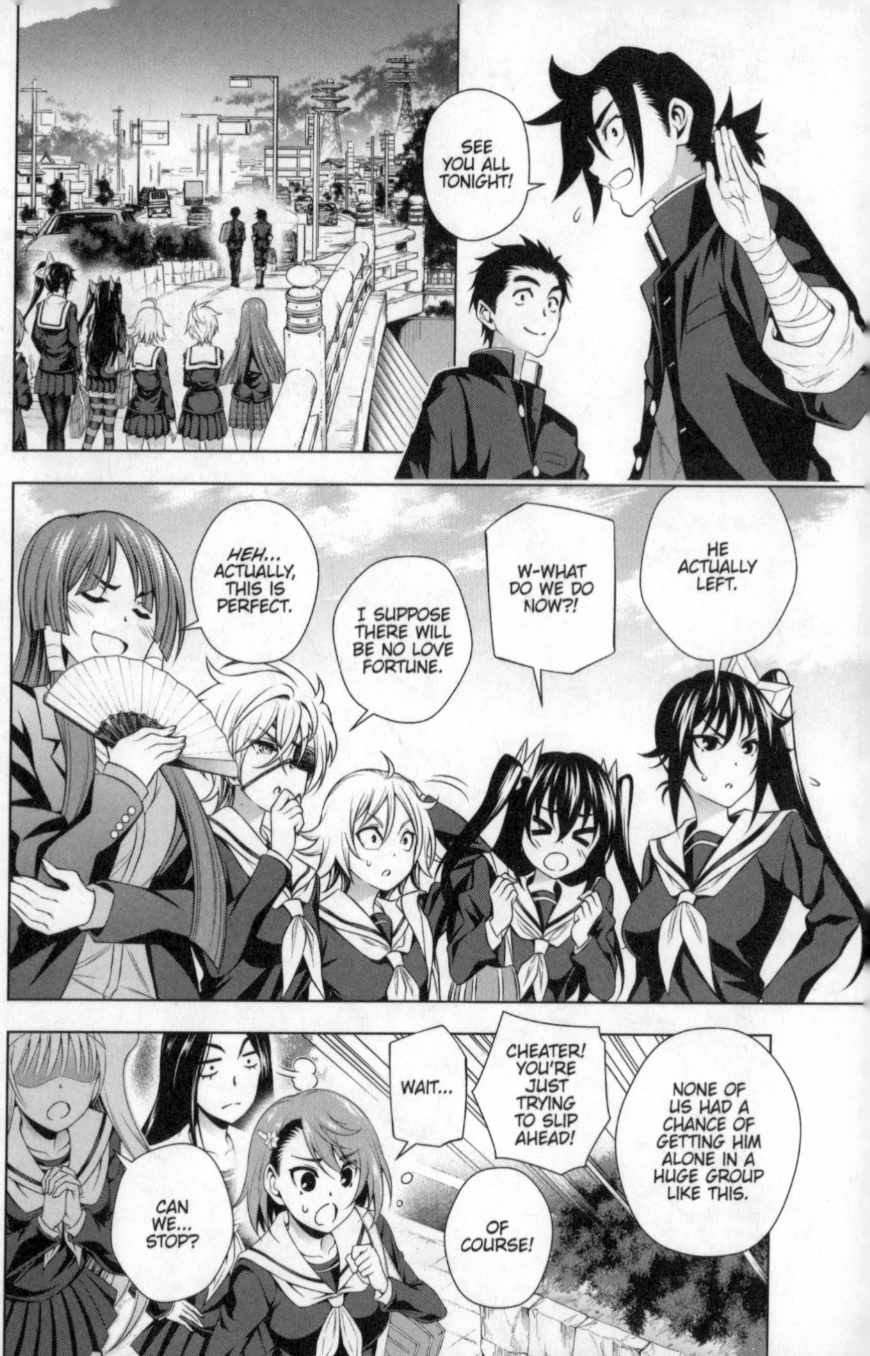
SEE YOU ALL TONIGHT!
HE ACTUALLY LEFT.
W-WHAT DO WE DO NOW?!
I SUPPOSE THERE WILL BE NO LOVE FORTUNE.
HEH... ACTUALLY, THIS IS PERFECT.
NONE OF US HAD A CHANCE OF GETTING HIM ALONE IN A HUGE GROUP LIKE THIS.
CHEATER! YOU'RE JUST TRYING TO SLIP AHEAD!
WAIT...
OF COURSE!
CAN WE... STOP?

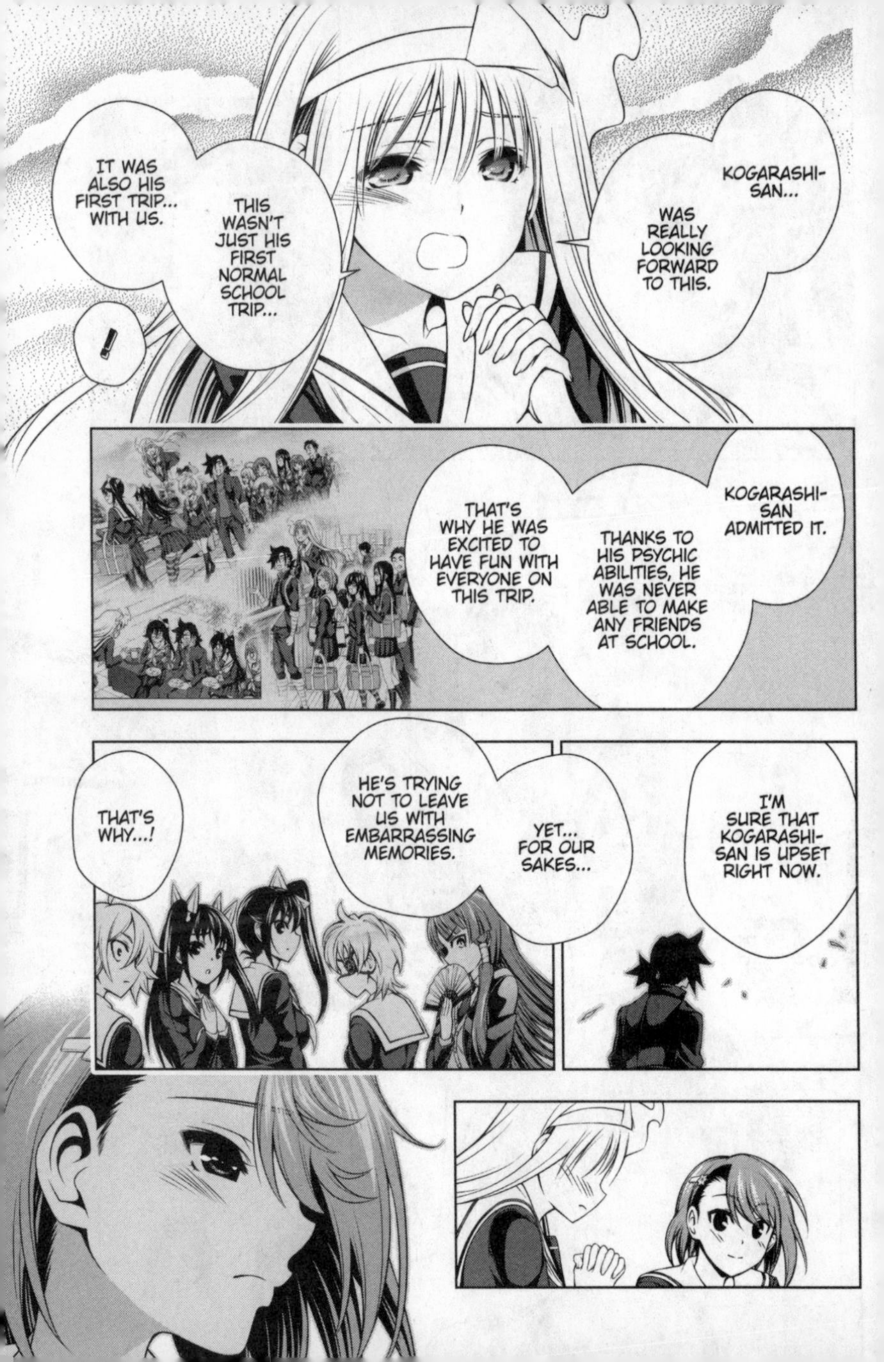
KOGARASHI-SAN...
WAS REALLY LOOKING FORWARD TO THIS.
THIS WASN'T JUST HIS FIRST NORMAL SCHOOL TRIP...
IT WAS ALSO HIS FIRST TRIP... WITH US.
!
KOGARASHI-SAN ADMITTED IT.
THANKS TO HIS PSYCHIC ABILITIES, HE WAS NEVER ABLE TO MAKE ANY FRIENDS AT SCHOOL.
THAT'S WHY HE WAS EXCITED TO HAVE FUN WITH EVERYONE ON THIS TRIP.
I'M SURE THAT KOGARASHI-SAN IS UPSET RIGHT NOW.
YET... FOR OUR SAKES...
HE'S TRYING NOT TO LEAVE US WITH EMBARRASSING MEMORIES.
THAT'S WHY...!

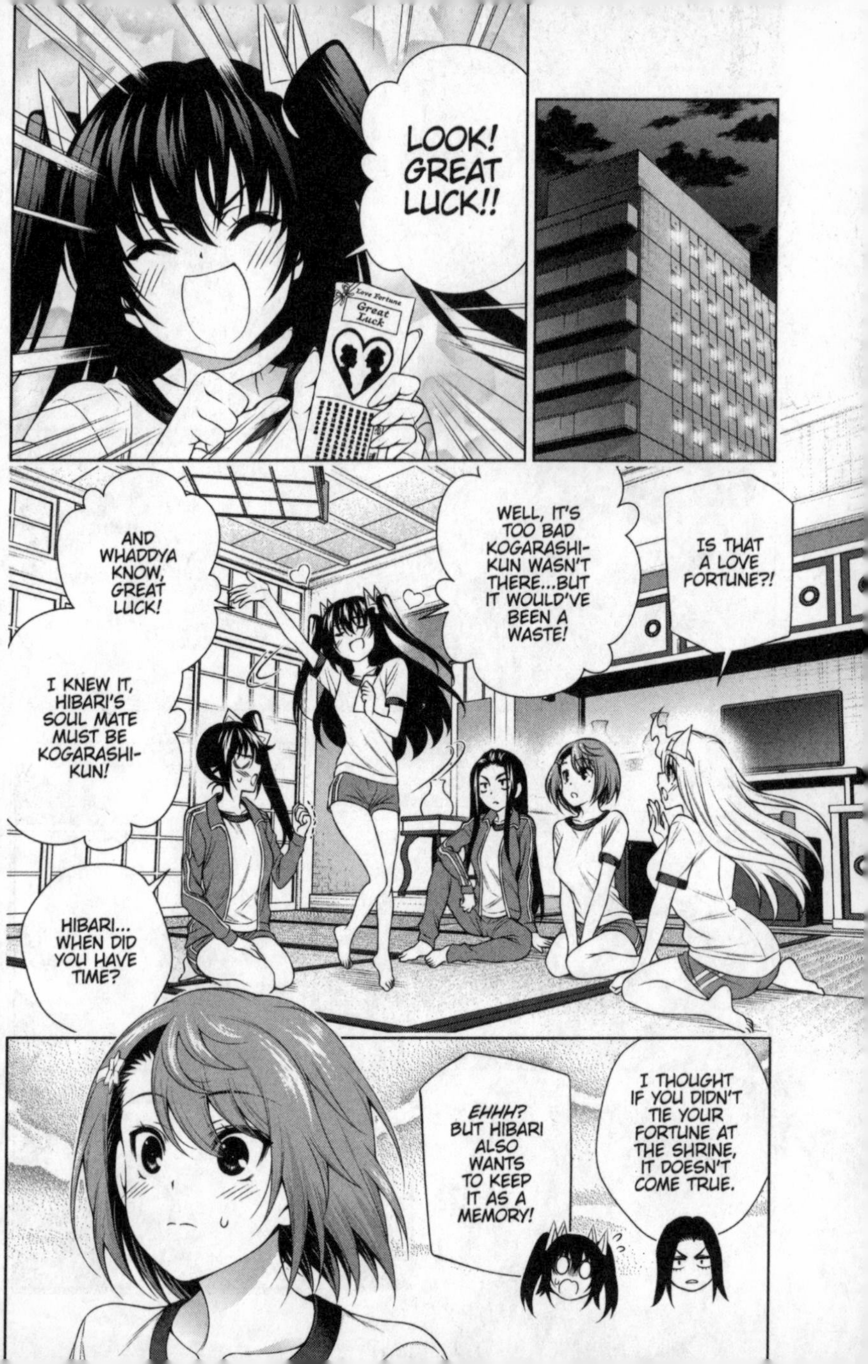
LOOK! GREAT LUCK!!
Love Fortune
Great Luck
IS THAT A LOVE FORTUNE?!
WELL, IT'S TOO BAD KOGARASHI-KUN WASN'T THERE...BUT IT WOULD'VE BEEN A WASTE!
AND WHADDYA KNOW, GREAT LUCK!
I KNEW IT, HIBARI'S SOUL MATE MUST BE KOGARASHI-KUN!
HIBARI... WHEN DID YOU HAVE TIME?
I THOUGHT IF YOU DIDN'T TIE YOUR FORTUNE AT THE SHRINE, IT DOESN'T COME TRUE.
EHHH? BUT HIBARI ALSO WANTS TO KEEP IT AS A MEMORY!

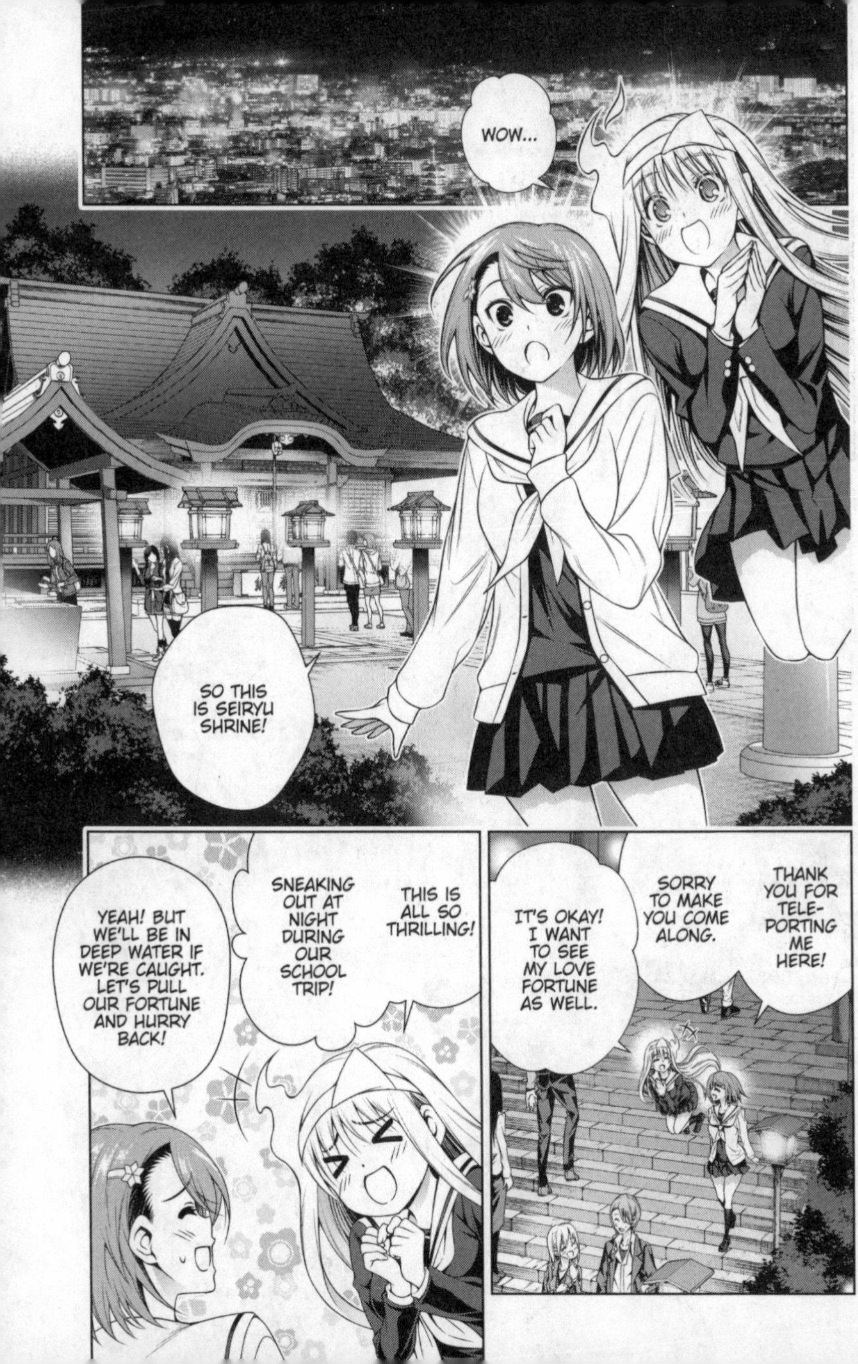
WOW...
SO THIS IS SEIRYU SHRINE!
THANK YOU FOR TELE-PORTING ME HERE!
SORRY TO MAKE YOU COME ALONG.
IT'S OKAY! I WANT TO SEE MY LOVE FORTUNE AS WELL.
THIS IS ALL SO THRILLING!
SNEAKING OUT AT NIGHT DURING OUR SCHOOL TRIP!
YEAH! BUT WE'LL BE IN DEEP WATER IF WE'RE CAUGHT. LET'S PULL OUR FORTUNE AND HURRY BACK!

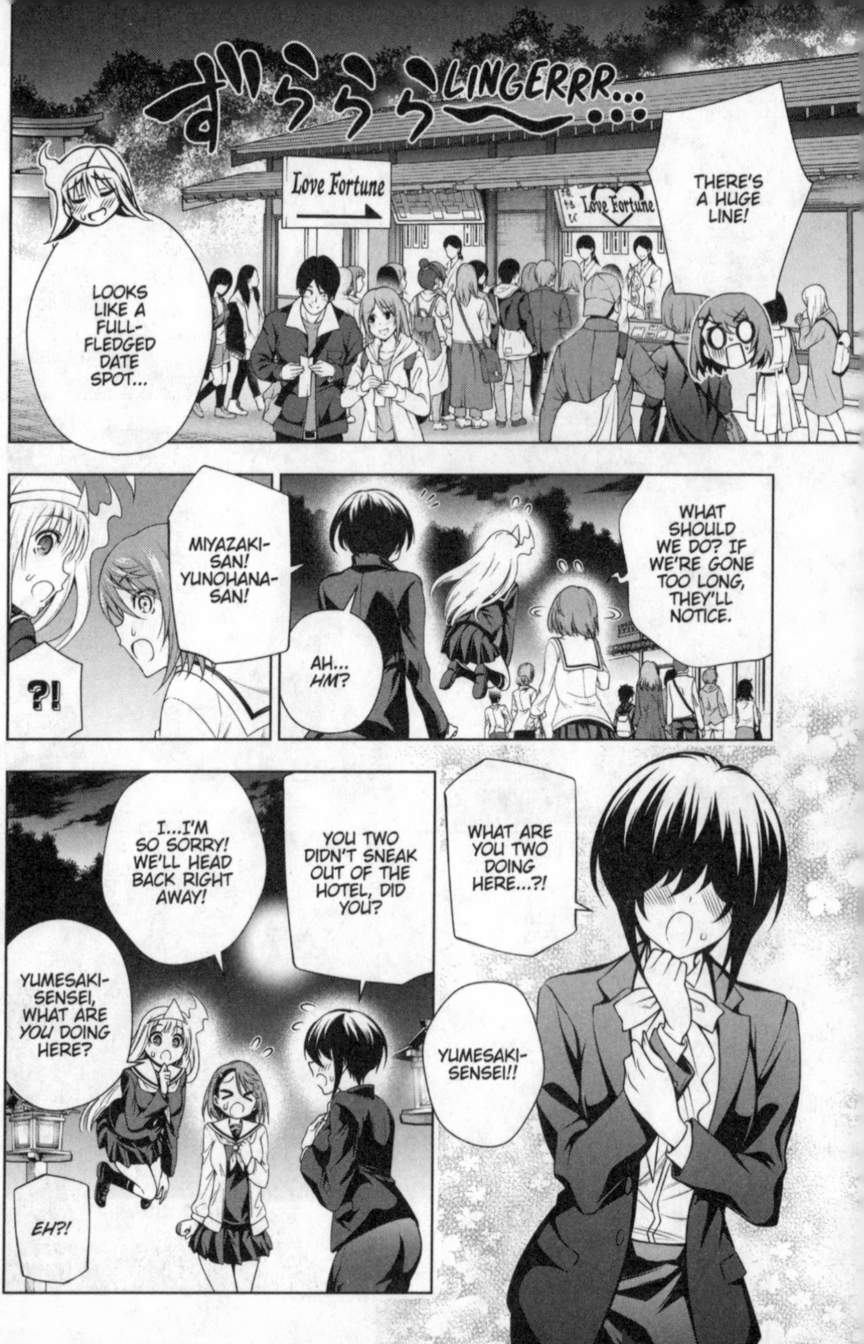

LINGERRR...
Love Fortune
Love Fortune
THERE'S A HUGE LINE!
LOOKS LIKE A FULL-FLEDGED DATE SPOT...
WHAT SHOULD WE DO? IF WE'RE GONE TOO LONG, THEY'LL NOTICE.
AH... HM?
MIYAZAKI-SAN! YUNOHANA-SAN!
?!
WHAT ARE YOU TWO DOING HERE...?!
YUMESAKI-SENSEI!!
YOU TWO DIDN'T SNEAK OUT OF THE HOTEL, DID YOU?
I...I'M SO SORRY! WE'LL HEAD BACK RIGHT AWAY!
YUMESAKI-SENSEI, WHAT ARE YOU DOING HERE?
EH?!

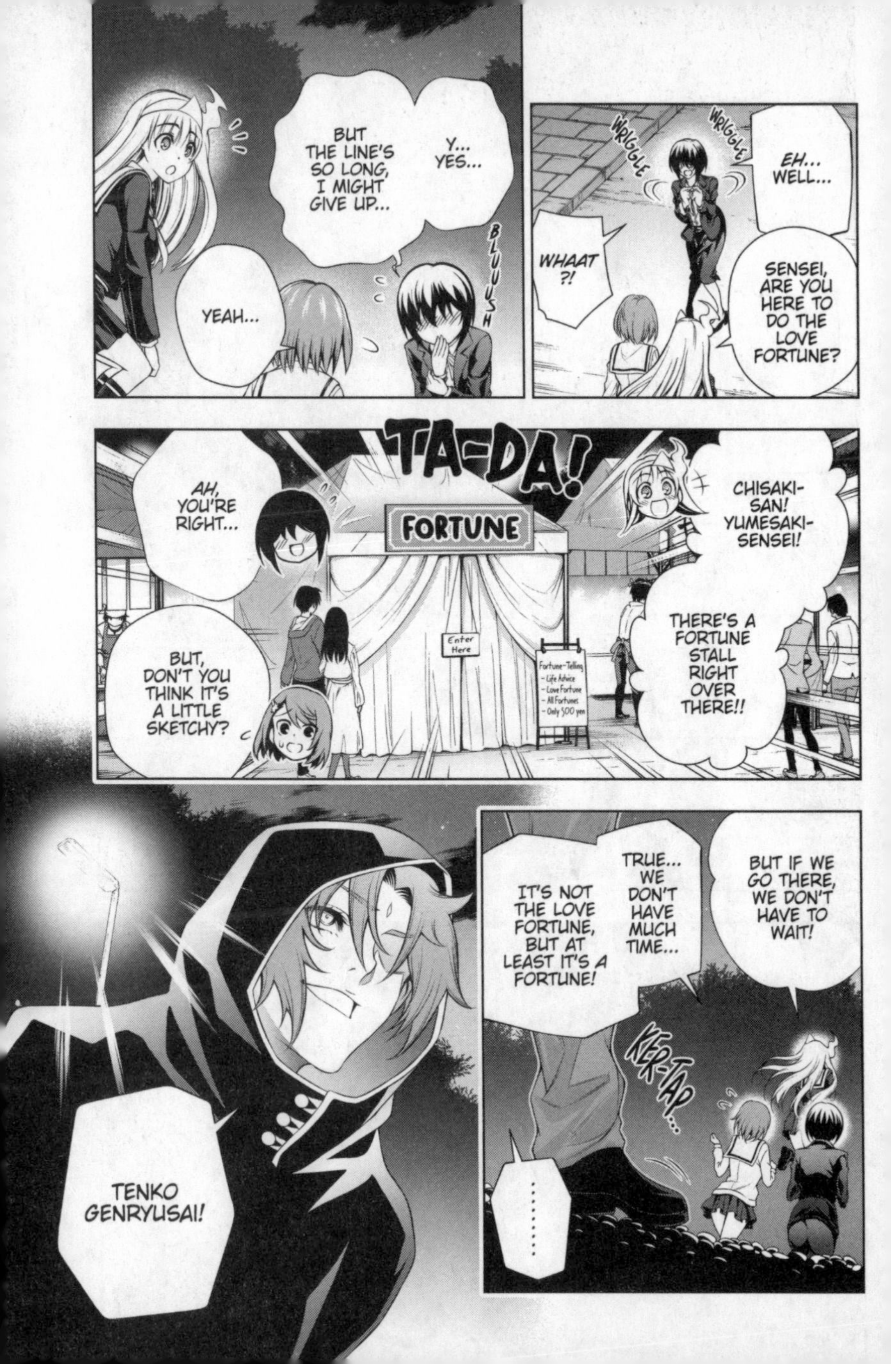
SENSEI, ARE YOU HERE TO DO THE LOVE FORTUNE?
EH... WELL...
WRIGGLE
WRIGGLE
WHAAT?!
Y... YES...
BUT THE LINE'S SO LONG, I MIGHT GIVE UP...
BLUUUSH
YEAH...
TA-DA!
CHISAKI-SAN! YUMESAKI-SENSEI!
THERE'S A FORTUNE STALL RIGHT OVER THERE!!
FORTUNE
AH, YOU'RE RIGHT...
Enter Here
Fortune-Telling
- Life Advice
- Love Fortune
- All Fortunes
- Only 500 yen
BUT, DON'T YOU THINK IT'S A LITTLE SKETCHY?
BUT IF WE GO THERE, WE DON'T HAVE TO WAIT!
TRUE... WE DON'T HAVE MUCH TIME...
IT'S NOT THE LOVE FORTUNE, BUT AT LEAST IT'S A FORTUNE!
KER-TAP...
......
TENKO GENRYUSAI!

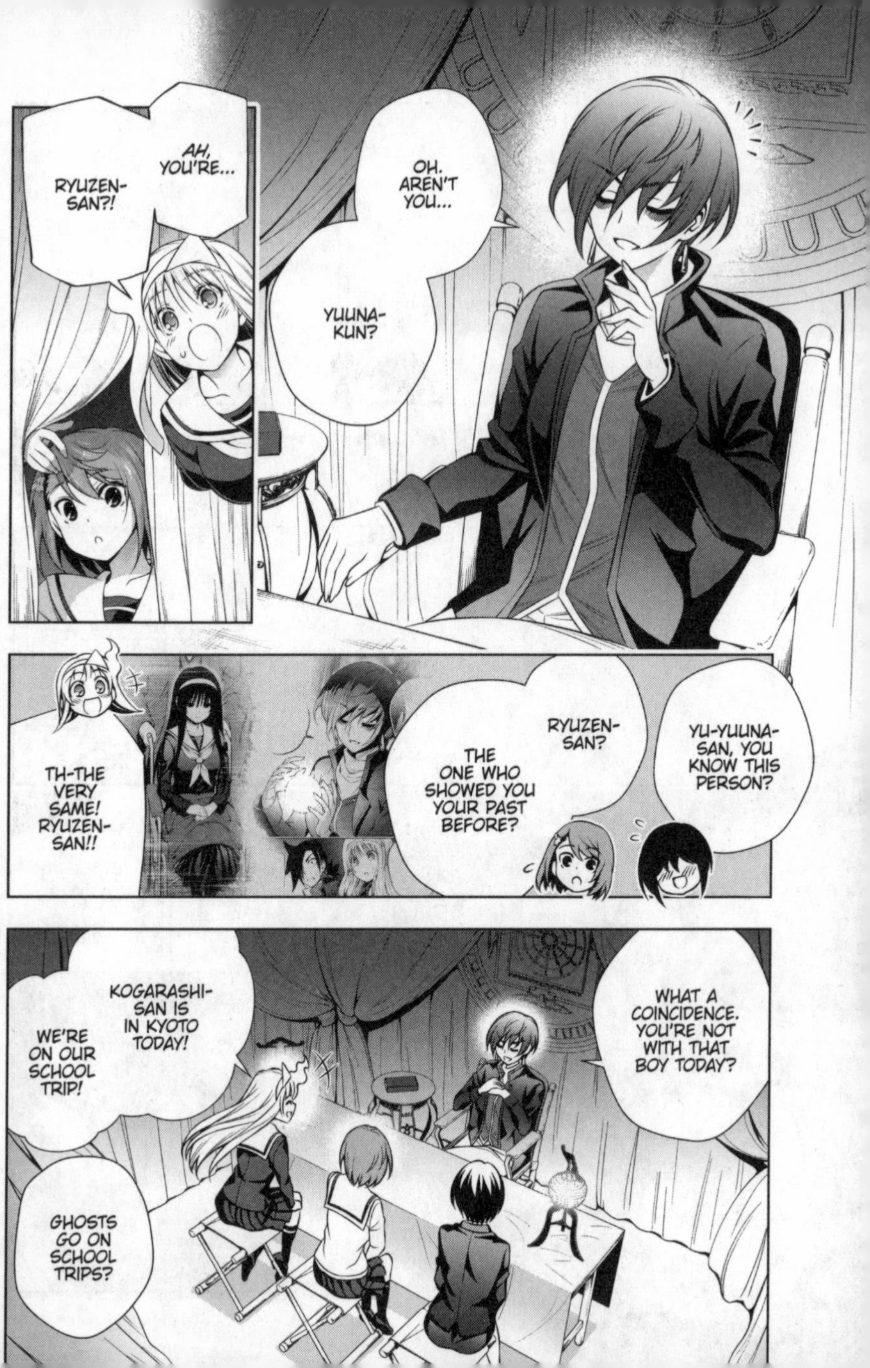
OH. AREN'T YOU...
YUUNA-KUN?
AH, YOU'RE...
RYUZEN-SAN?!
YU-YUUNA-SAN, YOU KNOW THIS PERSON?
RYUZEN-SAN?
THE ONE WHO SHOWED YOU YOUR PAST BEFORE?
TH-THE VERY SAME! RYUZEN-SAN!!
WHAT A COINCIDENCE. YOU'RE NOT WITH THAT BOY TODAY?
KOGARASHI-SAN IS IN KYOTO TODAY!
WE'RE ON OUR SCHOOL TRIP!
GHOSTS GO ON SCHOOL TRIPS?

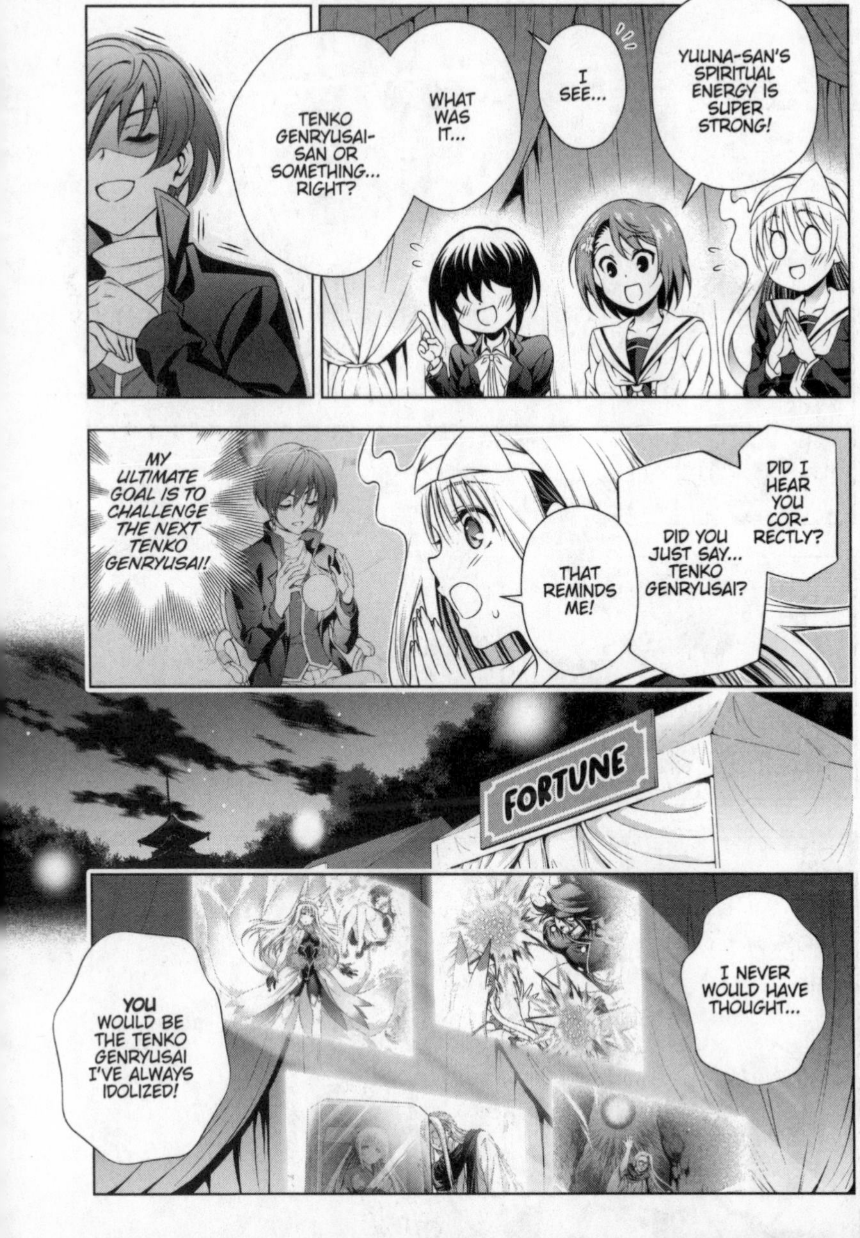
YUUNA-SAN'S SPIRITUAL ENERGY IS SUPER STRONG!
I SEE...
WHAT WAS IT...
TENKO GENRYUSAI-SAN OR SOMETHING... RIGHT?
DID I HEAR YOU COR-RECTLY?
DID YOU JUST SAY... TENKO GENRYUSAI?
THAT REMINDS ME!
MY ULTIMATE GOAL IS TO CHALLENGE THE NEXT TENKO GENRYUSAI!
FORTUNE
I NEVER WOULD HAVE THOUGHT...
YOU WOULD BE THE TENKO GENRYUSAI I'VE ALWAYS IDOLIZED!

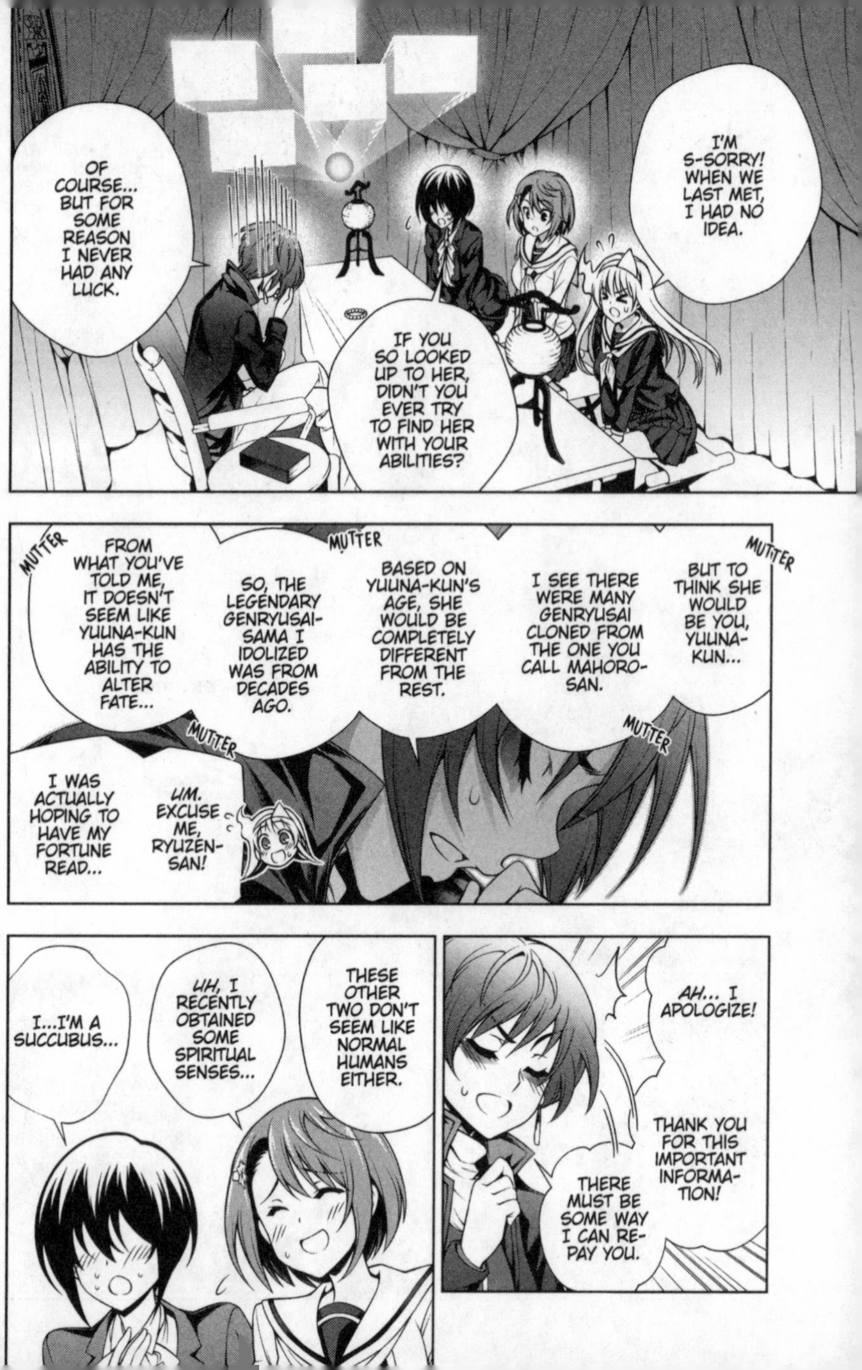
I'M S-SORRY! WHEN WE LAST MET, I HAD NO IDEA.
IF YOU SO LOOKED UP TO HER, DIDN'T YOU EVER TRY TO FIND HER WITH YOUR ABILITIES?
OF COURSE... BUT FOR SOME REASON I NEVER HAD ANY LUCK.
MUTTER
BUT TO THINK SHE WOULD BE YOU, YUUNA-KUN...
I SEE THERE WERE MANY GENRYUSAI CLONED FROM THE ONE YOU CALL MAHORO-SAN.
MUTTER
BASED ON YUUNA-KUN'S AGE, SHE WOULD BE COMPLETELY DIFFERENT FROM THE REST.
SO, THE LEGENDARY GENRYUSAI-SAMA I IDOLIZED WAS FROM DECADES AGO.
MUTTER
FROM WHAT YOU'VE TOLD ME, IT DOESN'T SEEM LIKE YUUNA-KUN HAS THE ABILITY TO ALTER FATE...
MUTTER
MUTTER
UM. EXCUSE ME, RYUZEN-SAN!
I WAS ACTUALLY HOPING TO HAVE MY FORTUNE READ...
AH... I APOLOGIZE!
THANK YOU FOR THIS IMPORTANT INFORMATION!
THERE MUST BE SOME WAY I CAN REPAY YOU.
THESE OTHER TWO DON'T SEEM LIKE NORMAL HUMANS EITHER.
UH, I RECENTLY OBTAINED SOME SPIRITUAL SENSES...
I...I'M A SUCCUBUS...

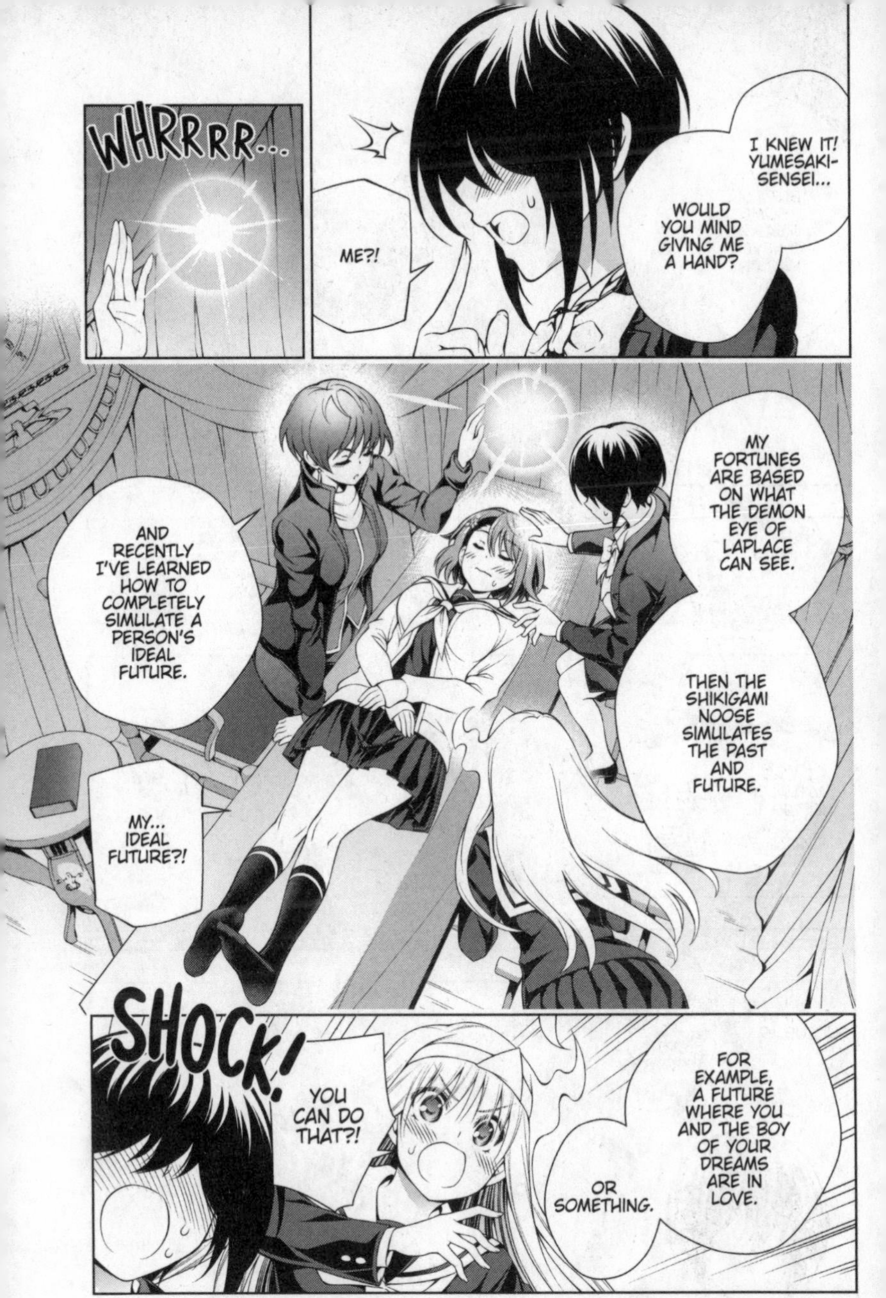
I KNEW IT! YUMESAKI-SENSEI...
WOULD YOU MIND GIVING ME A HAND?
ME?!
WHRRRR...
MY FORTUNES ARE BASED ON WHAT THE DEMON EYE OF LAPLACE CAN SEE.
THEN THE SHIKIGAMI NOOSE SIMULATES THE PAST AND FUTURE.
AND RECENTLY I'VE LEARNED HOW TO COMPLETELY SIMULATE A PERSON'S IDEAL FUTURE.
MY... IDEAL FUTURE?!
FOR EXAMPLE, A FUTURE WHERE YOU AND THE BOY OF YOUR DREAMS ARE IN LOVE.
OR SOMETHING.
YOU CAN DO THAT?!
SHOCK!

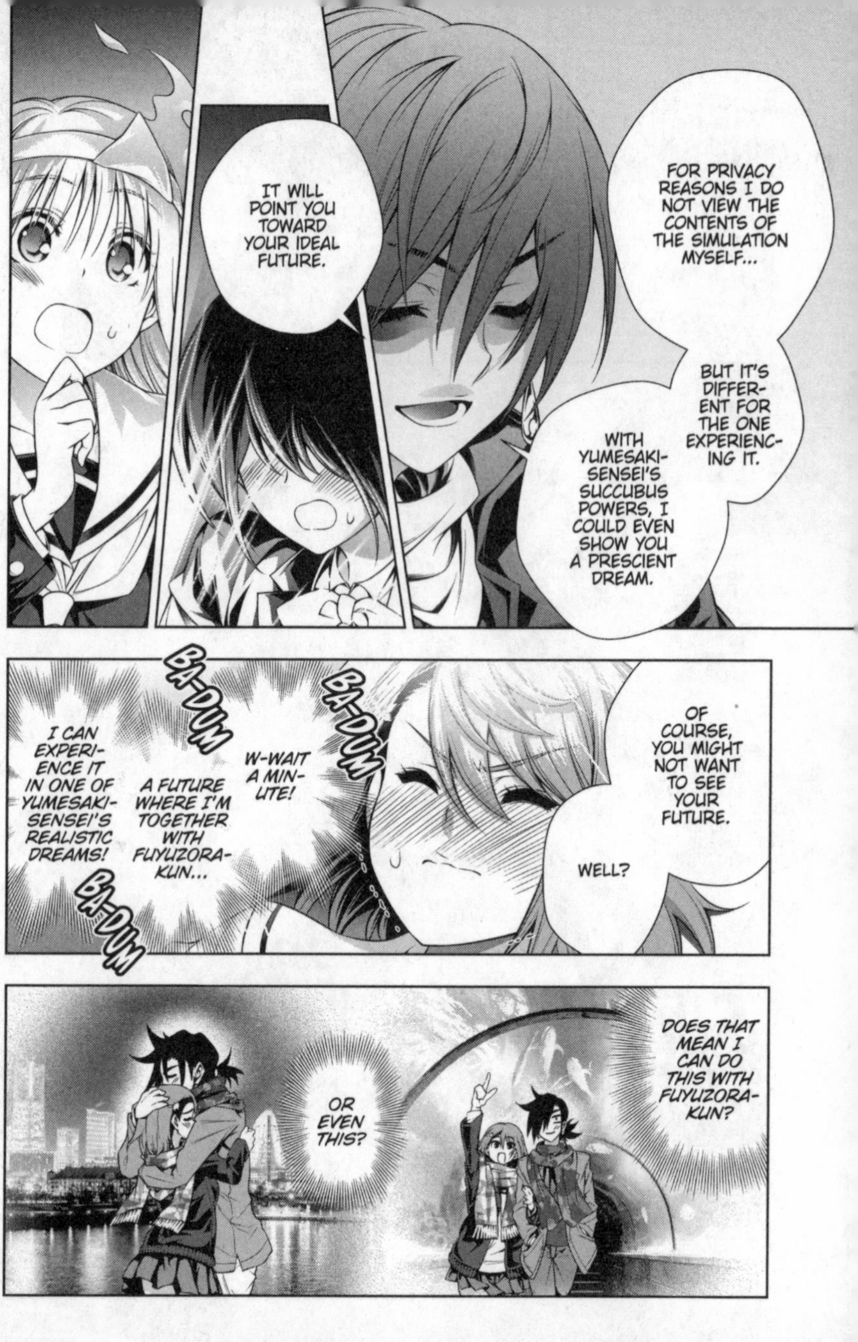
FOR PRIVACY REASONS I DO NOT VIEW THE CONTENTS OF THE SIMULATION MYSELF...
BUT IT'S DIFFER-ENT FOR THE ONE EXPERIENC-ING IT.
WITH YUMESAKI-SENSEI'S SUCCUBUS POWERS, I COULD EVEN SHOW YOU A PRESCIENT DREAM.
IT WILL POINT YOU TOWARD YOUR IDEAL FUTURE.
OF COURSE, YOU MIGHT NOT WANT TO SEE YOUR FUTURE.
WELL?
BA-DUM
W-WAIT A MIN-UTE!
BA-DUM
A FUTURE WHERE I'M TOGETHER WITH FUYUZORA-KUN...
I CAN EXPERI-ENCE IT IN ONE OF YUMESAKI-SENSEI'S REALISTIC DREAMS!
BA-DUM
DOES THAT MEAN I CAN DO THIS WITH FUYUZORA-KUN?
OR EVEN THIS?

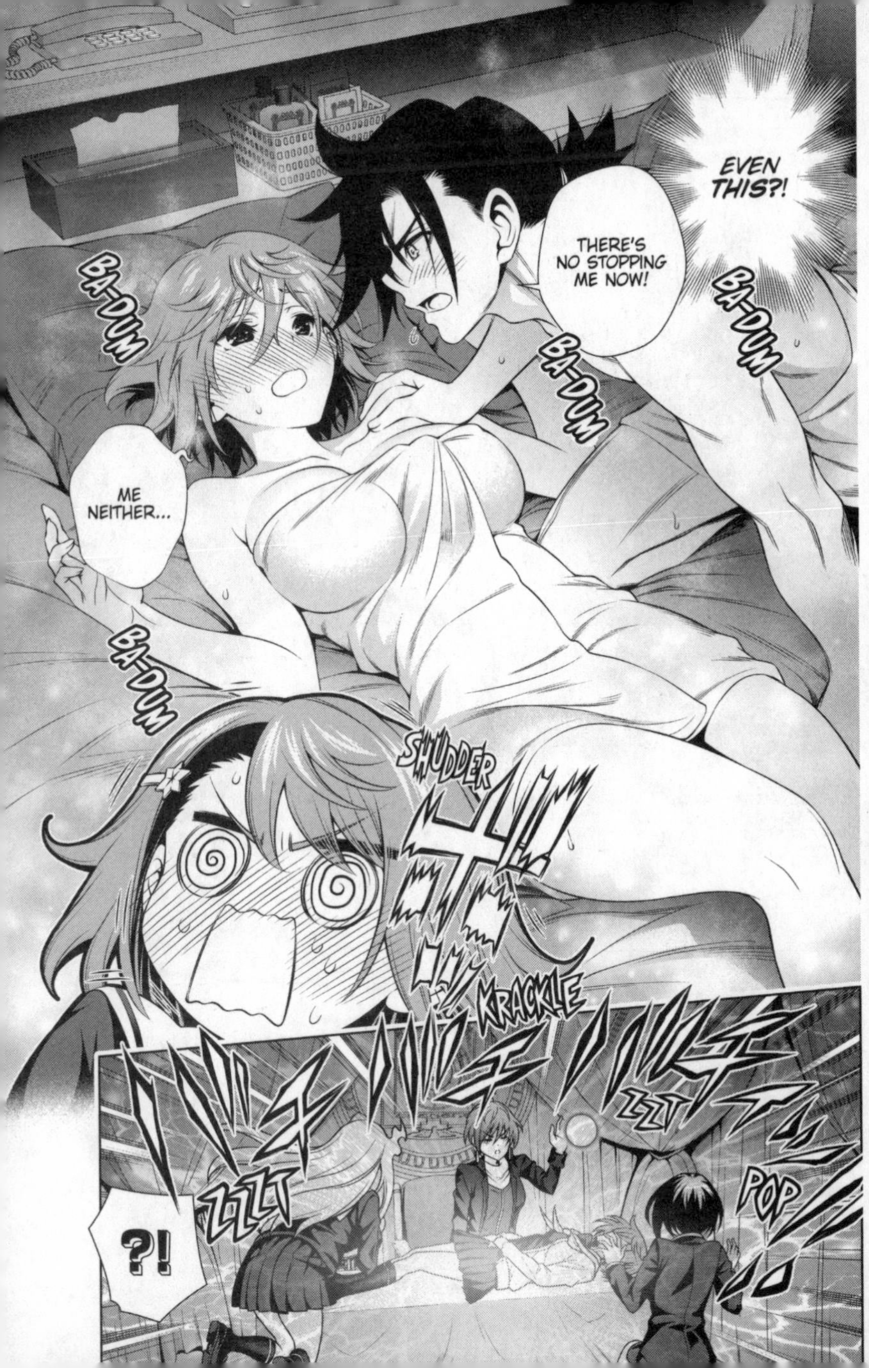
EVEN THIS?!
THERE'S NO STOPPING ME NOW!
BA-DUM
BA-DUM
BA-DUM
ME NEITHER...
BA-DUM
SHUDDER
KRACKLE
ZZZT
POP
ZZZT
?!

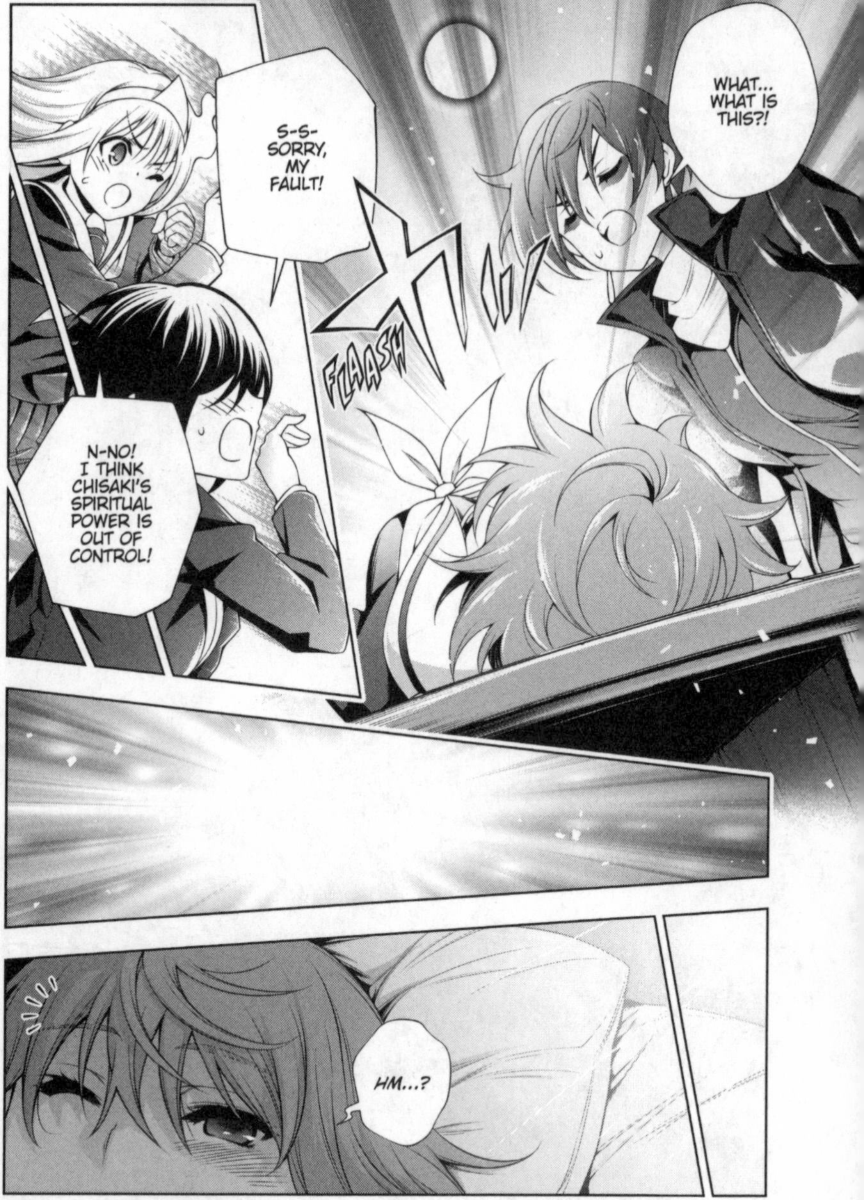
WHAT... WHAT IS THIS?!
FLAASH
S-S-SORRY, MY FAULT!
N-NO! I THINK CHISAKI'S SPIRITUAL POWER IS OUT OF CONTROL!
HM...?

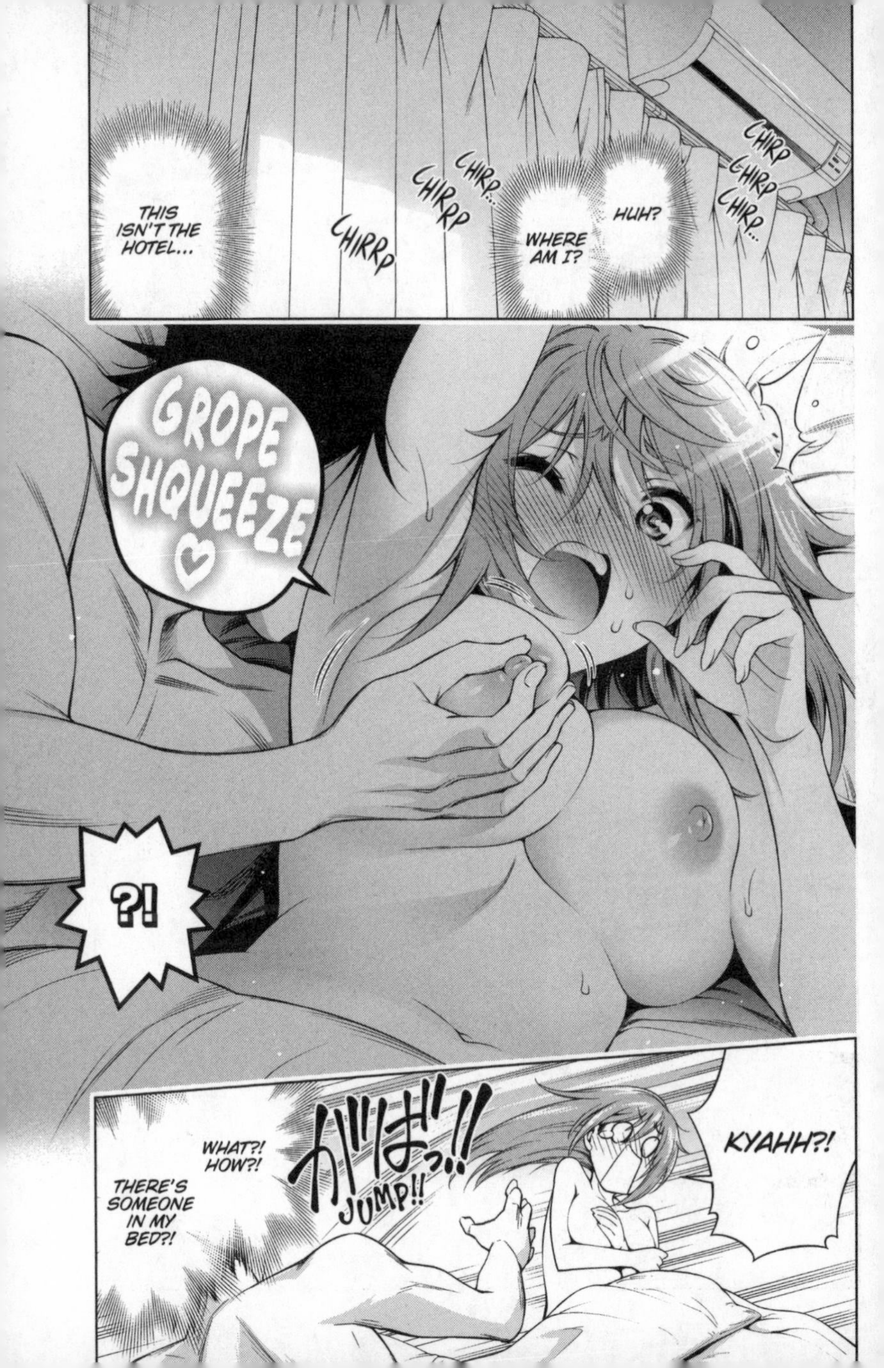
CHIRP CHIRP CHIRP...
HUH?
WHERE AM I?
CHIRP... CHIRRP
CHIRRP
THIS ISN'T THE HOTEL...
GROPE SHQUEEZE ♡
?!
KYAHH?!
がばっ!!
JUMP!!
WHAT?! HOW?!
THERE'S SOMEONE IN MY BED?!

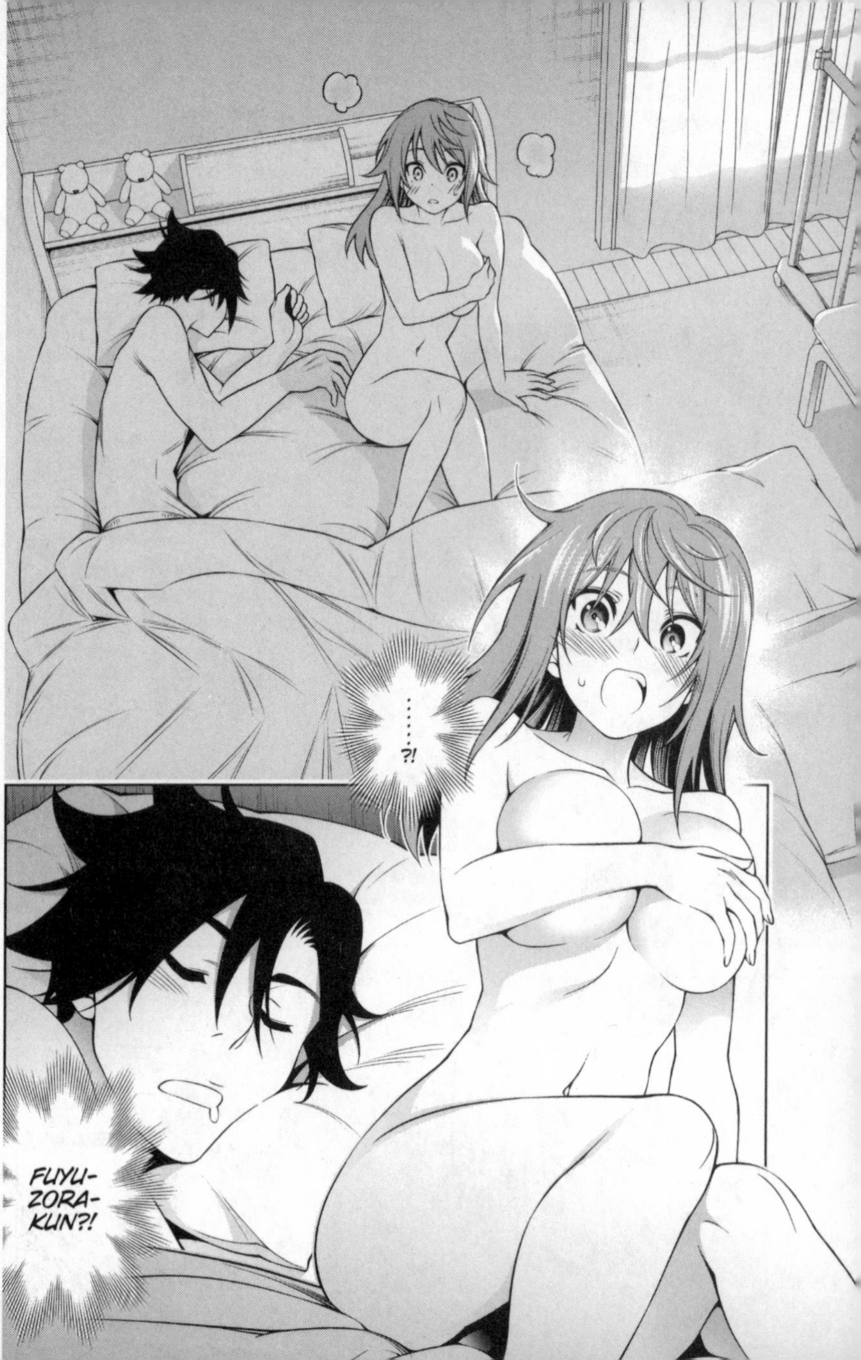
......?!
FUYU-ZORA-KUN?!

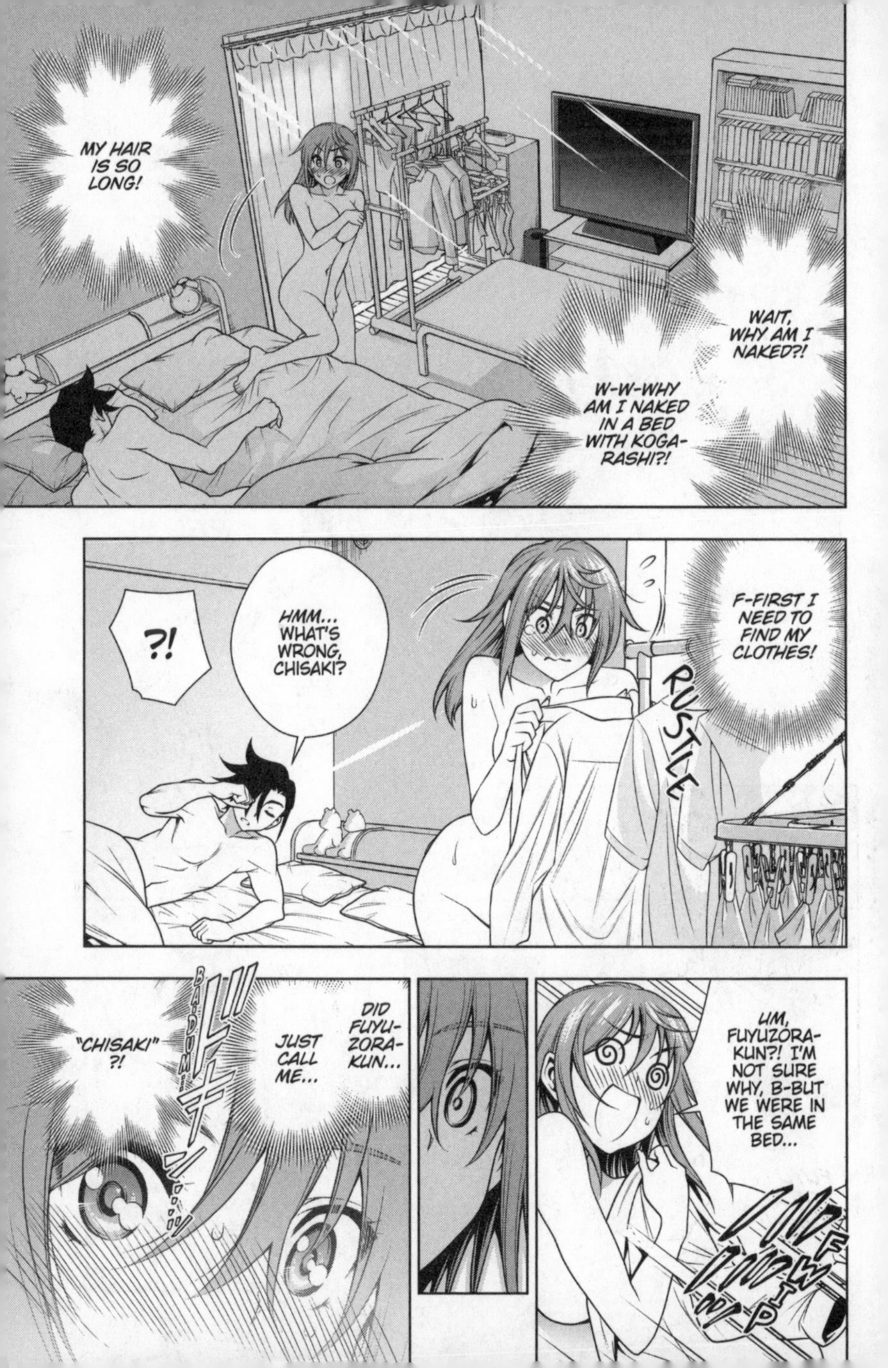
MY HAIR IS SO LONG!
WAIT, WHY AM I NAKED?!
W-W-WHY AM I NAKED IN A BED WITH KOGA-RASHI?!
F-FIRST I NEED TO FIND MY CLOTHES!
RUSTLE
HMM... WHAT'S WRONG, CHISAKI?
?!
UM, FUYUZORA-KUN?! I'M NOT SURE WHY, B-BUT WE WERE IN THE SAME BED...
FWIP
DID FUYUZORA-KUN...
JUST CALL ME...
"CHISAKI"?!
BADUMP!

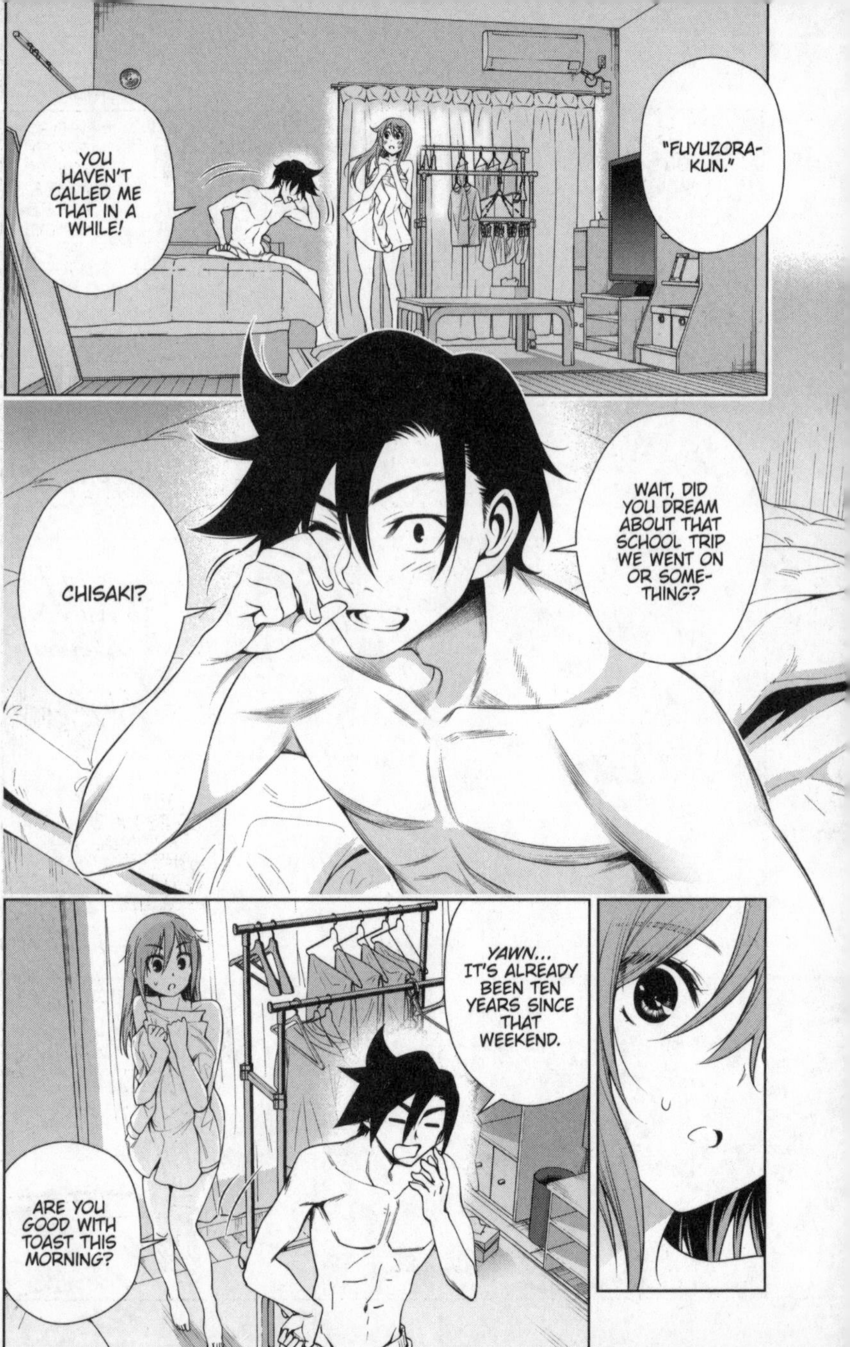
"FUYUZORA-KUN."
YOU HAVEN'T CALLED ME THAT IN A WHILE!
WAIT, DID YOU DREAM ABOUT THAT SCHOOL TRIP WE WENT ON OR SOME-THING?
CHISAKI?
YAWN... IT'S ALREADY BEEN TEN YEARS SINCE THAT WEEKEND.
ARE YOU GOOD WITH TOAST THIS MORNING?

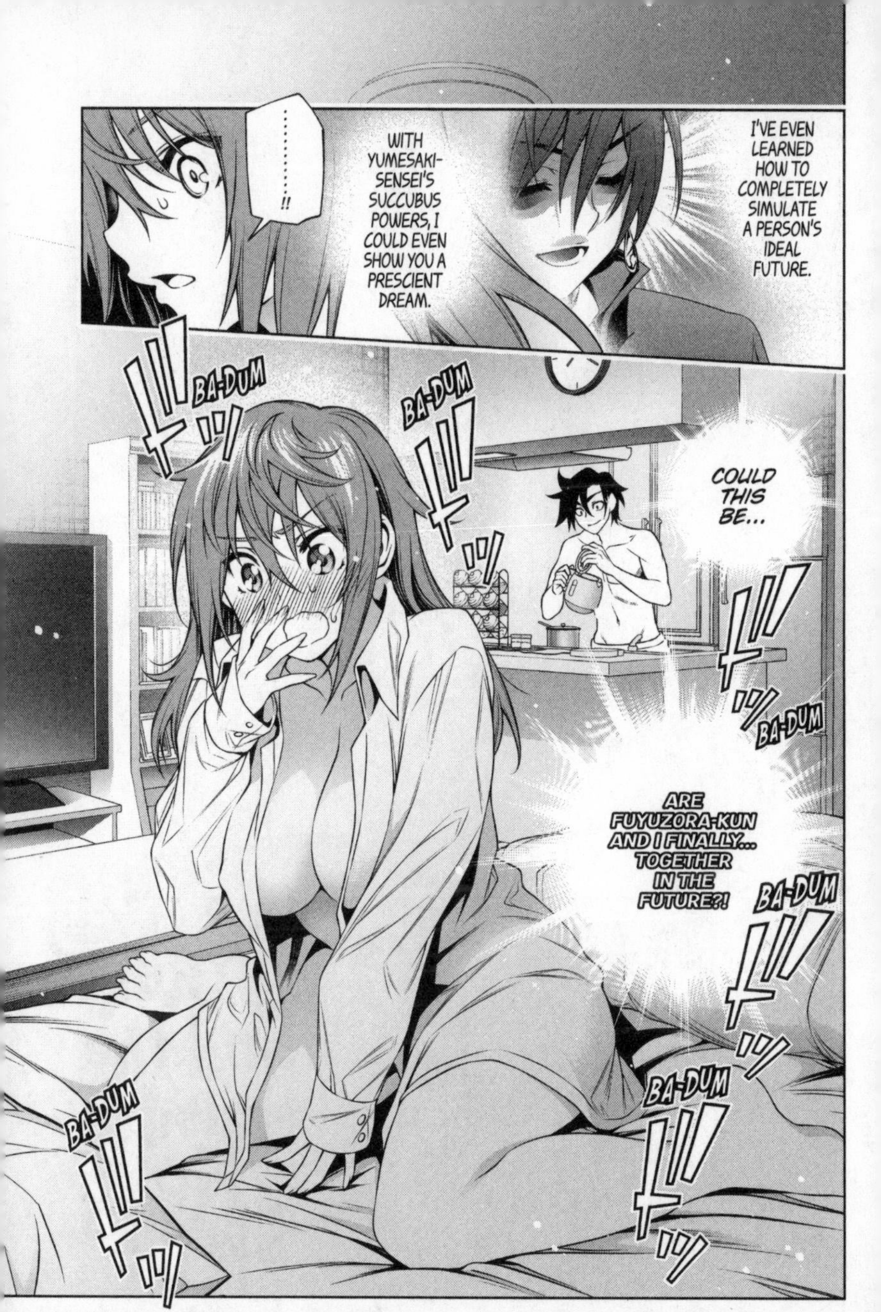
I'VE EVEN LEARNED HOW TO COMPLETELY SIMULATE A PERSON'S IDEAL FUTURE.
WITH YUMESAKI-SENSEI'S SUCCUBUS POWERS, I COULD EVEN SHOW YOU A PRESCIENT DREAM.
.......!!
COULD THIS BE...
BA-DUM
BA-DUM
BA-DUM
ARE FUYUZORA-KUN AND I FINALLY... TOGETHER IN THE FUTURE?!
BA-DUM
BA-DUM
BA-DUM

Yuuna
and the
Haunted
Hot
Springs

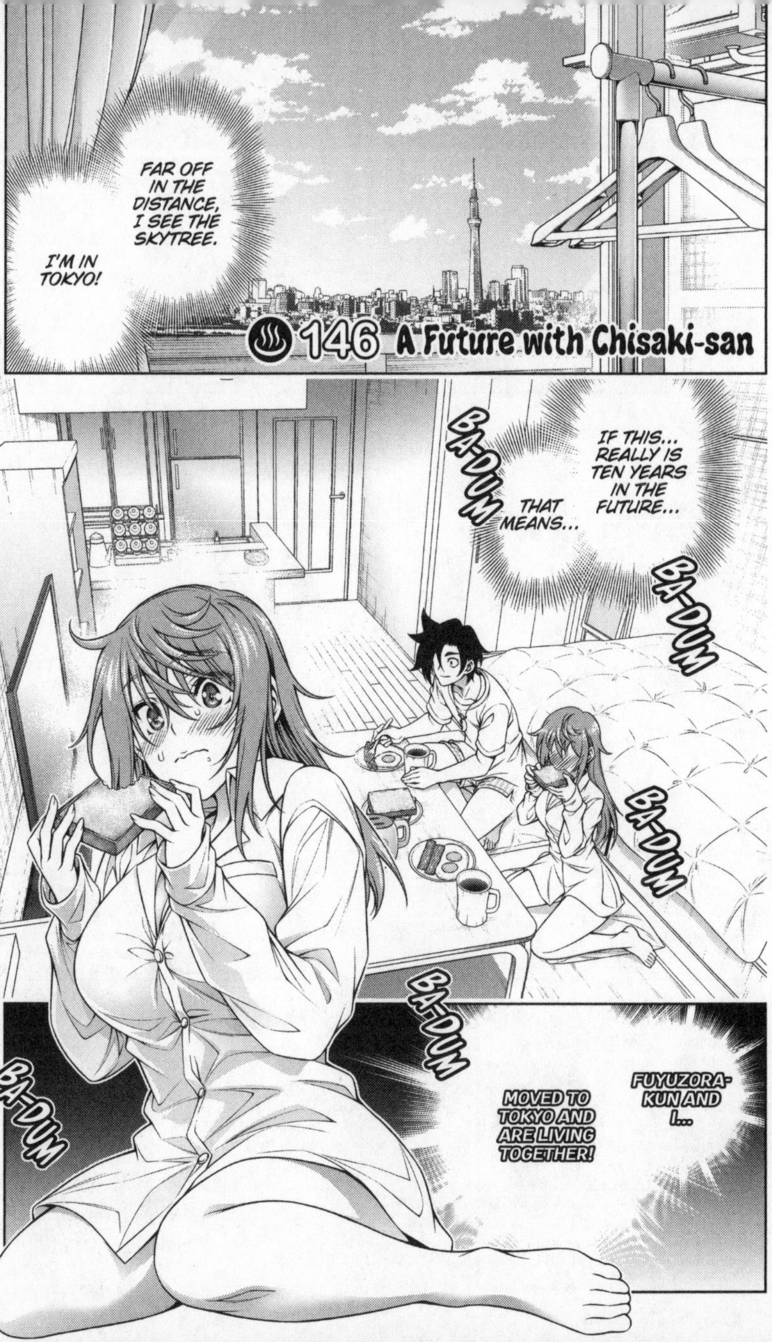
FAR OFF IN THE DISTANCE, I SEE THE SKYTREE.
I'M IN TOKYO!
146 A Future with Chisaki-san
IF THIS... REALLY IS TEN YEARS IN THE FUTURE...
THAT MEANS...
BA-DUM
BA-DUM
BA-DUM
BA-DUM
FUYUZORA-KUN AND I...
MOVED TO TOKYO AND ARE LIVING TOGETHER!
BA-DUM

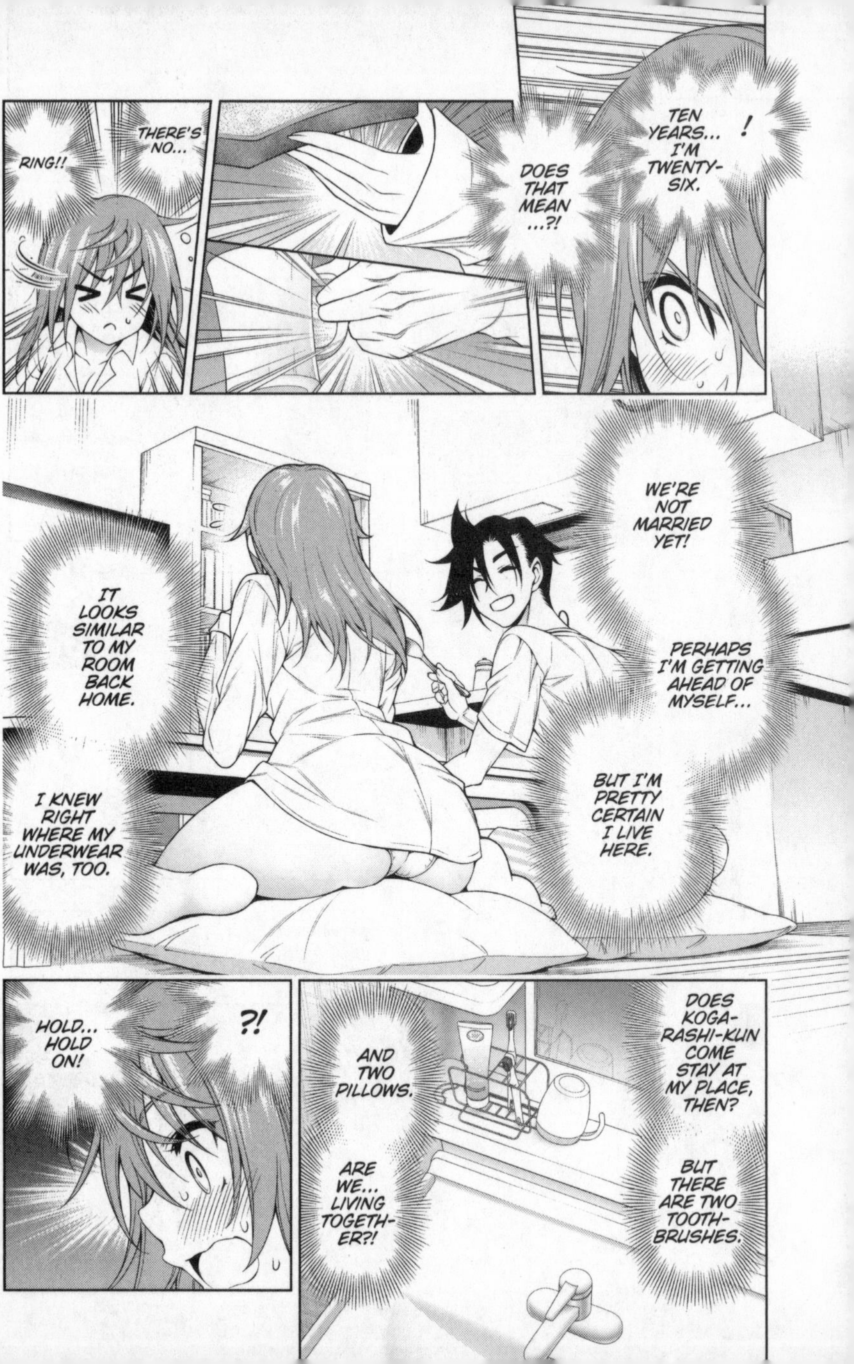
TEN YEARS... I'M TWENTY-SIX.
!
DOES THAT MEAN ...?!
THERE'S NO...
RING!!
WE'RE NOT MARRIED YET!
PERHAPS I'M GETTING AHEAD OF MYSELF...
BUT I'M PRETTY CERTAIN I LIVE HERE.
IT LOOKS SIMILAR TO MY ROOM BACK HOME.
I KNEW RIGHT WHERE MY UNDERWEAR WAS, TOO.
DOES KOGA-RASHI-KUN COME STAY AT MY PLACE, THEN?
BUT THERE ARE TWO TOOTH-BRUSHES.
AND TWO PILLOWS.
ARE WE... LIVING TOGETH-ER?!
?!
HOLD... HOLD ON!

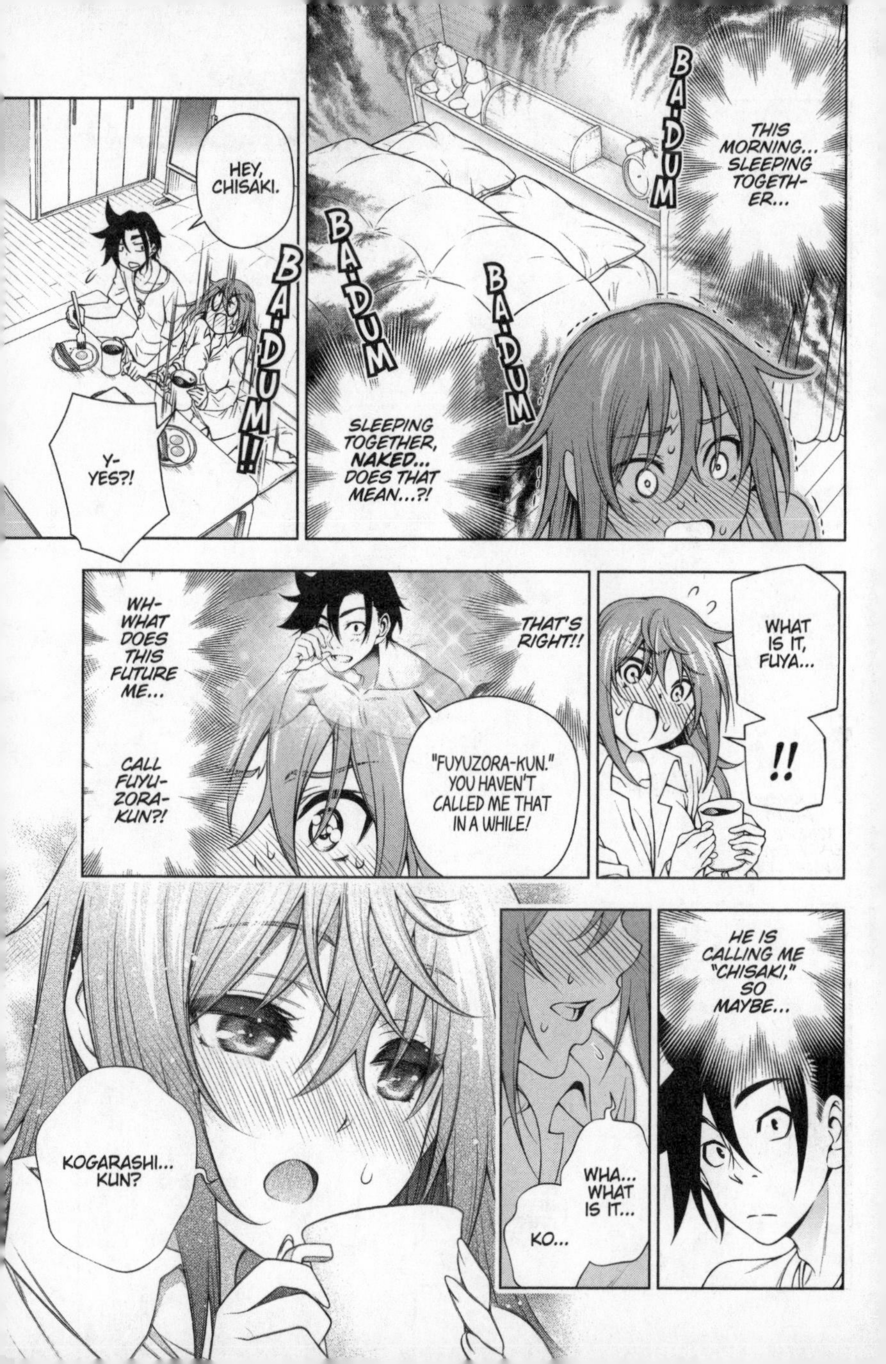
THIS MORNING... SLEEPING TOGETHER...
BA-DUM
BA-DUM
BA-DUM
SLEEPING TOGETHER, NAKED... DOES THAT MEAN...?!
HEY, CHISAKI.
BA-DUM!!
Y-YES?!
WHAT IS IT, FUYA...
!!
THAT'S RIGHT!!
"FUYUZORA-KUN." YOU HAVEN'T CALLED ME THAT IN A WHILE!
WH-WHAT DOES THIS FUTURE ME...
CALL FUYUZORA-KUN?!
HE IS CALLING ME "CHISAKI," SO MAYBE...
WHA... WHAT IS IT...
KO...
KOGARASHI... KUN?

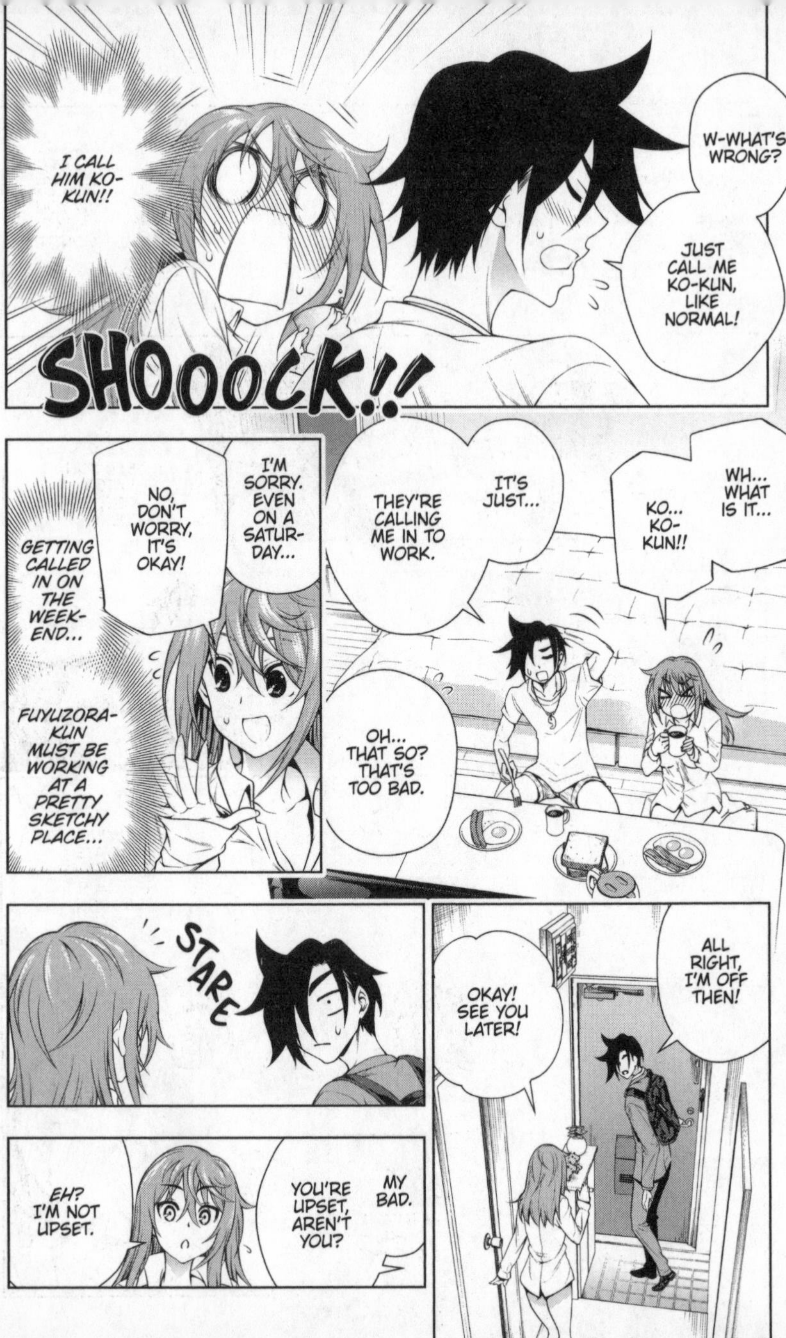
W-WHAT'S WRONG?
JUST CALL ME KO-KUN, LIKE NORMAL!
I CALL HIM KO-KUN!!
SHOOOCK!!
WH... WHAT IS IT...
KO... KO-KUN!!
IT'S JUST...
THEY'RE CALLING ME IN TO WORK.
OH... THAT SO? THAT'S TOO BAD.
I'M SORRY. EVEN ON A SATURDAY...
NO, DON'T WORRY, IT'S OKAY!
GETTING CALLED IN ON THE WEEKEND...
FUYUZORA-KUN MUST BE WORKING AT A PRETTY SKETCHY PLACE...
ALL RIGHT, I'M OFF THEN!
OKAY! SEE YOU LATER!
STARE
MY BAD.
YOU'RE UPSET, AREN'T YOU?
EH? I'M NOT UPSET.

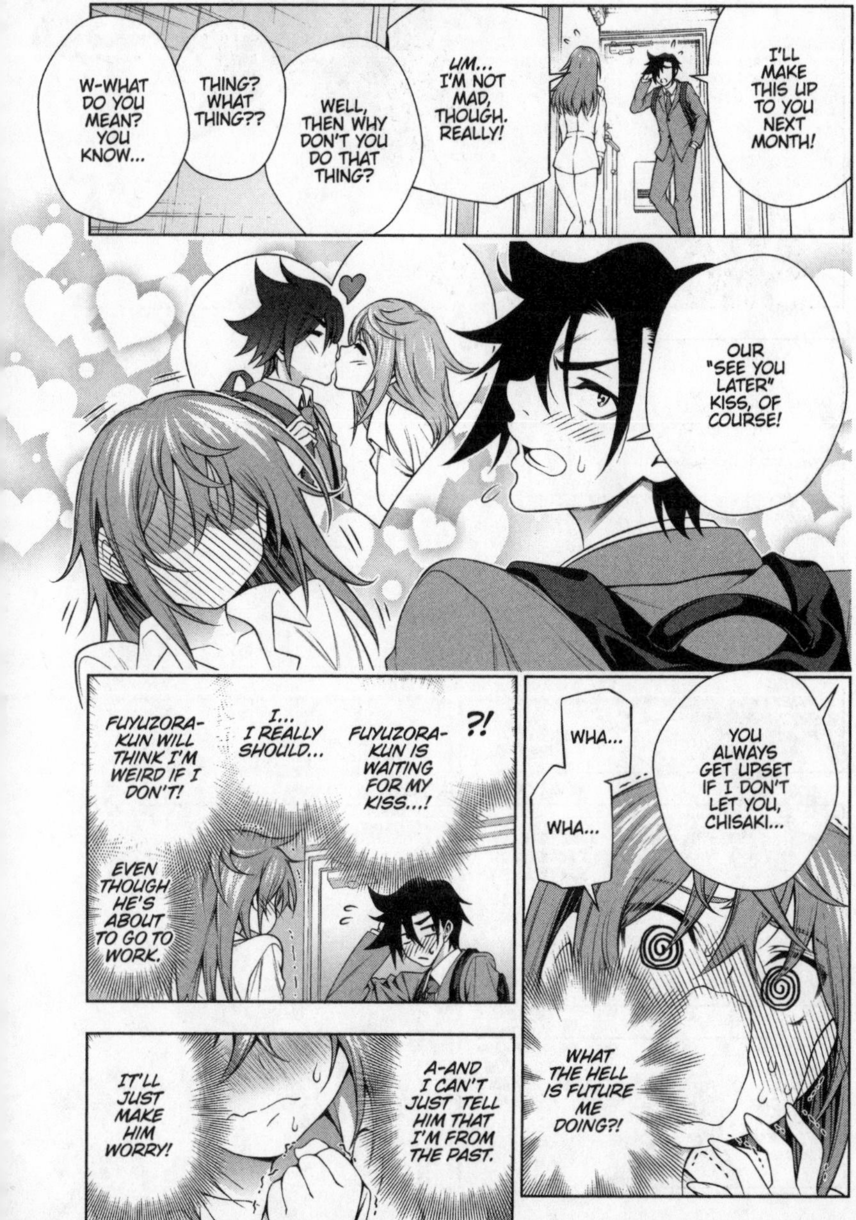
I'LL MAKE THIS UP TO YOU NEXT MONTH!
UM... I'M NOT MAD, THOUGH. REALLY!
WELL, THEN WHY DON'T YOU DO THAT THING?
THING? WHAT THING??
W-WHAT DO YOU MEAN? YOU KNOW...
OUR "SEE YOU LATER" KISS, OF COURSE!
YOU ALWAYS GET UPSET IF I DON'T LET YOU, CHISAKI...
WHA...
WHA...
WHAT THE HELL IS FUTURE ME DOING?!
?!
FUYUZORA-KUN IS WAITING FOR MY KISS...!
I... I REALLY SHOULD...
FUYUZORA-KUN WILL THINK I'M WEIRD IF I DON'T!
EVEN THOUGH HE'S ABOUT TO GO TO WORK.
A-AND I CAN'T JUST TELL HIM THAT I'M FROM THE PAST.
IT'LL JUST MAKE HIM WORRY!

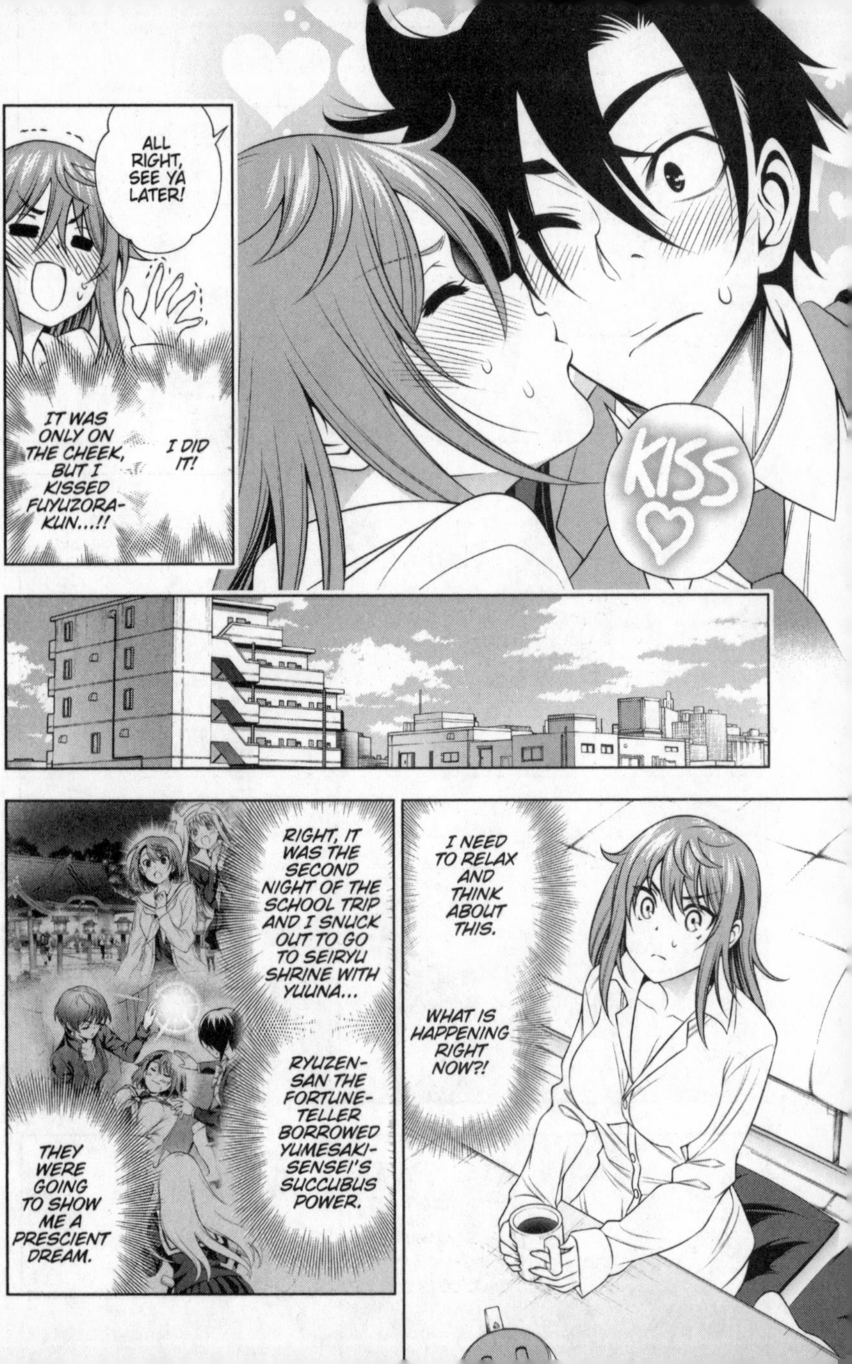
KISS ♡

ALL RIGHT, SEE YA LATER!
I DID IT!
IT WAS ONLY ON THE CHEEK, BUT I KISSED FUYUZORA-KUN...!!
I NEED TO RELAX AND THINK ABOUT THIS.
WHAT IS HAPPENING RIGHT NOW?!
RIGHT, IT WAS THE SECOND NIGHT OF THE SCHOOL TRIP AND I SNUCK OUT TO GO TO SEIRYU SHRINE WITH YUUNA...
RYUZEN-SAN THE FORTUNE-TELLER BORROWED YUMESAKI-SENSEI'S SUCCUBUS POWER.
THEY WERE GOING TO SHOW ME A PRESCIENT DREAM.

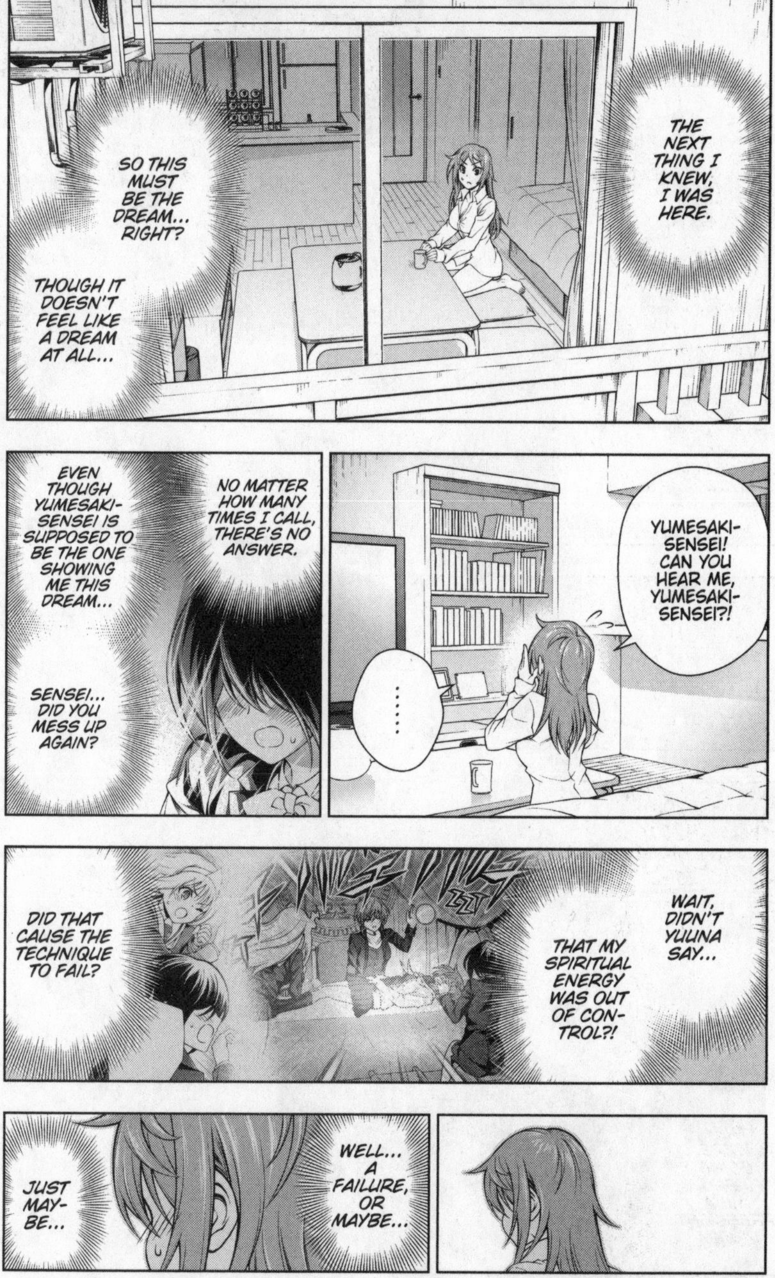
THE NEXT THING I KNEW, I WAS HERE.
SO THIS MUST BE THE DREAM... RIGHT?
THOUGH IT DOESN'T FEEL LIKE A DREAM AT ALL...
YUMESAKI-SENSEI! CAN YOU HEAR ME, YUMESAKI-SENSEI?!
......
NO MATTER HOW MANY TIMES I CALL, THERE'S NO ANSWER.
EVEN THOUGH YUMESAKI-SENSEI IS SUPPOSED TO BE THE ONE SHOWING ME THIS DREAM...
SENSEI... DID YOU MESS UP AGAIN?
WAIT, DIDN'T YUUNA SAY...
THAT MY SPIRITUAL ENERGY WAS OUT OF CON-TROL?!
ZZZT
DID THAT CAUSE THE TECHNIQUE TO FAIL?
WELL... A FAILURE, OR MAYBE...
JUST MAY-BE...

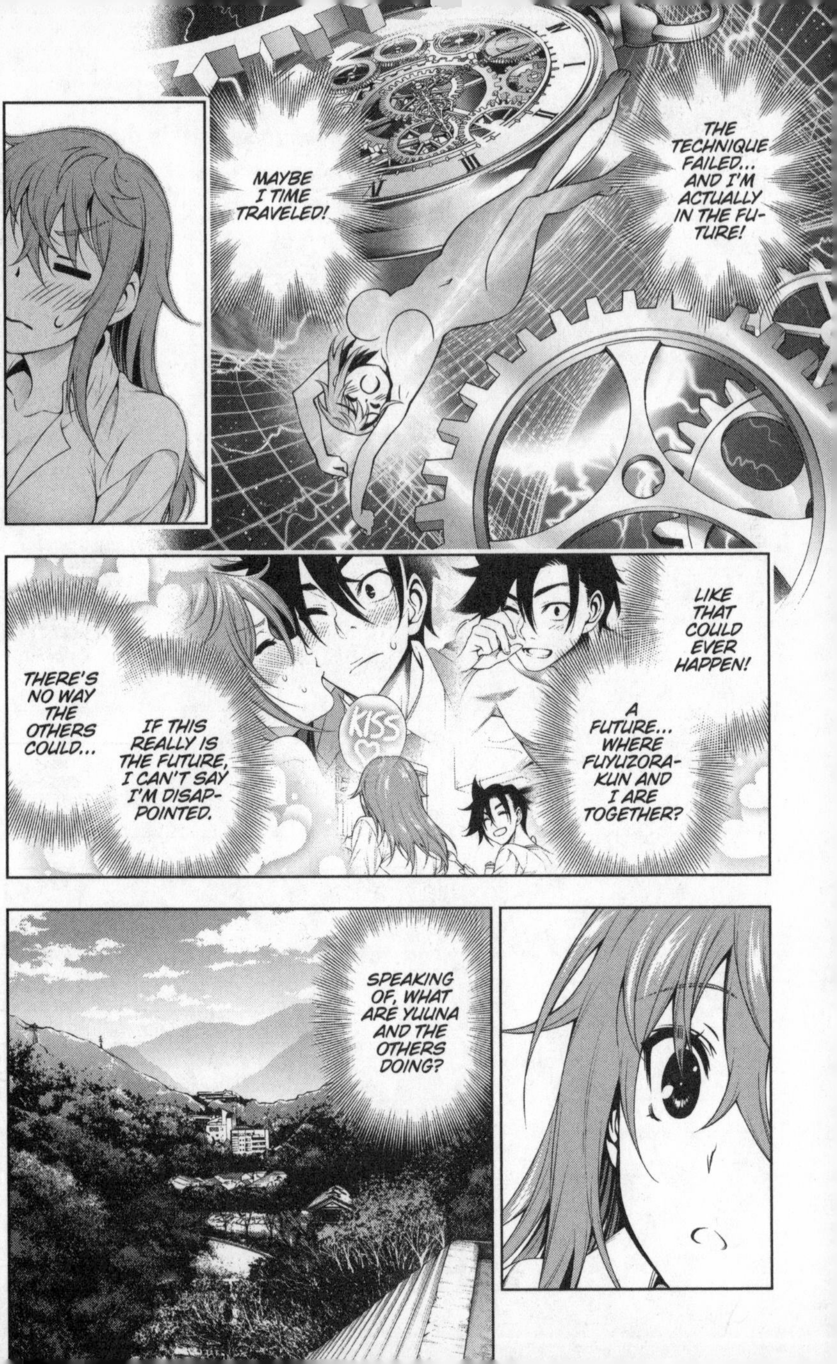
THE TECHNIQUE FAILED... AND I'M ACTUALLY IN THE FU-TURE!
MAYBE I TIME TRAVELED!
LIKE THAT COULD EVER HAPPEN!
A FUTURE... WHERE FUYUZORA-KUN AND I ARE TOGETHER?
KISS
IF THIS REALLY IS THE FUTURE, I CAN'T SAY I'M DISAP-POINTED.
THERE'S NO WAY THE OTHERS COULD...
SPEAKING OF, WHAT ARE YUUNA AND THE OTHERS DOING?

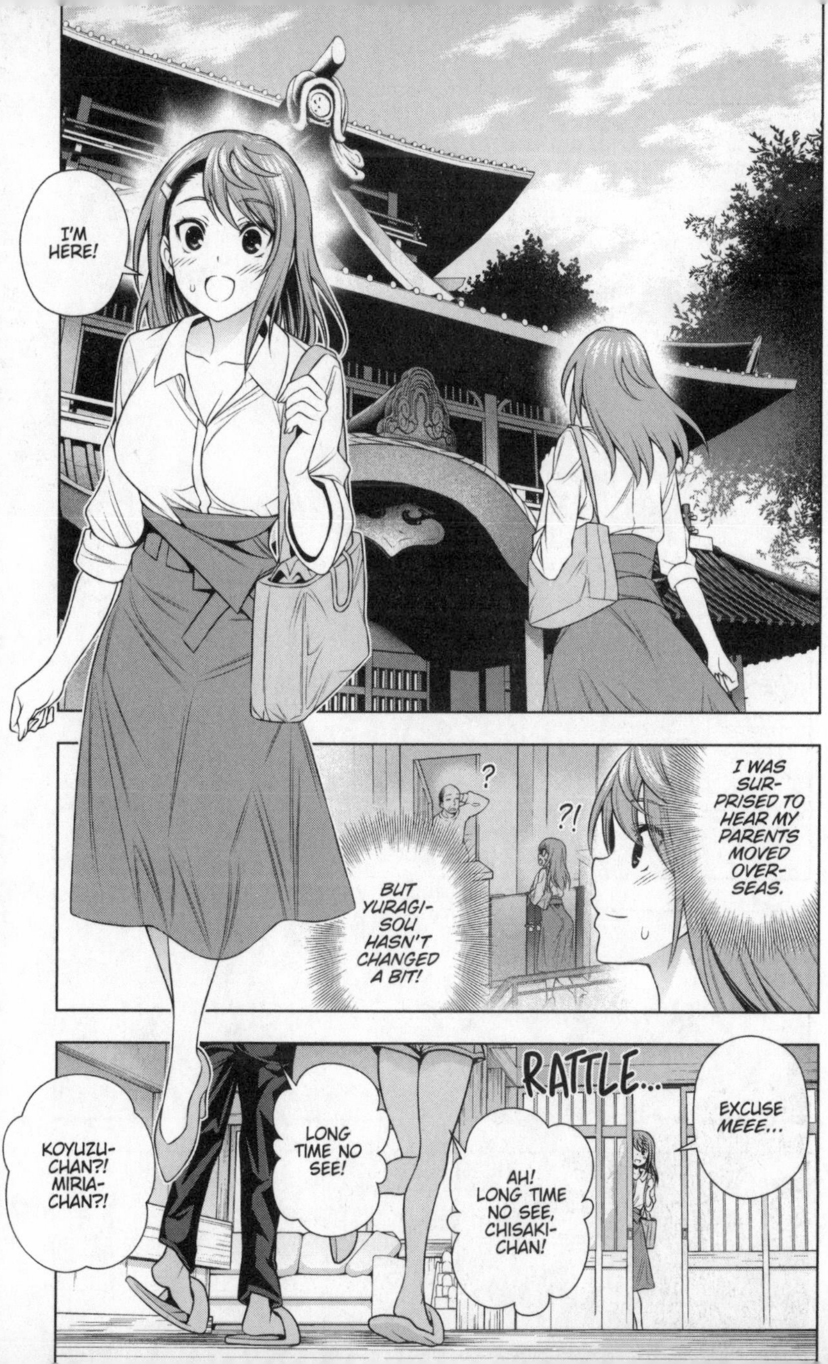
I'M HERE!
I WAS SUR-PRISED TO HEAR MY PARENTS MOVED OVER-SEAS.
?
?!
BUT YURAGI-SOU HASN'T CHANGED A BIT!
EXCUSE MEEE...
RATTLE...
AH! LONG TIME NO SEE, CHISAKI-CHAN!
LONG TIME NO SEE!
KOYUZU-CHAN?! MIRIA-CHAN?!

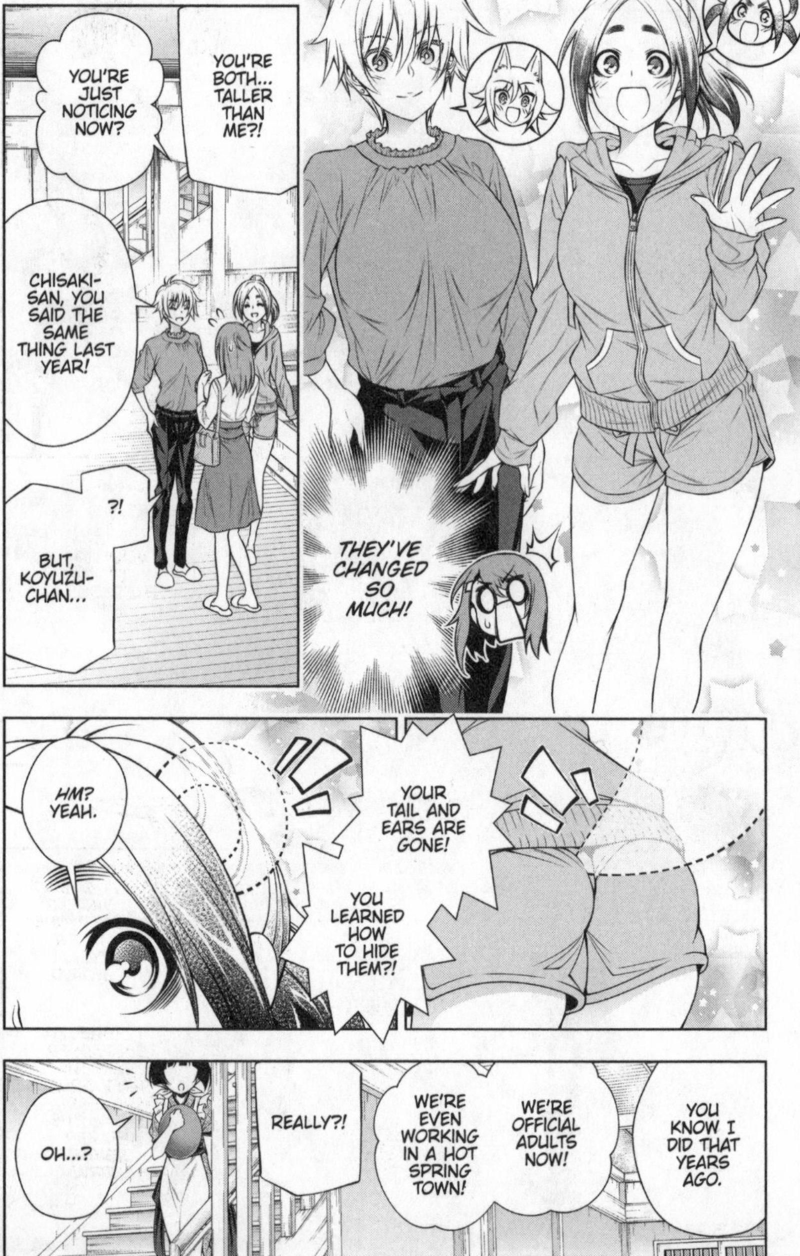
THEY'VE CHANGED SO MUCH!
YOU'RE BOTH... TALLER THAN ME?!
YOU'RE JUST NOTICING NOW?
CHISAKI-SAN, YOU SAID THE SAME THING LAST YEAR!
?!
BUT, KOYUZU-CHAN...
YOUR TAIL AND EARS ARE GONE!
YOU LEARNED HOW TO HIDE THEM?!
HM? YEAH.
YOU KNOW I DID THAT YEARS AGO.
WE'RE OFFICIAL ADULTS NOW!
WE'RE EVEN WORKING IN A HOT SPRING TOWN!
REALLY?!
OH...?

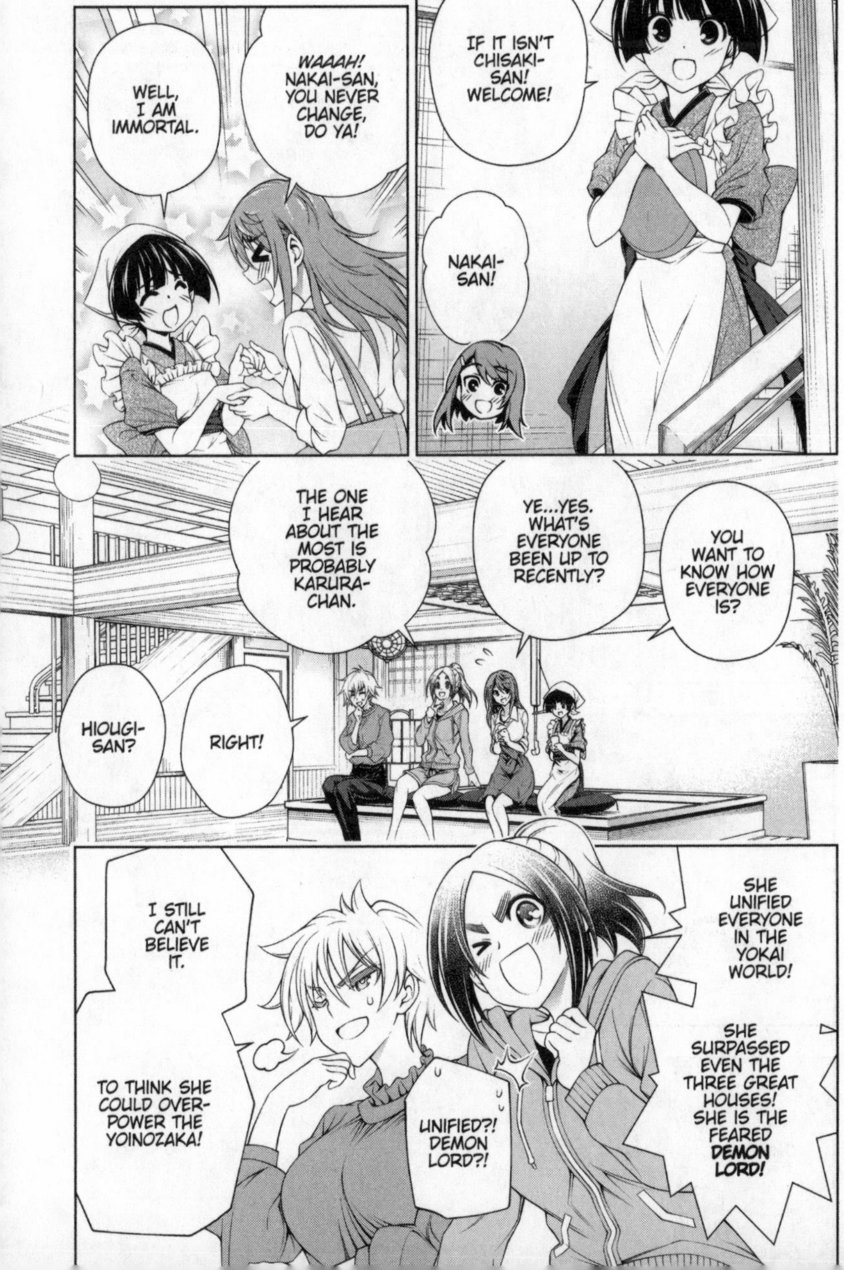
IF IT ISN'T CHISAKI-SAN! WELCOME!
NAKAI-SAN!
WAAAH! NAKAI-SAN, YOU NEVER CHANGE, DO YA!
WELL, I AM IMMORTAL.
YOU WANT TO KNOW HOW EVERYONE IS?
YE...YES. WHAT'S EVERYONE BEEN UP TO RECENTLY?
THE ONE I HEAR ABOUT THE MOST IS PROBABLY KARURA-CHAN.
RIGHT!
HIOUGI-SAN?
SHE UNIFIED EVERYONE IN THE YOKAI WORLD!
SHE SURPASSED EVEN THE THREE GREAT HOUSES! SHE IS THE FEARED **DEMON LORD!**
UNIFIED?! DEMON LORD?!
I STILL CAN'T BELIEVE IT.
TO THINK SHE COULD OVERPOWER THE YOINOZAKA!

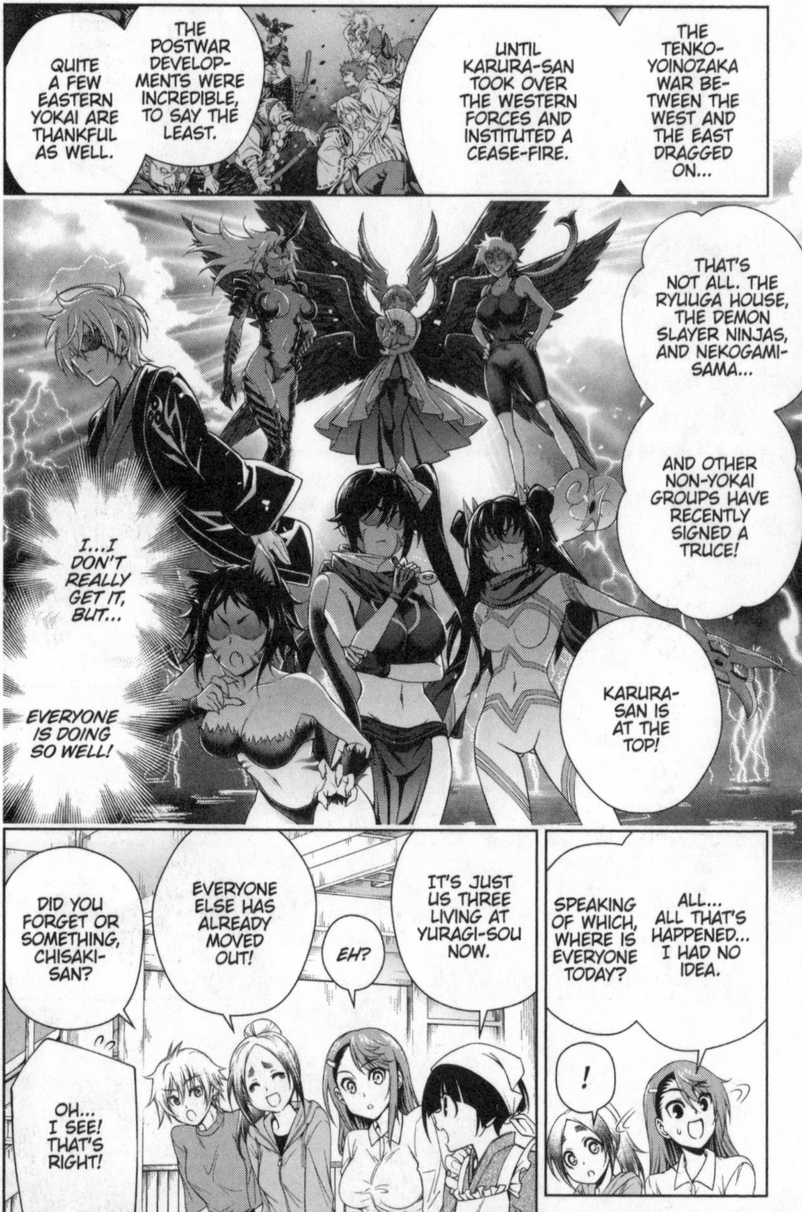
THE TENKO-YOINOZAKA WAR BETWEEN THE WEST AND THE EAST DRAGGED ON...
UNTIL KARURA-SAN TOOK OVER THE WESTERN FORCES AND INSTITUTED A CEASE-FIRE.
THE POSTWAR DEVELOPMENTS WERE INCREDIBLE, TO SAY THE LEAST.
QUITE A FEW EASTERN YOKAI ARE THANKFUL AS WELL.
THAT'S NOT ALL. THE RYUUGA HOUSE, THE DEMON SLAYER NINJAS, AND NEKOGAMI-SAMA...
AND OTHER NON-YOKAI GROUPS HAVE RECENTLY SIGNED A TRUCE!
KARURA-SAN IS AT THE TOP!
I...I DON'T REALLY GET IT, BUT...
EVERYONE IS DOING SO WELL!
ALL... ALL THAT'S HAPPENED... I HAD NO IDEA.
SPEAKING OF WHICH, WHERE IS EVERYONE TODAY?
!
IT'S JUST US THREE LIVING AT YURAGI-SOU NOW.
EH?
EVERYONE ELSE HAS ALREADY MOVED OUT!
DID YOU FORGET OR SOMETHING, CHISAKI-SAN?
OH... I SEE! THAT'S RIGHT!

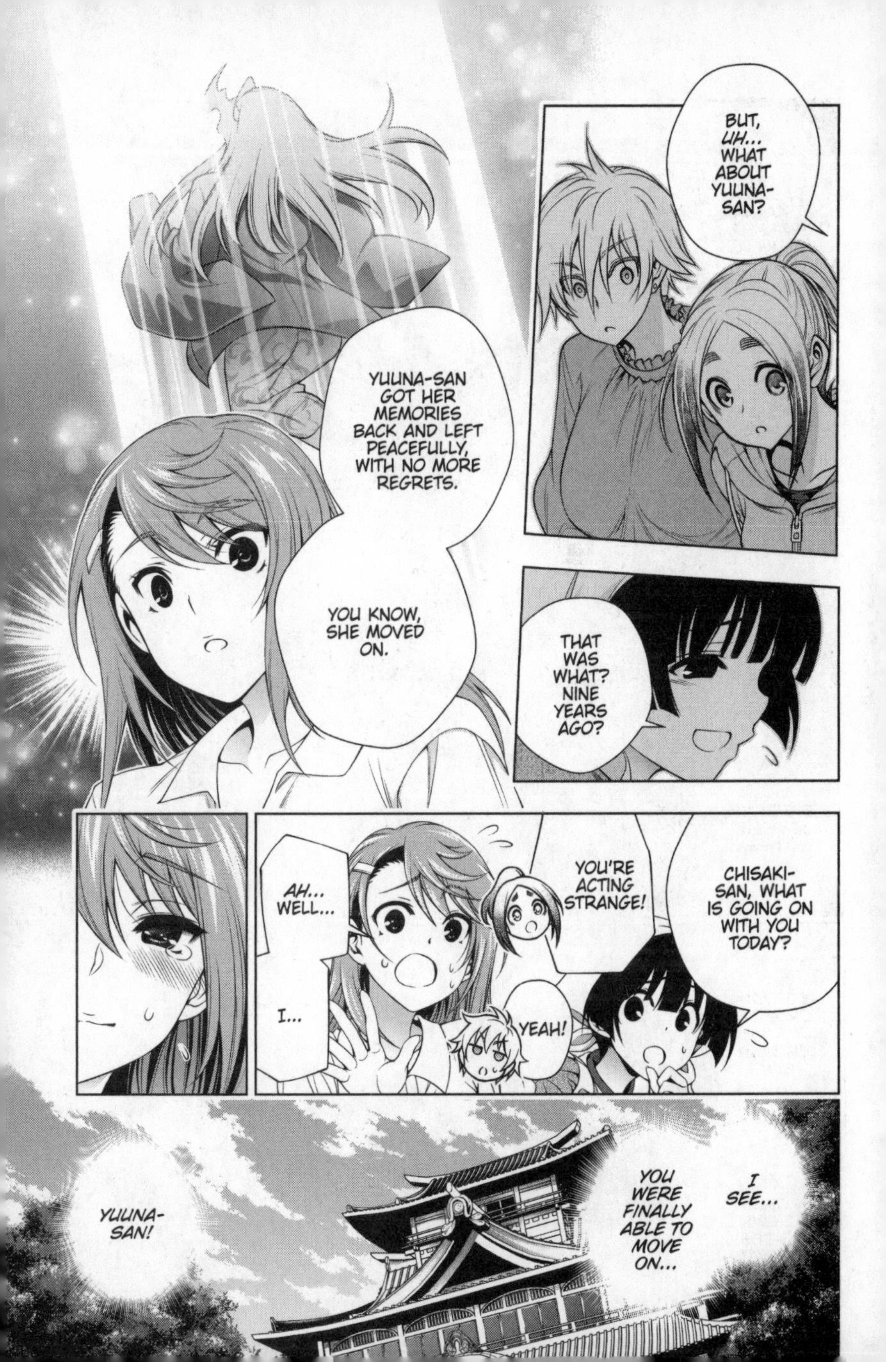
BUT, UH... WHAT ABOUT YUUNA-SAN?
THAT WAS WHAT? NINE YEARS AGO?
YUUNA-SAN GOT HER MEMORIES BACK AND LEFT PEACEFULLY, WITH NO MORE REGRETS.
YOU KNOW, SHE MOVED ON.
CHISAKI-SAN, WHAT IS GOING ON WITH YOU TODAY?
YOU'RE ACTING STRANGE!
YEAH!
AH... WELL...
I...
I SEE...
YOU WERE FINALLY ABLE TO MOVE ON...
YUUNA-SAN!

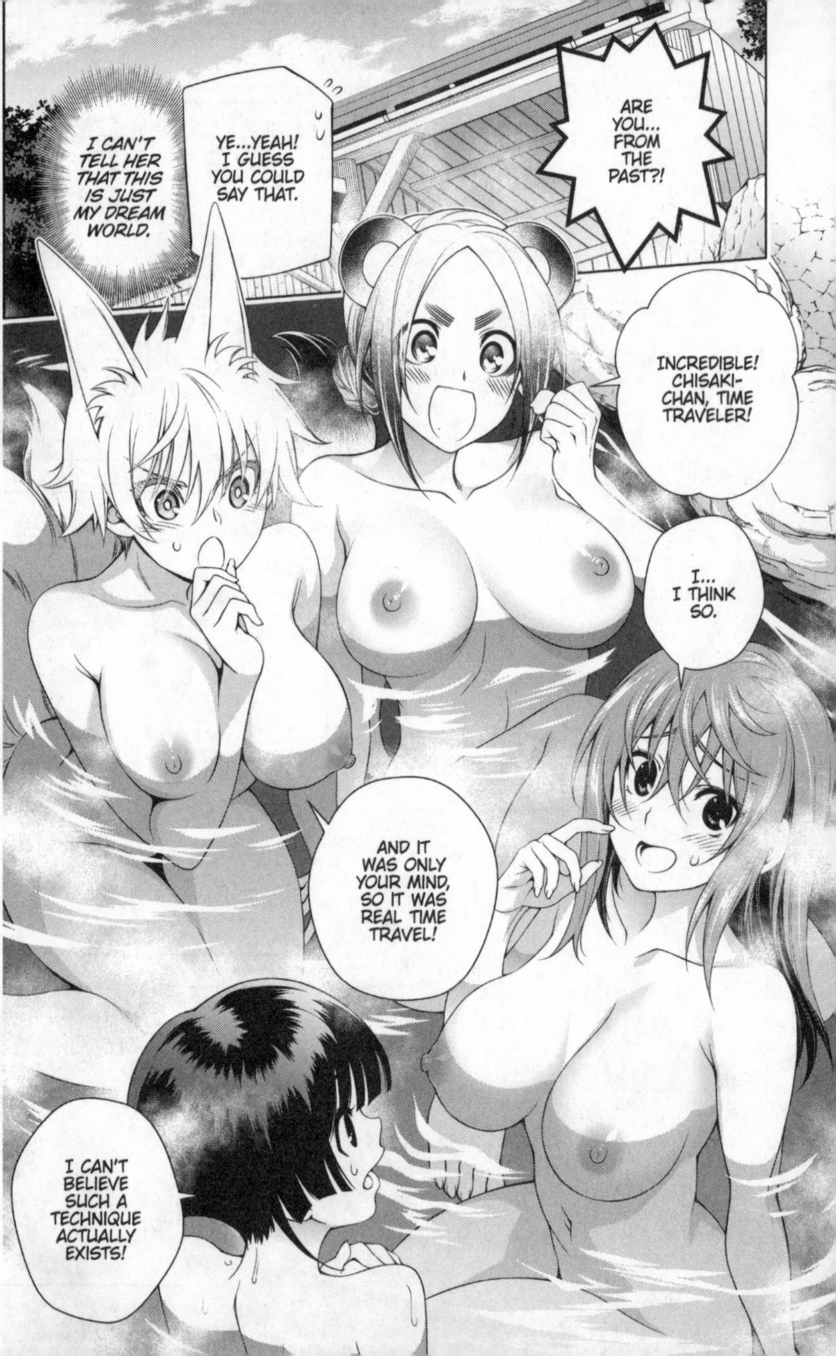
ARE YOU... FROM THE PAST?!
YE...YEAH! I GUESS YOU COULD SAY THAT.
I CAN'T TELL HER THAT THIS IS JUST MY DREAM WORLD.
INCREDIBLE! CHISAKI-CHAN, TIME TRAVELER!
I... I THINK SO.
AND IT WAS ONLY YOUR MIND, SO IT WAS REAL TIME TRAVEL!
I CAN'T BELIEVE SUCH A TECHNIQUE ACTUALLY EXISTS!

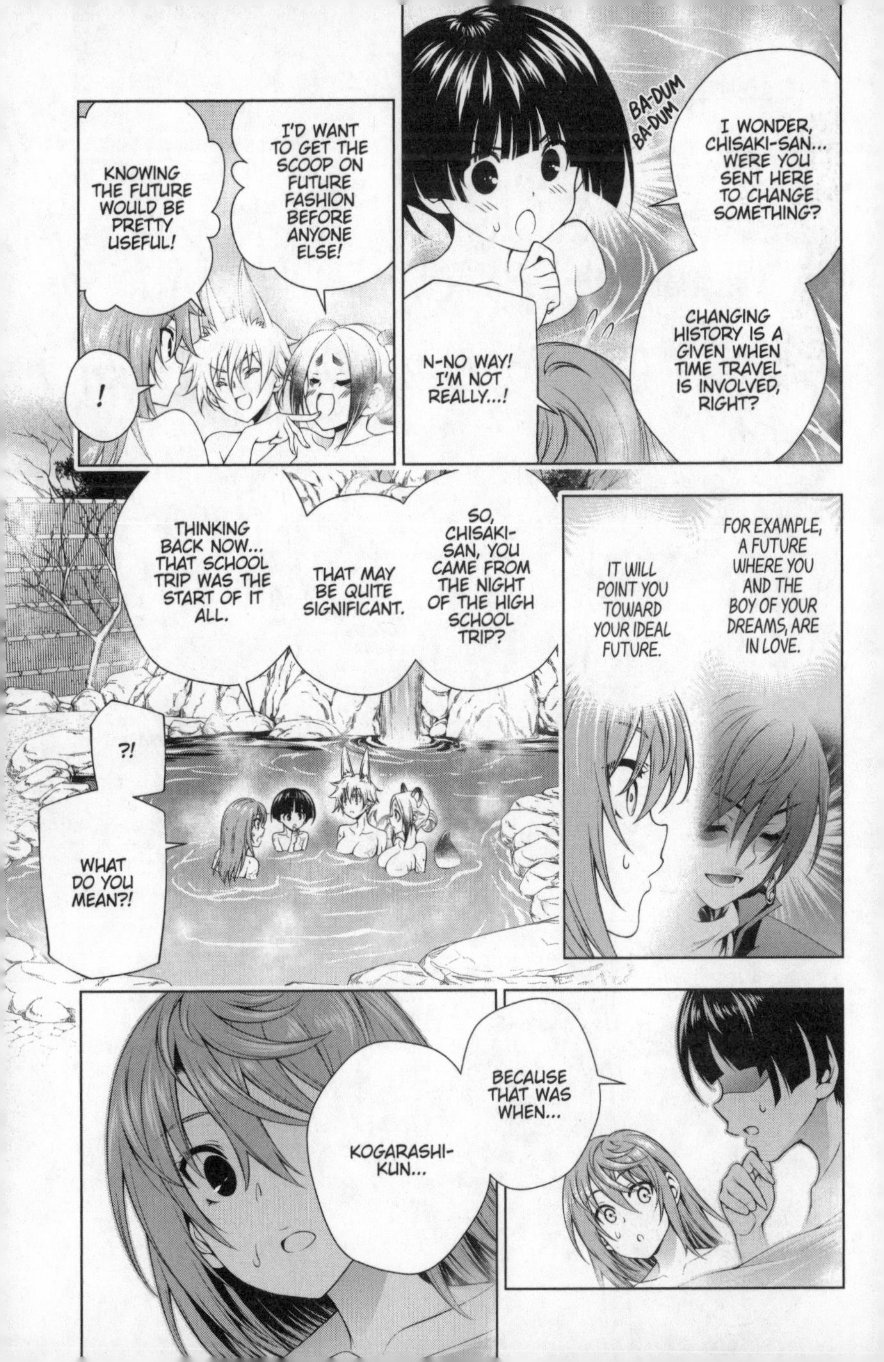
BA-DUM BA-DUM
I WONDER, CHISAKI-SAN... WERE YOU SENT HERE TO CHANGE SOMETHING?
CHANGING HISTORY IS A GIVEN WHEN TIME TRAVEL IS INVOLVED, RIGHT?
N-NO WAY! I'M NOT REALLY...!
I'D WANT TO GET THE SCOOP ON FUTURE FASHION BEFORE ANYONE ELSE!
KNOWING THE FUTURE WOULD BE PRETTY USEFUL!
!
FOR EXAMPLE, A FUTURE WHERE YOU AND THE BOY OF YOUR DREAMS, ARE IN LOVE.
IT WILL POINT YOU TOWARD YOUR IDEAL FUTURE.
SO, CHISAKI-SAN, YOU CAME FROM THE NIGHT OF THE HIGH SCHOOL TRIP?
THAT MAY BE QUITE SIGNIFICANT.
THINKING BACK NOW... THAT SCHOOL TRIP WAS THE START OF IT ALL.
?!
WHAT DO YOU MEAN?!
BECAUSE THAT WAS WHEN...
KOGARASHI-KUN...

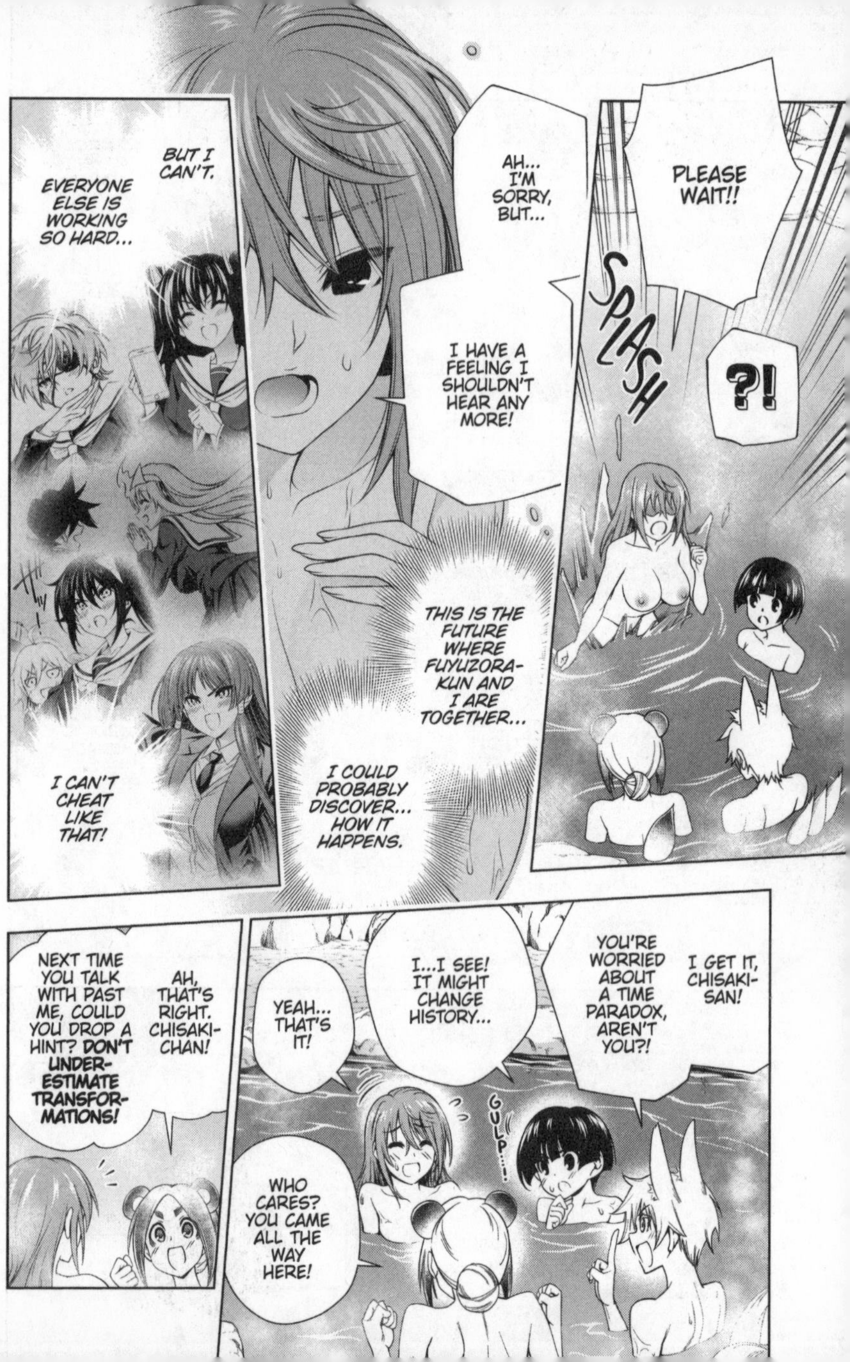
PLEASE WAIT!!
SPLASH
?!
AH... I'M SORRY, BUT...
I HAVE A FEELING I SHOULDN'T HEAR ANY MORE!
THIS IS THE FUTURE WHERE FUYUZORA-KUN AND I ARE TOGETHER...
I COULD PROBABLY DISCOVER... HOW IT HAPPENS.
BUT I CAN'T.
EVERYONE ELSE IS WORKING SO HARD...
I CAN'T CHEAT LIKE THAT!
I GET IT, CHISAKI-SAN!
YOU'RE WORRIED ABOUT A TIME PARADOX, AREN'T YOU?!
I...I SEE! IT MIGHT CHANGE HISTORY...
YEAH... THAT'S IT!
GULP...
WHO CARES? YOU CAME ALL THE WAY HERE!
AH, THAT'S RIGHT. CHISAKI-CHAN!
NEXT TIME YOU TALK WITH PAST ME, COULD YOU DROP A HINT? DON'T UNDERESTIMATE TRANSFORMATIONS!

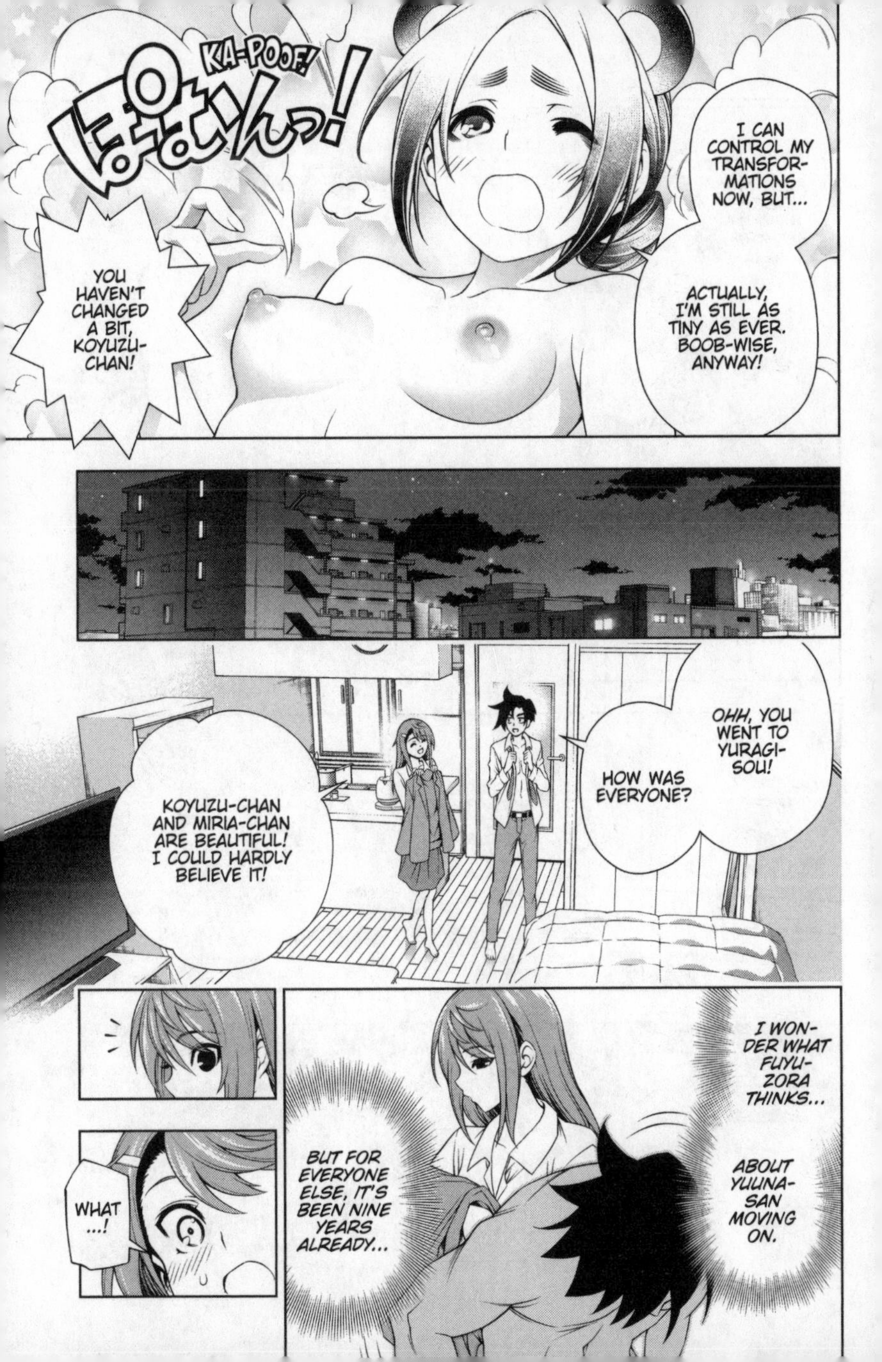
I CAN CONTROL MY TRANSFORMATIONS NOW, BUT...
ほわんっ!
KA-POOF!
ACTUALLY, I'M STILL AS TINY AS EVER. BOOB-WISE, ANYWAY!
YOU HAVEN'T CHANGED A BIT, KOYUZU-CHAN!
OHH, YOU WENT TO YURAGI-SOU!
HOW WAS EVERYONE?
KOYUZU-CHAN AND MIRIA-CHAN ARE BEAUTIFUL! I COULD HARDLY BELIEVE IT!
I WONDER WHAT FUYUZORA THINKS...
ABOUT YUUNA-SAN MOVING ON.
BUT FOR EVERYONE ELSE, IT'S BEEN NINE YEARS ALREADY...
WHAT ...!

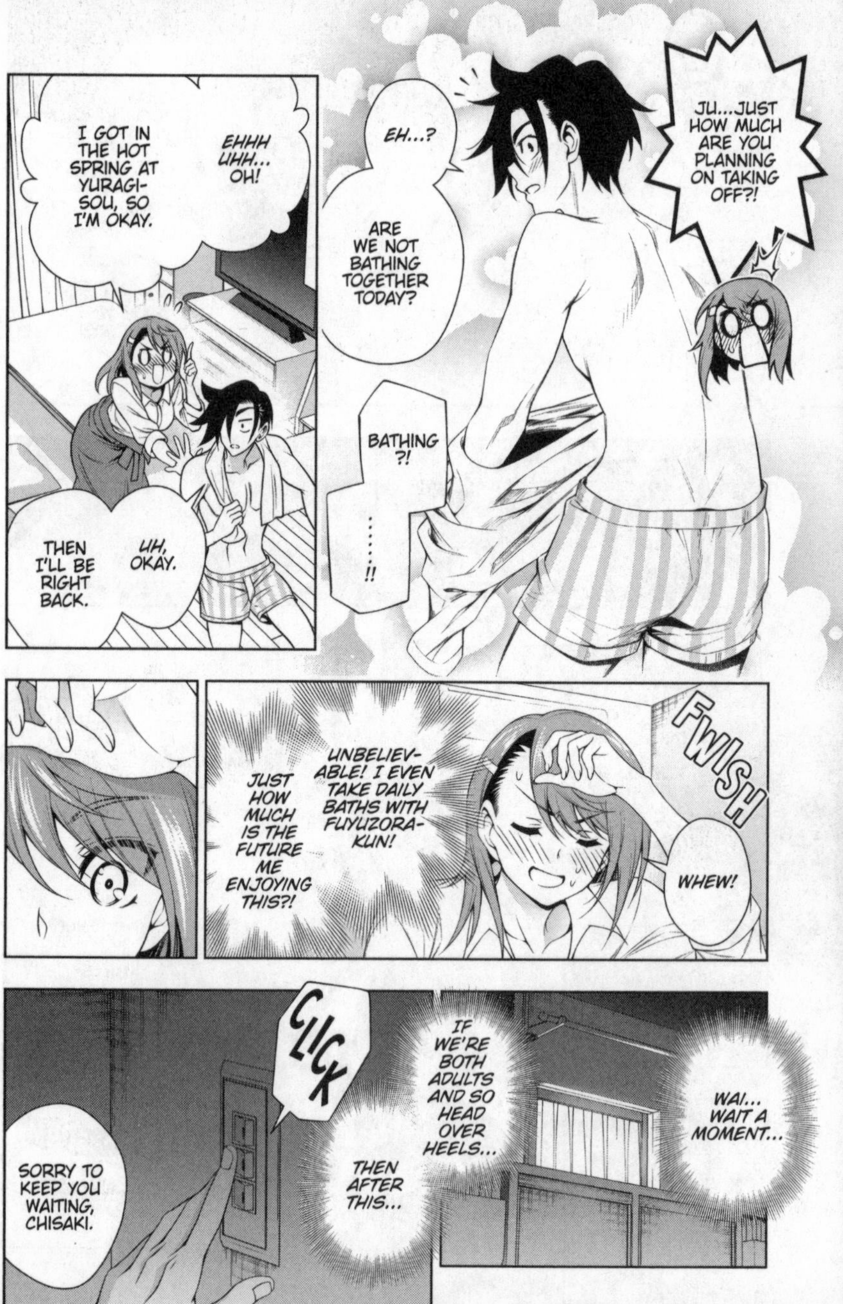

JU...JUST HOW MUCH ARE YOU PLANNING ON TAKING OFF?!
EH...?
ARE WE NOT BATHING TOGETHER TODAY?
BATHING?!
......!!
EHHH UHH... OH!
I GOT IN THE HOT SPRING AT YURAGI-SOU, SO I'M OKAY.
UH, OKAY.
THEN I'LL BE RIGHT BACK.
FWISH
WHEW!
UNBELIEV-ABLE! I EVEN TAKE DAILY BATHS WITH FUYUZORA-KUN!
JUST HOW MUCH IS THE FUTURE ME ENJOYING THIS?!
WAI... WAIT A MOMENT...
IF WE'RE BOTH ADULTS AND SO HEAD OVER HEELS...
THEN AFTER THIS...
CLICK
SORRY TO KEEP YOU WAITING, CHISAKI.

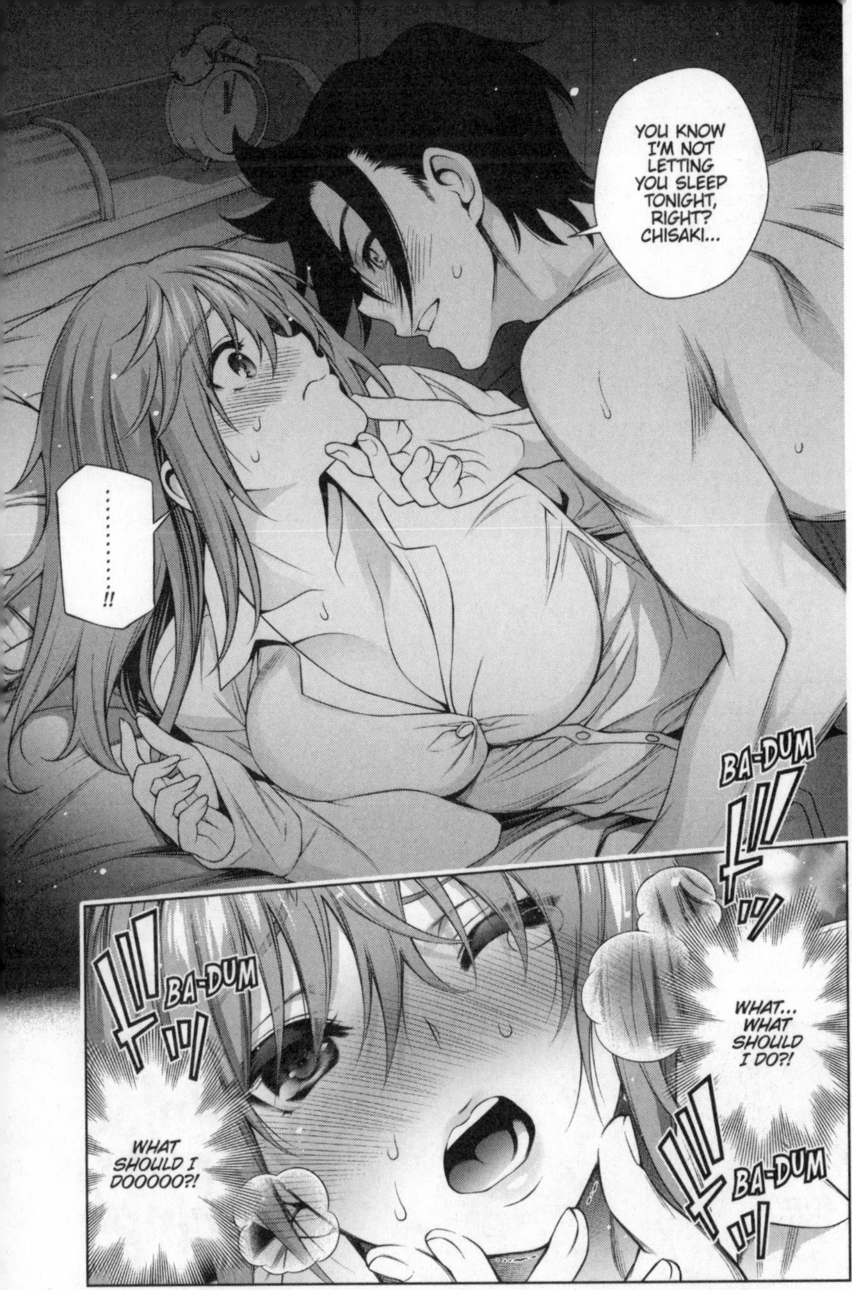
YOU KNOW I'M NOT LETTING YOU SLEEP TONIGHT, RIGHT? CHISAKI...
.........!!
BA-DUM
BA-DUM
WHAT... WHAT SHOULD I DO?!
BA-DUM
BA-DUM
WHAT SHOULD I DOOOOO?!

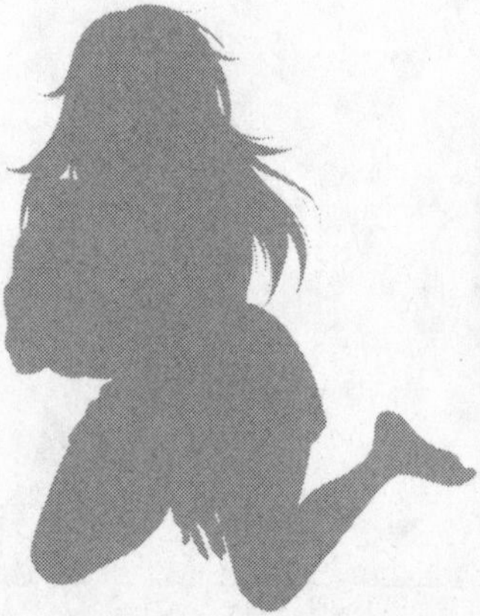

Yuuna and the Haunted Hot Springs

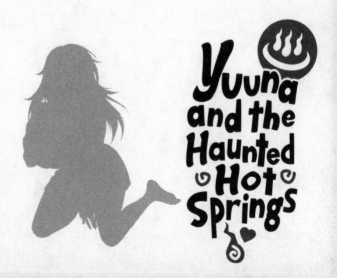

147 These Ten Years with Chisaki-san

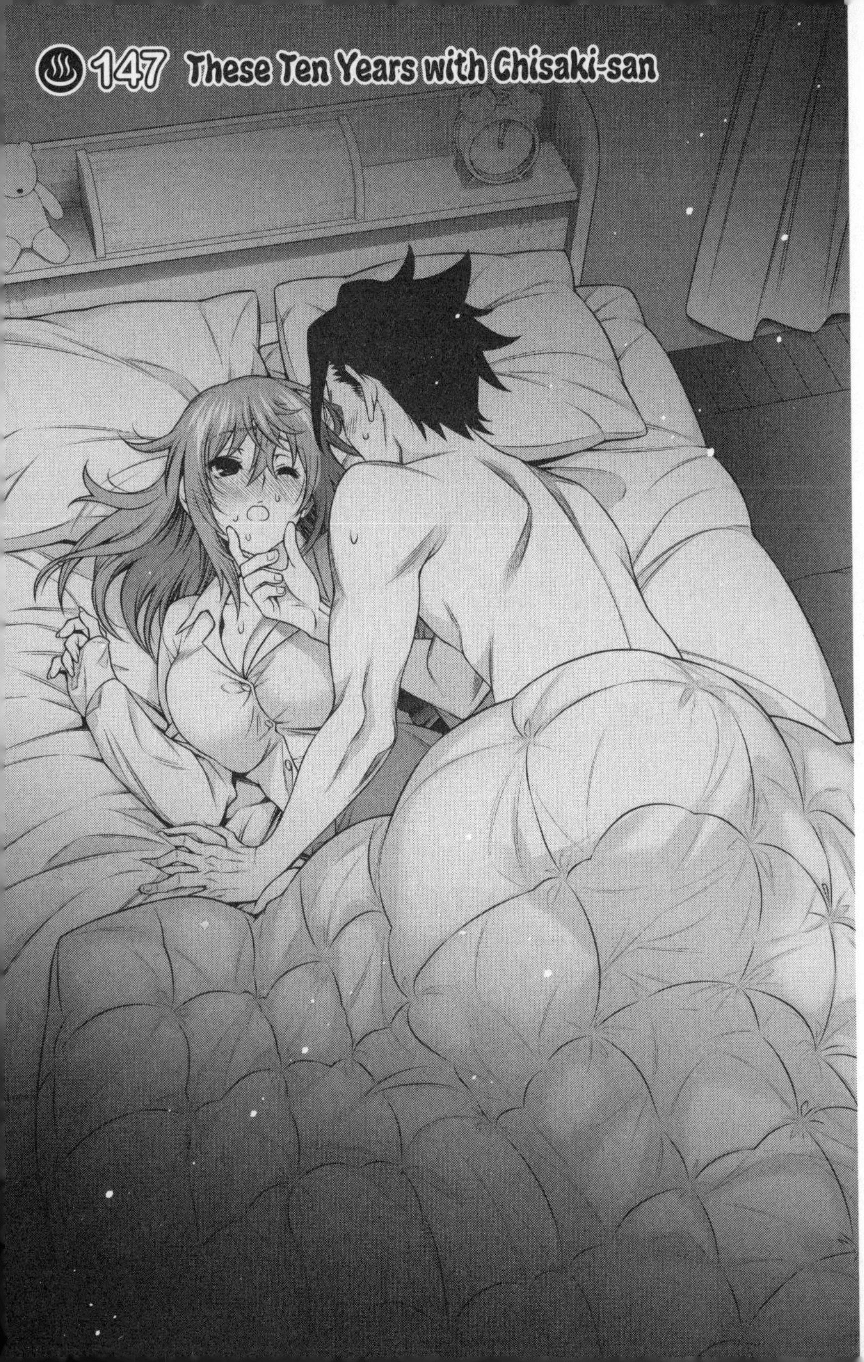

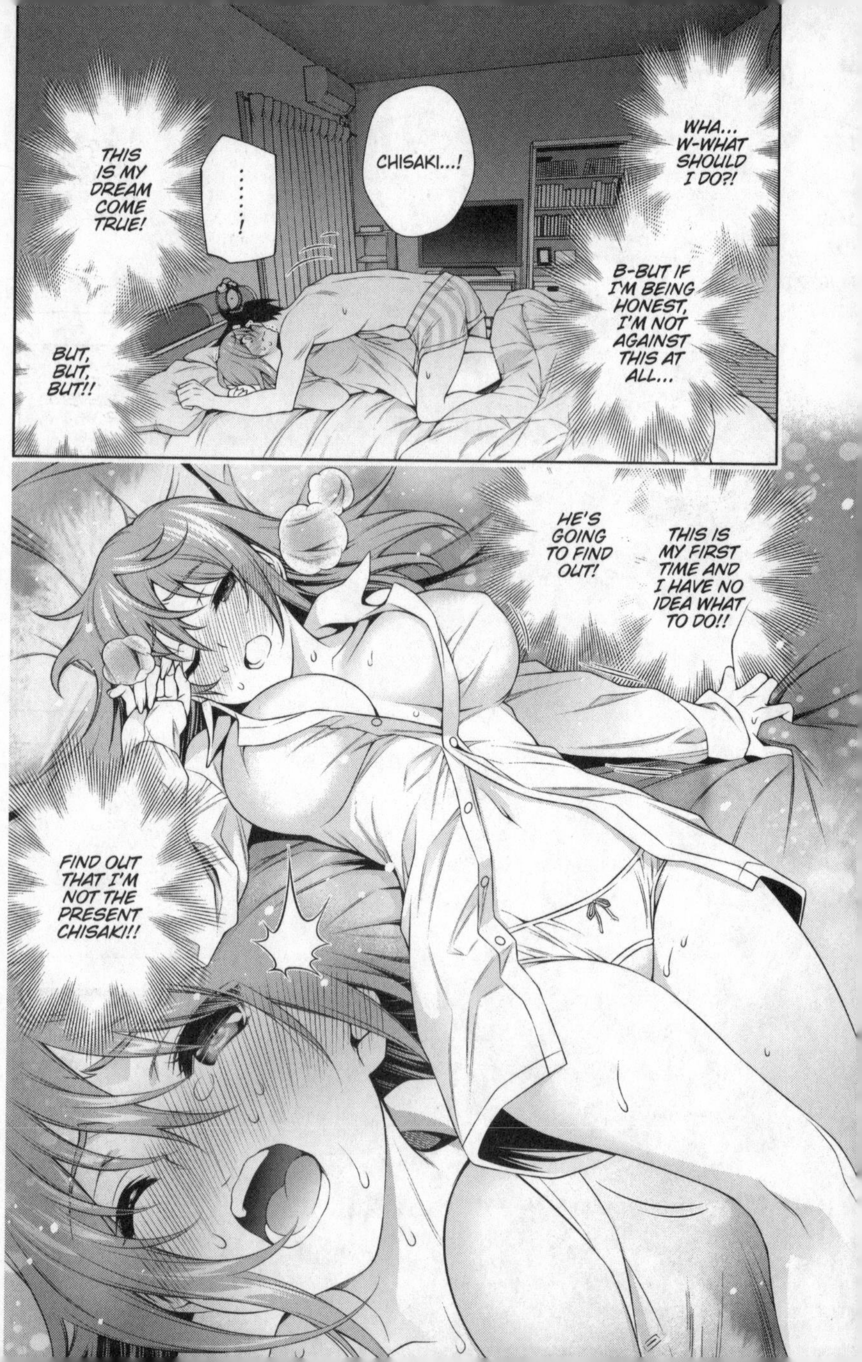
WHA... W-WHAT SHOULD I DO?!
B-BUT IF I'M BEING HONEST, I'M NOT AGAINST THIS AT ALL...
CHISAKI...!
......!
THIS IS MY DREAM COME TRUE!
BUT, BUT, BUT!!
THIS IS MY FIRST TIME AND I HAVE NO IDEA WHAT TO DO!!
HE'S GOING TO FIND OUT!
FIND OUT THAT I'M NOT THE PRESENT CHISAKI!!

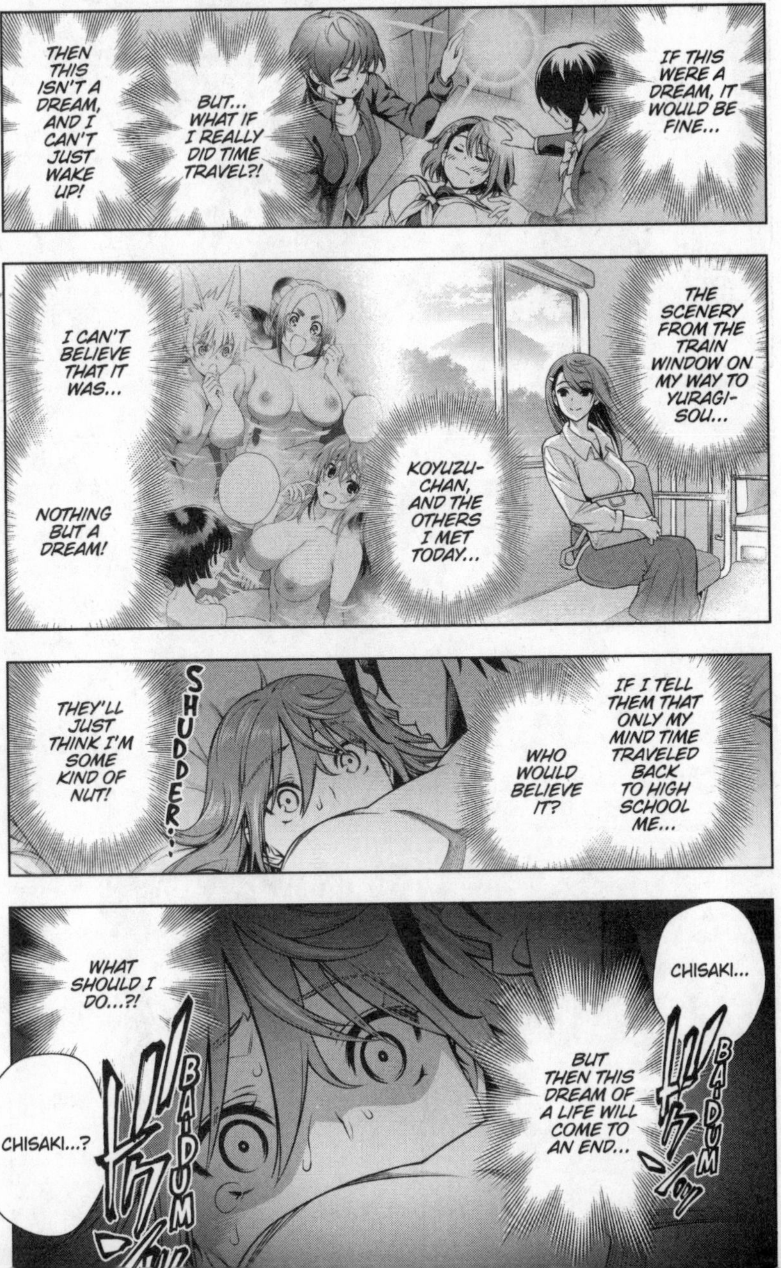
IF THIS WERE A DREAM, IT WOULD BE FINE...
BUT... WHAT IF I REALLY DID TIME TRAVEL?!
THEN THIS ISN'T A DREAM, AND I CAN'T JUST WAKE UP!
THE SCENERY FROM THE TRAIN WINDOW ON MY WAY TO YURAGI-SOU...
KOYUZU-CHAN, AND THE OTHERS I MET TODAY...
I CAN'T BELIEVE THAT IT WAS...
NOTHING BUT A DREAM!
IF I TELL THEM THAT ONLY MY MIND TIME TRAVELED BACK TO HIGH SCHOOL ME...
WHO WOULD BELIEVE IT?
SHUDDER...
THEY'LL JUST THINK I'M SOME KIND OF NUT!
CHISAKI...
BADUM
BUT THEN THIS DREAM OF A LIFE WILL COME TO AN END...
WHAT SHOULD I DO...?!
BADUM
CHISAKI...?

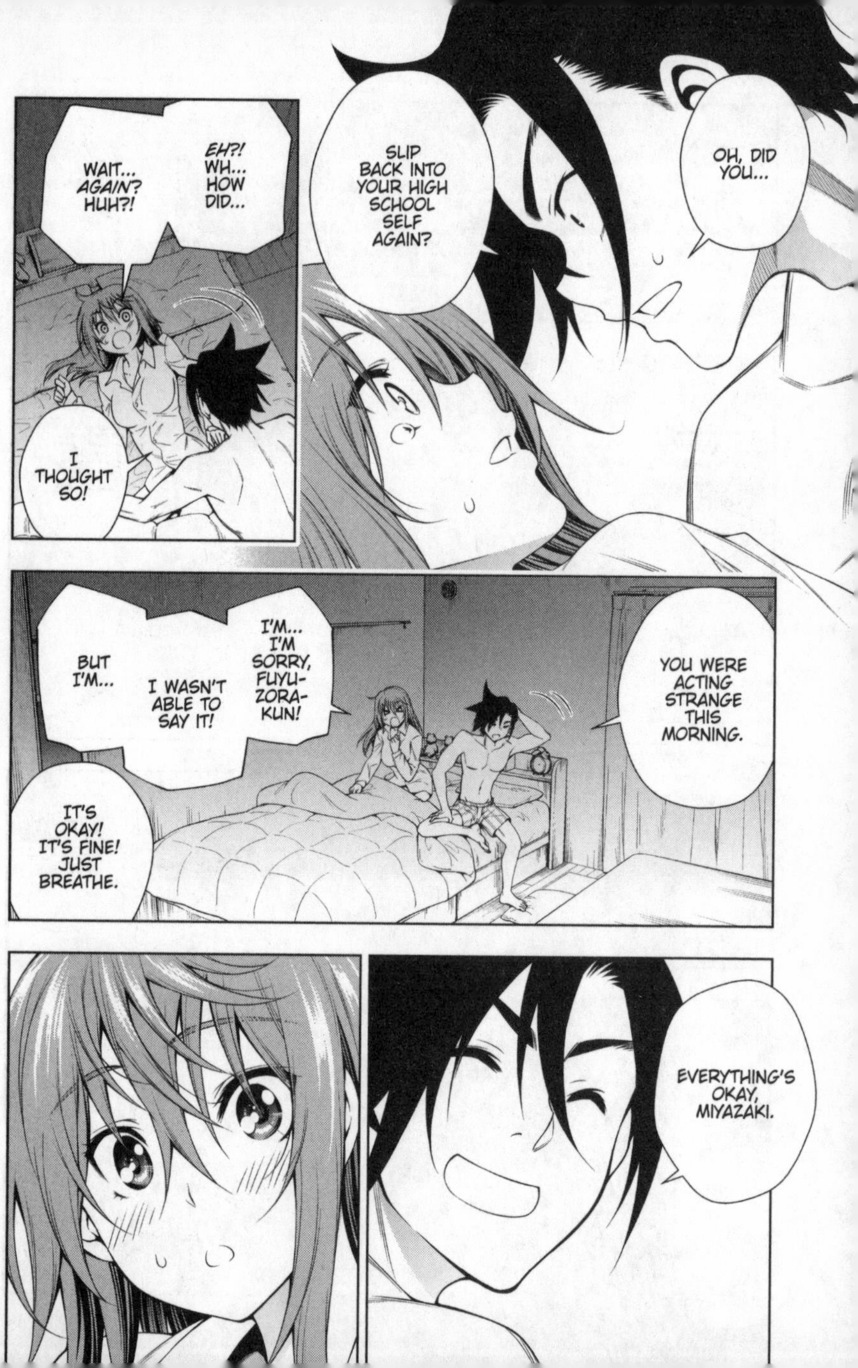
OH, DID YOU...
SLIP BACK INTO YOUR HIGH SCHOOL SELF AGAIN?
EH?! WH... HOW DID...
WAIT... AGAIN? HUH?!
I THOUGHT SO!
YOU WERE ACTING STRANGE THIS MORNING.
I'M... I'M SORRY, FUYU-ZORA-KUN!
I WASN'T ABLE TO SAY IT!
BUT I'M...
IT'S OKAY! IT'S FINE! JUST BREATHE.
EVERYTHING'S OKAY, MIYAZAKI.

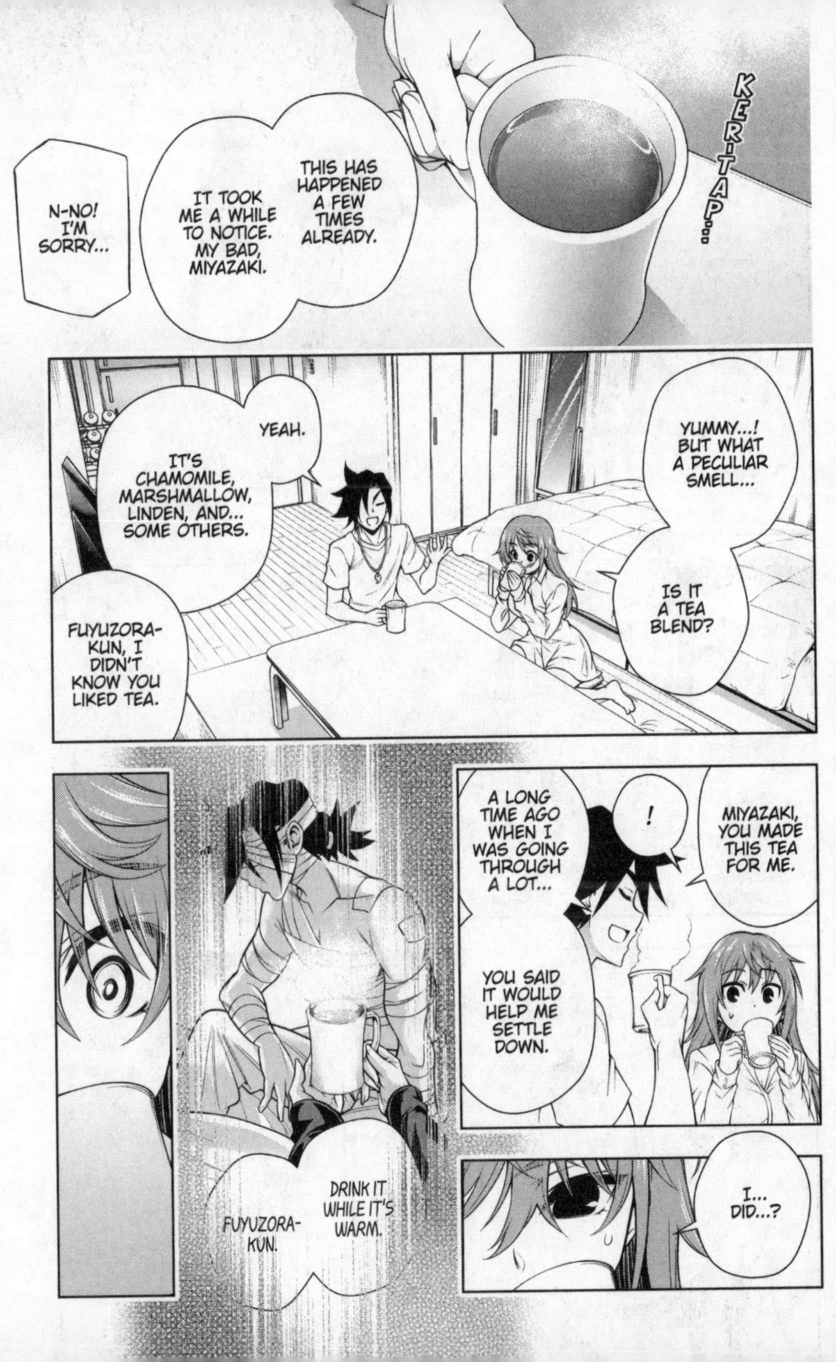
KERITAP..
THIS HAS HAPPENED A FEW TIMES ALREADY.
IT TOOK ME A WHILE TO NOTICE. MY BAD, MIYAZAKI.
N-NO! I'M SORRY...
YUMMY...! BUT WHAT A PECULIAR SMELL...
IS IT A TEA BLEND?
YEAH.
IT'S CHAMOMILE, MARSHMALLOW, LINDEN, AND... SOME OTHERS.
FUYUZORA-KUN, I DIDN'T KNOW YOU LIKED TEA.
MIYAZAKI, YOU MADE THIS TEA FOR ME.
!
A LONG TIME AGO WHEN I WAS GOING THROUGH A LOT...
YOU SAID IT WOULD HELP ME SETTLE DOWN.
I... DID...?
DRINK IT WHILE IT'S WARM.
FUYUZORA-KUN.

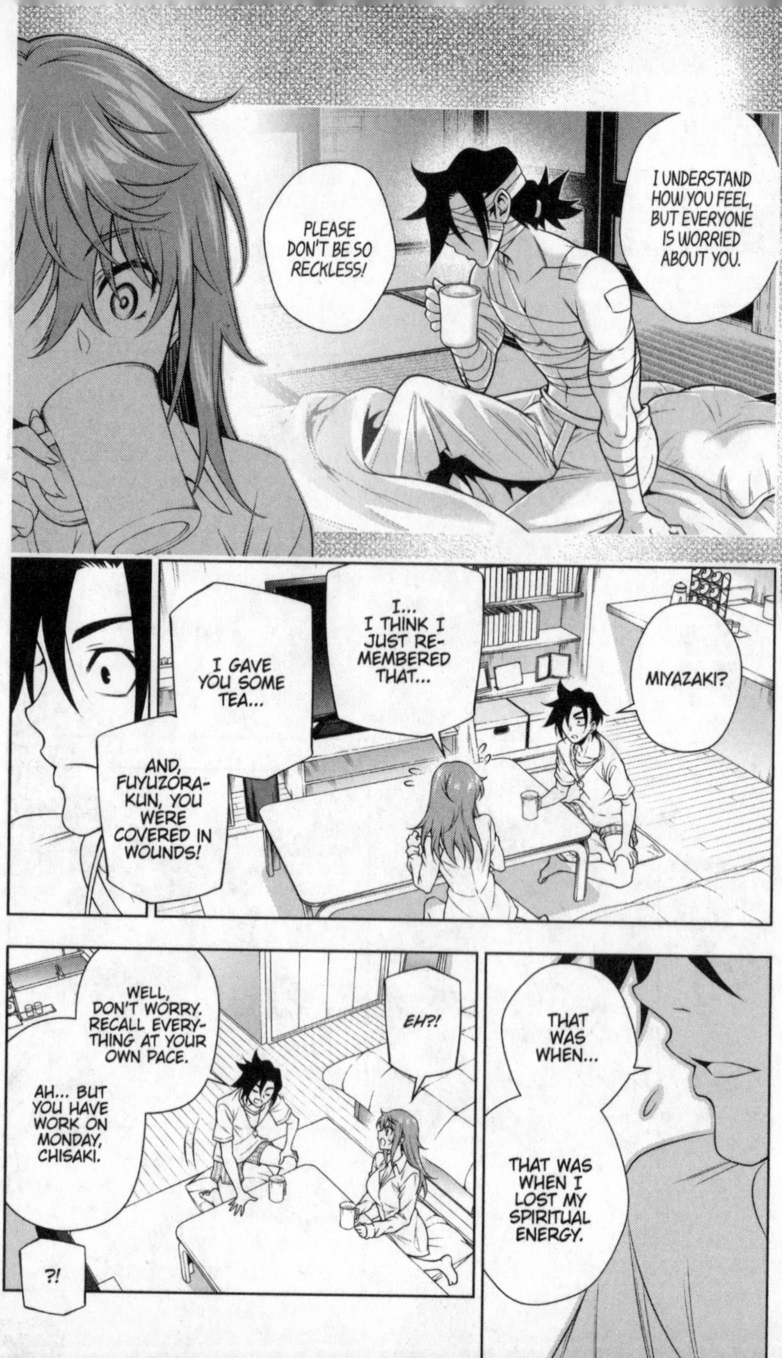
I UNDERSTAND HOW YOU FEEL, BUT EVERYONE IS WORRIED ABOUT YOU.
PLEASE DON'T BE SO RECKLESS!
MIYAZAKI?
I... I THINK I JUST RE-MEMBERED THAT...
I GAVE YOU SOME TEA...
AND, FUYUZORA-KUN, YOU WERE COVERED IN WOUNDS!
THAT WAS WHEN...
THAT WAS WHEN I LOST MY SPIRITUAL ENERGY.
EH?!
WELL, DON'T WORRY. RECALL EVERY-THING AT YOUR OWN PACE.
AH... BUT YOU HAVE WORK ON MONDAY, CHISAKI.
?!

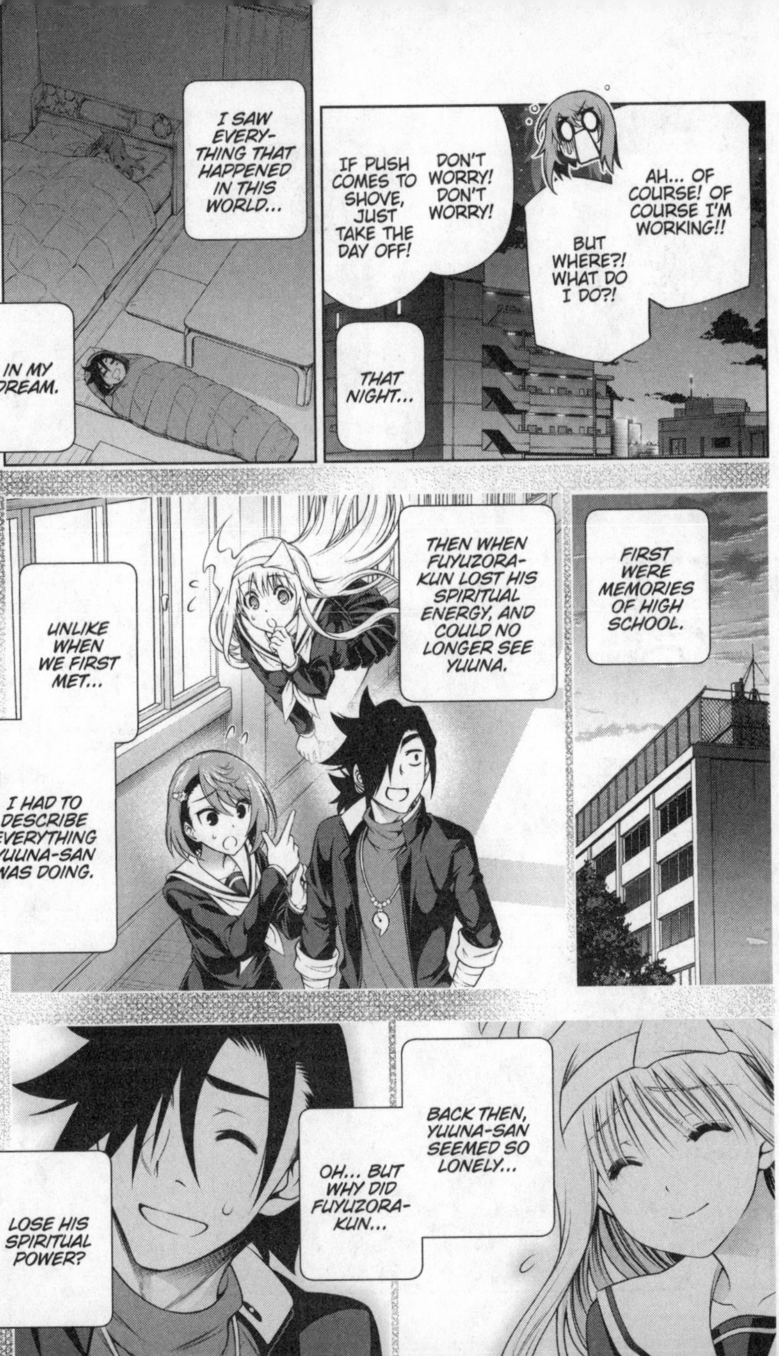
AH... OF COURSE! OF COURSE I'M WORKING!!
BUT WHERE?! WHAT DO I DO?!
DON'T WORRY! DON'T WORRY!
IF PUSH COMES TO SHOVE, JUST TAKE THE DAY OFF!
THAT NIGHT...
I SAW EVERYTHING THAT HAPPENED IN THIS WORLD...
IN MY DREAM.
FIRST WERE MEMORIES OF HIGH SCHOOL.
THEN WHEN FUYUZORA-KUN LOST HIS SPIRITUAL ENERGY, AND COULD NO LONGER SEE YUUNA.
UNLIKE WHEN WE FIRST MET...
I HAD TO DESCRIBE EVERYTHING YUUNA-SAN WAS DOING.
BACK THEN, YUUNA-SAN SEEMED SO LONELY...
OH... BUT WHY DID FUYUZORA-KUN...
LOSE HIS SPIRITUAL POWER?

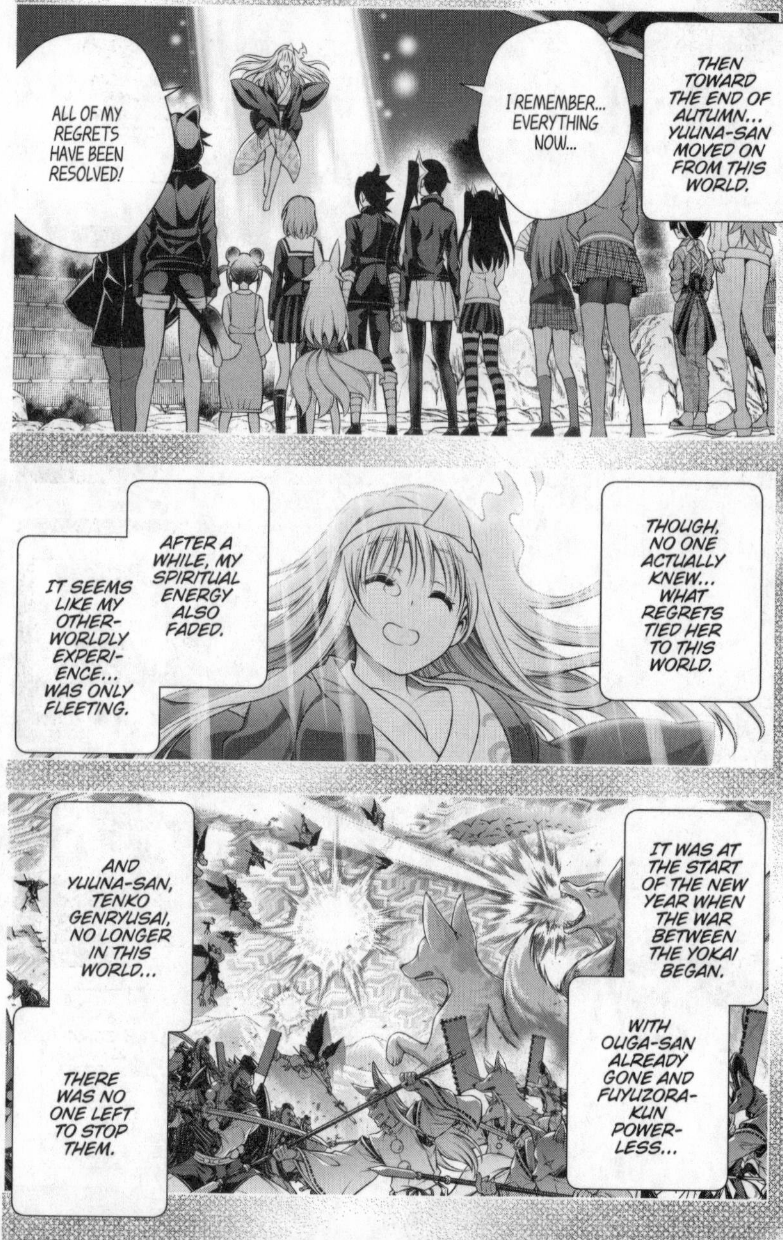
THEN TOWARD THE END OF AUTUMN... YUUNA-SAN MOVED ON FROM THIS WORLD.
I REMEMBER... EVERYTHING NOW...
ALL OF MY REGRETS HAVE BEEN RESOLVED!
THOUGH, NO ONE ACTUALLY KNEW... WHAT REGRETS TIED HER TO THIS WORLD.
AFTER A WHILE, MY SPIRITUAL ENERGY ALSO FADED.
IT SEEMS LIKE MY OTHER-WORLDLY EXPERIENCE... WAS ONLY FLEETING.
IT WAS AT THE START OF THE NEW YEAR WHEN THE WAR BETWEEN THE YOKAI BEGAN.
WITH OUGA-SAN ALREADY GONE AND FUYUZORA-KUN POWERLESS...
AND YUUNA-SAN, TENKO GENRYUSAI, NO LONGER IN THIS WORLD...
THERE WAS NO ONE LEFT TO STOP THEM.

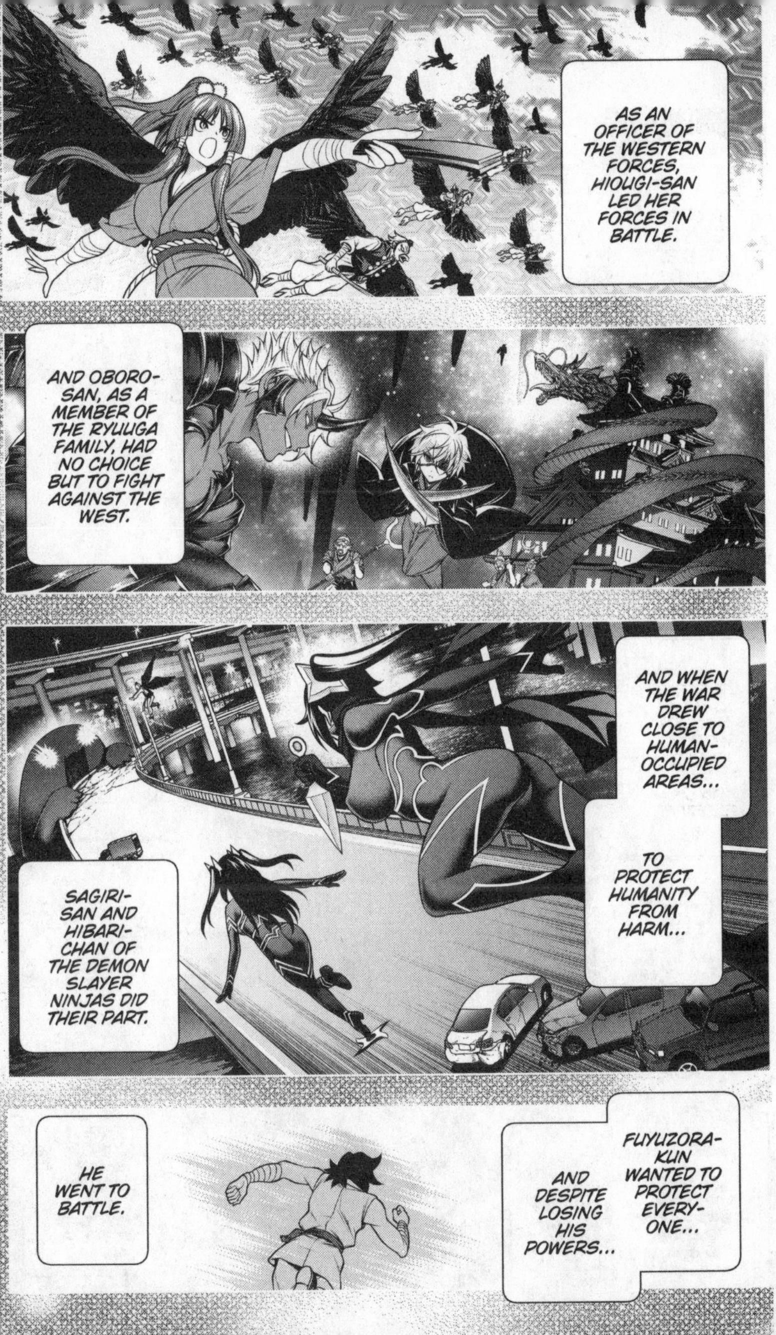
AS AN OFFICER OF THE WESTERN FORCES, HIOUGI-SAN LED HER FORCES IN BATTLE.
AND OBORO-SAN, AS A MEMBER OF THE RYUUGA FAMILY, HAD NO CHOICE BUT TO FIGHT AGAINST THE WEST.
AND WHEN THE WAR DREW CLOSE TO HUMAN-OCCUPIED AREAS...
TO PROTECT HUMANITY FROM HARM...
SAGIRI-SAN AND HIBARI-CHAN OF THE DEMON SLAYER NINJAS DID THEIR PART.
FUYUZORA-KUN WANTED TO PROTECT EVERY-ONE...
AND DESPITE LOSING HIS POWERS...
HE WENT TO BATTLE.

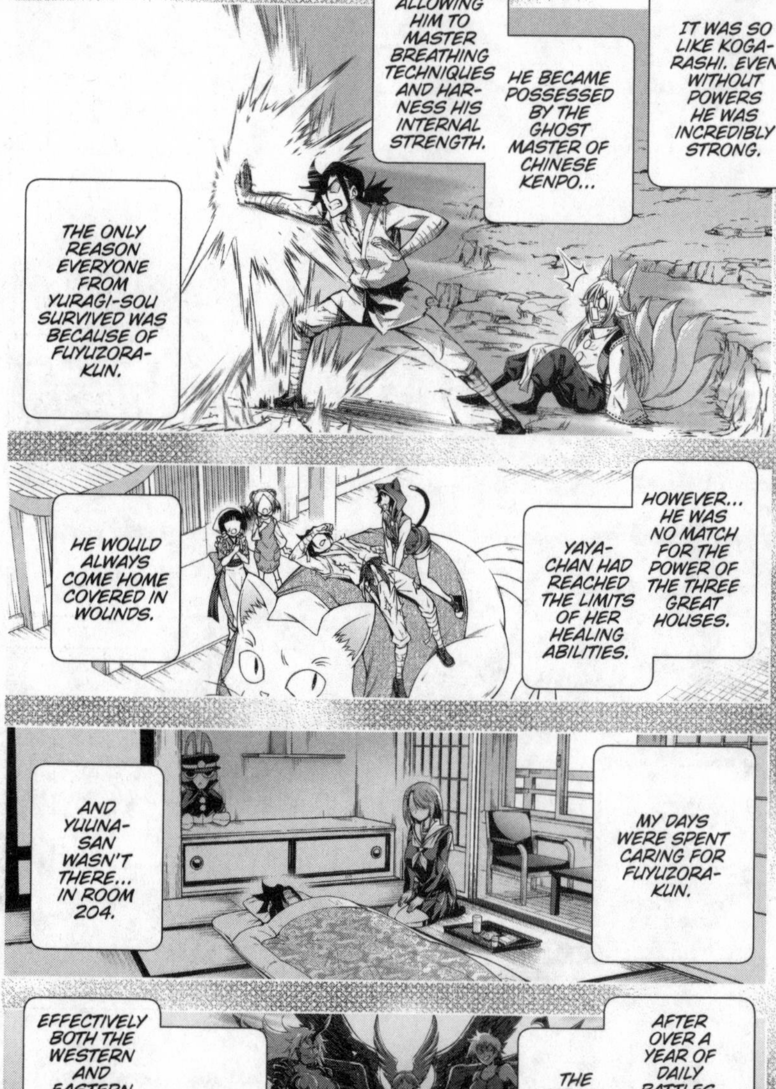
IT WAS SO LIKE KOGA-RASHI. EVEN WITHOUT POWERS HE WAS INCREDIBLY STRONG.
HE BECAME POSSESSED BY THE GHOST MASTER OF CHINESE KENPO...
ALLOWING HIM TO MASTER BREATHING TECHNIQUES AND HAR-NESS HIS INTERNAL STRENGTH.
THE ONLY REASON EVERYONE FROM YURAGI-SOU SURVIVED WAS BECAUSE OF FUYUZORA-KUN.
HOWEVER... HE WAS NO MATCH FOR THE POWER OF THE THREE GREAT HOUSES.
YAYA-CHAN HAD REACHED THE LIMITS OF HER HEALING ABILITIES.
HE WOULD ALWAYS COME HOME COVERED IN WOUNDS.
MY DAYS WERE SPENT CARING FOR FUYUZORA-KUN.
AND YUUNA-SAN WASN'T THERE... IN ROOM 204.
AFTER OVER A YEAR OF DAILY BATTLES, WITH EVERYONE AT THEIR LIMITS...
THE WAR WAS FINALLY BROUGHT TO AN END.
A CEASE-FIRE WAS CALLED.
EFFECTIVELY BOTH THE WESTERN AND EASTERN FORCES WERE NOW UNDER HIOUGI-SAN'S FLAG.

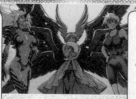

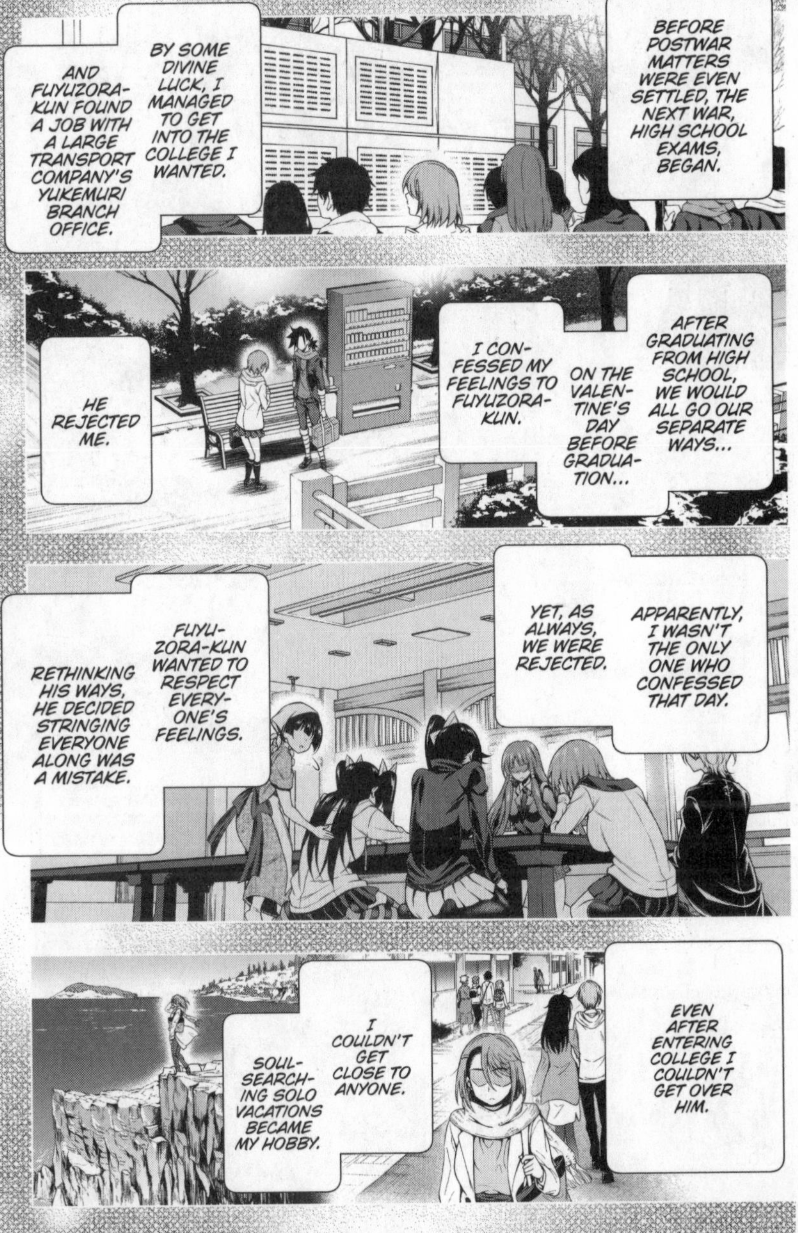

BEFORE POSTWAR MATTERS WERE EVEN SETTLED, THE NEXT WAR, HIGH SCHOOL EXAMS, BEGAN.
BY SOME DIVINE LUCK, I MANAGED TO GET INTO THE COLLEGE I WANTED.
AND FUYUZORA-KUN FOUND A JOB WITH A LARGE TRANSPORT COMPANY'S YUKEMURI BRANCH OFFICE.
AFTER GRADUATING FROM HIGH SCHOOL, WE WOULD ALL GO OUR SEPARATE WAYS...
ON THE VALENTINE'S DAY BEFORE GRADUATION...
I CONFESSED MY FEELINGS TO FUYUZORA-KUN.
HE REJECTED ME.
APPARENTLY, I WASN'T THE ONLY ONE WHO CONFESSED THAT DAY.
YET, AS ALWAYS, WE WERE REJECTED.
FUYUZORA-KUN WANTED TO RESPECT EVERYONE'S FEELINGS.
RETHINKING HIS WAYS, HE DECIDED STRINGING EVERYONE ALONG WAS A MISTAKE.
EVEN AFTER ENTERING COLLEGE I COULDN'T GET OVER HIM.
I COULDN'T GET CLOSE TO ANYONE.
SOUL-SEARCHING SOLO VACATIONS BECAME MY HOBBY.

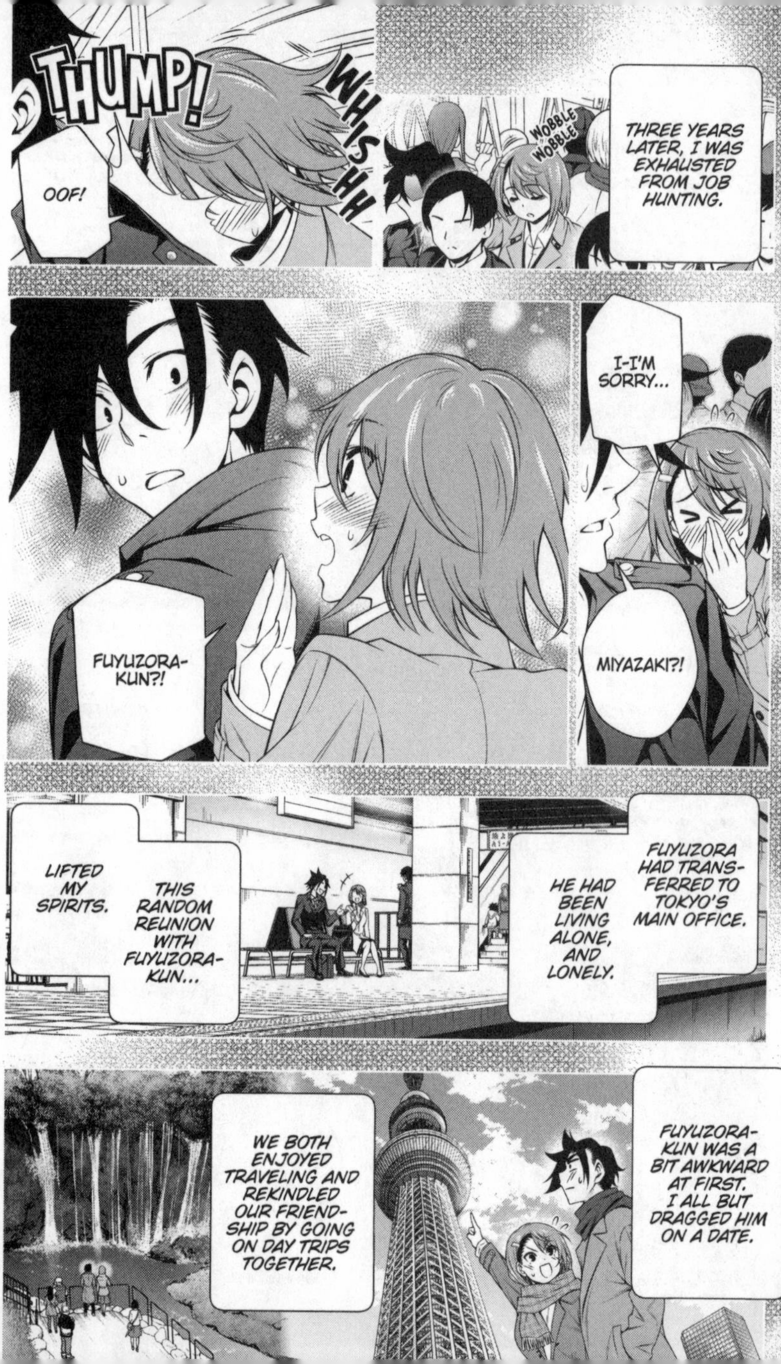
THREE YEARS LATER, I WAS EXHAUSTED FROM JOB HUNTING.
WOBBLE WOBBLE
THUMP!
WHISHH
OOF!
I-I'M SORRY...
MIYAZAKI?!
FUYUZORA-KUN?!
FUYUZORA HAD TRANSFERRED TO TOKYO'S MAIN OFFICE.
HE HAD BEEN LIVING ALONE, AND LONELY.
THIS RANDOM REUNION WITH FUYUZORA-KUN...
LIFTED MY SPIRITS.
FUYUZORA-KUN WAS A BIT AWKWARD AT FIRST. I ALL BUT DRAGGED HIM ON A DATE.
WE BOTH ENJOYED TRAVELING AND REKINDLED OUR FRIENDSHIP BY GOING ON DAY TRIPS TOGETHER.

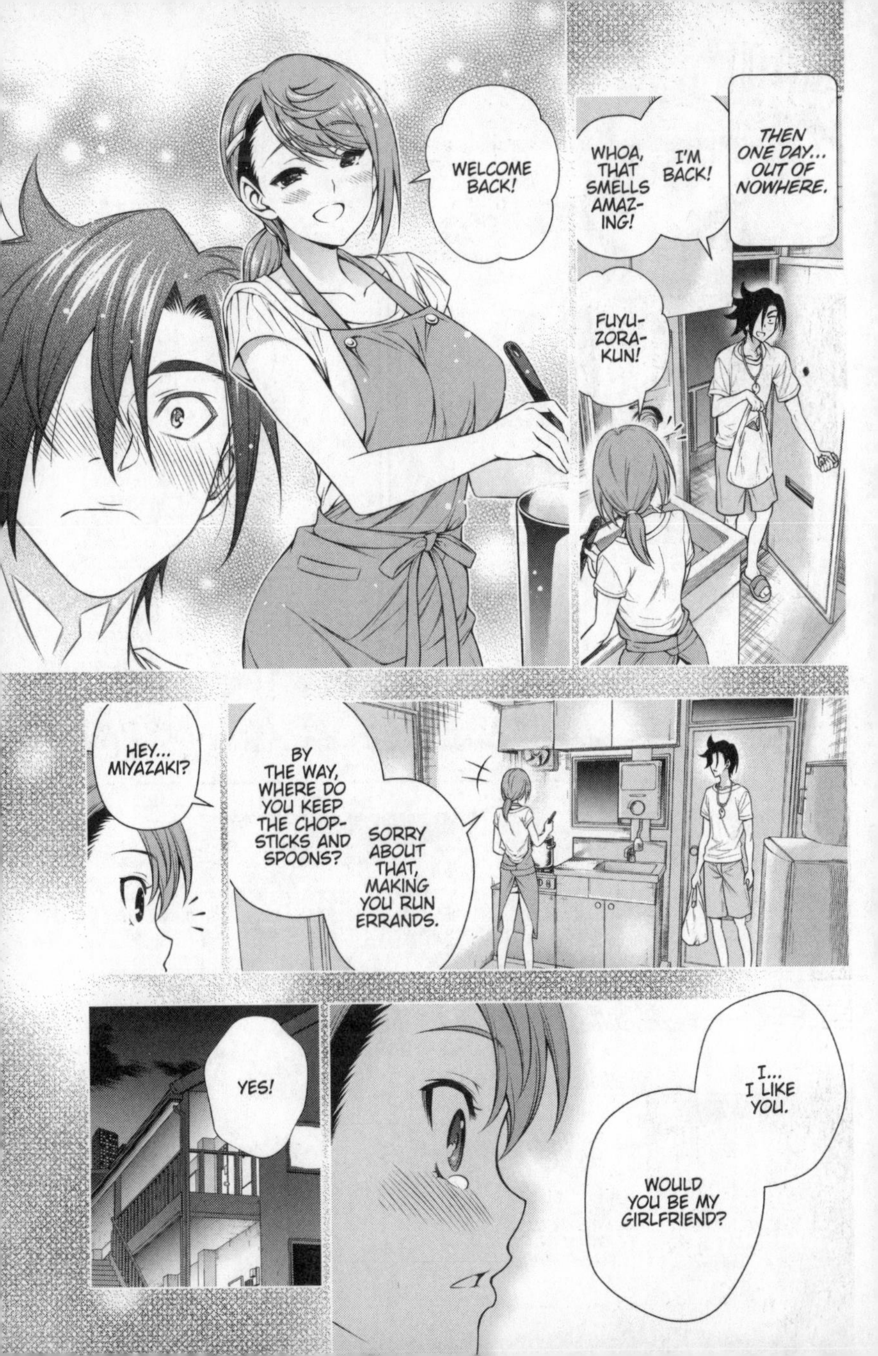
THEN ONE DAY... OUT OF NOWHERE.
I'M BACK!
WHOA, THAT SMELLS AMAZ-ING!
FUYU-ZORA-KUN!
WELCOME BACK!
SORRY ABOUT THAT, MAKING YOU RUN ERRANDS.
BY THE WAY, WHERE DO YOU KEEP THE CHOP-STICKS AND SPOONS?
HEY... MIYAZAKI?
I... I LIKE YOU.
WOULD YOU BE MY GIRLFRIEND?
YES!

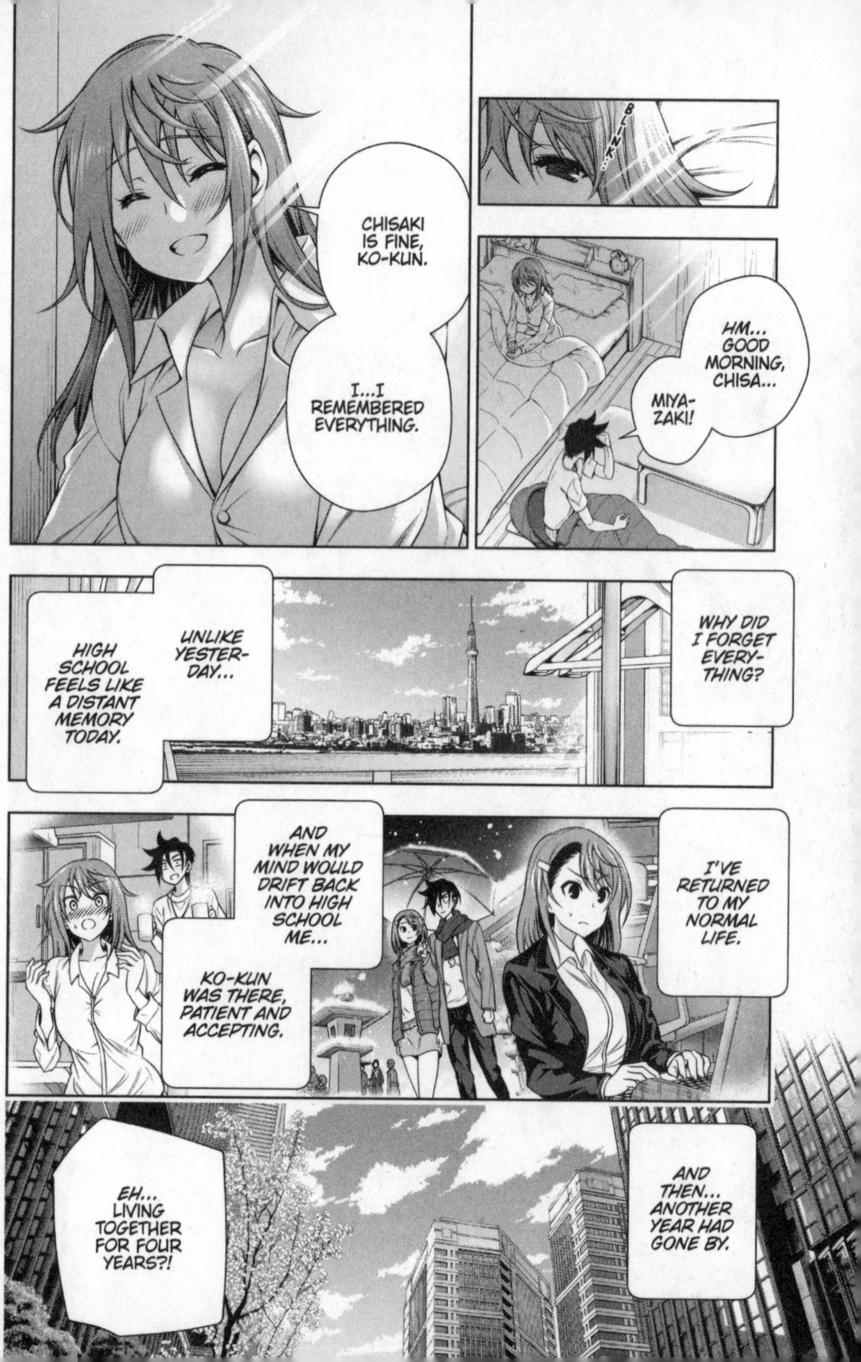
BLINK...
HM... GOOD MORNING, CHISA...
MIYAZAKI!
CHISAKI IS FINE, KO-KUN.
I...I REMEMBERED EVERYTHING.
WHY DID I FORGET EVERYTHING?
UNLIKE YESTERDAY...
HIGH SCHOOL FEELS LIKE A DISTANT MEMORY TODAY.
I'VE RETURNED TO MY NORMAL LIFE.
AND WHEN MY MIND WOULD DRIFT BACK INTO HIGH SCHOOL ME...
KO-KUN WAS THERE, PATIENT AND ACCEPTING.
AND THEN... ANOTHER YEAR HAD GONE BY.
EH... LIVING TOGETHER FOR FOUR YEARS?!

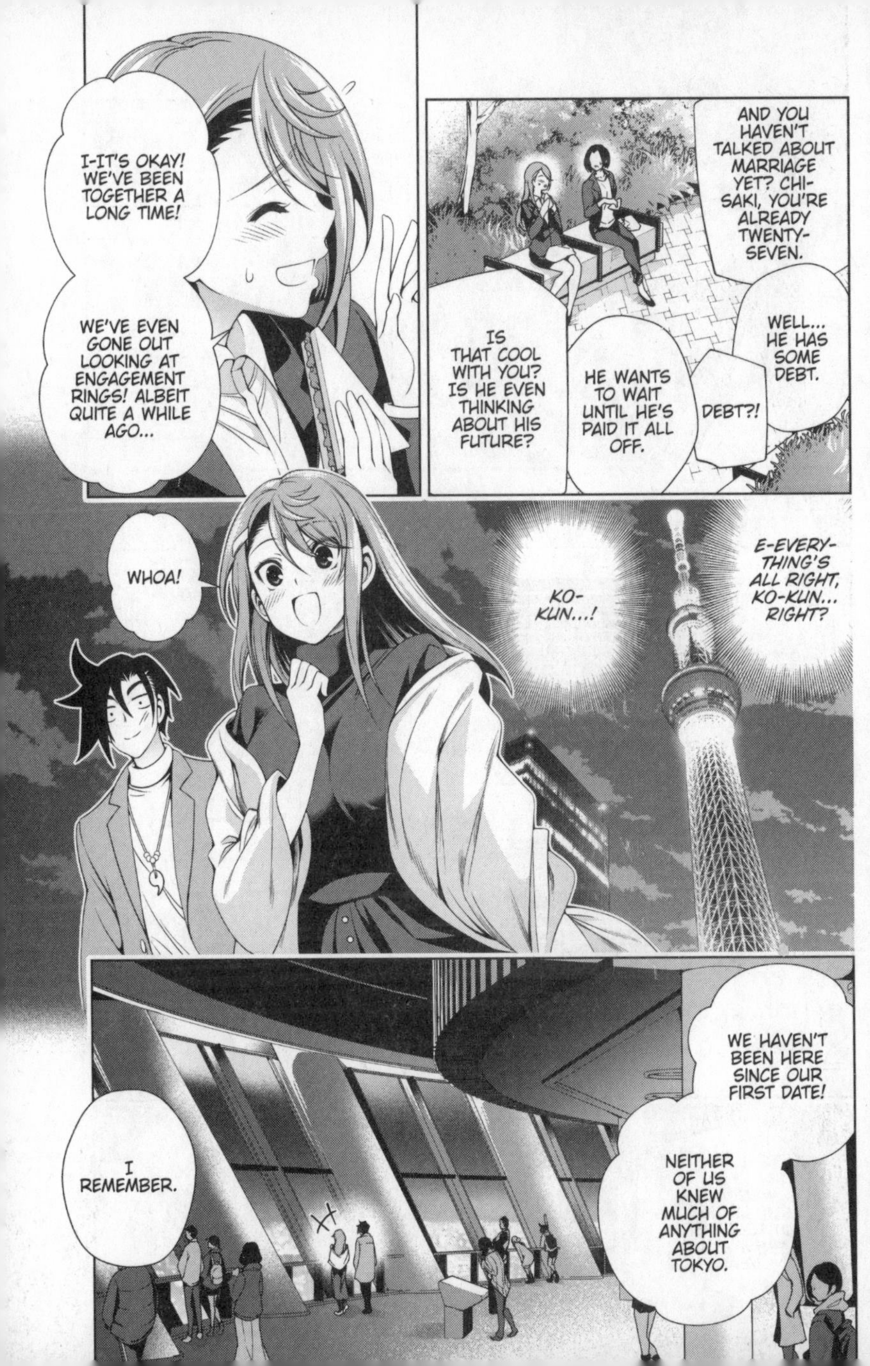
AND YOU HAVEN'T TALKED ABOUT MARRIAGE YET? CHI-SAKI, YOU'RE ALREADY TWENTY-SEVEN.
WELL... HE HAS SOME DEBT.
DEBT?!
HE WANTS TO WAIT UNTIL HE'S PAID IT ALL OFF.
IS THAT COOL WITH YOU? IS HE EVEN THINKING ABOUT HIS FUTURE?
I-IT'S OKAY! WE'VE BEEN TOGETHER A LONG TIME!
WE'VE EVEN GONE OUT LOOKING AT ENGAGEMENT RINGS! ALBEIT QUITE A WHILE AGO...
E-EVERYTHING'S ALL RIGHT, KO-KUN... RIGHT?
KO-KUN...!
WHOA!
WE HAVEN'T BEEN HERE SINCE OUR FIRST DATE!
NEITHER OF US KNEW MUCH OF ANYTHING ABOUT TOKYO.
I REMEMBER.

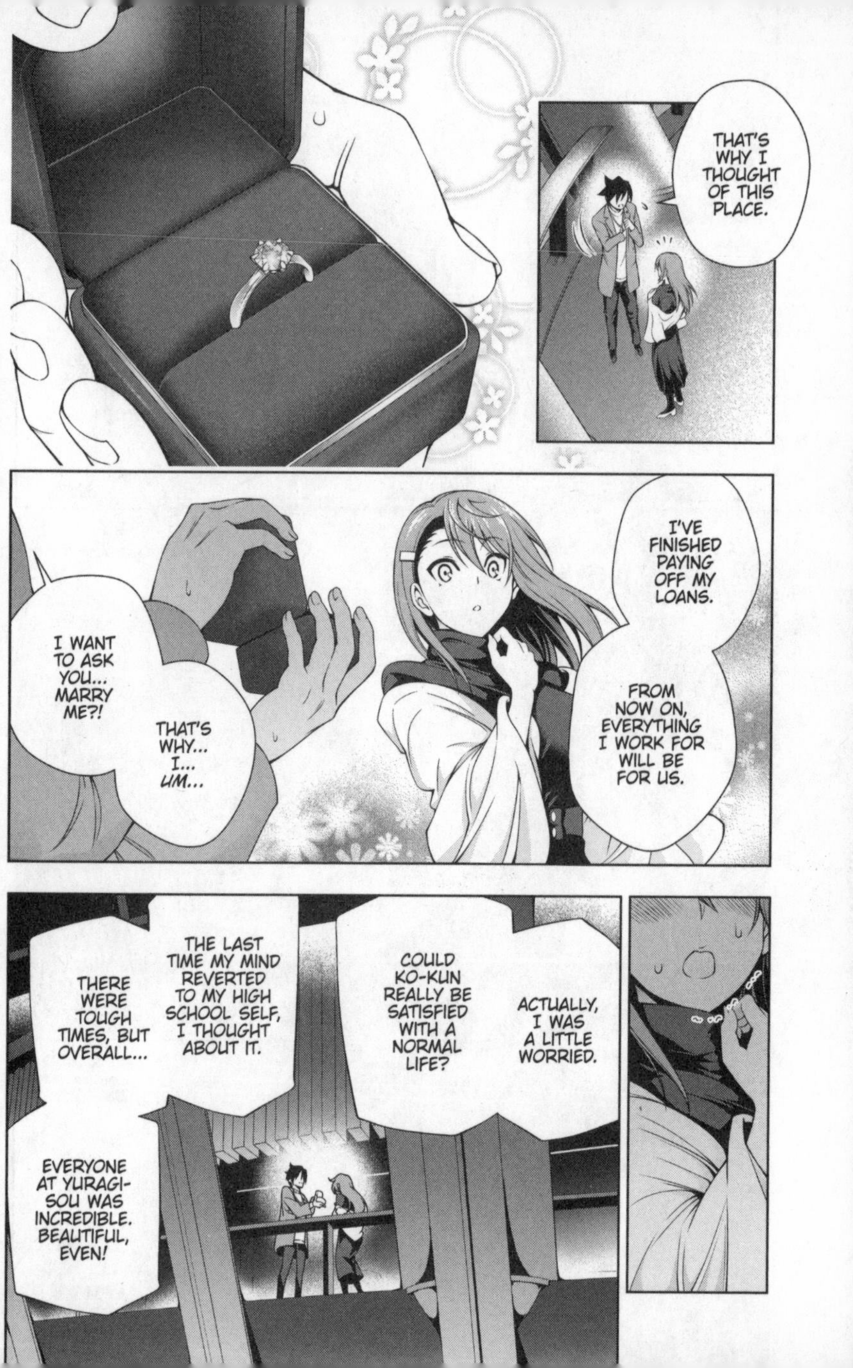
THAT'S WHY I THOUGHT OF THIS PLACE.
I'VE FINISHED PAYING OFF MY LOANS.
FROM NOW ON, EVERYTHING I WORK FOR WILL BE FOR US.
THAT'S WHY... I... UM...
I WANT TO ASK YOU... MARRY ME?!
ACTUALLY, I WAS A LITTLE WORRIED.
COULD KO-KUN REALLY BE SATISFIED WITH A NORMAL LIFE?
THE LAST TIME MY MIND REVERTED TO MY HIGH SCHOOL SELF, I THOUGHT ABOUT IT.
THERE WERE TOUGH TIMES, BUT OVERALL...
EVERYONE AT YURAGI-SOU WAS INCREDIBLE. BEAUTIFUL, EVEN!

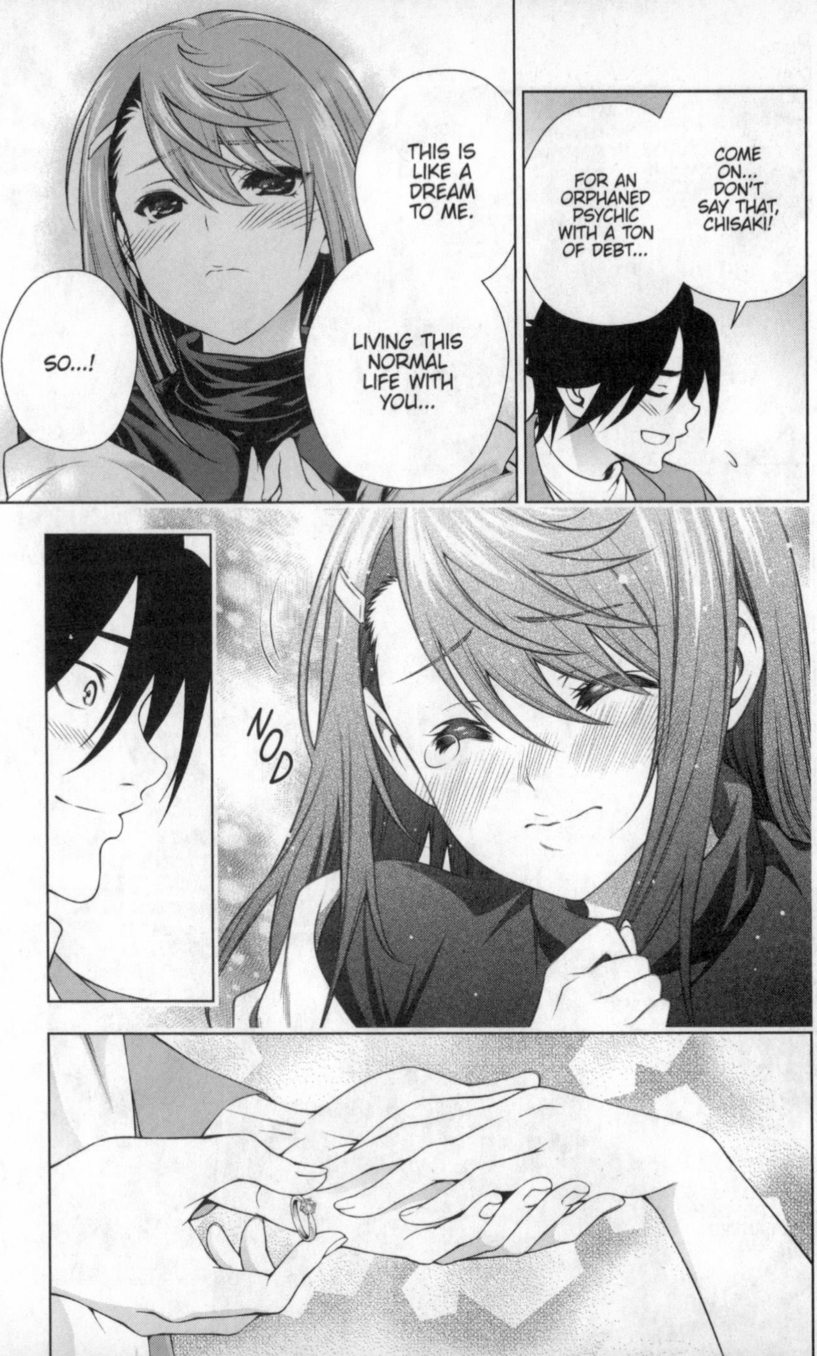
COME ON... DON'T SAY THAT, CHISAKI!
FOR AN ORPHANED PSYCHIC WITH A TON OF DEBT...
THIS IS LIKE A DREAM TO ME.
LIVING THIS NORMAL LIFE WITH YOU...
SO...!
NOD

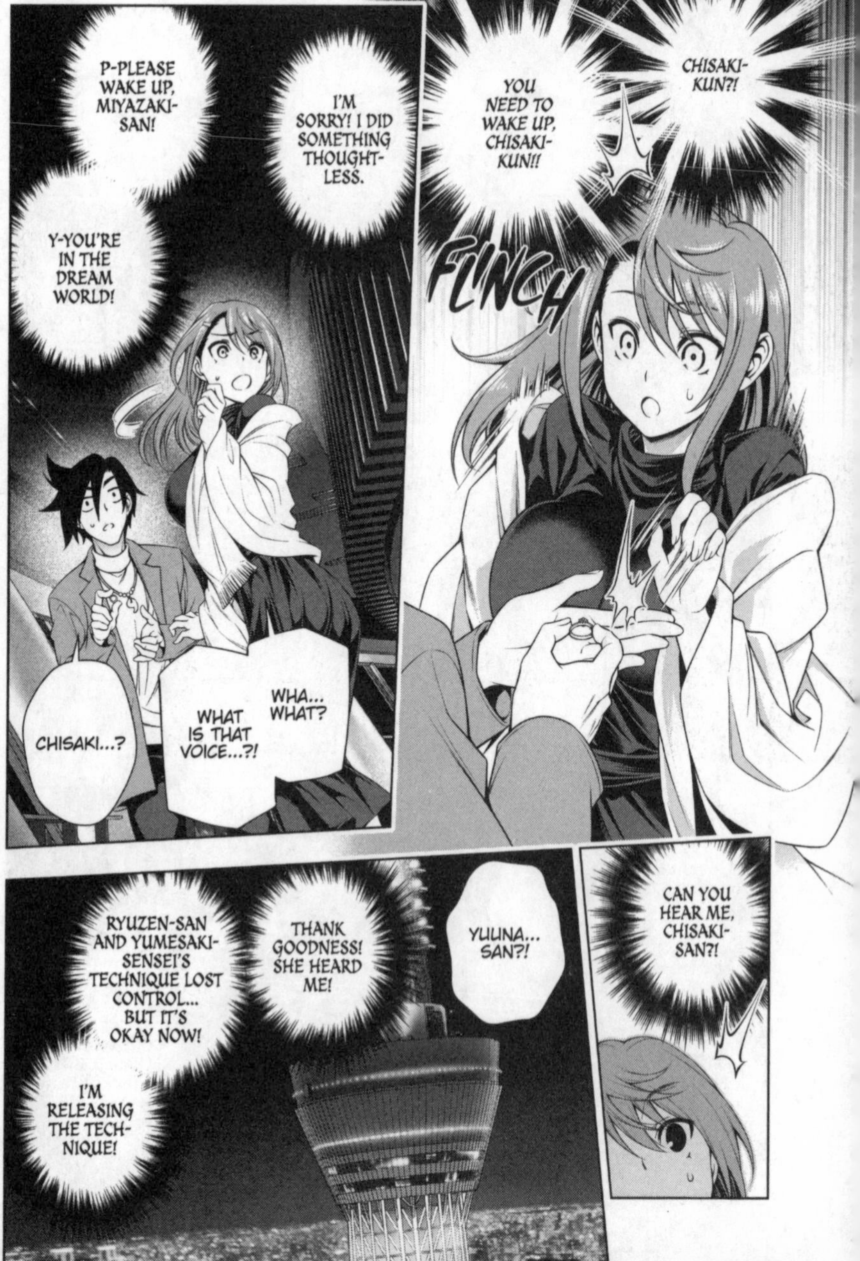
CHISAKI-KUN?!
YOU NEED TO WAKE UP, CHISAKI-KUN!!
FLINCH
I'M SORRY! I DID SOMETHING THOUGHT-LESS.
P-PLEASE WAKE UP, MIYAZAKI-SAN!
Y-YOU'RE IN THE DREAM WORLD!
WHA... WHAT?
WHAT IS THAT VOICE...?!
CHISAKI...?
CAN YOU HEAR ME, CHISAKI-SAN?!
YUUNA... SAN?!
THANK GOODNESS! SHE HEARD ME!
RYUZEN-SAN AND YUMESAKI-SENSEI'S TECHNIQUE LOST CONTROL... BUT IT'S OKAY NOW!
I'M RELEASING THE TECH-NIQUE!

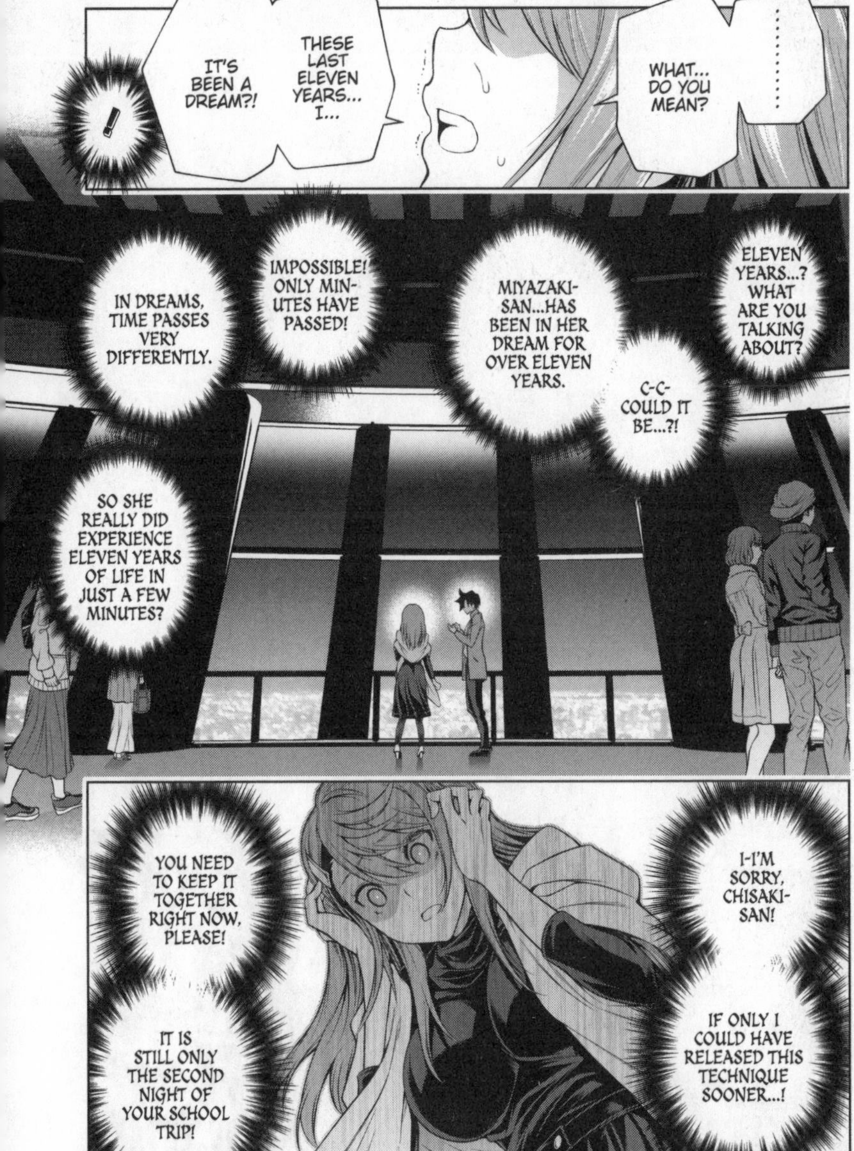
......
WHAT... DO YOU MEAN?
THESE LAST ELEVEN YEARS... I...
IT'S BEEN A DREAM?!
!
ELEVEN YEARS...? WHAT ARE YOU TALKING ABOUT?
C-C-COULD IT BE...?!
MIYAZAKI-SAN...HAS BEEN IN HER DREAM FOR OVER ELEVEN YEARS.
IMPOSSIBLE! ONLY MIN-UTES HAVE PASSED!
IN DREAMS, TIME PASSES VERY DIFFERENTLY.
SO SHE REALLY DID EXPERIENCE ELEVEN YEARS OF LIFE IN JUST A FEW MINUTES?
I-I'M SORRY, CHISAKI-SAN!
YOU NEED TO KEEP IT TOGETHER RIGHT NOW, PLEASE!
IF ONLY I COULD HAVE RELEASED THIS TECHNIQUE SOONER...!
IT IS STILL ONLY THE SECOND NIGHT OF YOUR SCHOOL TRIP!

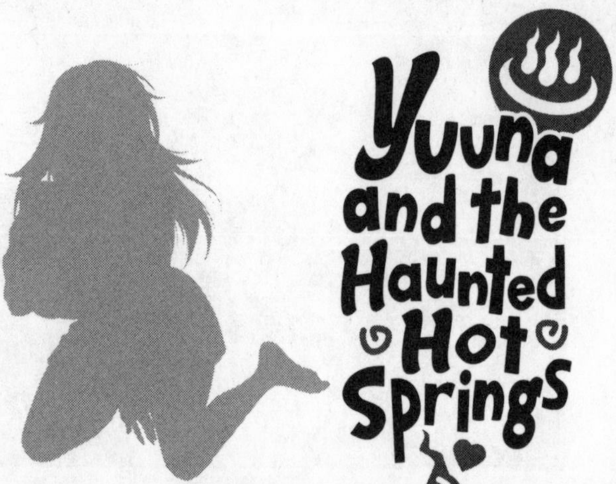

Yuuna and the Haunted Hot Springs

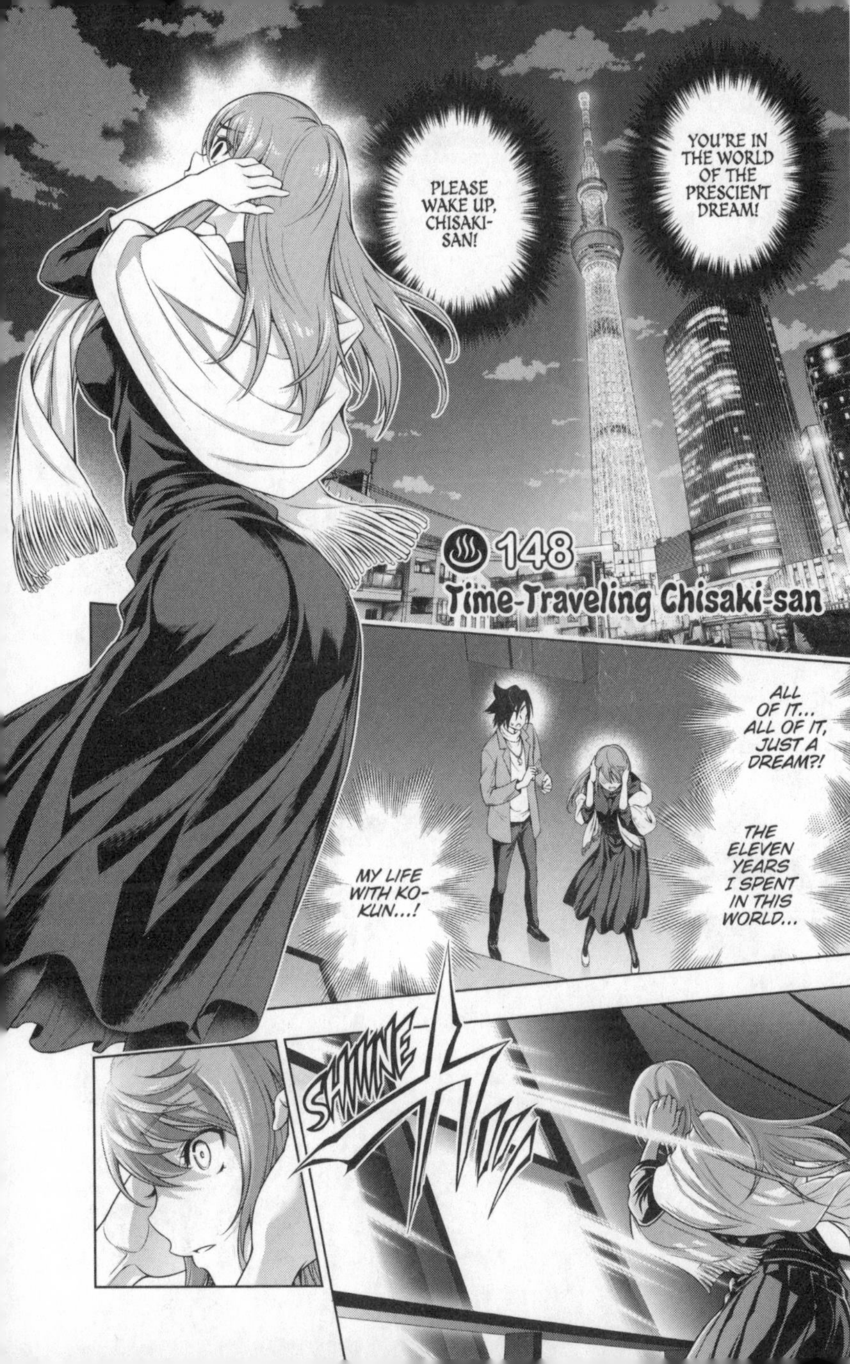
YOU'RE IN THE WORLD OF THE PRESCIENT DREAM!
PLEASE WAKE UP, CHISAKI-SAN!
148
Time-Traveling Chisaki-san
ALL OF IT... ALL OF IT, JUST A DREAM?!
THE ELEVEN YEARS I SPENT IN THIS WORLD...
MY LIFE WITH KO-KUN...!
SHIIINE

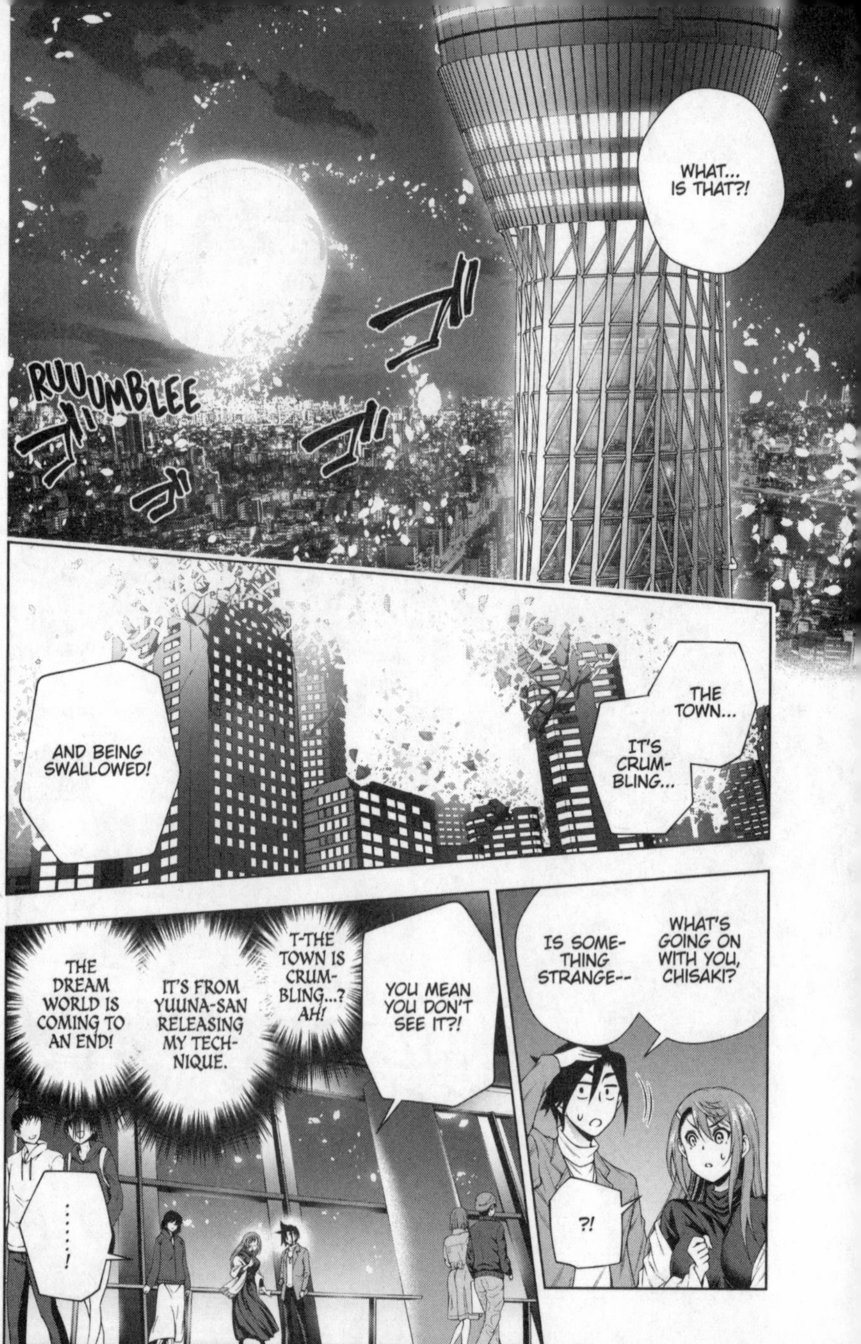
WHAT... IS THAT?!
RUUUMBLEE
THE TOWN...
IT'S CRUMBLING...
AND BEING SWALLOWED!
WHAT'S GOING ON WITH YOU, CHISAKI?
IS SOMETHING STRANGE--
?!
YOU MEAN YOU DON'T SEE IT?!
T-THE TOWN IS CRUMBLING...? AH!
IT'S FROM YUUNA-SAN RELEASING MY TECHNIQUE.
THE DREAM WORLD IS COMING TO AN END!
......!

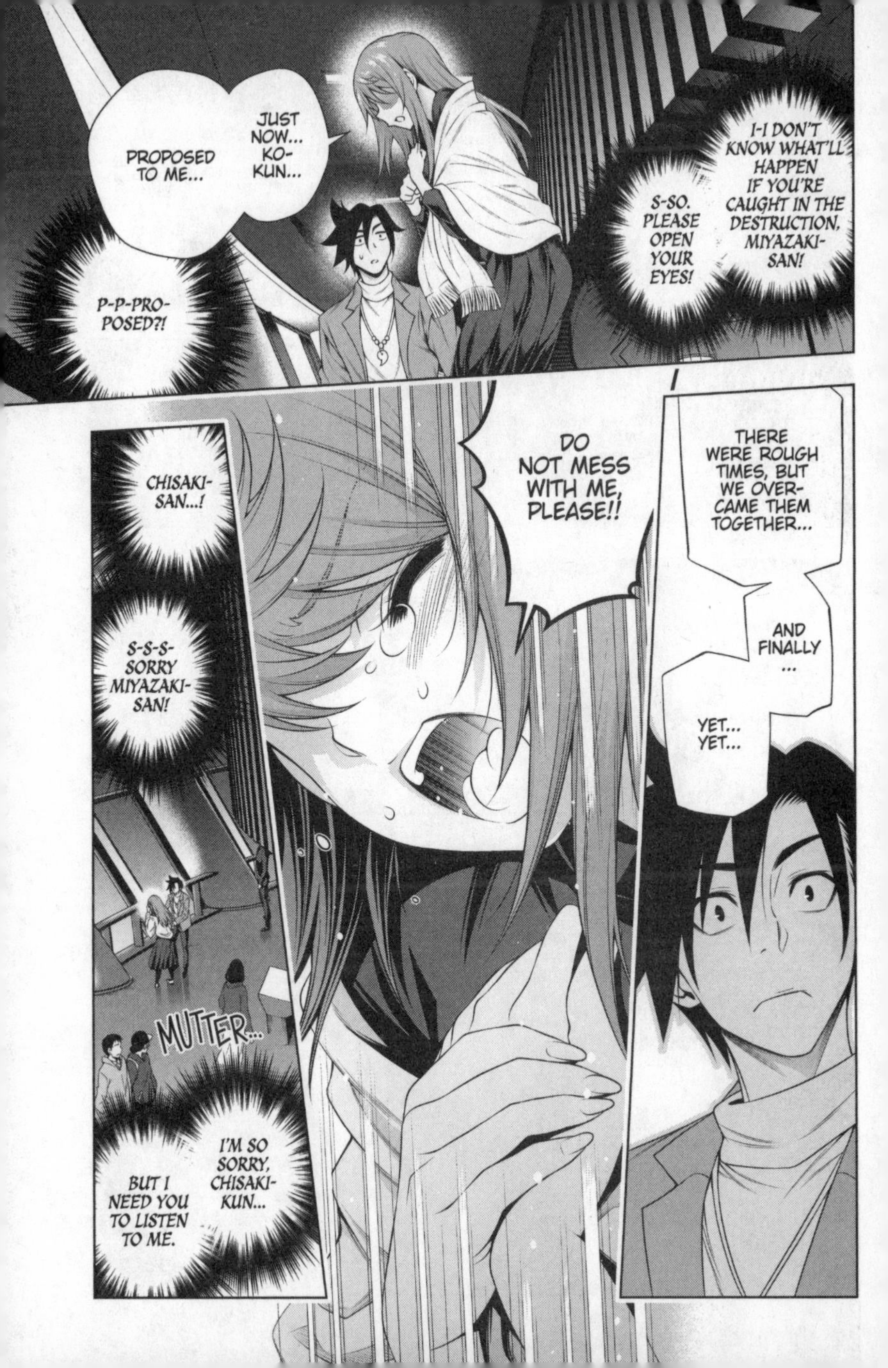

I-I DON'T KNOW WHAT'LL HAPPEN IF YOU'RE CAUGHT IN THE DESTRUCTION, MIYAZAKI-SAN!
S-SO. PLEASE OPEN YOUR EYES!
JUST NOW... KO-KUN...
PROPOSED TO ME...
P-P-PRO-POSED?!
THERE WERE ROUGH TIMES, BUT WE OVER-CAME THEM TOGETHER...
AND FINALLY ...
YET... YET...
DO NOT MESS WITH ME, PLEASE!!
CHISAKI-SAN...!
S-S-S-SORRY MIYAZAKI-SAN!
MUTTER...
I'M SO SORRY, CHISAKI-KUN...
BUT I NEED YOU TO LISTEN TO ME.

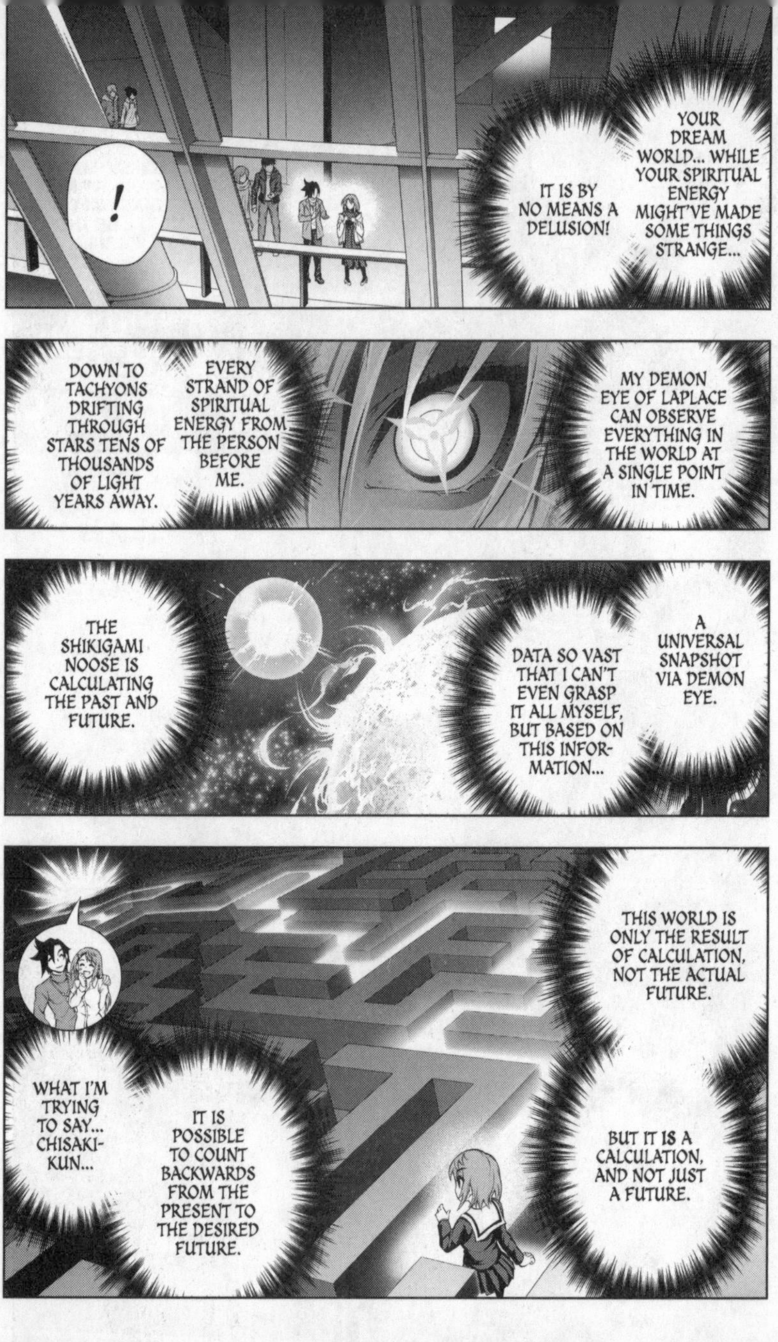
YOUR DREAM WORLD... WHILE YOUR SPIRITUAL ENERGY MIGHT'VE MADE SOME THINGS STRANGE...
IT IS BY NO MEANS A DELUSION!
!
MY DEMON EYE OF LAPLACE CAN OBSERVE EVERYTHING IN THE WORLD AT A SINGLE POINT IN TIME.
EVERY STRAND OF SPIRITUAL ENERGY FROM THE PERSON BEFORE ME.
DOWN TO TACHYONS DRIFTING THROUGH STARS TENS OF THOUSANDS OF LIGHT YEARS AWAY.
A UNIVERSAL SNAPSHOT VIA DEMON EYE.
DATA SO VAST THAT I CAN'T EVEN GRASP IT ALL MYSELF, BUT BASED ON THIS INFOR-MATION...
THE SHIKIGAMI NOOSE IS CALCULATING THE PAST AND FUTURE.
THIS WORLD IS ONLY THE RESULT OF CALCULATION, NOT THE ACTUAL FUTURE.
BUT IT IS A CALCULATION, AND NOT JUST A FUTURE.
WHAT I'M TRYING TO SAY... CHISAKI-KUN...
IT IS POSSIBLE TO COUNT BACKWARDS FROM THE PRESENT TO THE DESIRED FUTURE.

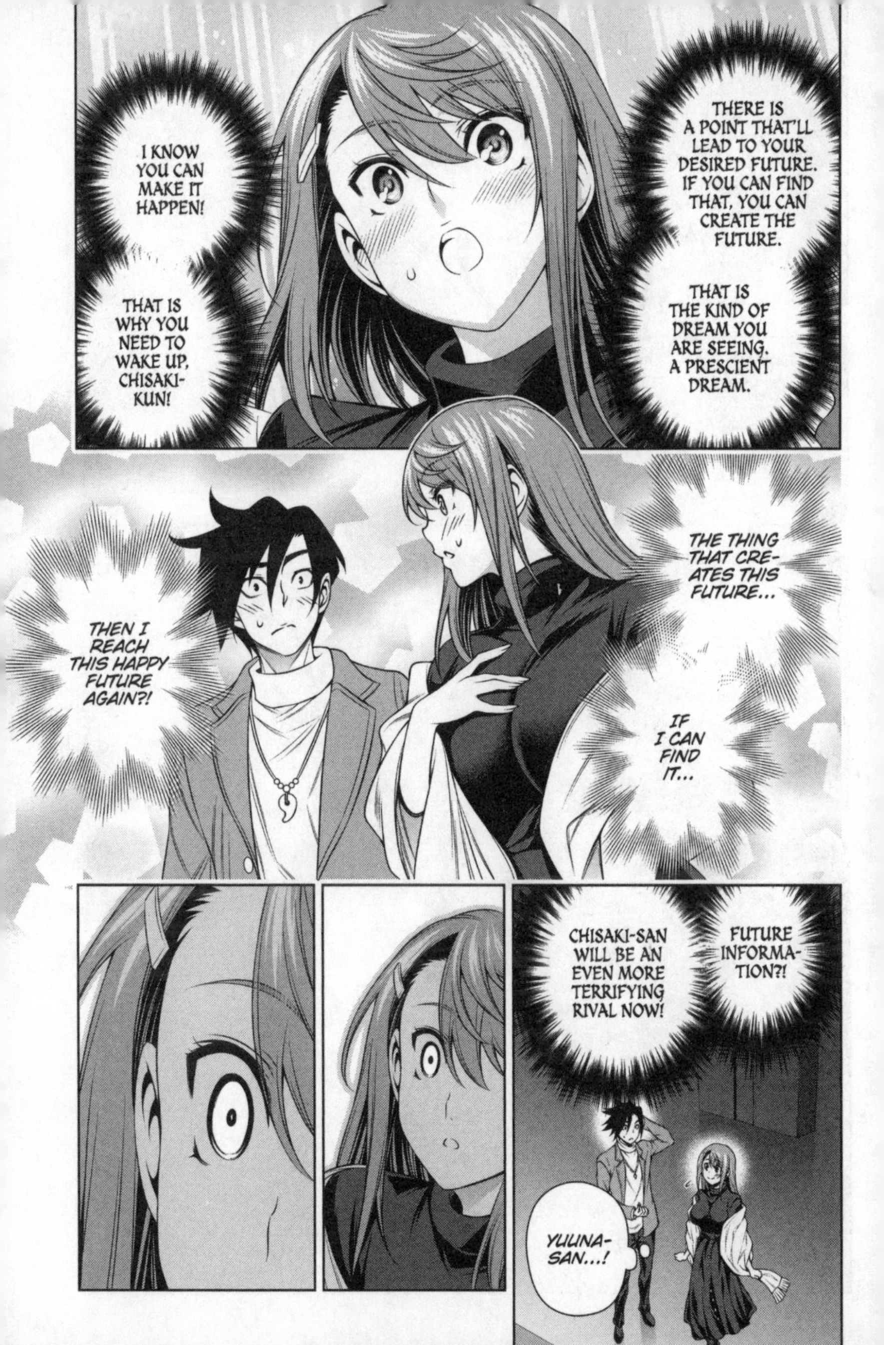
THERE IS A POINT THAT'LL LEAD TO YOUR DESIRED FUTURE. IF YOU CAN FIND THAT, YOU CAN CREATE THE FUTURE.
THAT IS THE KIND OF DREAM YOU ARE SEEING. A PRESCIENT DREAM.
I KNOW YOU CAN MAKE IT HAPPEN!
THAT IS WHY YOU NEED TO WAKE UP, CHISAKI-KUN!
THE THING THAT CRE-ATES THIS FUTURE...
IF I CAN FIND IT...
THEN I REACH THIS HAPPY FUTURE AGAIN?!
FUTURE INFORMA-TION?!
CHISAKI-SAN WILL BE AN EVEN MORE TERRIFYING RIVAL NOW!
YUUNA-SAN...!

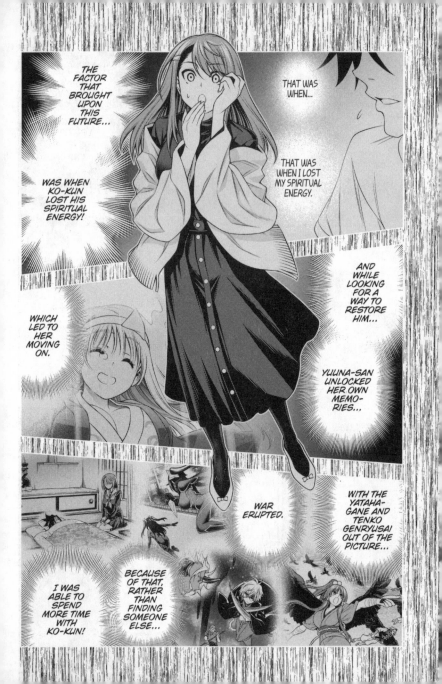

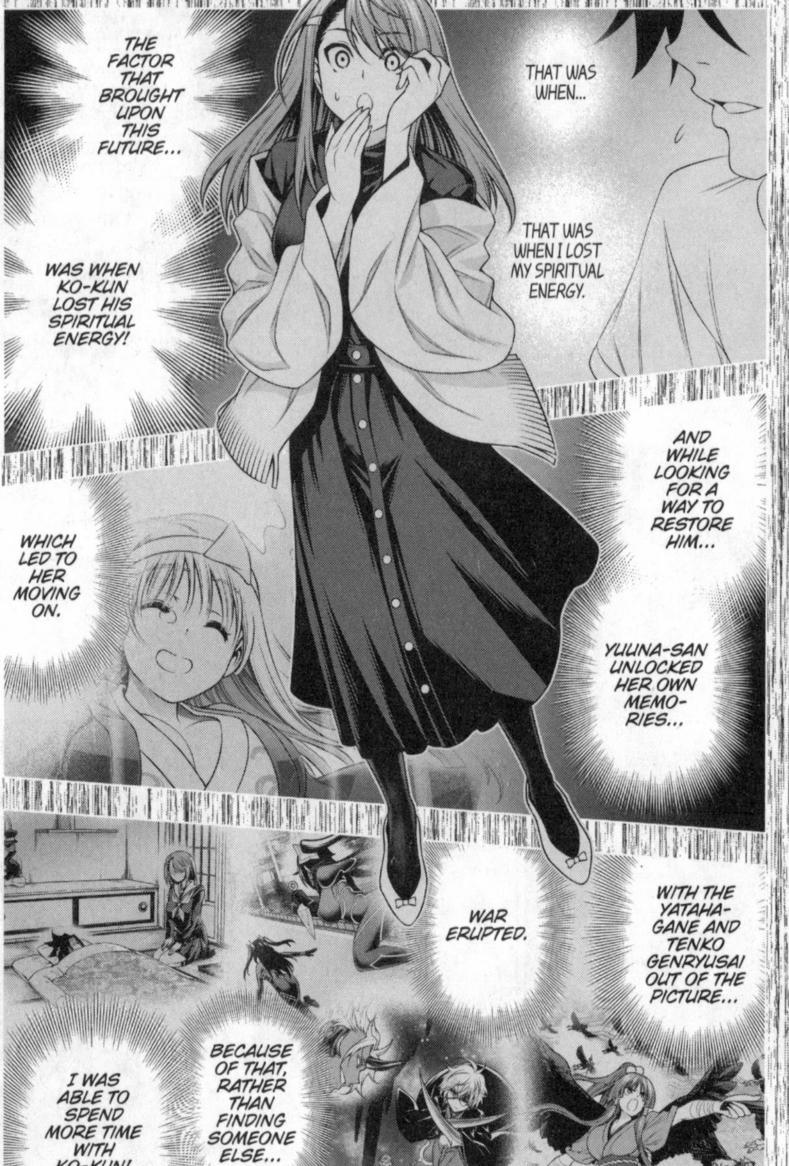
THAT WAS WHEN...
THAT WAS WHEN I LOST MY SPIRITUAL ENERGY.
THE FACTOR THAT BROUGHT UPON THIS FUTURE...
WAS WHEN KO-KUN LOST HIS SPIRITUAL ENERGY!
AND WHILE LOOKING FOR A WAY TO RESTORE HIM...
YUUNA-SAN UNLOCKED HER OWN MEMO-RIES...
WHICH LED TO HER MOVING ON.
WITH THE YATAHA-GANE AND TENKO GENRYUSAI OUT OF THE PICTURE...
WAR ERUPTED.
BECAUSE OF THAT, RATHER THAN FINDING SOMEONE ELSE...
I WAS ABLE TO SPEND MORE TIME WITH KO-KUN!

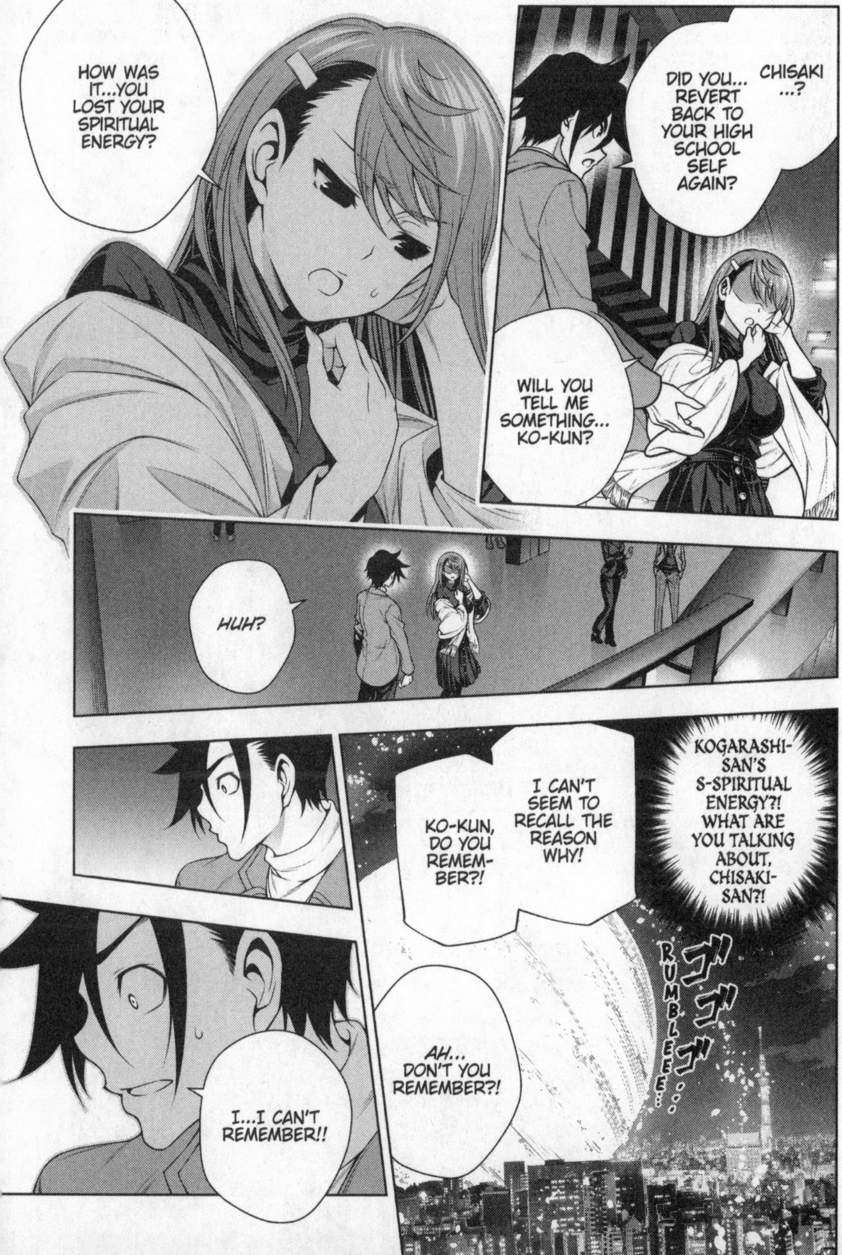
CHISAKI ...?
DID YOU... REVERT BACK TO YOUR HIGH SCHOOL SELF AGAIN?
WILL YOU TELL ME SOMETHING... KO-KUN?
HOW WAS IT...YOU LOST YOUR SPIRITUAL ENERGY?
HUH?
KOGARASHI-SAN'S S-SPIRITUAL ENERGY?! WHAT ARE YOU TALKING ABOUT, CHISAKI-SAN?!
I CAN'T SEEM TO RECALL THE REASON WHY!
KO-KUN, DO YOU REMEMBER?!
RUMBLEEE...
AH... DON'T YOU REMEMBER?!
I...I CAN'T REMEMBER!!

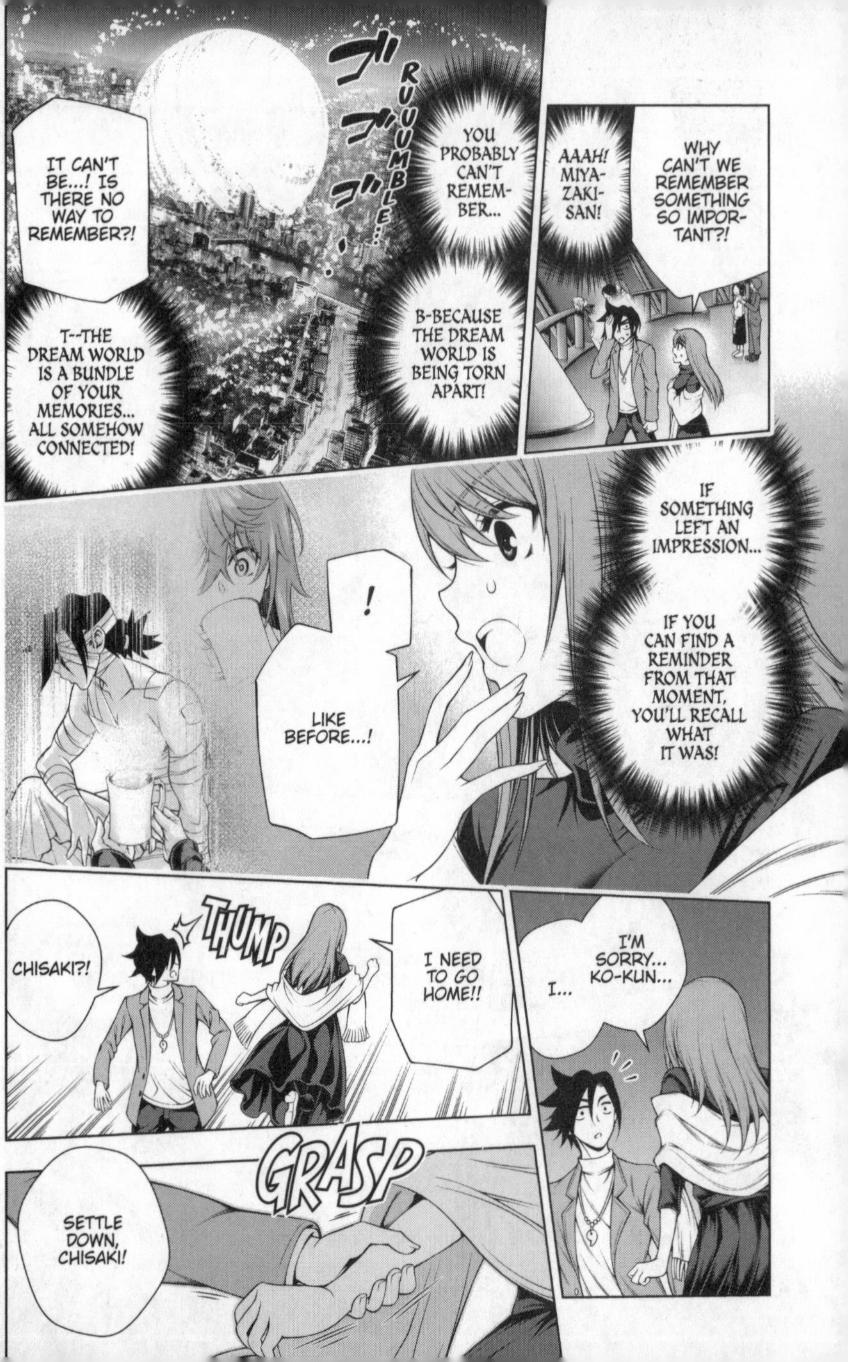
WHY CAN'T WE REMEMBER SOMETHING SO IMPORTANT?!
AAAH! MIYA-ZAKI-SAN!
RUUUMBLE...
YOU PROBABLY CAN'T REMEMBER...
IT CAN'T BE...! IS THERE NO WAY TO REMEMBER?!
B-BECAUSE THE DREAM WORLD IS BEING TORN APART!
T--THE DREAM WORLD IS A BUNDLE OF YOUR MEMORIES... ALL SOMEHOW CONNECTED!
IF SOMETHING LEFT AN IMPRESSION...
IF YOU CAN FIND A REMINDER FROM THAT MOMENT, YOU'LL RECALL WHAT IT WAS!
!
LIKE BEFORE...!
I'M SORRY... KO-KUN...
I...
I NEED TO GO HOME!!
THUMP
CHISAKI?!
GRASP
SETTLE DOWN, CHISAKI!

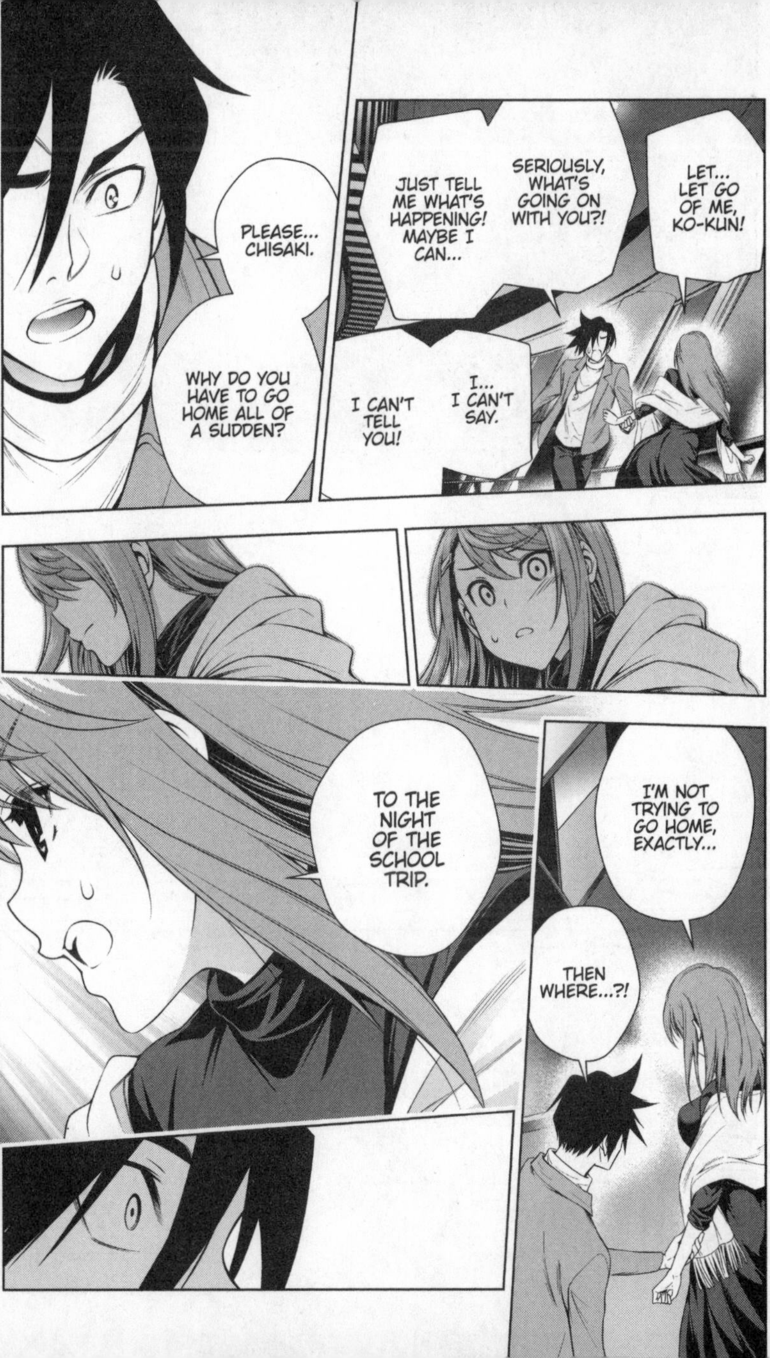
LET... LET GO OF ME, KO-KUN!
SERIOUSLY, WHAT'S GOING ON WITH YOU?!
JUST TELL ME WHAT'S HAPPENING! MAYBE I CAN...
I... I CAN'T SAY.
I CAN'T TELL YOU!
PLEASE... CHISAKI.
WHY DO YOU HAVE TO GO HOME ALL OF A SUDDEN?
I'M NOT TRYING TO GO HOME, EXACTLY...
THEN WHERE...?!
TO THE NIGHT OF THE SCHOOL TRIP.

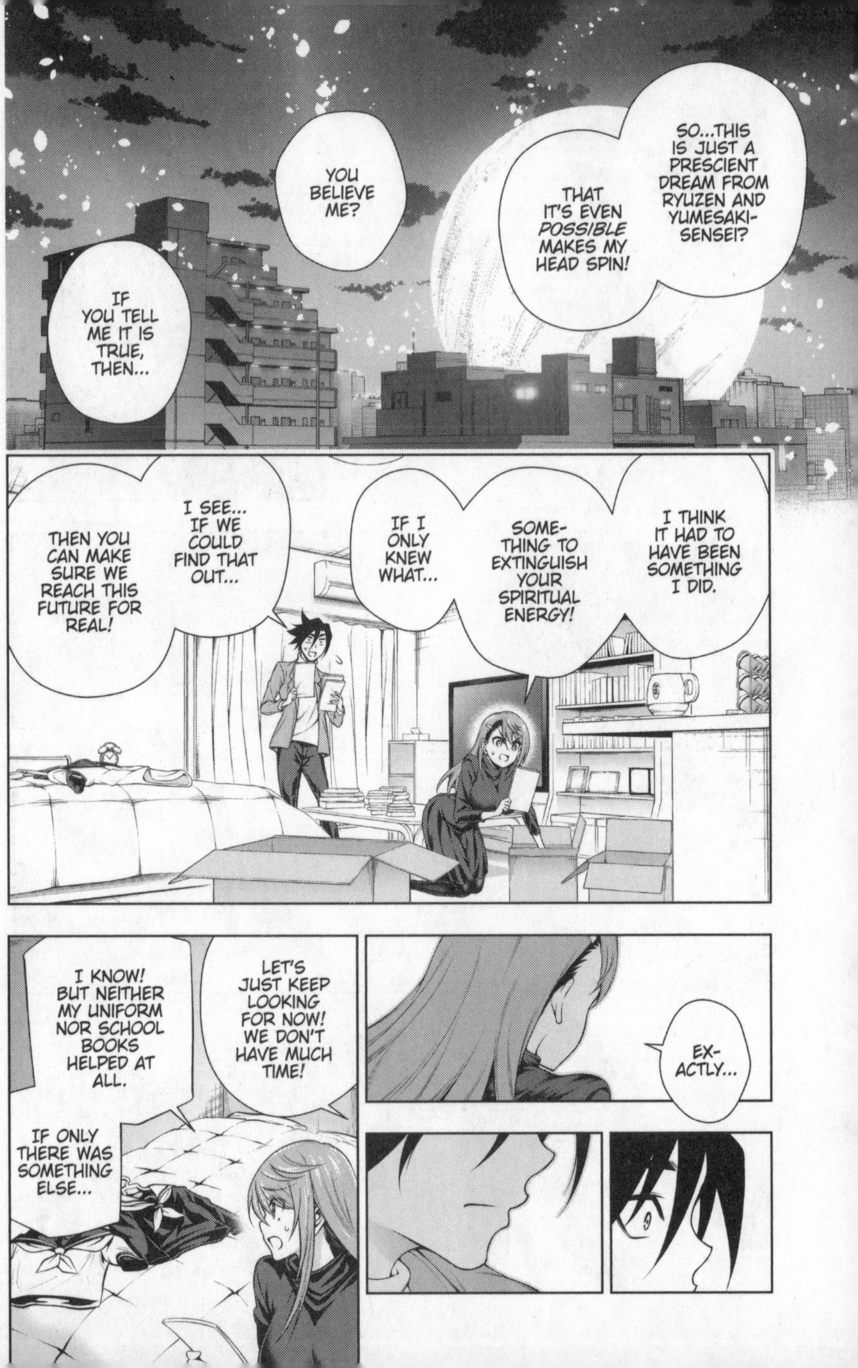
SO...THIS IS JUST A PRESCIENT DREAM FROM RYUZEN AND YUMESAKI-SENSEI?
THAT IT'S EVEN *POSSIBLE* MAKES MY HEAD SPIN!
YOU BELIEVE ME?
IF YOU TELL ME IT IS TRUE, THEN...
I THINK IT HAD TO HAVE BEEN SOMETHING I DID.
SOME-THING TO EXTINGUISH YOUR SPIRITUAL ENERGY!
IF I ONLY KNEW WHAT...
I SEE... IF WE COULD FIND THAT OUT...
THEN YOU CAN MAKE SURE WE REACH THIS FUTURE FOR REAL!
EX-ACTLY...
LET'S JUST KEEP LOOKING FOR NOW! WE DON'T HAVE MUCH TIME!
I KNOW! BUT NEITHER MY UNIFORM NOR SCHOOL BOOKS HELPED AT ALL.
IF ONLY THERE WAS SOMETHING ELSE...

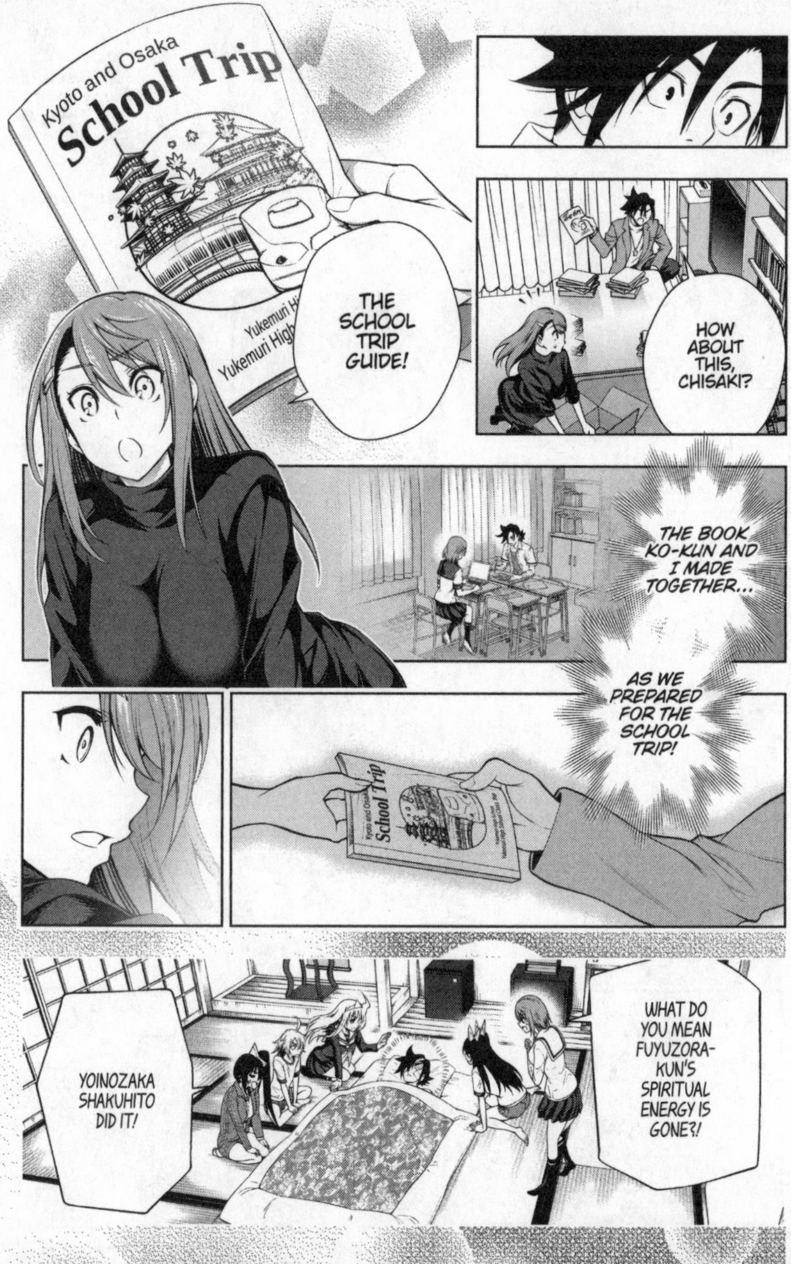
HOW ABOUT THIS, CHISAKI?
Kyoto and Osaka
School Trip
THE SCHOOL TRIP GUIDE!
THE BOOK KO-KUN AND I MADE TOGETHER...
AS WE PREPARED FOR THE SCHOOL TRIP!
WHAT DO YOU MEAN FUYUZORA-KUN'S SPIRITUAL ENERGY IS GONE?!
YOINOZAKA SHAKUHITO DID IT!

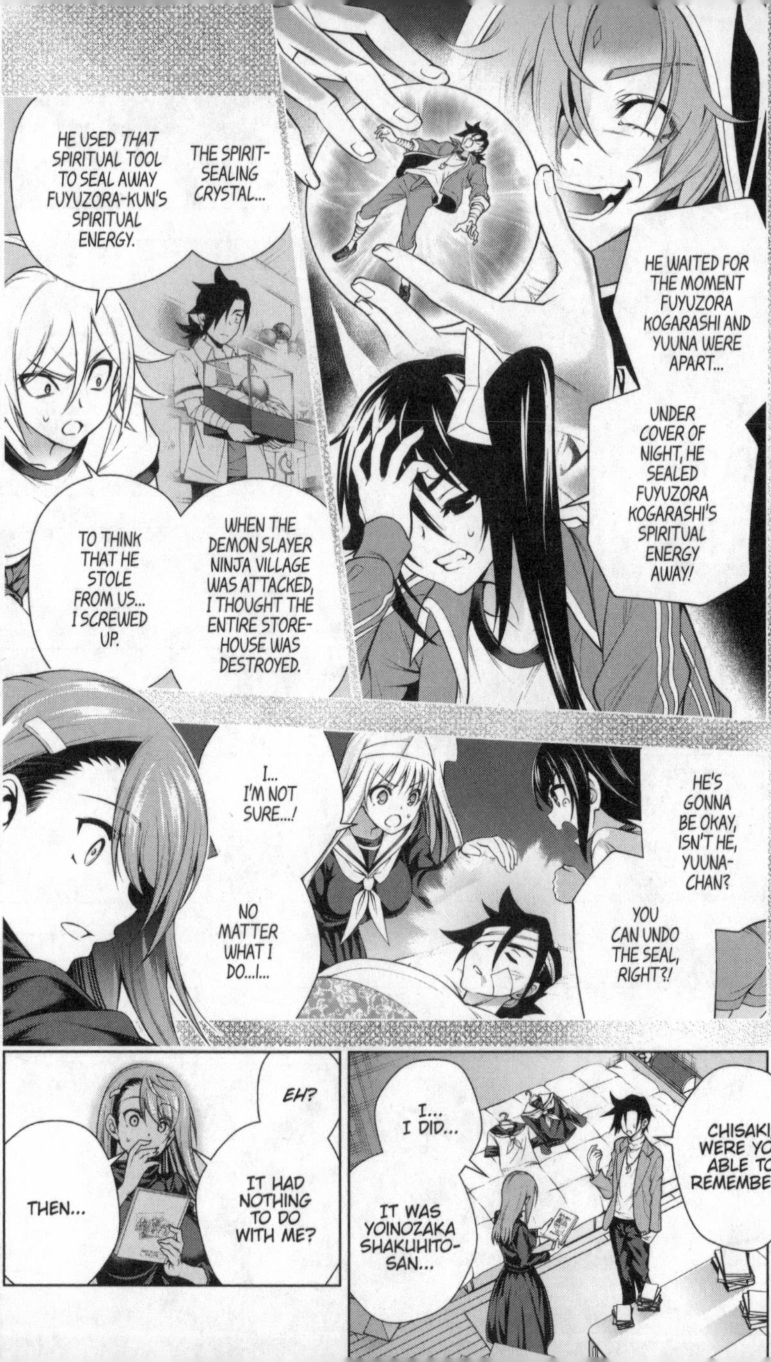
HE WAITED FOR THE MOMENT FUYUZORA KOGARASHI AND YUUNA WERE APART...
UNDER COVER OF NIGHT, HE SEALED FUYUZORA KOGARASHI'S SPIRITUAL ENERGY AWAY!
THE SPIRIT-SEALING CRYSTAL...
HE USED *THAT* SPIRITUAL TOOL TO SEAL AWAY FUYUZORA-KUN'S SPIRITUAL ENERGY.
WHEN THE DEMON SLAYER NINJA VILLAGE WAS ATTACKED, I THOUGHT THE ENTIRE STORE-HOUSE WAS DESTROYED.
TO THINK THAT HE STOLE FROM US... I SCREWED UP.
HE'S GONNA BE OKAY, ISN'T HE, YUUNA-CHAN?
YOU CAN UNDO THE SEAL, RIGHT?!
I... I'M NOT SURE...!
NO MATTER WHAT I DO...I...
CHISAKI, WERE YOU ABLE TO REMEMBER?
I... I DID...
IT WAS YOINOZAKA SHAKUHITO-SAN...
EH?
IT HAD NOTHING TO DO WITH ME?
THEN...

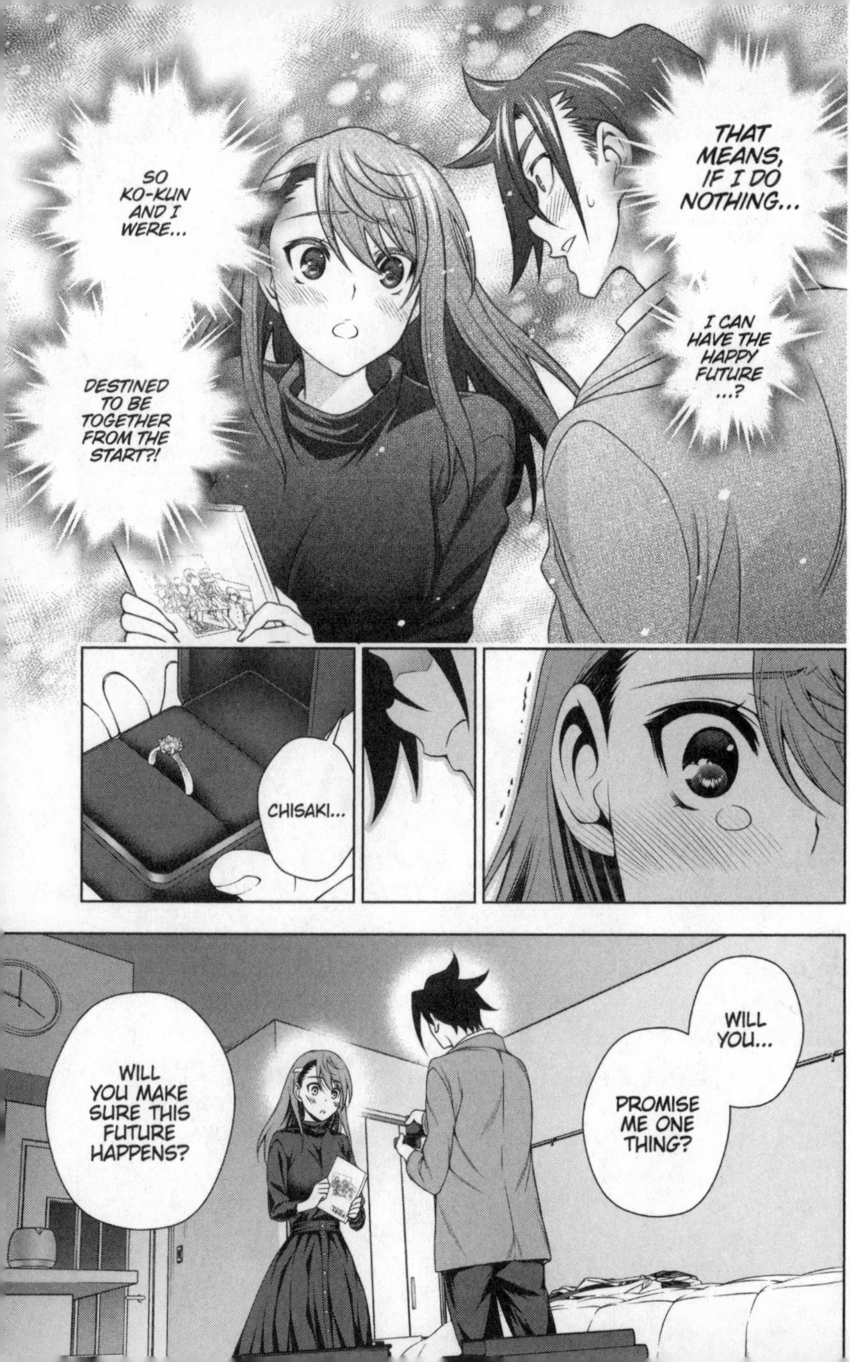
THAT MEANS, IF I DO NOTHING...
I CAN HAVE THE HAPPY FUTURE ...?
SO KO-KUN AND I WERE...
DESTINED TO BE TOGETHER FROM THE START?!
......
CHISAKI...
WILL YOU...
PROMISE ME ONE THING?
WILL YOU MAKE SURE THIS FUTURE HAPPENS?

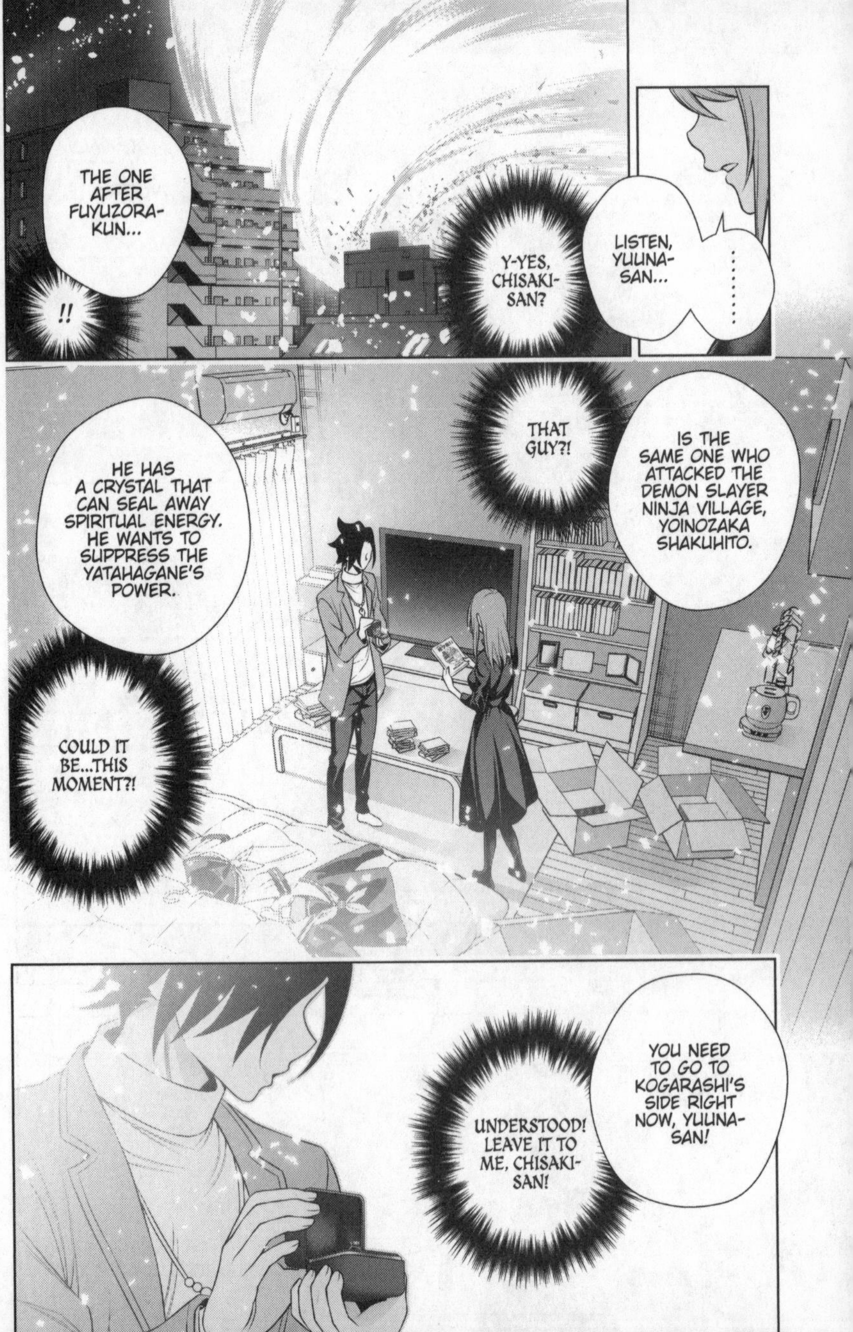
LISTEN, YUUNA-SAN...
......
Y-YES, CHISAKI-SAN?
THE ONE AFTER FUYUZORA-KUN...
!!
IS THE SAME ONE WHO ATTACKED THE DEMON SLAYER NINJA VILLAGE, YOINOZAKA SHAKUHITO.
THAT GUY?!
HE HAS A CRYSTAL THAT CAN SEAL AWAY SPIRITUAL ENERGY. HE WANTS TO SUPPRESS THE YATAHAGANE'S POWER.
COULD IT BE...THIS MOMENT?!
YOU NEED TO GO TO KOGARASHI'S SIDE RIGHT NOW, YUUNA-SAN!
UNDERSTOOD! LEAVE IT TO ME, CHISAKI-SAN!

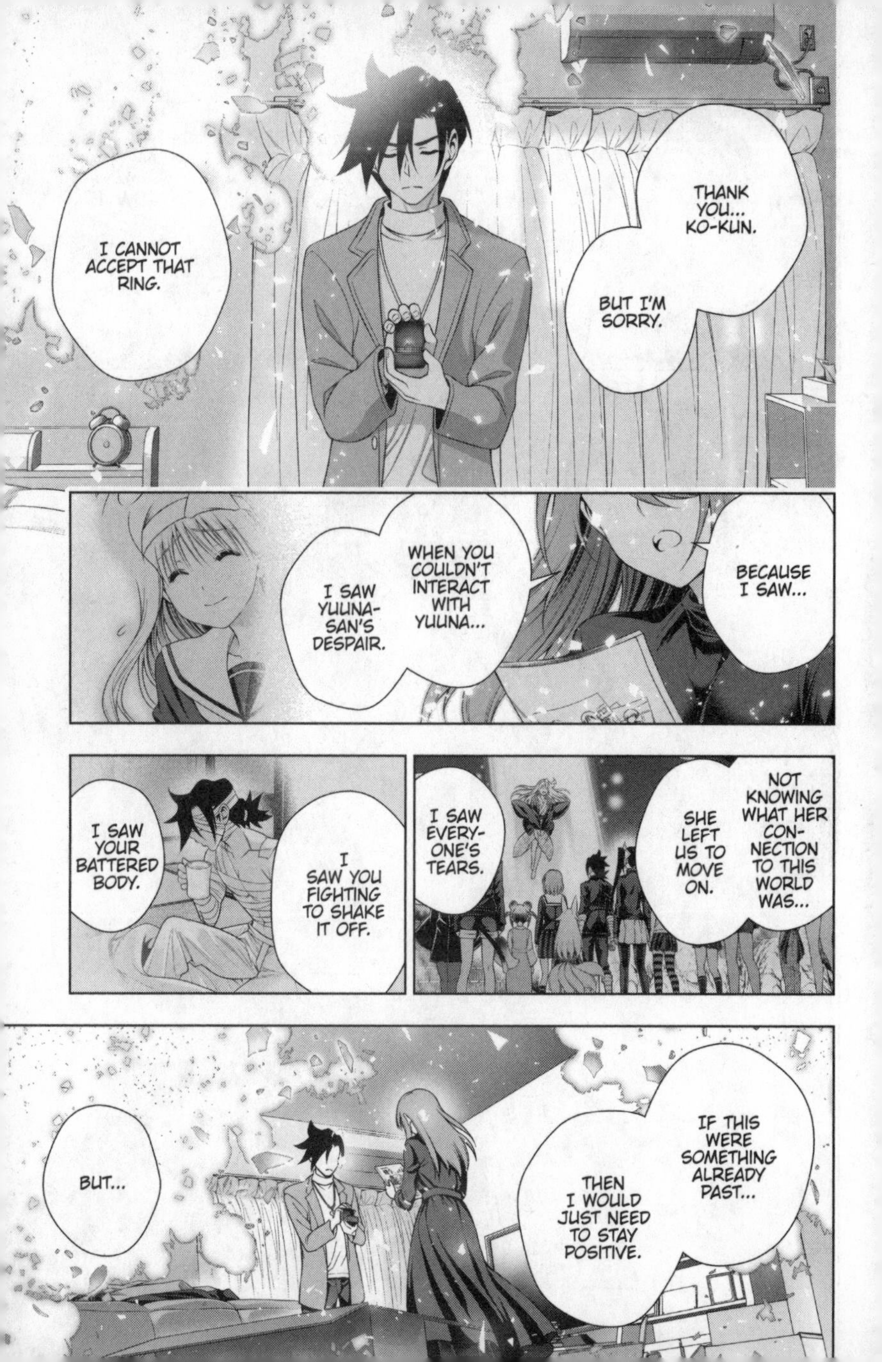
THANK YOU... KO-KUN.
BUT I'M SORRY.
I CANNOT ACCEPT THAT RING.
BECAUSE I SAW...
WHEN YOU COULDN'T INTERACT WITH YUUNA...
I SAW YUUNA-SAN'S DESPAIR.
NOT KNOWING WHAT HER CON-NECTION TO THIS WORLD WAS...
SHE LEFT US TO MOVE ON.
I SAW EVERY-ONE'S TEARS.
I SAW YOU FIGHTING TO SHAKE IT OFF.
I SAW YOUR BATTERED BODY.
IF THIS WERE SOMETHING ALREADY PAST...
THEN I WOULD JUST NEED TO STAY POSITIVE.
BUT...

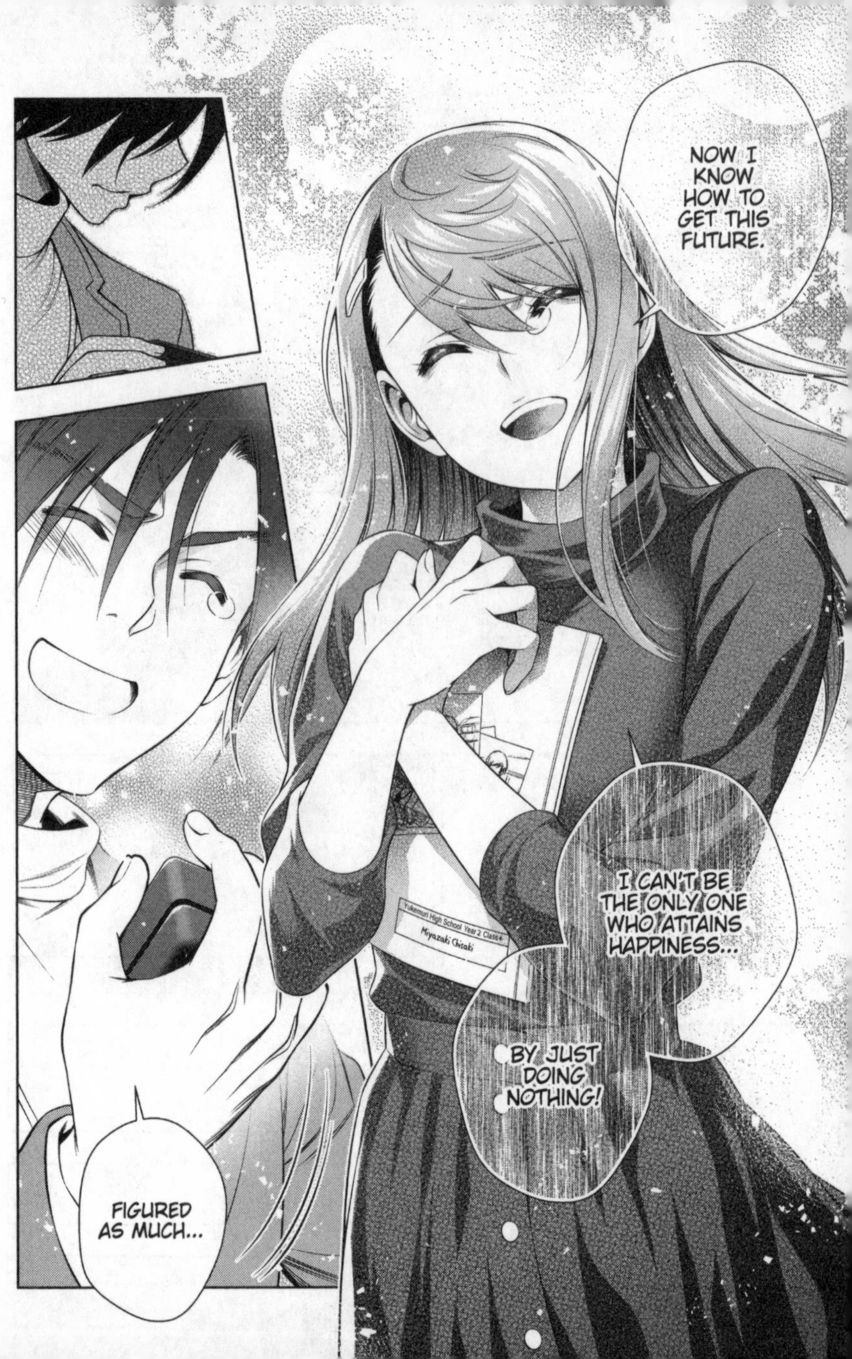
NOW I KNOW HOW TO GET THIS FUTURE.
I CAN'T BE THE ONLY ONE WHO ATTAINS HAPPINESS...
BY JUST DOING NOTHING!
Yukemuri High School Year 2 Class 4
Miyazaki Chisaki
FIGURED AS MUCH...

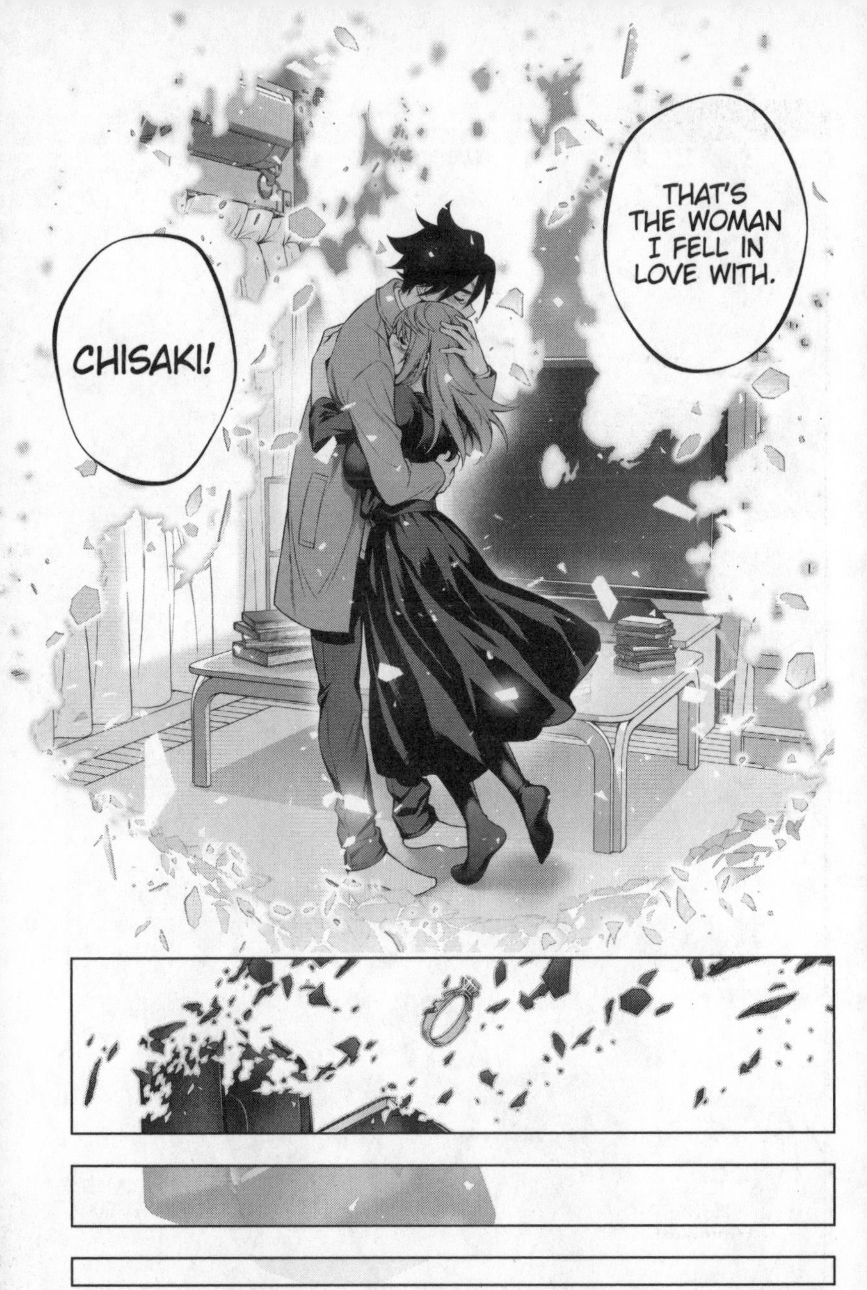
THAT'S THE WOMAN I FELL IN LOVE WITH.
CHISAKI!

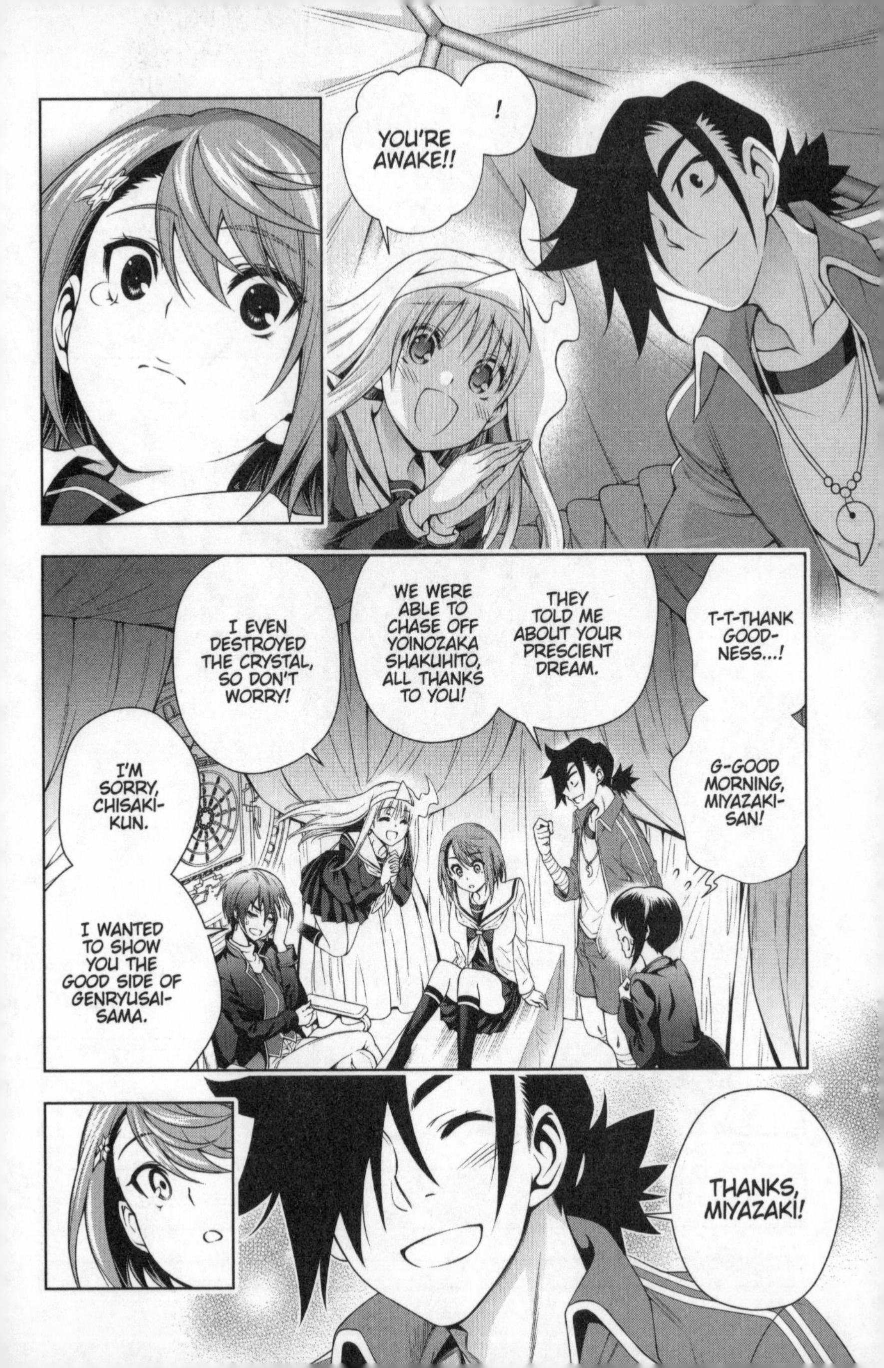
!
YOU'RE AWAKE!!
T-T-THANK GOOD-NESS...!
G-GOOD MORNING, MIYAZAKI-SAN!
THEY TOLD ME ABOUT YOUR PRESCIENT DREAM.
WE WERE ABLE TO CHASE OFF YOINOZAKA SHAKUHITO, ALL THANKS TO YOU!
I EVEN DESTROYED THE CRYSTAL, SO DON'T WORRY!
I'M SORRY, CHISAKI-KUN.
I WANTED TO SHOW YOU THE GOOD SIDE OF GENRYUSAI-SAMA.
THANKS, MIYAZAKI!

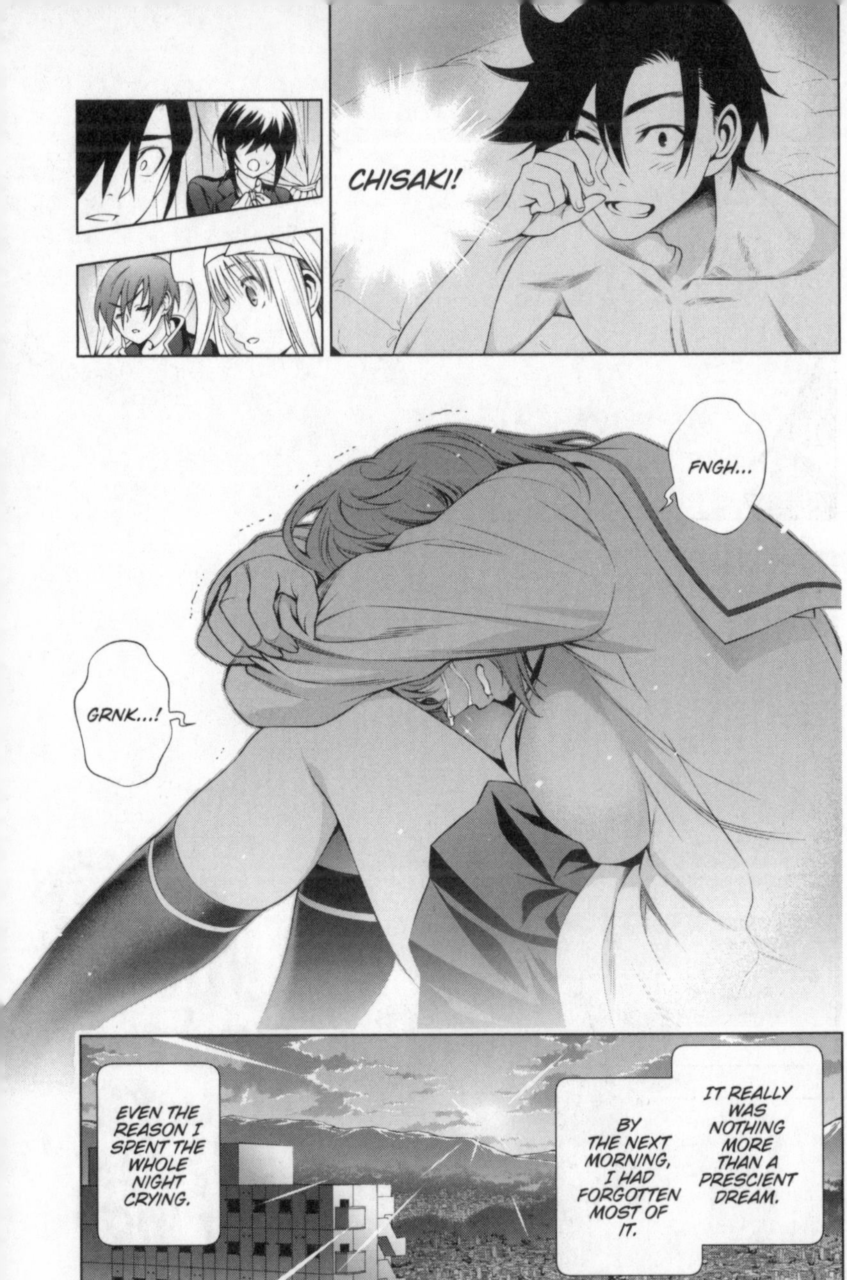
CHISAKI!
FNGH...
GRNK...!
IT REALLY WAS NOTHING MORE THAN A PRESCIENT DREAM.
BY THE NEXT MORNING, I HAD FORGOTTEN MOST OF IT.
EVEN THE REASON I SPENT THE WHOLE NIGHT CRYING.

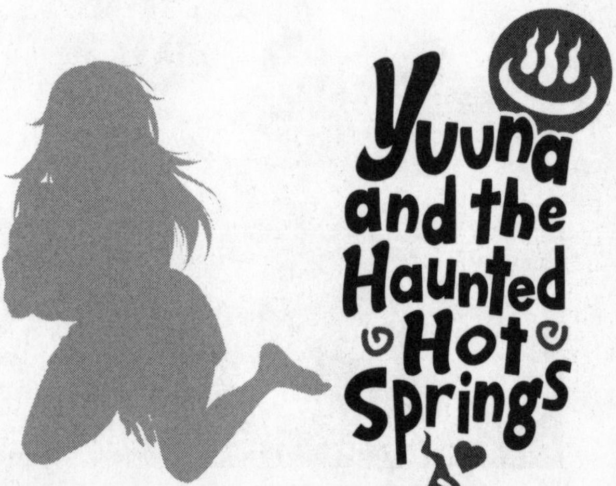

Yuuna and the Haunted Hot Springs

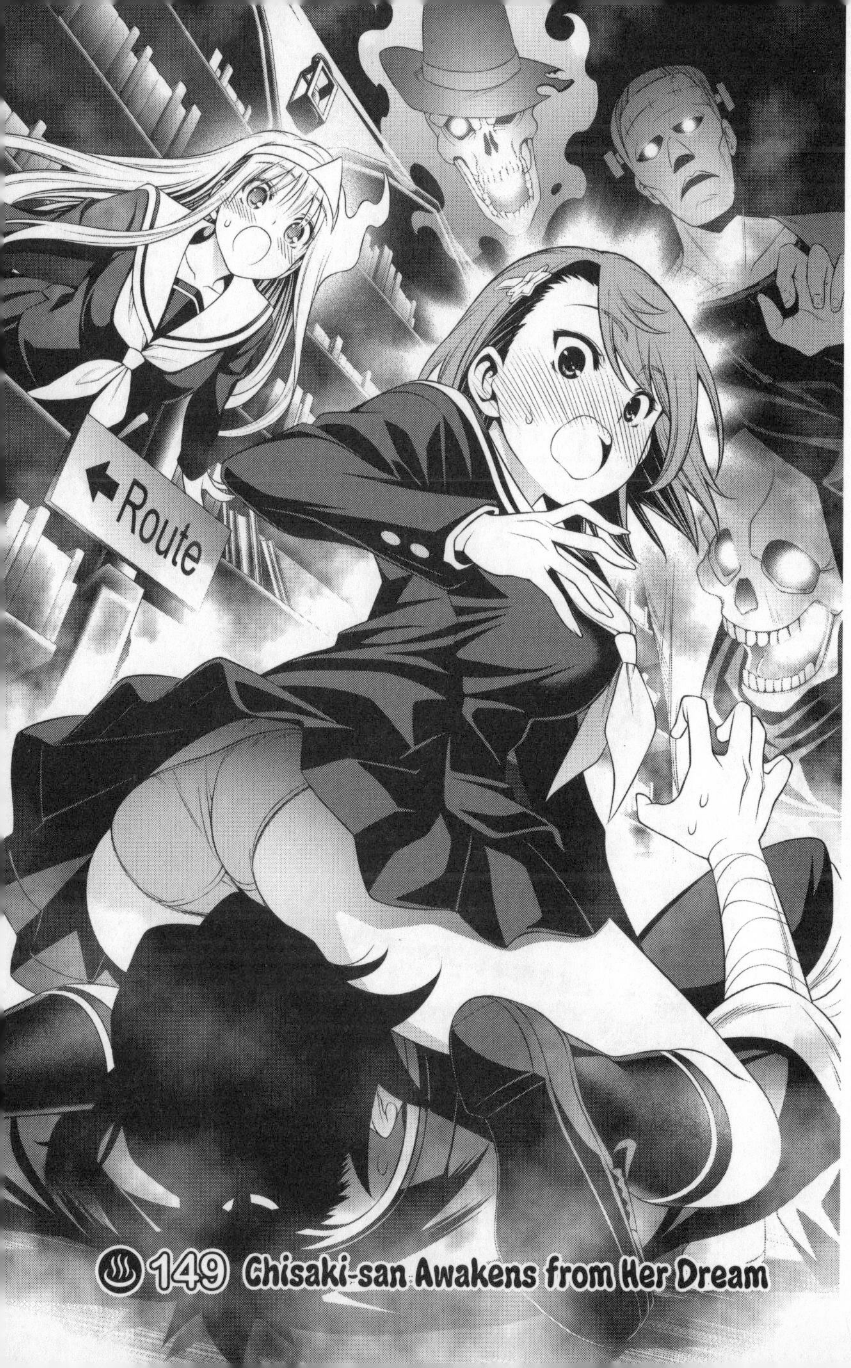
← Route

♨149 Chisaki-san Awakens from Her Dream

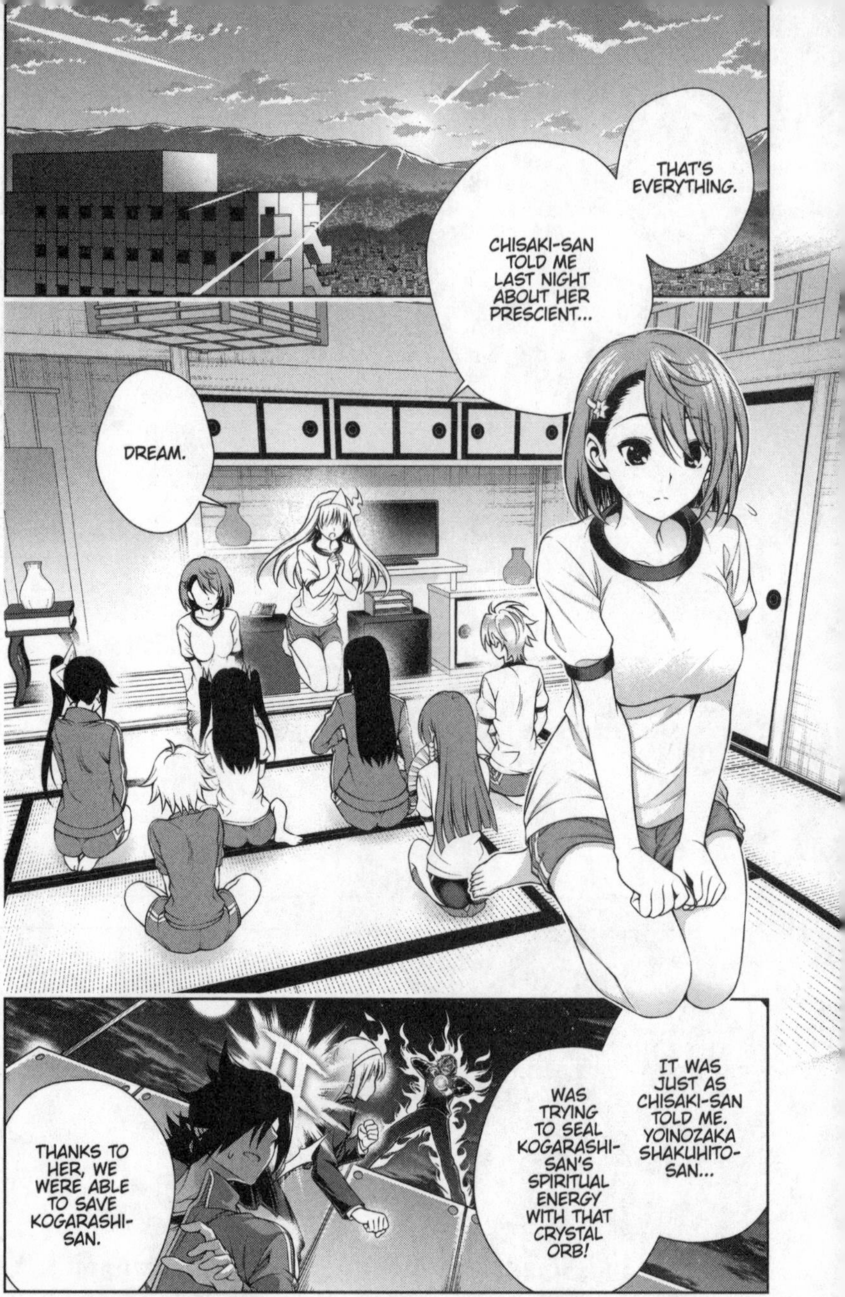
THAT'S EVERYTHING.
CHISAKI-SAN TOLD ME LAST NIGHT ABOUT HER PRESCIENT...
DREAM.
IT WAS JUST AS CHISAKI-SAN TOLD ME. YOINOZAKA SHAKUHITO-SAN...
WAS TRYING TO SEAL KOGARASHI-SAN'S SPIRITUAL ENERGY WITH THAT CRYSTAL ORB!
THANKS TO HER, WE WERE ABLE TO SAVE KOGARASHI-SAN.

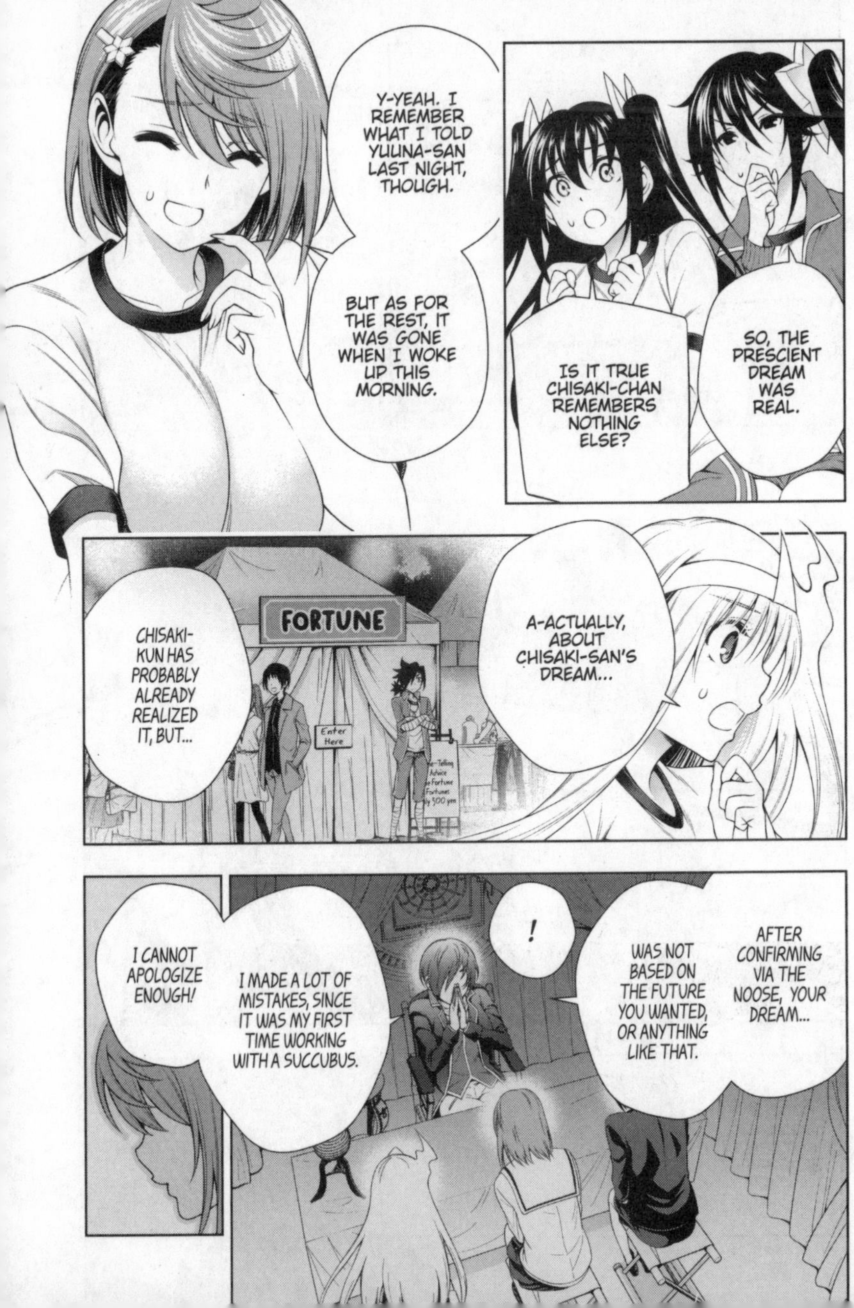
SO, THE PRESCIENT DREAM WAS REAL.
IS IT TRUE CHISAKI-CHAN REMEMBERS NOTHING ELSE?
Y-YEAH. I REMEMBER WHAT I TOLD YUUNA-SAN LAST NIGHT, THOUGH.
BUT AS FOR THE REST, IT WAS GONE WHEN I WOKE UP THIS MORNING.
A-ACTUALLY, ABOUT CHISAKI-SAN'S DREAM...
FORTUNE
Enter Here
CHISAKI-KUN HAS PROBABLY ALREADY REALIZED IT, BUT...
AFTER CONFIRMING VIA THE NOOSE, YOUR DREAM...
WAS NOT BASED ON THE FUTURE YOU WANTED, OR ANYTHING LIKE THAT.
!
I MADE A LOT OF MISTAKES, SINCE IT WAS MY FIRST TIME WORKING WITH A SUCCUBUS.
I CANNOT APOLOGIZE ENOUGH!

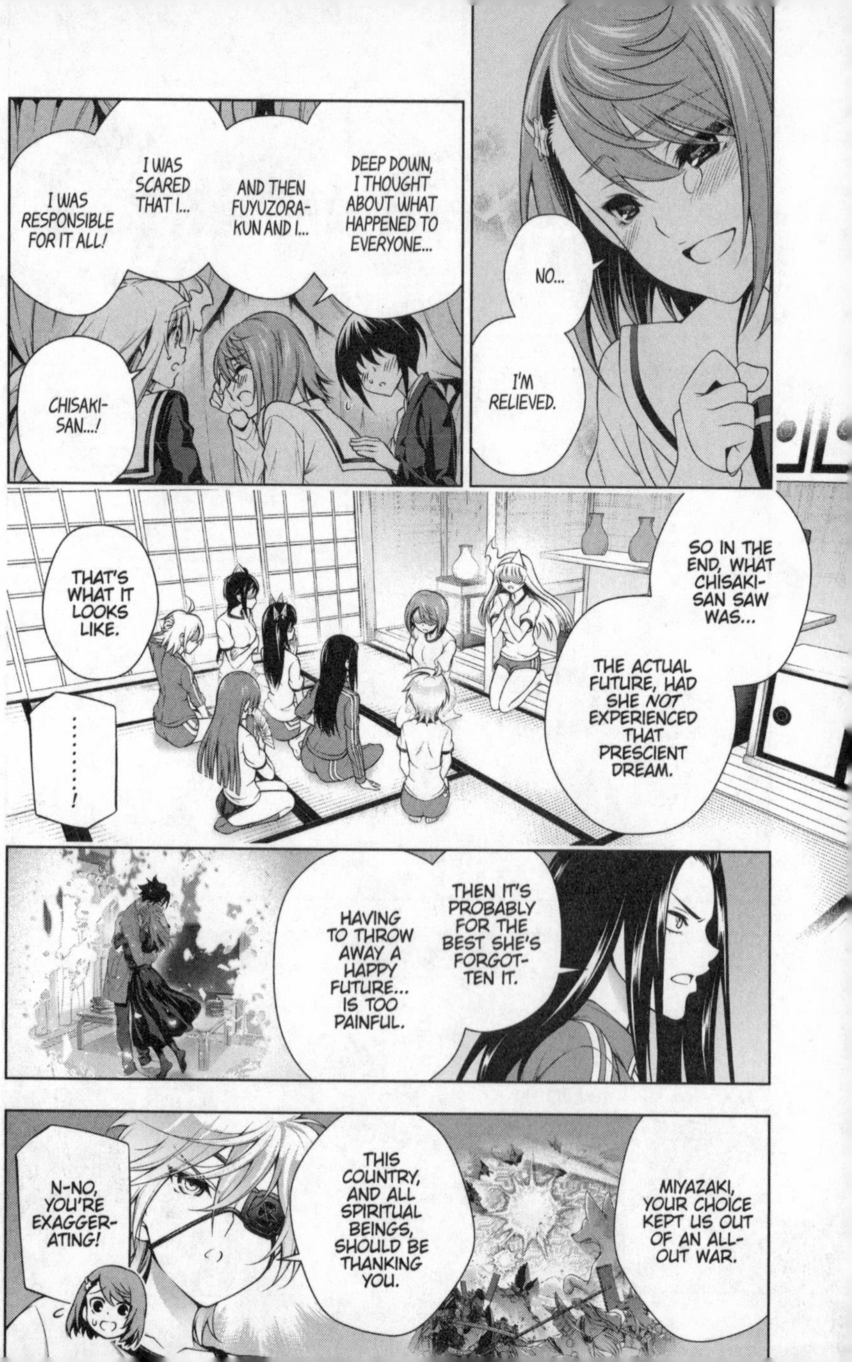
NO...
I'M RELIEVED.
DEEP DOWN, I THOUGHT ABOUT WHAT HAPPENED TO EVERYONE...
AND THEN FUYUZORA-KUN AND I...
I WAS SCARED THAT I...
I WAS RESPONSIBLE FOR IT ALL!
CHISAKI-SAN...!
SO IN THE END, WHAT CHISAKI-SAN SAW WAS...
THE ACTUAL FUTURE, HAD SHE *NOT* EXPERIENCED THAT PRESCIENT DREAM.
THAT'S WHAT IT LOOKS LIKE.
........!
THEN IT'S PROBABLY FOR THE BEST SHE'S FORGOTTEN IT.
HAVING TO THROW AWAY A HAPPY FUTURE... IS TOO PAINFUL.
MIYAZAKI, YOUR CHOICE KEPT US OUT OF AN ALL-OUT WAR.
THIS COUNTRY, AND ALL SPIRITUAL BEINGS, SHOULD BE THANKING YOU.
N-NO, YOU'RE EXAGGERATING!

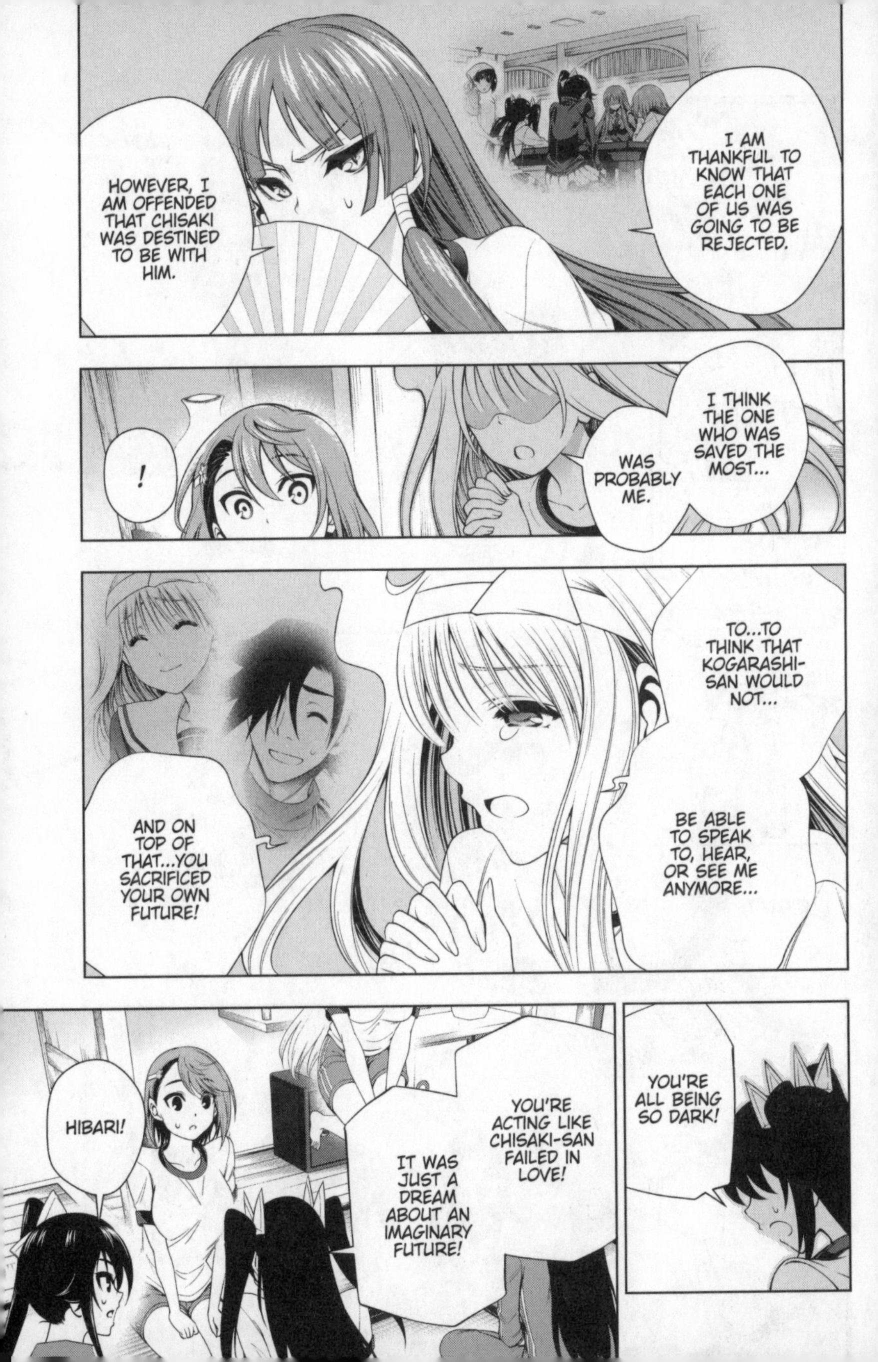
I AM THANKFUL TO KNOW THAT EACH ONE OF US WAS GOING TO BE REJECTED.
HOWEVER, I AM OFFENDED THAT CHISAKI WAS DESTINED TO BE WITH HIM.
I THINK THE ONE WHO WAS SAVED THE MOST...
WAS PROBABLY ME.
!
TO...TO THINK THAT KOGARASHI-SAN WOULD NOT...
BE ABLE TO SPEAK TO, HEAR, OR SEE ME ANYMORE...
AND ON TOP OF THAT...YOU SACRIFICED YOUR OWN FUTURE!
YOU'RE ALL BEING SO DARK!
YOU'RE ACTING LIKE CHISAKI-SAN FAILED IN LOVE!
IT WAS JUST A DREAM ABOUT AN IMAGINARY FUTURE!
HIBARI!

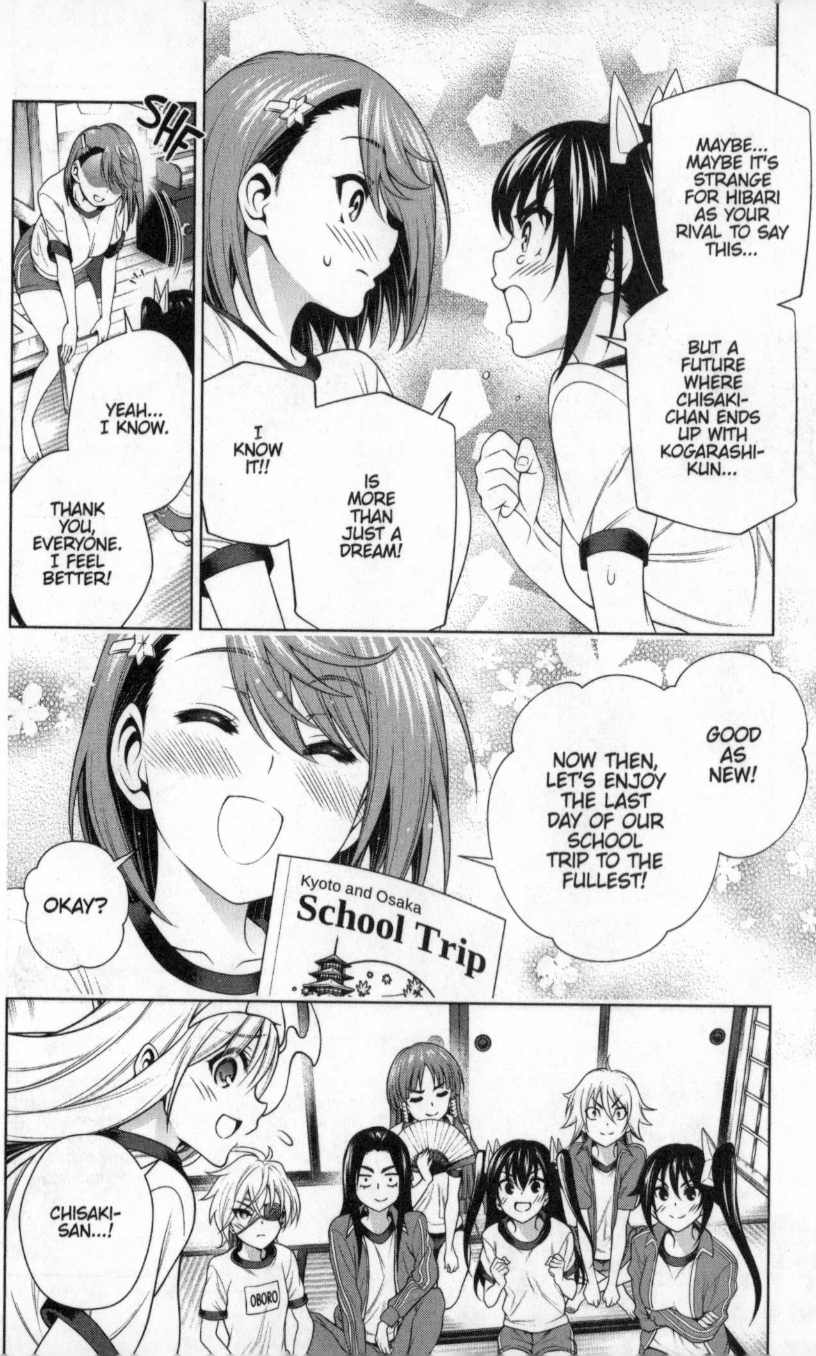
MAYBE... MAYBE IT'S STRANGE FOR HIBARI AS YOUR RIVAL TO SAY THIS...
BUT A FUTURE WHERE CHISAKI-CHAN ENDS UP WITH KOGARASHI-KUN...
IS MORE THAN JUST A DREAM!
I KNOW IT!!
SHF
YEAH... I KNOW.
THANK YOU, EVERYONE. I FEEL BETTER!
GOOD AS NEW!
NOW THEN, LET'S ENJOY THE LAST DAY OF OUR SCHOOL TRIP TO THE FULLEST!
Kyoto and Osaka
School Trip
OKAY?
CHISAKI-SAN...!
OBORO

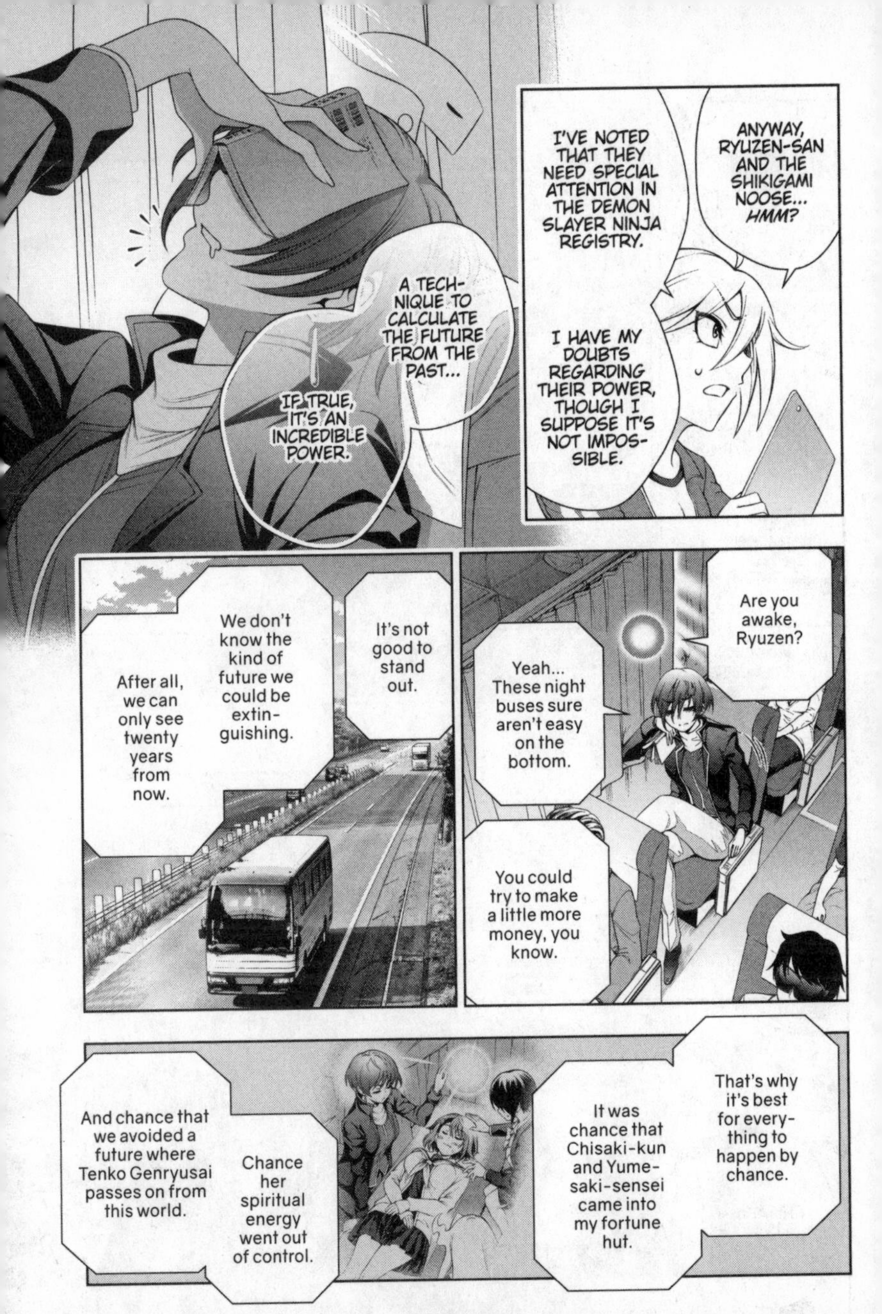
ANYWAY, RYUZEN-SAN AND THE SHIKIGAMI NOOSE... *HMM?*
I'VE NOTED THAT THEY NEED SPECIAL ATTENTION IN THE DEMON SLAYER NINJA REGISTRY.
I HAVE MY DOUBTS REGARDING THEIR POWER, THOUGH I SUPPOSE IT'S NOT IMPOSSIBLE.
A TECHNIQUE TO CALCULATE THE FUTURE FROM THE PAST...
IF TRUE, IT'S AN INCREDIBLE POWER.
Are you awake, Ryuzen?
Yeah... These night buses sure aren't easy on the bottom.
You could try to make a little more money, you know.
It's not good to stand out.
We don't know the kind of future we could be extinguishing.
After all, we can only see twenty years from now.
That's why it's best for everything to happen by chance.
It was chance that Chisaki-kun and Yumesaki-sensei came into my fortune hut.
Chance her spiritual energy went out of control.
And chance that we avoided a future where Tenko Genryusai passes on from this world.

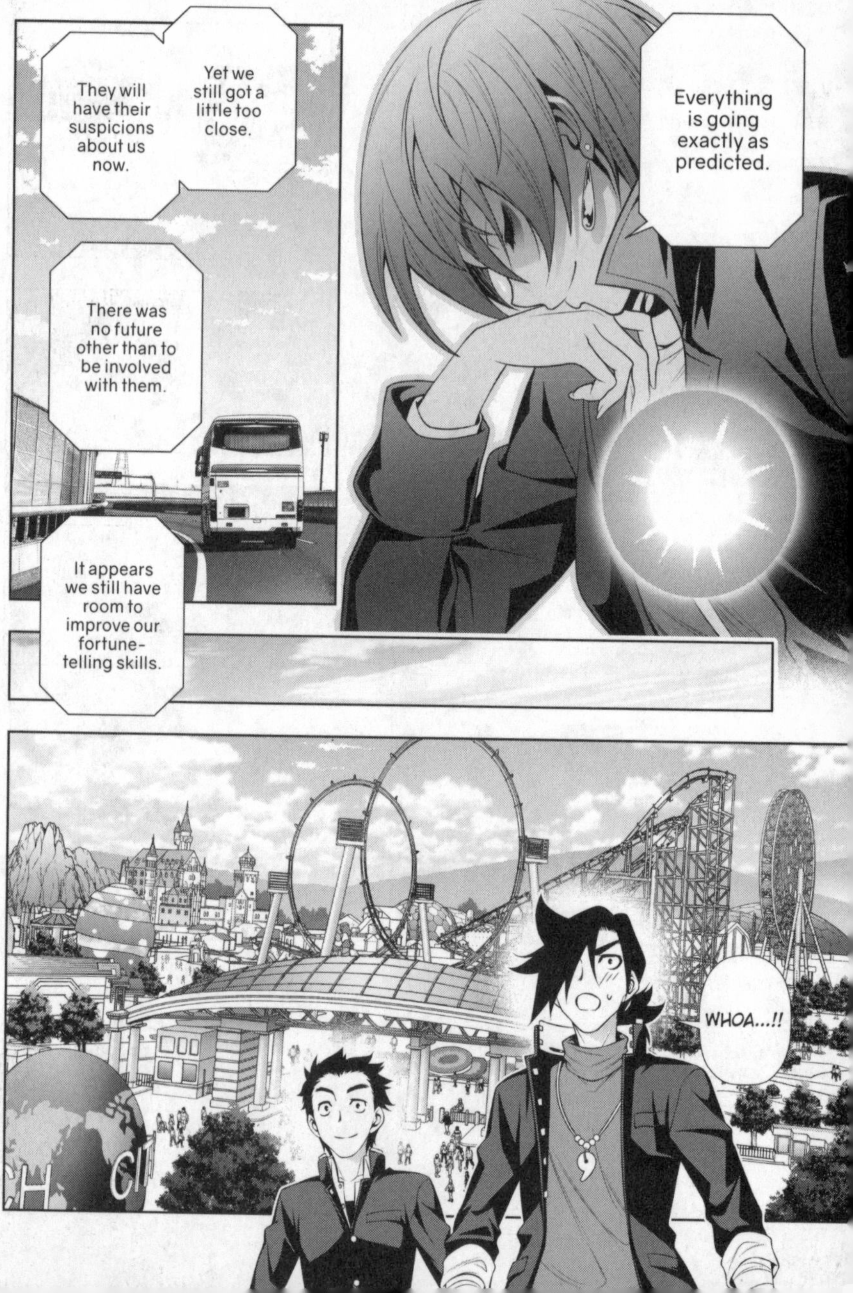
Everything is going exactly as predicted.
Yet we still got a little too close.
They will have their suspicions about us now.
There was no future other than to be involved with them.
It appears we still have room to improve our fortune-telling skills.
WHOA...!!

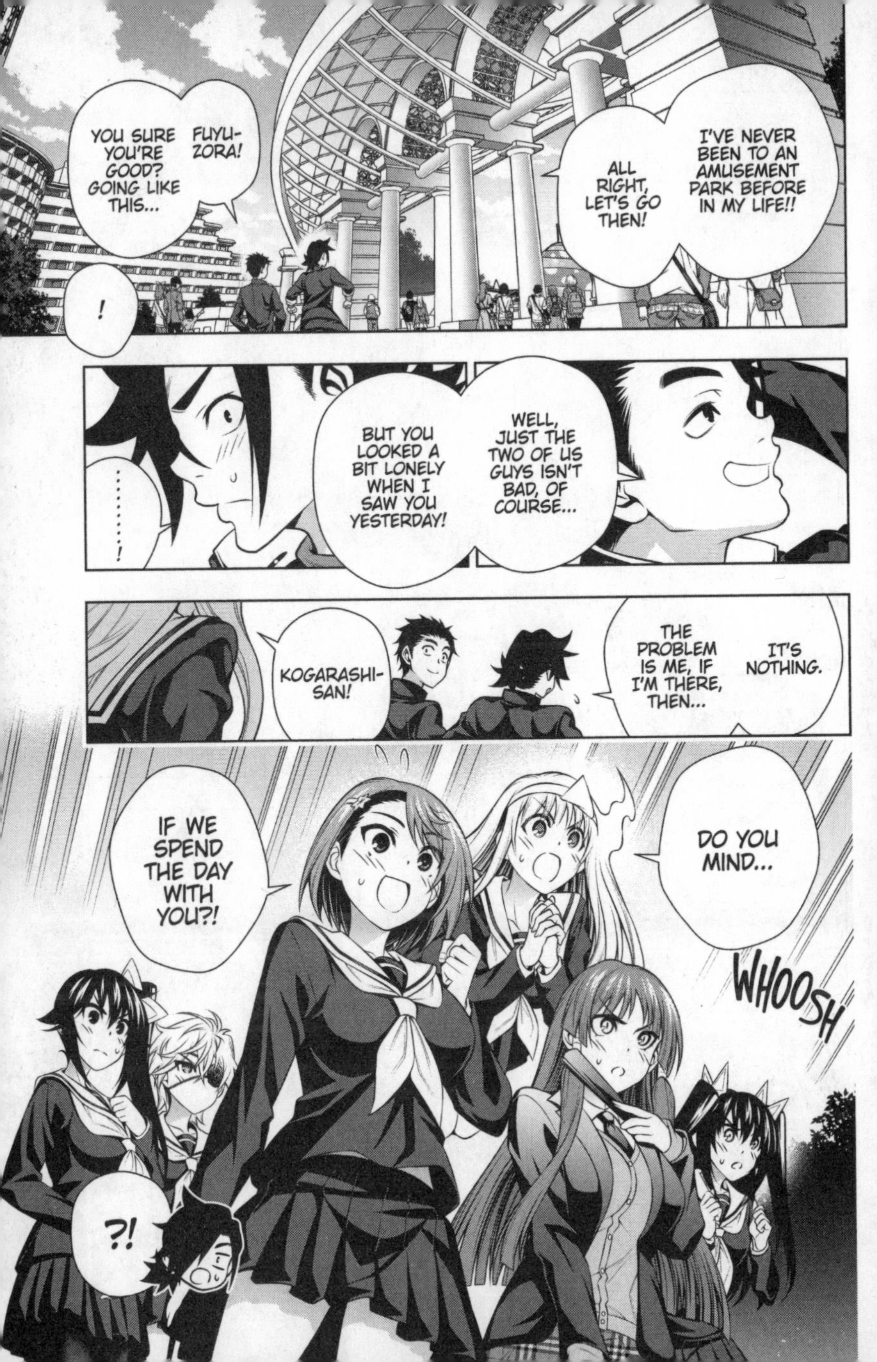
I'VE NEVER BEEN TO AN AMUSEMENT PARK BEFORE IN MY LIFE!!
ALL RIGHT, LET'S GO THEN!
FUYU-ZORA!
YOU SURE YOU'RE GOOD? GOING LIKE THIS...
!
WELL, JUST THE TWO OF US GUYS ISN'T BAD, OF COURSE...
BUT YOU LOOKED A BIT LONELY WHEN I SAW YOU YESTERDAY!
......!
IT'S NOTHING.
THE PROBLEM IS ME, IF I'M THERE, THEN...
KOGARASHI-SAN!
DO YOU MIND...
IF WE SPEND THE DAY WITH YOU?!
WHOOSH
?!

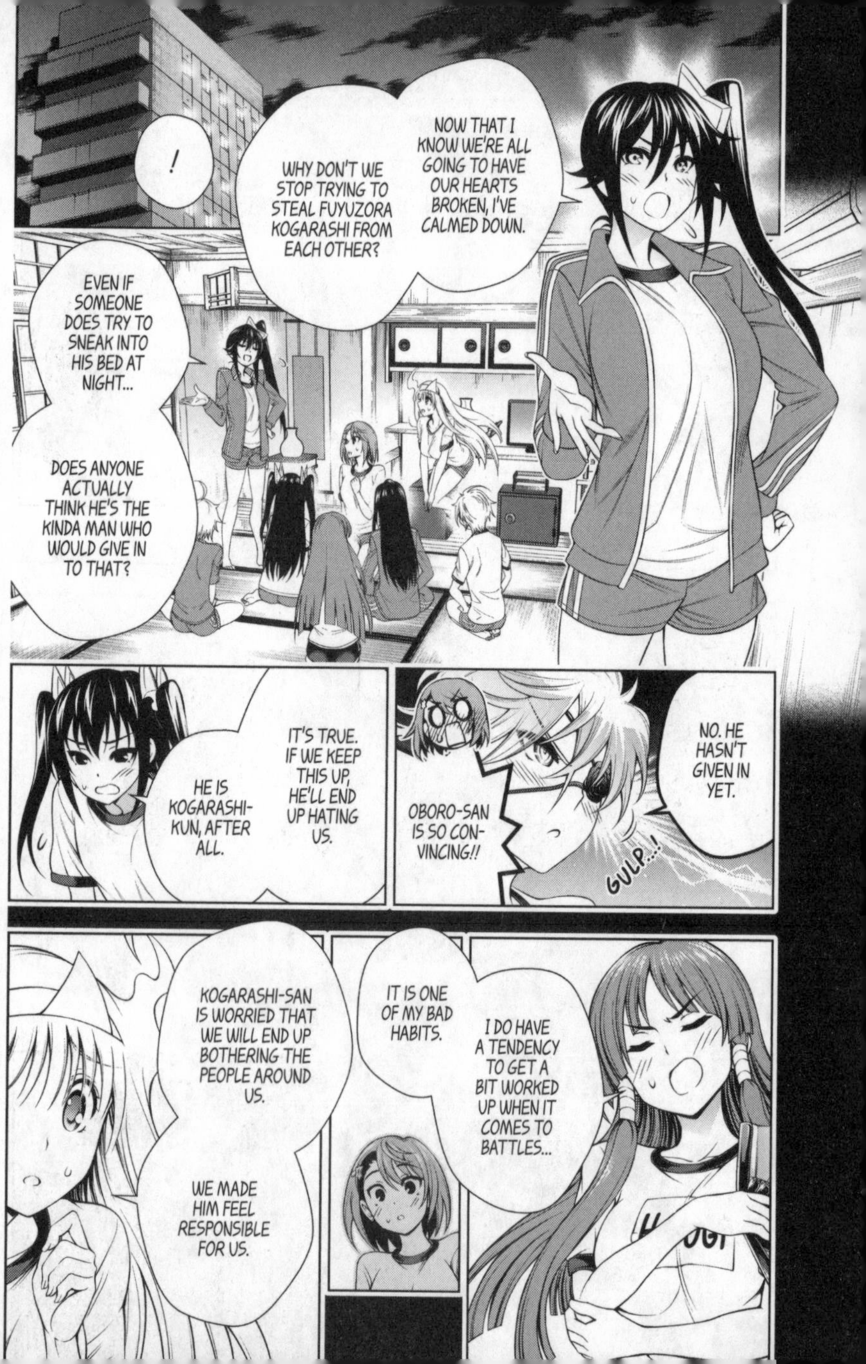
NOW THAT I KNOW WE'RE ALL GOING TO HAVE OUR HEARTS BROKEN, I'VE CALMED DOWN.
WHY DON'T WE STOP TRYING TO STEAL FUYUZORA KOGARASHI FROM EACH OTHER?
!
EVEN IF SOMEONE DOES TRY TO SNEAK INTO HIS BED AT NIGHT...
DOES ANYONE ACTUALLY THINK HE'S THE KINDA MAN WHO WOULD GIVE IN TO THAT?
NO. HE HASN'T GIVEN IN YET.
OBORO-SAN IS SO CONVINCING!!
GULP...!
IT'S TRUE. IF WE KEEP THIS UP, HE'LL END UP HATING US.
HE IS KOGARASHI-KUN, AFTER ALL.
I DO HAVE A TENDENCY TO GET A BIT WORKED UP WHEN IT COMES TO BATTLES...
IT IS ONE OF MY BAD HABITS.
KOGARASHI-SAN IS WORRIED THAT WE WILL END UP BOTHERING THE PEOPLE AROUND US.
WE MADE HIM FEEL RESPONSIBLE FOR US.

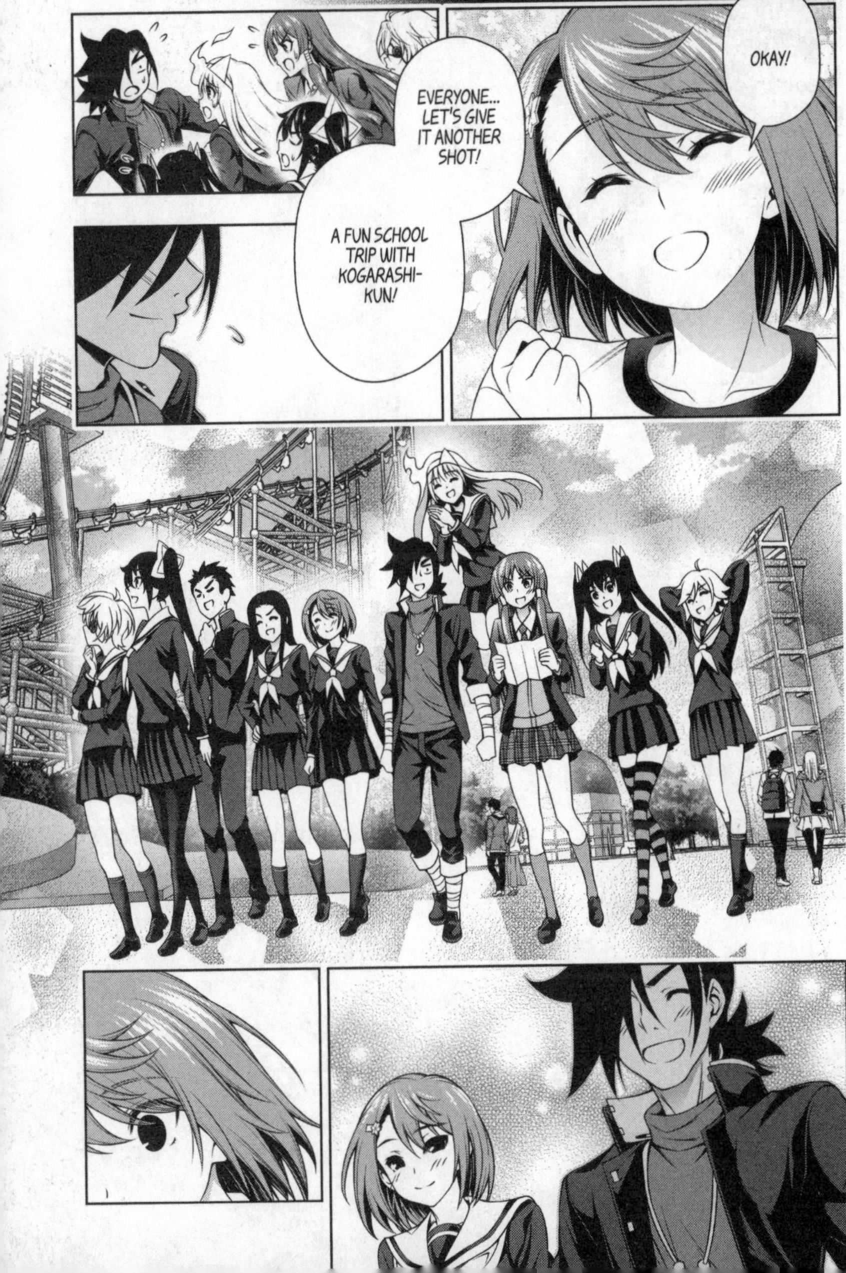
OKAY!
EVERYONE... LET'S GIVE IT ANOTHER SHOT!
A FUN SCHOOL TRIP WITH KOGARASHI-KUN!

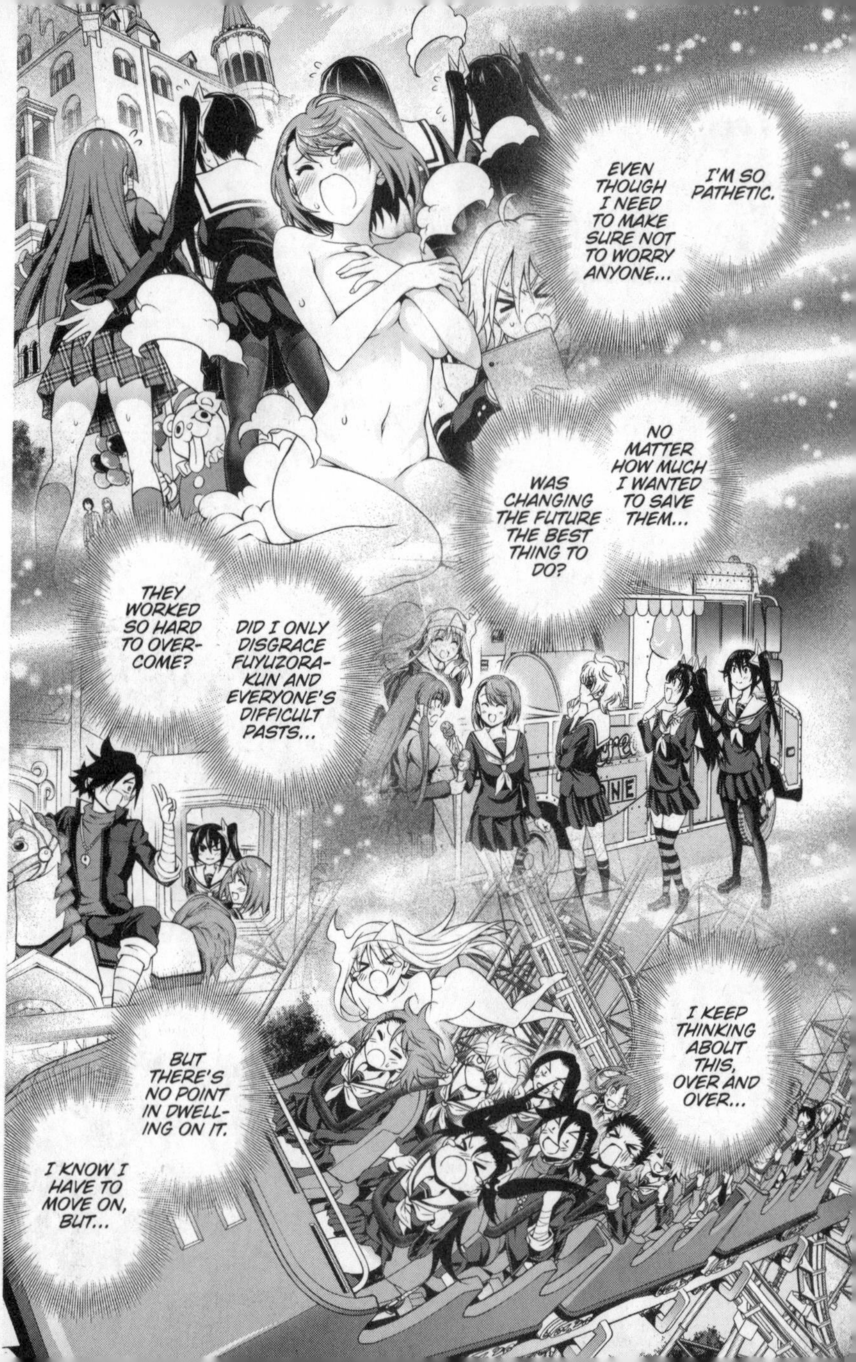
I'M SO PATHETIC.
EVEN THOUGH I NEED TO MAKE SURE NOT TO WORRY ANYONE...
NO MATTER HOW MUCH I WANTED TO SAVE THEM...
WAS CHANGING THE FUTURE THE BEST THING TO DO?
DID I ONLY DISGRACE FUYUZORA-KUN AND EVERYONE'S DIFFICULT PASTS...
THEY WORKED SO HARD TO OVER-COME?
I KEEP THINKING ABOUT THIS, OVER AND OVER...
BUT THERE'S NO POINT IN DWELL-ING ON IT.
I KNOW I HAVE TO MOVE ON, BUT...

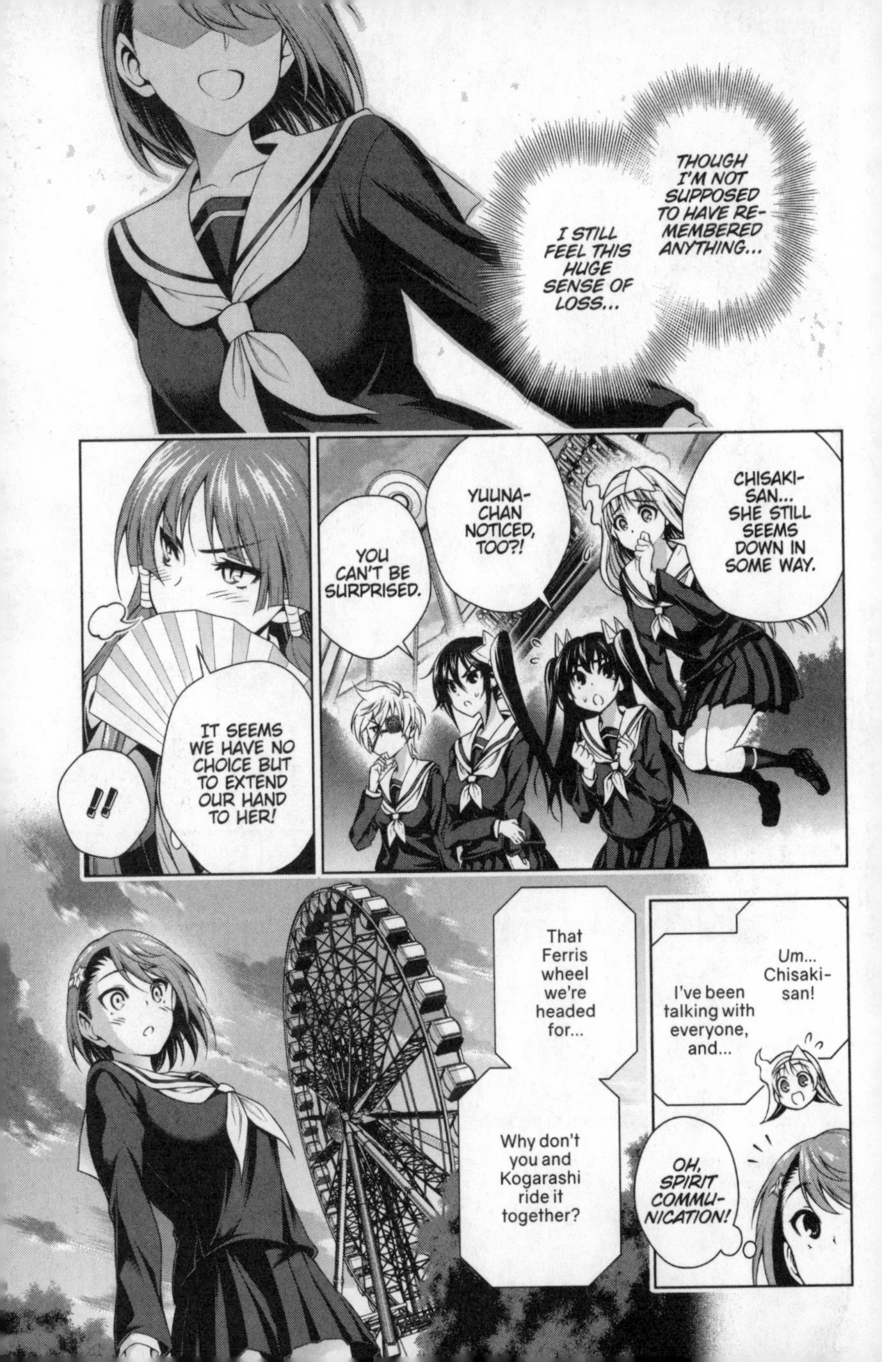
THOUGH I'M NOT SUPPOSED TO HAVE RE-MEMBERED ANYTHING...
I STILL FEEL THIS HUGE SENSE OF LOSS...
CHISAKI-SAN... SHE STILL SEEMS DOWN IN SOME WAY.
YUUNA-CHAN NOTICED, TOO?!
YOU CAN'T BE SURPRISED.
IT SEEMS WE HAVE NO CHOICE BUT TO EXTEND OUR HAND TO HER!
!!
Um... Chisaki-san!
I've been talking with everyone, and...
OH, SPIRIT COMMUNICATION!
That Ferris wheel we're headed for...
Why don't you and Kogarashi ride it together?

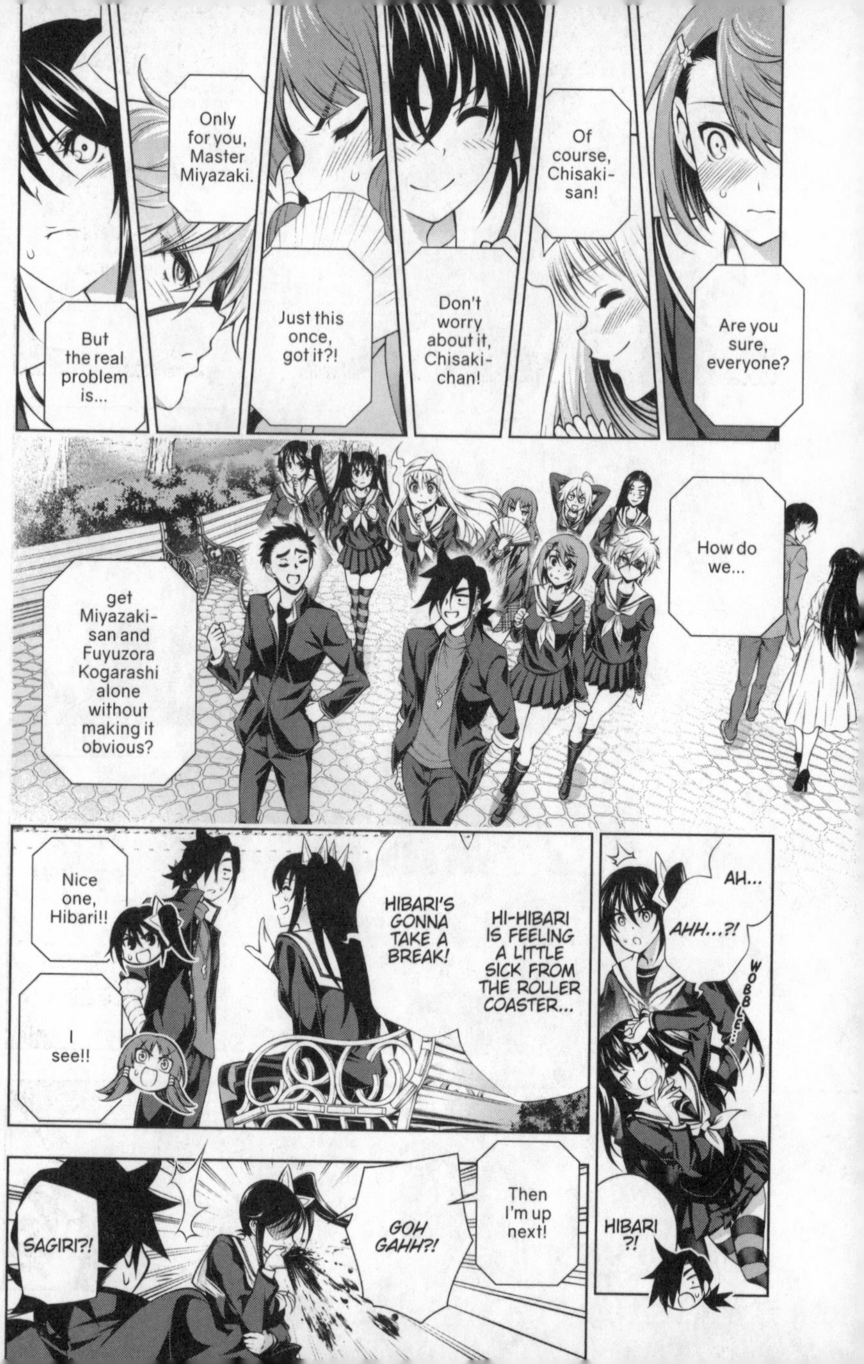

Are you sure, everyone?
Of course, Chisaki-san!
Don't worry about it, Chisaki-chan!
Just this once, got it?!
Only for you, Master Miyazaki.
But the real problem is...
How do we...
get Miyazaki-san and Fuyuzora Kogarashi alone without making it obvious?
AH...
AHH...?!
WOBBLE...
HIBARI ?!
HI-HIBARI IS FEELING A LITTLE SICK FROM THE ROLLER COASTER...
HIBARI'S GONNA TAKE A BREAK!
Nice one, Hibari!!
I see!!
Then I'm up next!
GOH GAHH?!
SAGIRI?!

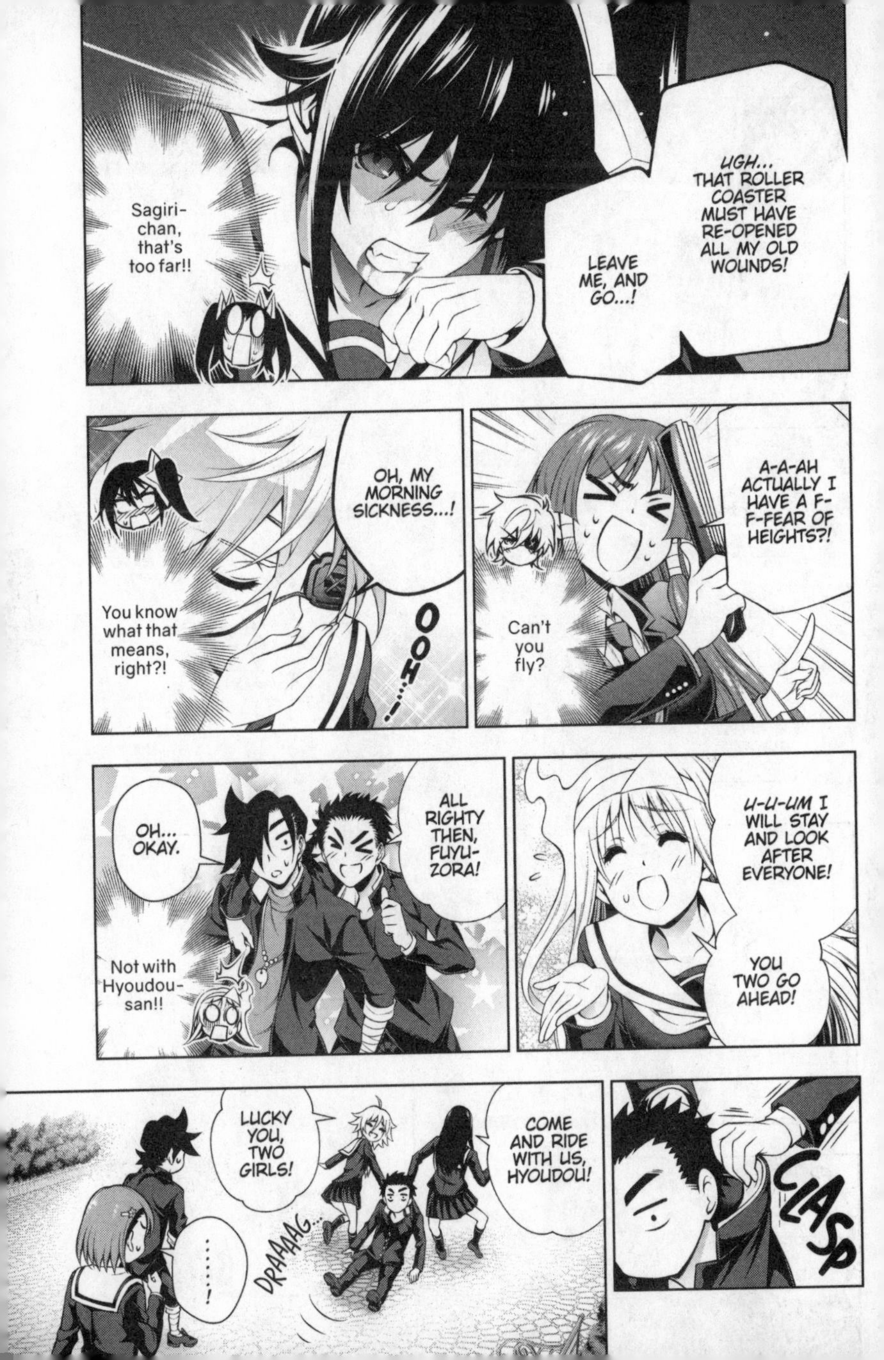

UGH... THAT ROLLER COASTER MUST HAVE RE-OPENED ALL MY OLD WOUNDS!
LEAVE ME, AND GO...!
Sagiri-chan, that's too far!!
A-A-AH ACTUALLY I HAVE A F-F-FEAR OF HEIGHTS?!
Can't you fly?
OH, MY MORNING SICKNESS...!
OOH...!
You know what that means, right?!
U-U-UM I WILL STAY AND LOOK AFTER EVERYONE!
YOU TWO GO AHEAD!
ALL RIGHTY THEN, FUYUZORA!
OH... OKAY.
Not with Hyoudou-san!!
CLASP
COME AND RIDE WITH US, HYOUDOU!
DRAAAAG...
LUCKY YOU, TWO GIRLS!
......!

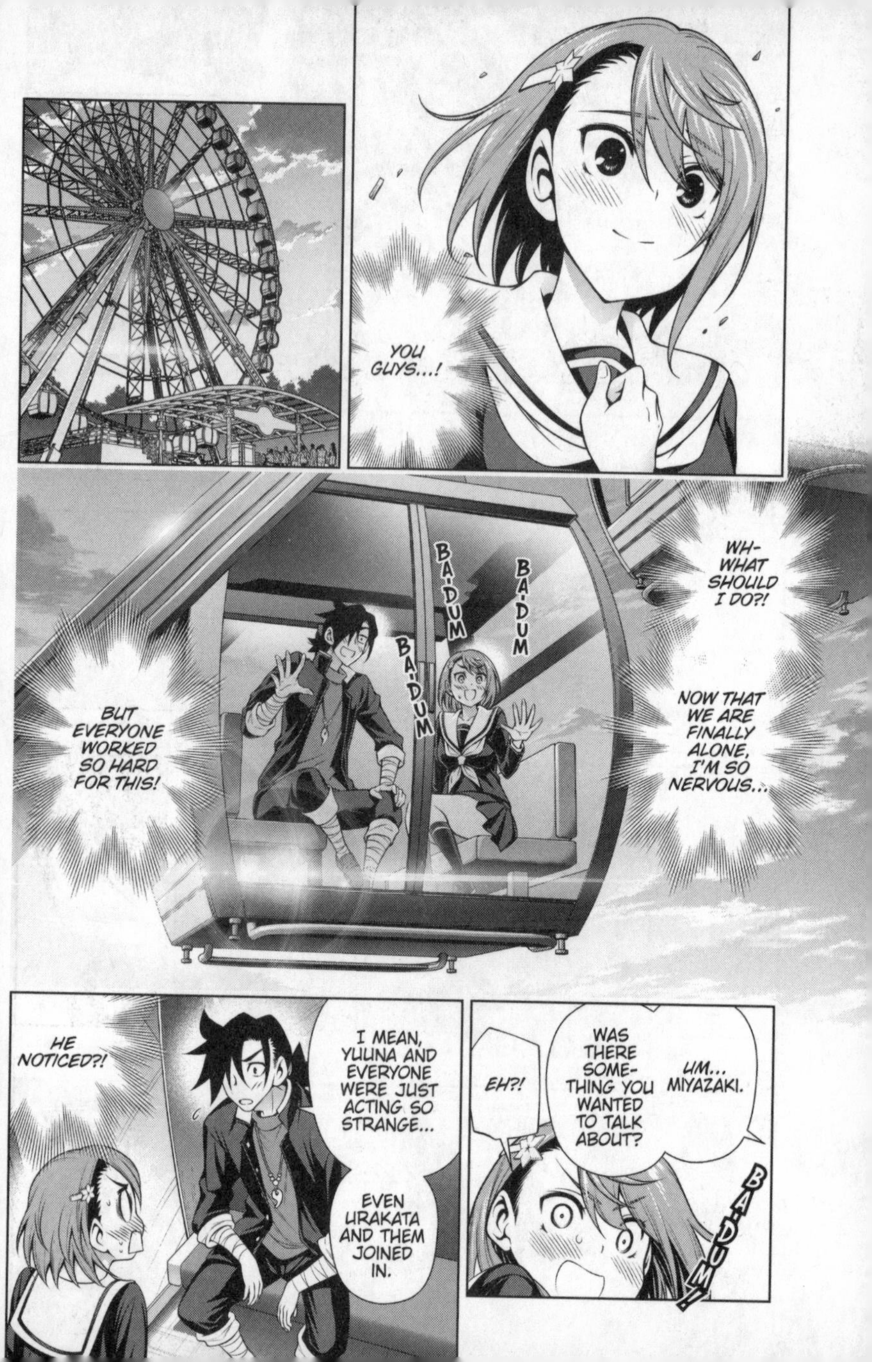
YOU GUYS...!
WH-WHAT SHOULD I DO?!
BA-DUM
BA-DUM
NOW THAT WE ARE FINALLY ALONE, I'M SO NERVOUS...
BA-DUM
BUT EVERYONE WORKED SO HARD FOR THIS!
UM... MIYAZAKI.
WAS THERE SOME-THING YOU WANTED TO TALK ABOUT?
EH?!
BA-DUM!
I MEAN, YUUNA AND EVERYONE WERE JUST ACTING SO STRANGE...
HE NOTICED?!
EVEN URAKATA AND THEM JOINED IN.

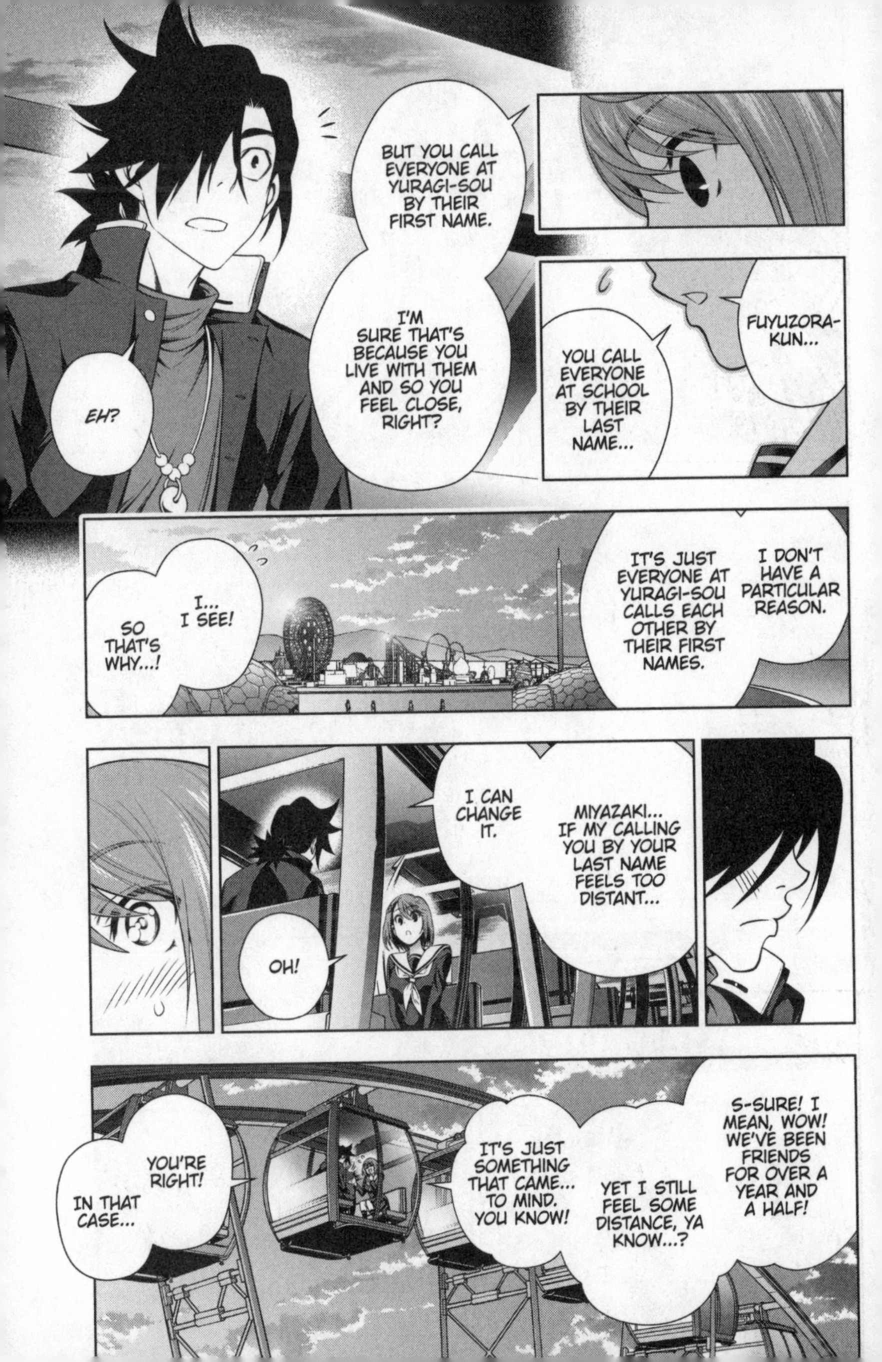
FUYUZORA-KUN...
YOU CALL EVERYONE AT SCHOOL BY THEIR LAST NAME...
BUT YOU CALL EVERYONE AT YURAGI-SOU BY THEIR FIRST NAME.
I'M SURE THAT'S BECAUSE YOU LIVE WITH THEM AND SO YOU FEEL CLOSE, RIGHT?
EH?
I DON'T HAVE A PARTICULAR REASON.
IT'S JUST EVERYONE AT YURAGI-SOU CALLS EACH OTHER BY THEIR FIRST NAMES.
I... I SEE!
SO THAT'S WHY...!
MIYAZAKI... IF MY CALLING YOU BY YOUR LAST NAME FEELS TOO DISTANT...
I CAN CHANGE IT.
OH!
S-SURE! I MEAN, WOW! WE'VE BEEN FRIENDS FOR OVER A YEAR AND A HALF!
YET I STILL FEEL SOME DISTANCE, YA KNOW...?
IT'S JUST SOMETHING THAT CAME... TO MIND. YOU KNOW!
YOU'RE RIGHT!
IN THAT CASE...

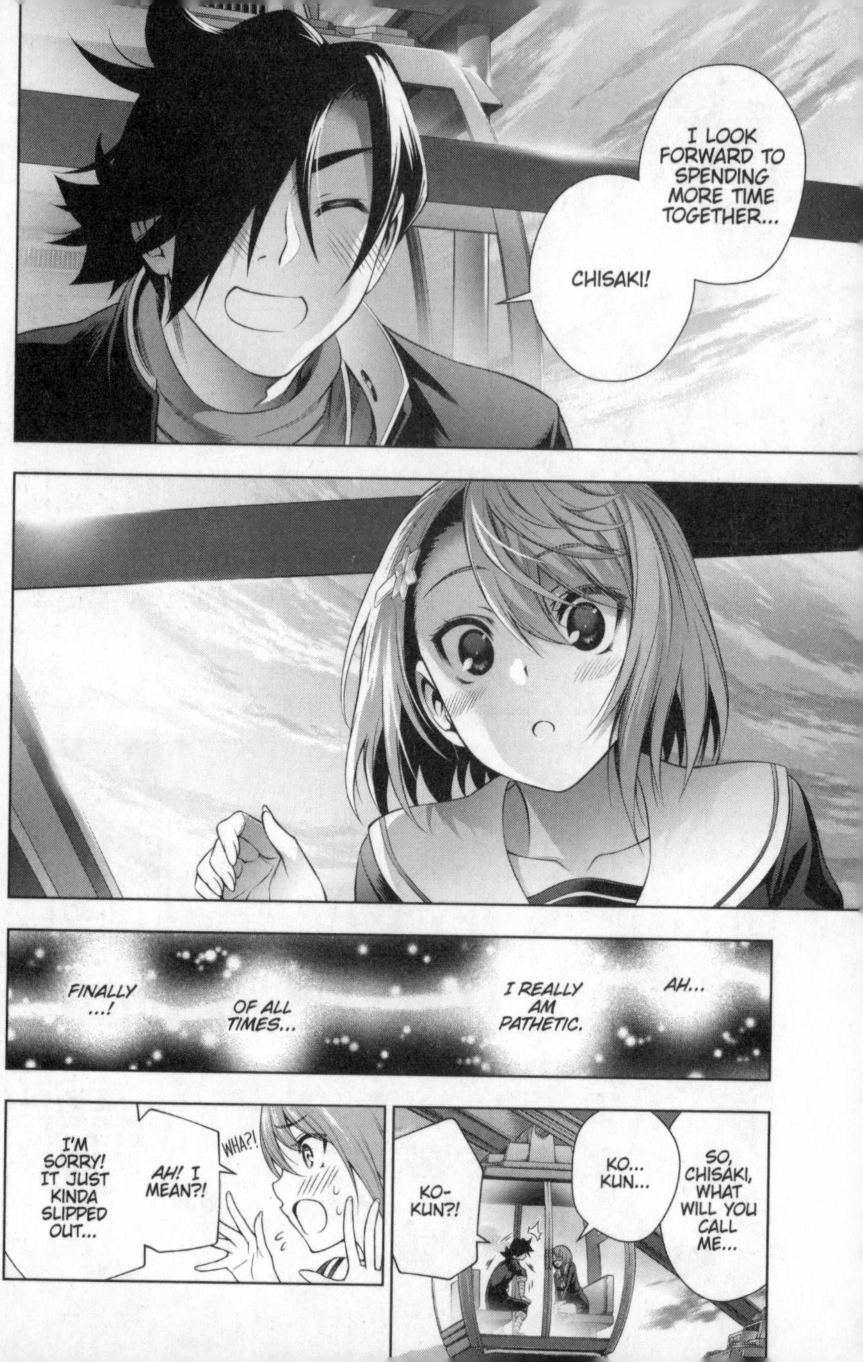
I LOOK FORWARD TO SPENDING MORE TIME TOGETHER...
CHISAKI!
AH...
I REALLY AM PATHETIC.
OF ALL TIMES...
FINALLY ...!
SO, CHISAKI, WHAT WILL YOU CALL ME...
KO... KUN...
KO-KUN?!
WHA?!
AH! I MEAN?!
I'M SORRY! IT JUST KINDA SLIPPED OUT...

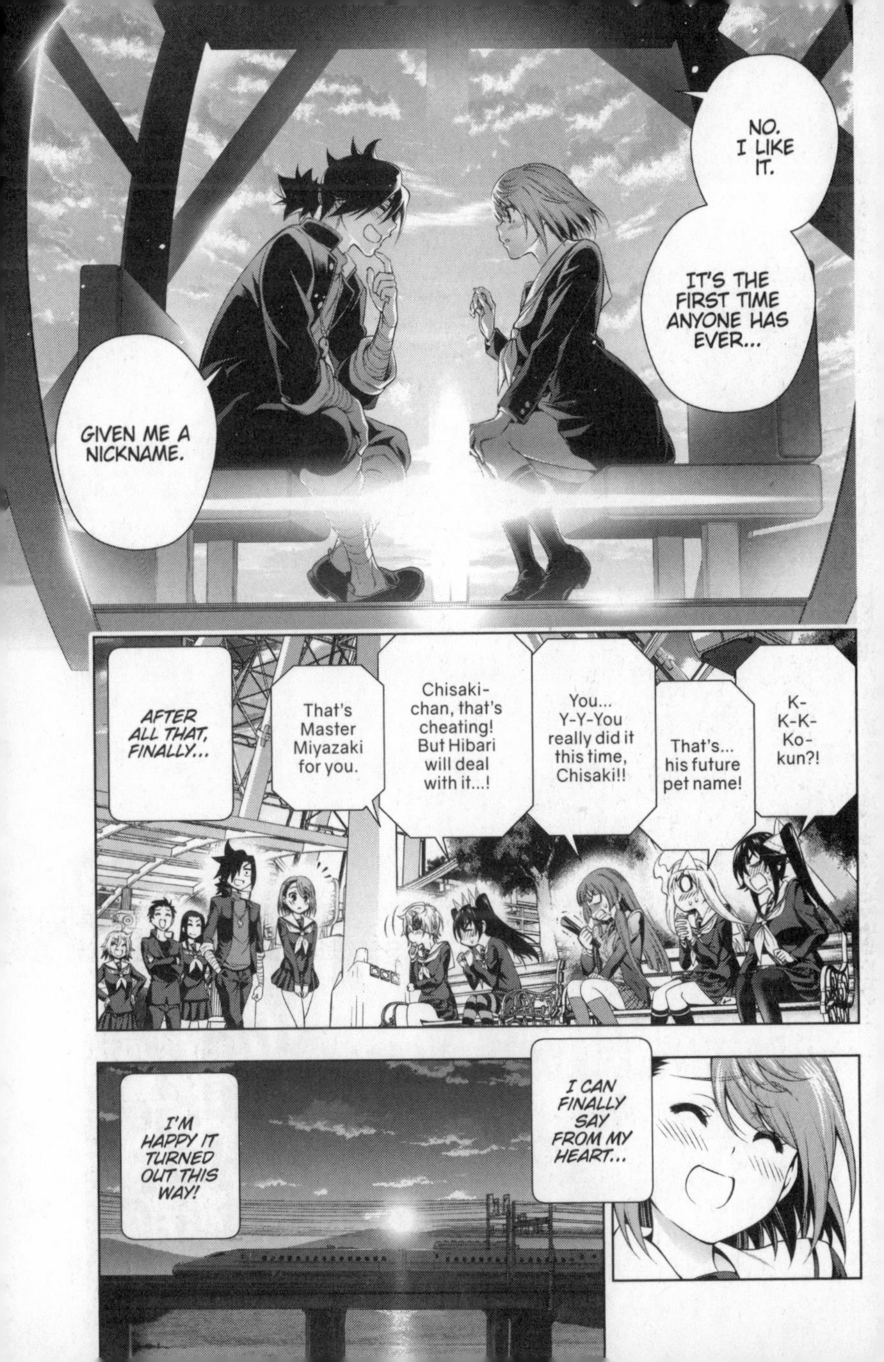
NO. I LIKE IT.
IT'S THE FIRST TIME ANYONE HAS EVER...
GIVEN ME A NICKNAME.
K-K-K-Ko-kun?!
That's... his future pet name!
You... Y-Y-You really did it this time, Chisaki!!
Chisaki-chan, that's cheating! But Hibari will deal with it...!
That's Master Miyazaki for you.
AFTER ALL THAT, FINALLY...
I CAN FINALLY SAY FROM MY HEART...
I'M HAPPY IT TURNED OUT THIS WAY!

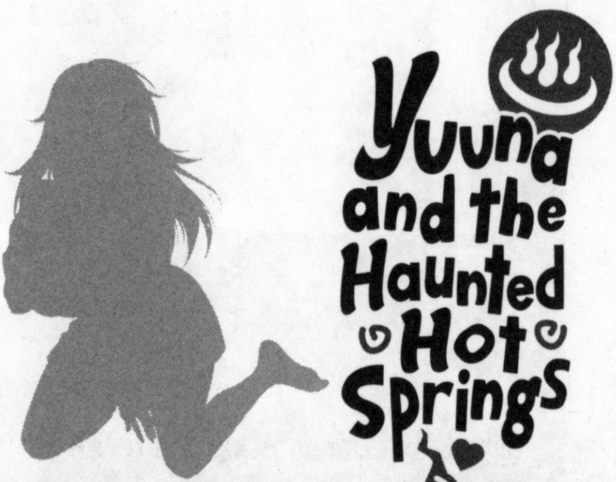

Yuuna and the Haunted Hot Springs

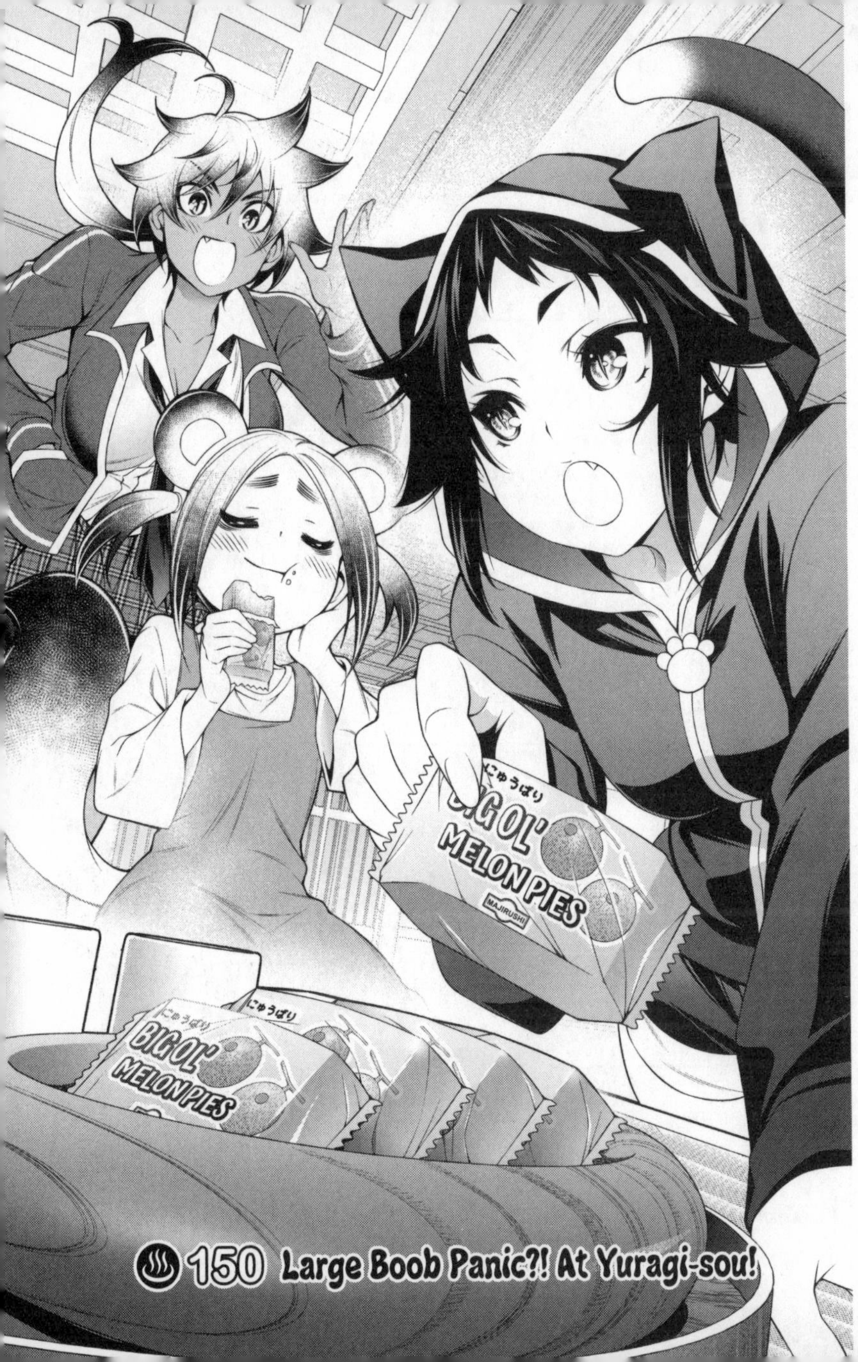

にゅうばり
BIG OL'
MELON PIES
MAJIRUSHI
にゅうばり
にゅうばり
BIG OL'
MELON PIES
150 Large Boob Panic?! At Yuragi-sou!

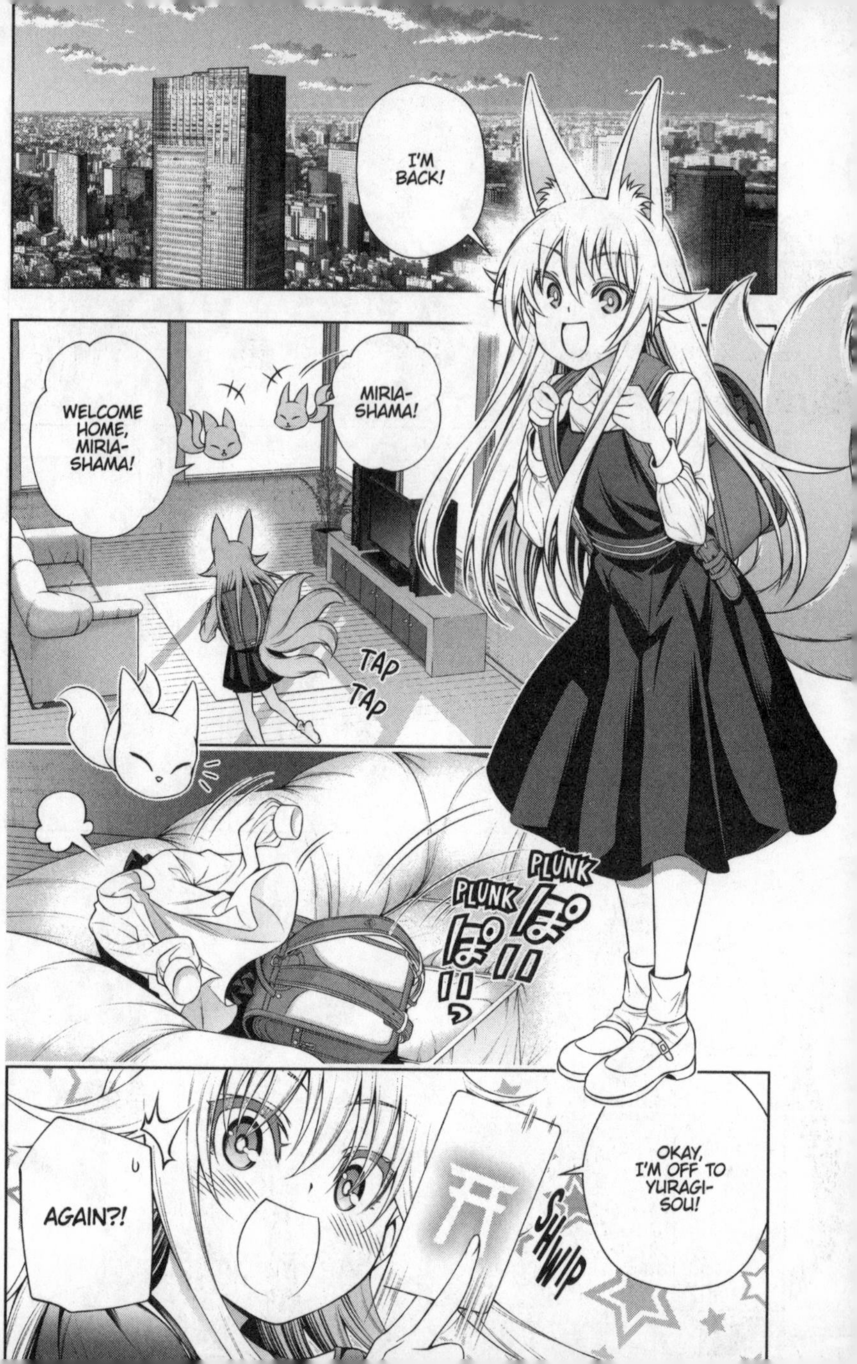
I'M BACK!
MIRIA-SHAMA!
WELCOME HOME, MIRIA-SHAMA!
TAP TAP
PLUNK
PLUNK
OKAY, I'M OFF TO YURAGI-SOU!
SHWIP
AGAIN?!

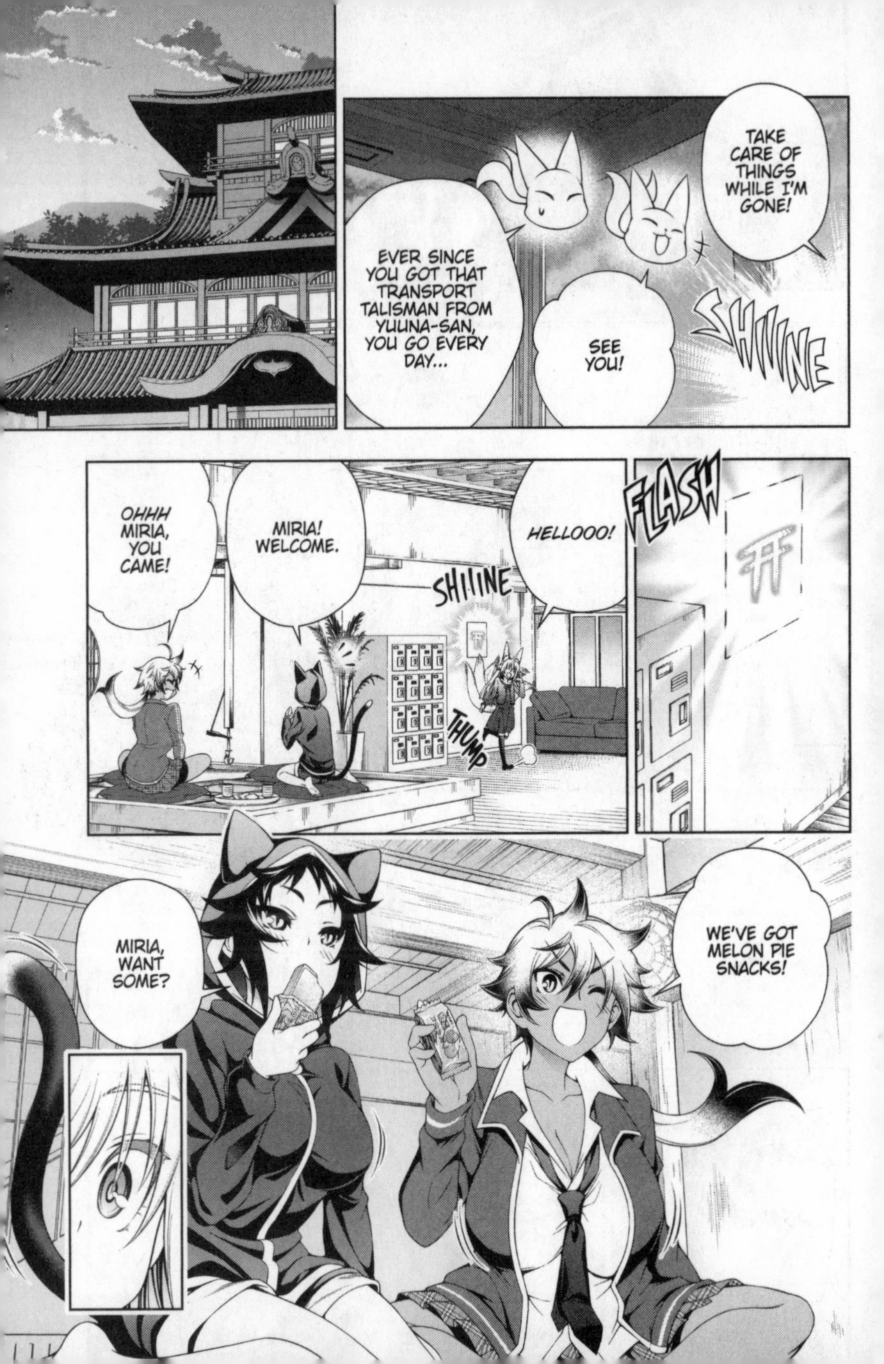
TAKE CARE OF THINGS WHILE I'M GONE!
SHIIINE
SEE YOU!
EVER SINCE YOU GOT THAT TRANSPORT TALISMAN FROM YUUNA-SAN, YOU GO EVERY DAY...
FLASH
HELLOOO!
SHIIINE
THUMP
MIRIA! WELCOME.
OHHH MIRIA, YOU CAME!
WE'VE GOT MELON PIE SNACKS!
MIRIA, WANT SOME?

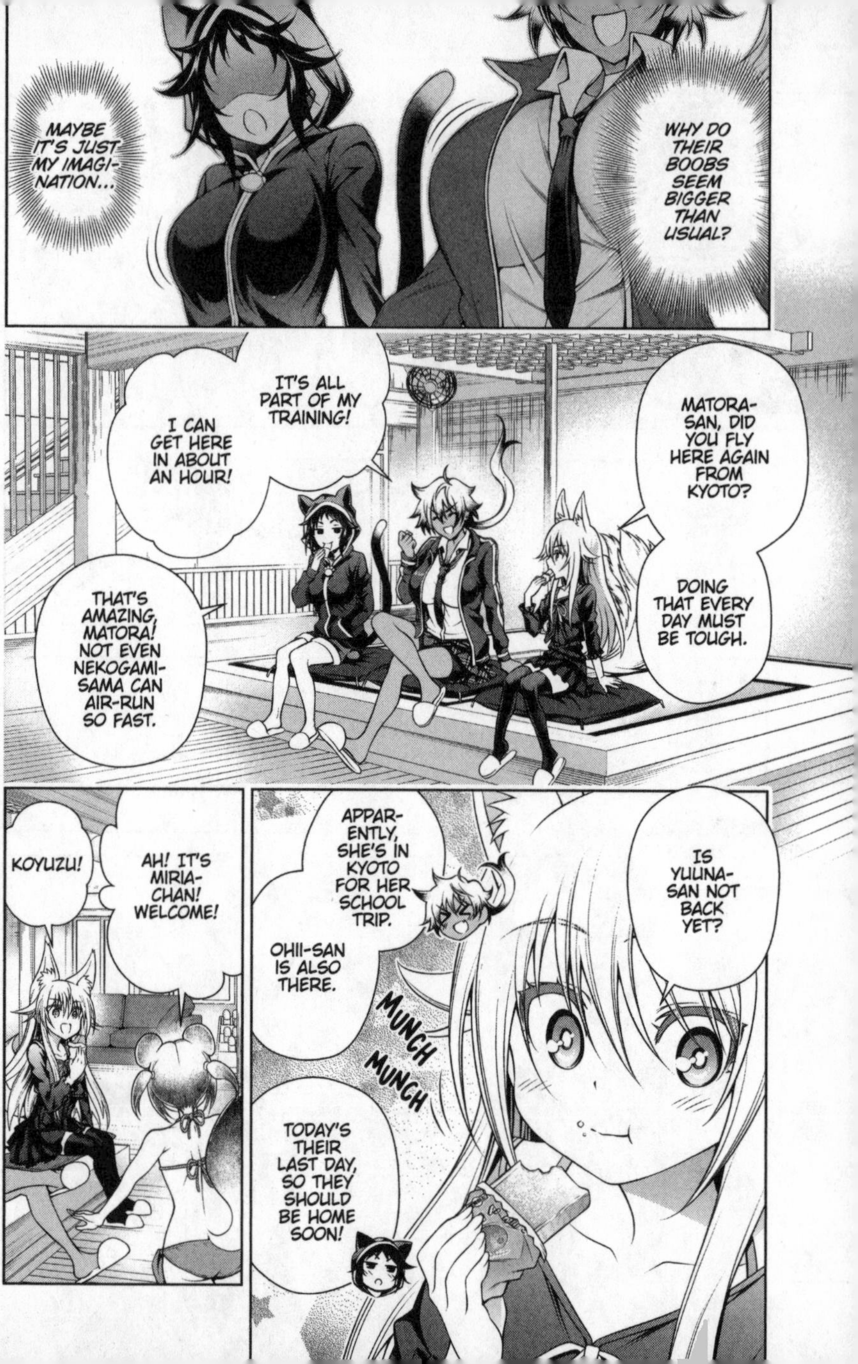
WHY DO THEIR BOOBS SEEM BIGGER THAN USUAL?
MAYBE IT'S JUST MY IMAGI-NATION...
MATORA-SAN, DID YOU FLY HERE AGAIN FROM KYOTO?
DOING THAT EVERY DAY MUST BE TOUGH.
IT'S ALL PART OF MY TRAINING!
I CAN GET HERE IN ABOUT AN HOUR!
THAT'S AMAZING, MATORA! NOT EVEN NEKOGAMI-SAMA CAN AIR-RUN SO FAST.
IS YUUNA-SAN NOT BACK YET?
APPAR-ENTLY, SHE'S IN KYOTO FOR HER SCHOOL TRIP.
OHII-SAN IS ALSO THERE.
MUNCH MUNCH
TODAY'S THEIR LAST DAY, SO THEY SHOULD BE HOME SOON!
AH! IT'S MIRIA-CHAN! WELCOME!
KOYUZU!

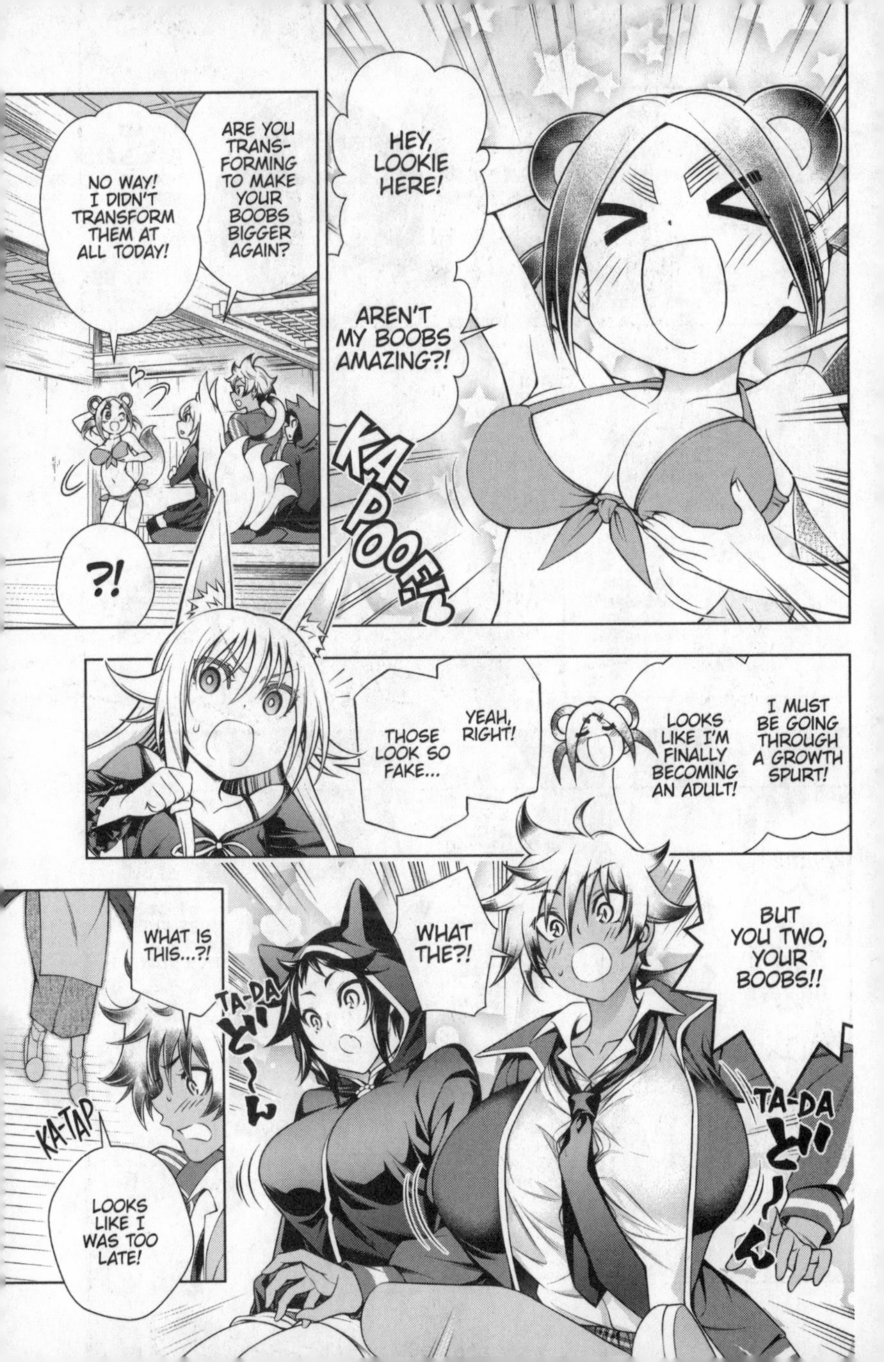
HEY, LOOKIE HERE!
AREN'T MY BOOBS AMAZING?!
KA-POOF!♥
ARE YOU TRANSFORMING TO MAKE YOUR BOOBS BIGGER AGAIN?
NO WAY! I DIDN'T TRANSFORM THEM AT ALL TODAY!
?!
I MUST BE GOING THROUGH A GROWTH SPURT!
LOOKS LIKE I'M FINALLY BECOMING AN ADULT!
YEAH, RIGHT!
THOSE LOOK SO FAKE...
BUT YOU TWO, YOUR BOOBS!!
TA-DA
WHAT THE?!
TA-DA
WHAT IS THIS...?!
KA-TAP
LOOKS LIKE I WAS TOO LATE!

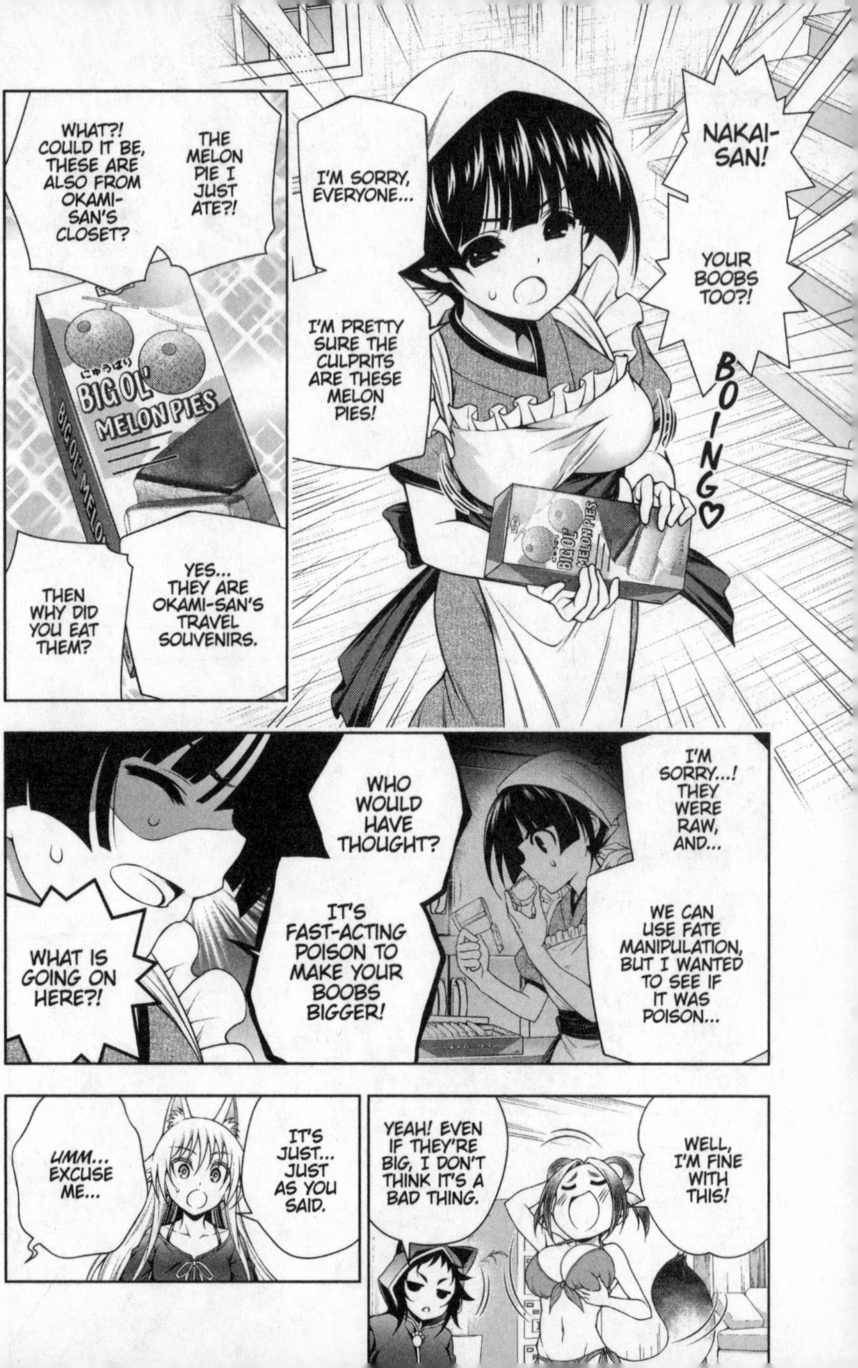
NAKAI-SAN!
YOUR BOOBS TOO?!
BOING♡
I'M SORRY, EVERYONE...
I'M PRETTY SURE THE CULPRITS ARE THESE MELON PIES!
BIG OL' MELON PIES
THE MELON PIE I JUST ATE?!
WHAT?! COULD IT BE, THESE ARE ALSO FROM OKAMI-SAN'S CLOSET?
BIG OL' MELON PIES
YES... THEY ARE OKAMI-SAN'S TRAVEL SOUVENIRS.
THEN WHY DID YOU EAT THEM?
I'M SORRY...! THEY WERE RAW, AND...
WE CAN USE FATE MANIPULATION, BUT I WANTED TO SEE IF IT WAS POISON...
WHO WOULD HAVE THOUGHT?
IT'S FAST-ACTING POISON TO MAKE YOUR BOOBS BIGGER!
WHAT IS GOING ON HERE?!
WELL, I'M FINE WITH THIS!
YEAH! EVEN IF THEY'RE BIG, I DON'T THINK IT'S A BAD THING.
IT'S JUST... JUST AS YOU SAID.
UMM... EXCUSE ME...

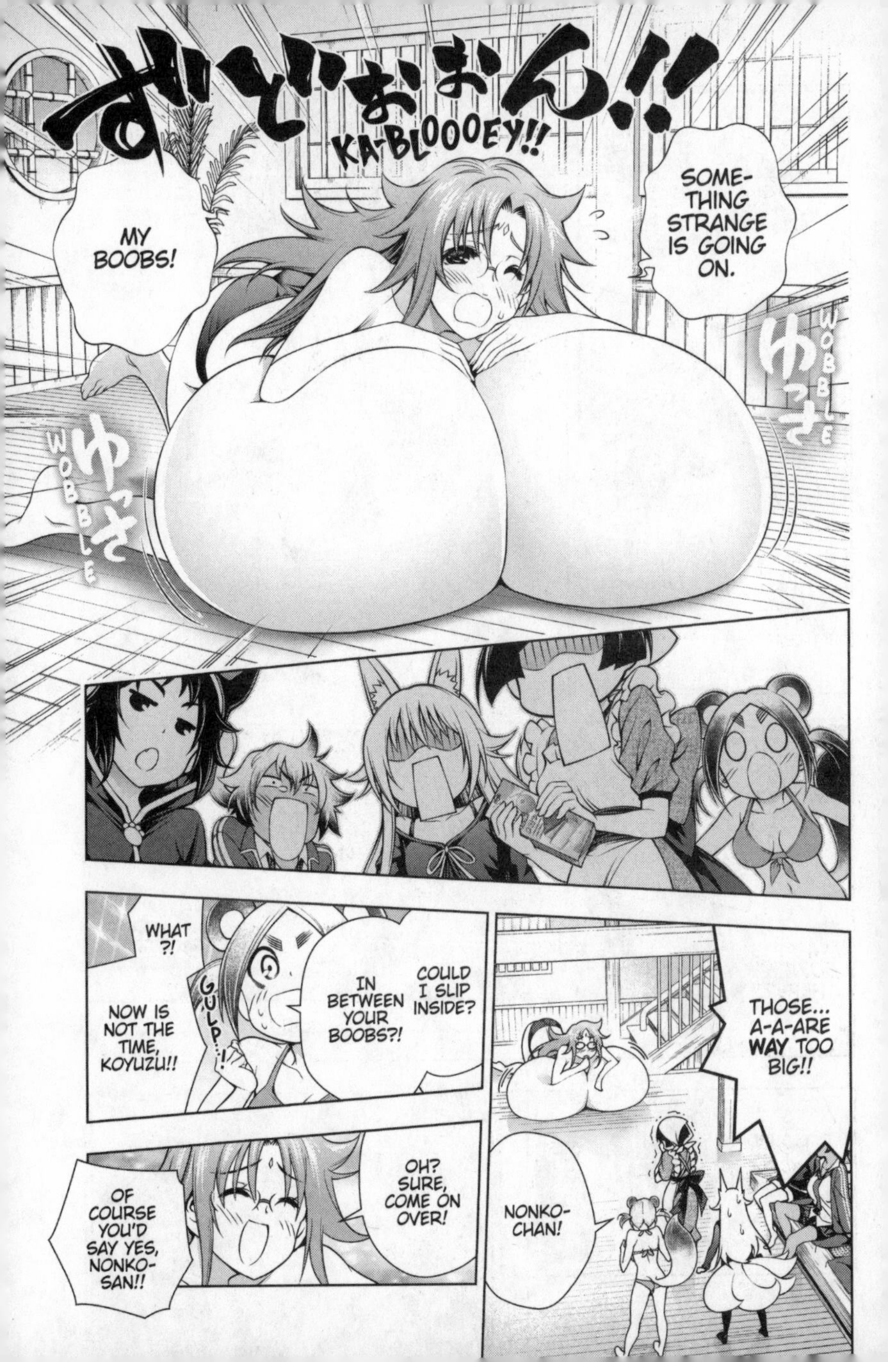
KA-BLOOOEY!!
SOME-THING STRANGE IS GOING ON.
MY BOOBS!
WOBBLE
WOBBLE
THOSE... A-A-ARE WAY TOO BIG!!
NONKO-CHAN!
COULD I SLIP INSIDE?
IN BETWEEN YOUR BOOBS?!
GULP...!
WHAT ?!
NOW IS NOT THE TIME, KOYUZU!!
OH? SURE, COME ON OVER!
OF COURSE YOU'D SAY YES, NONKO-SAN!!

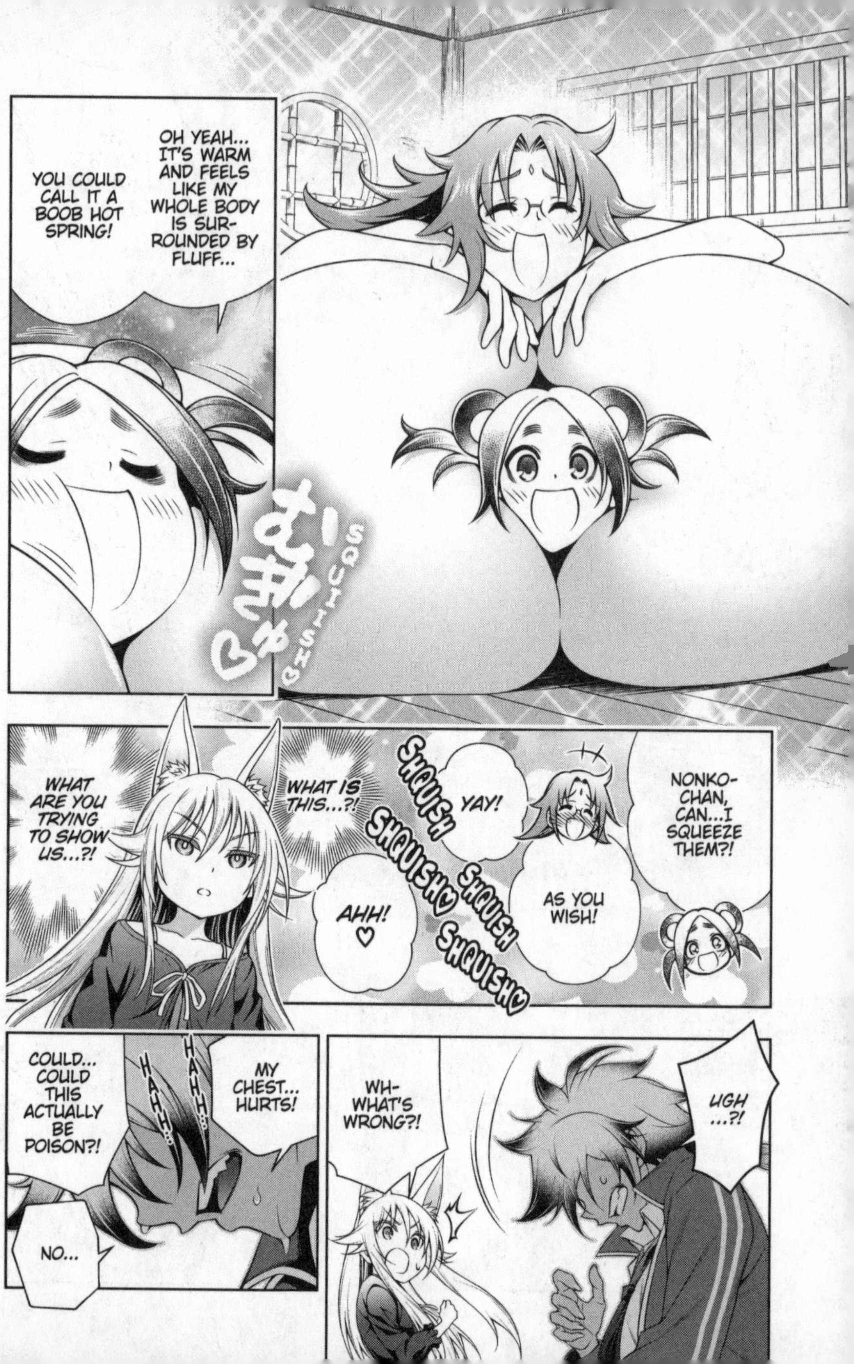
OH YEAH... IT'S WARM AND FEELS LIKE MY WHOLE BODY IS SURROUNDED BY FLUFF...
YOU COULD CALL IT A BOOB HOT SPRING!
むぎゅ♡
SQUIISH♡
NONKO-CHAN, CAN...I SQUEEZE THEM?!
AS YOU WISH!
YAY!
SHQUISH
SHQUISH
SHQUISH♡
SHQUISH
SHQUISH♡
AHH! ♡
WHAT IS THIS...?!
WHAT ARE YOU TRYING TO SHOW US...?!
UGH ...?!
WH-WHAT'S WRONG?!
MY CHEST... HURTS!
HAHH... HAHH...
COULD... COULD THIS ACTUALLY BE POISON?!
NO...

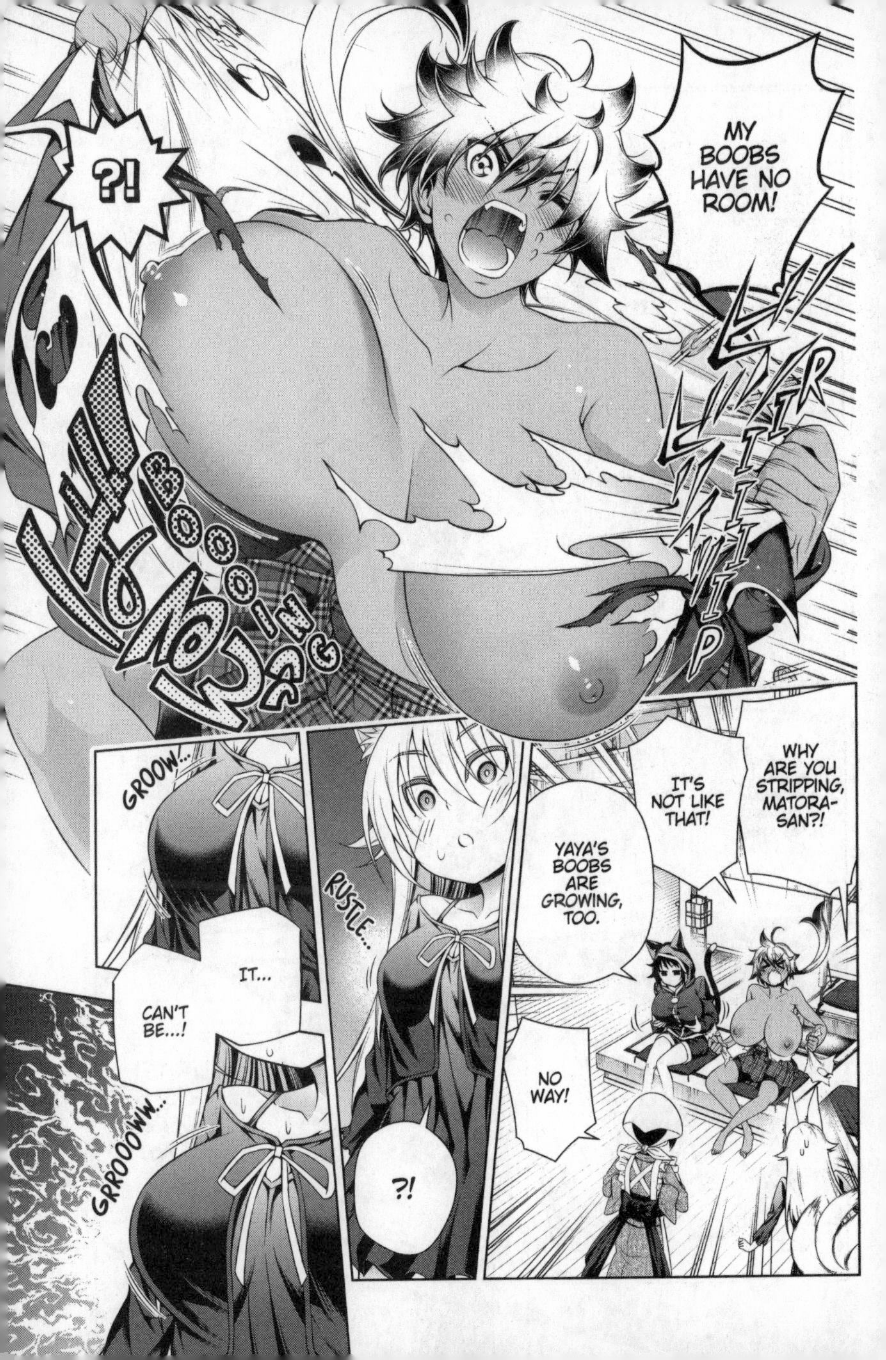
MY BOOBS HAVE NO ROOM!
RIIIIIIP
?!
BOOOING
WHY ARE YOU STRIPPING, MATORA-SAN?!
IT'S NOT LIKE THAT!
YAYA'S BOOBS ARE GROWING, TOO.
NO WAY!
RUSTLE...
?!
GROOW...
IT...
CAN'T BE...!
GRROOOWW...

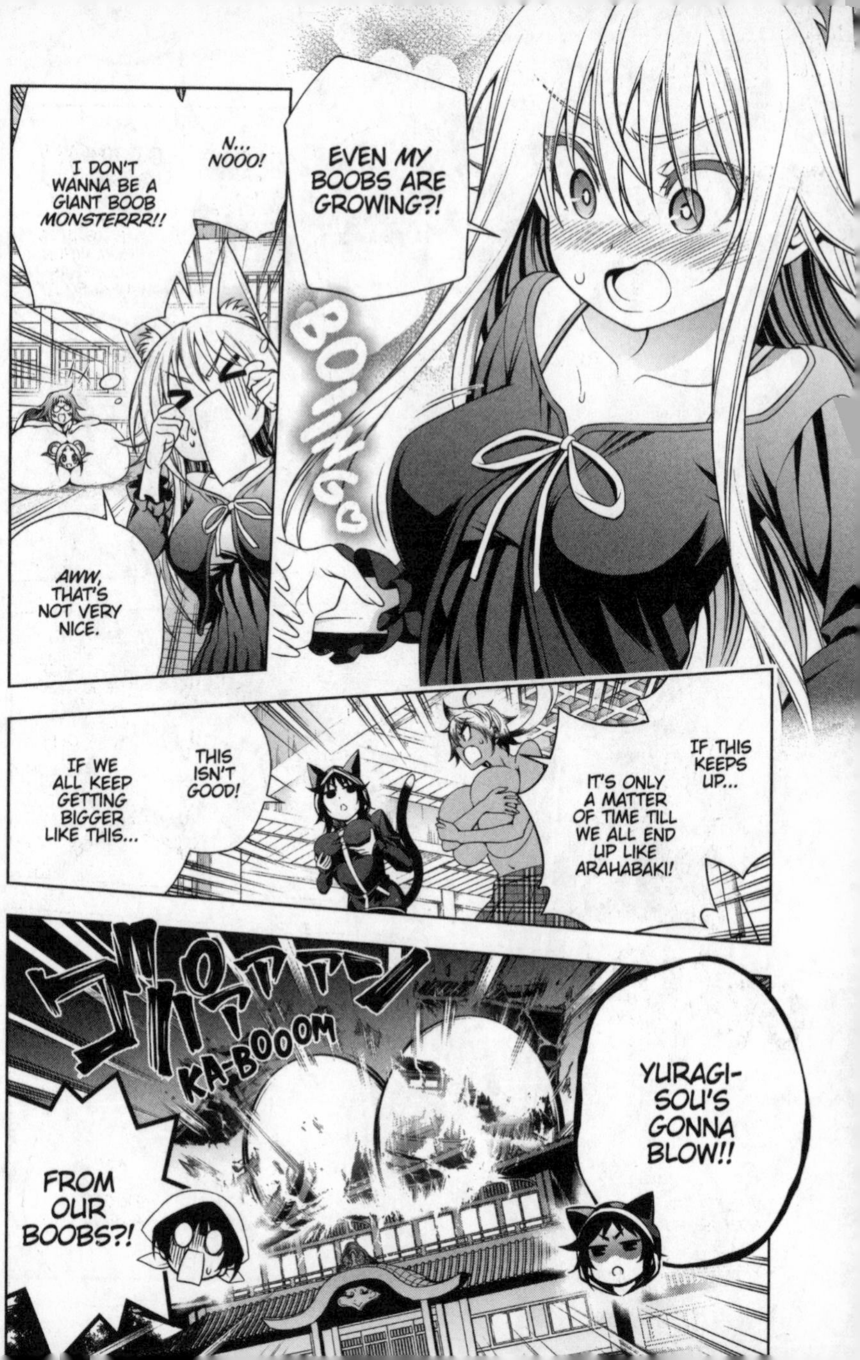
EVEN MY BOOBS ARE GROWING?!
BOINGG♡
N... NOOO!
I DON'T WANNA BE A GIANT BOOB MONSTERRR!!
AWW, THAT'S NOT VERY NICE.
IF THIS KEEPS UP...
IT'S ONLY A MATTER OF TIME TILL WE ALL END UP LIKE ARAHABAKI!
THIS ISN'T GOOD!
IF WE ALL KEEP GETTING BIGGER LIKE THIS...
YURAGI-SOU'S GONNA BLOW!!
KA-BOOOM
FROM OUR BOOBS?!

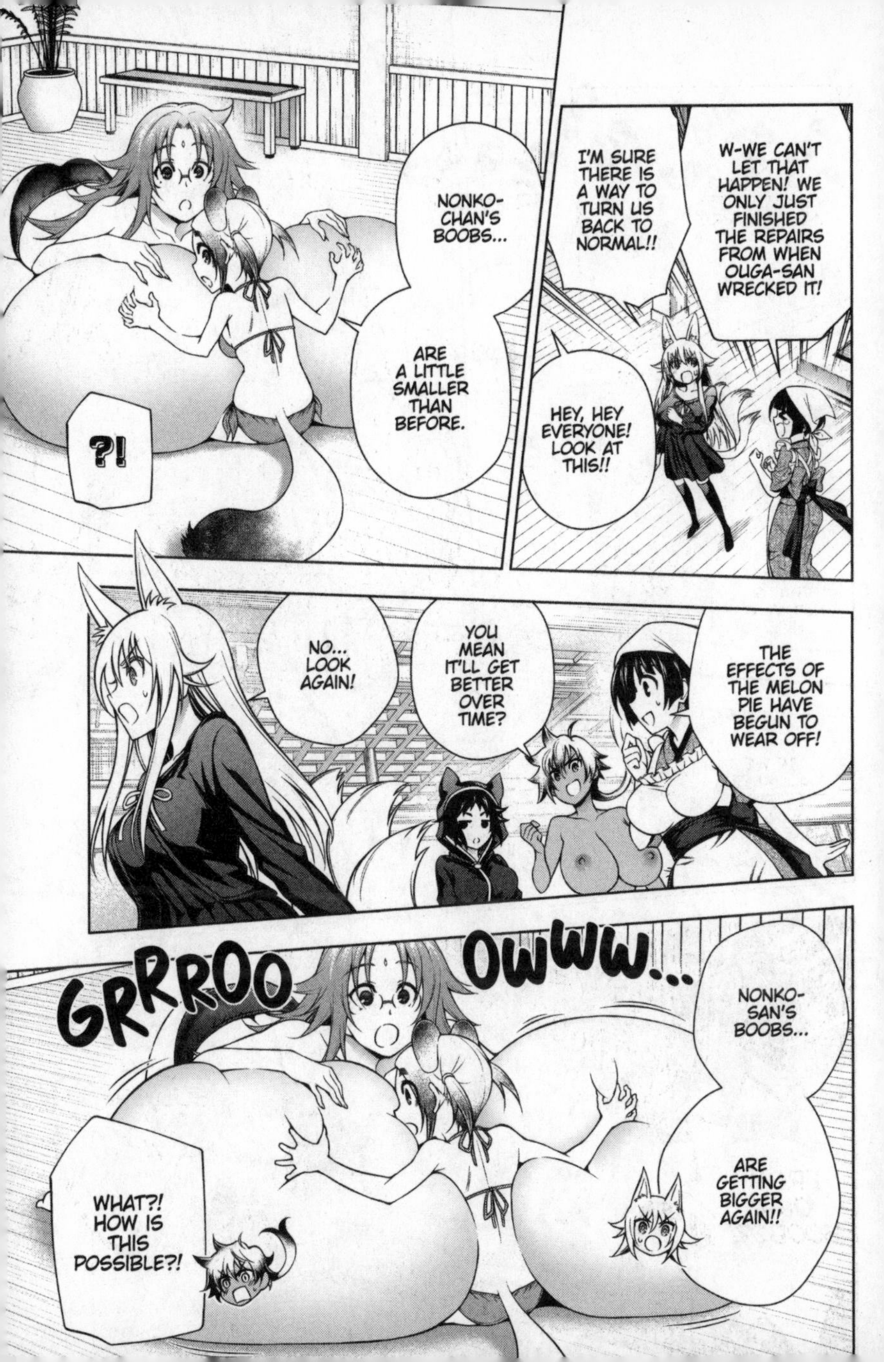
W-WE CAN'T LET THAT HAPPEN! WE ONLY JUST FINISHED THE REPAIRS FROM WHEN OUGA-SAN WRECKED IT!
I'M SURE THERE IS A WAY TO TURN US BACK TO NORMAL!!
HEY, HEY EVERYONE! LOOK AT THIS!!
NONKO-CHAN'S BOOBS...
ARE A LITTLE SMALLER THAN BEFORE.
?!
THE EFFECTS OF THE MELON PIE HAVE BEGUN TO WEAR OFF!
YOU MEAN IT'LL GET BETTER OVER TIME?
NO... LOOK AGAIN!
NONKO-SAN'S BOOBS...
ARE GETTING BIGGER AGAIN!!
GRRROO OWWW...
WHAT?! HOW IS THIS POSSIBLE?!

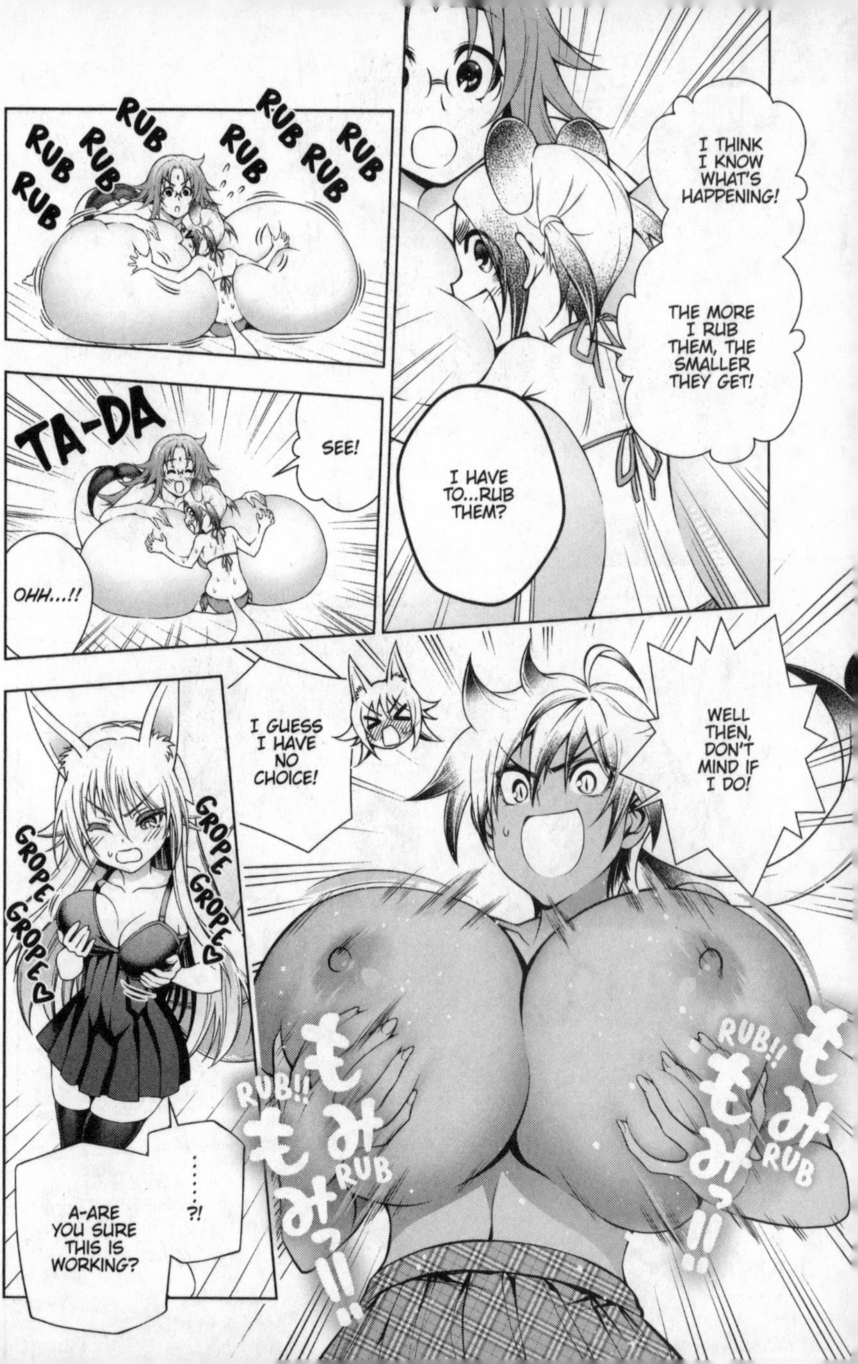
I THINK I KNOW WHAT'S HAPPENING!
THE MORE I RUB THEM, THE SMALLER THEY GET!
I HAVE TO...RUB THEM?
RUB RUB RUB RUB RUB RUB RUB RUB
TA-DA
SEE!
OHH...!!
WELL THEN, DON'T MIND IF I DO!
I GUESS I HAVE NO CHOICE!
RUB!! RUB
もみもみっ!!
RUB!! RUB
もみもみっ!!
GROPE GROPE GROPE GROPE♡
......?!
A-ARE YOU SURE THIS IS WORKING?

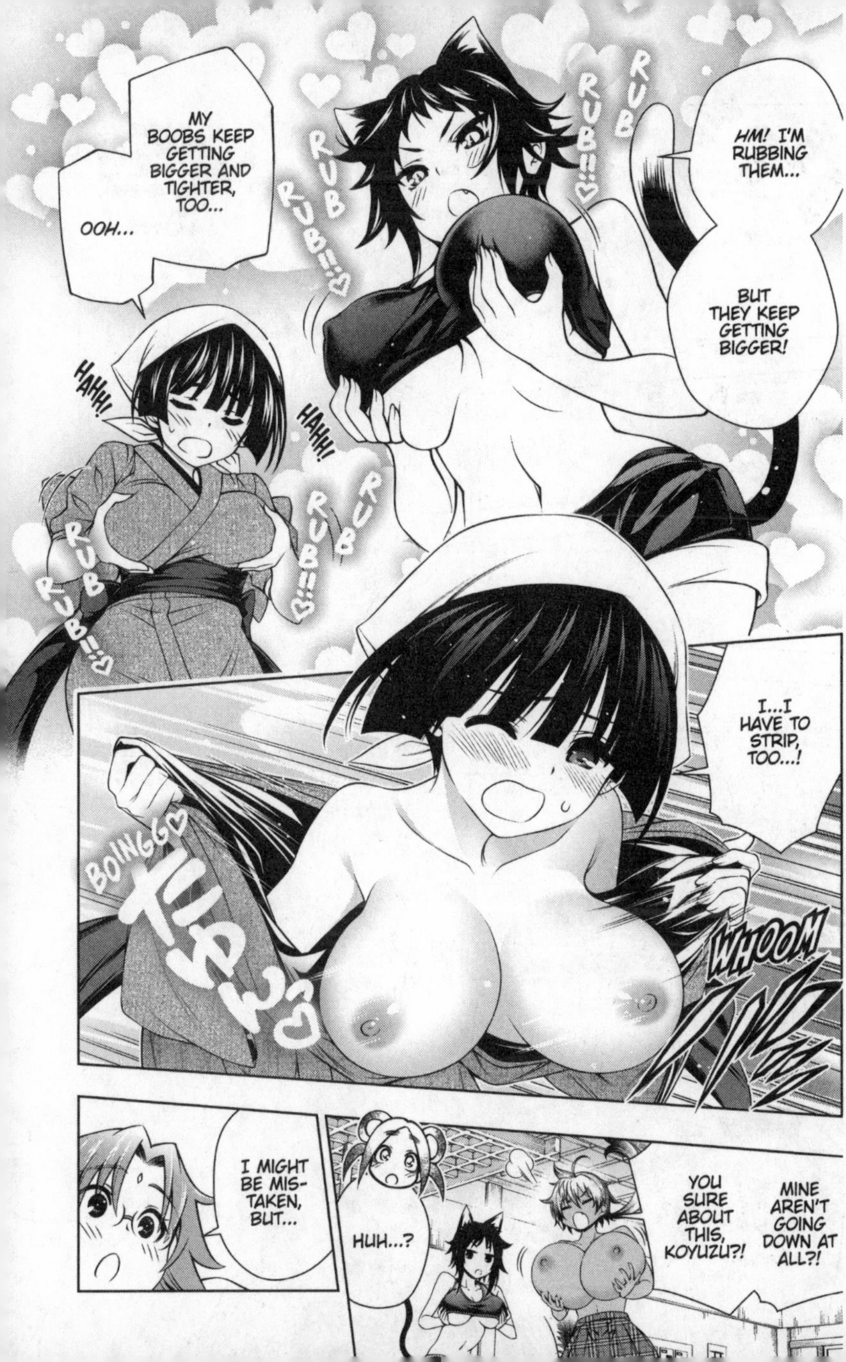
HM! I'M RUBBING THEM...
BUT THEY KEEP GETTING BIGGER!
RUB RUB!!♡
RUB RUB!!♡
MY BOOBS KEEP GETTING BIGGER AND TIGHTER, TOO...
OOH...
HAHH!
HAHH!
RUB RUB!!♡
RUB RUB!!♡
I...I HAVE TO STRIP, TOO...!
WHOOM
BOINGG♡
MINE AREN'T GOING DOWN AT ALL?!
YOU SURE ABOUT THIS, KOYUZU?!
HUH...?
I MIGHT BE MIS-TAKEN, BUT...

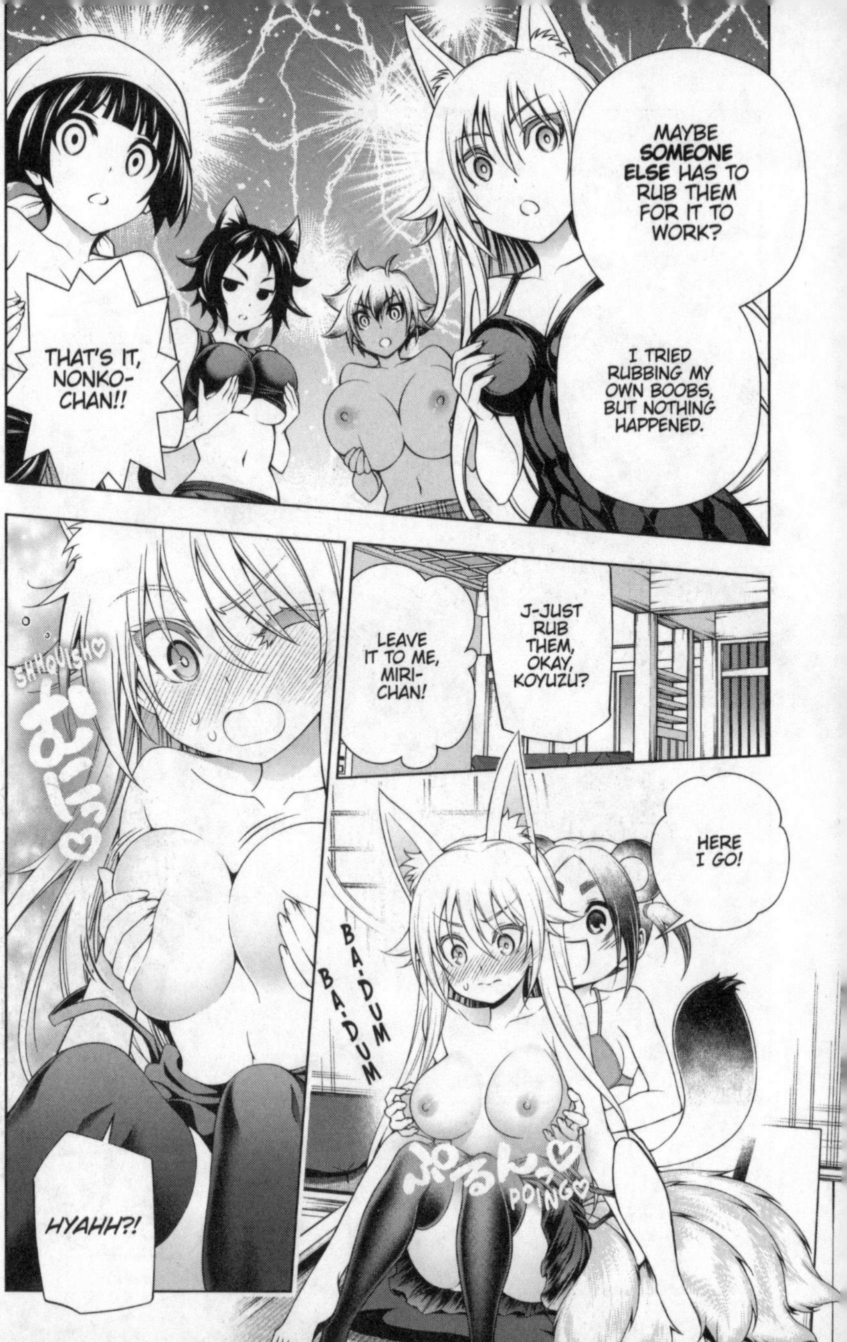
MAYBE SOMEONE ELSE HAS TO RUB THEM FOR IT TO WORK?
I TRIED RUBBING MY OWN BOOBS, BUT NOTHING HAPPENED.
THAT'S IT, NONKO-CHAN!!
J-JUST RUB THEM, OKAY, KOYUZU?
LEAVE IT TO ME, MIRI-CHAN!
HERE I GO!
BA-DUM BA-DUM
ぷるんっ
POING
SHHQUISH
HYAHH?!

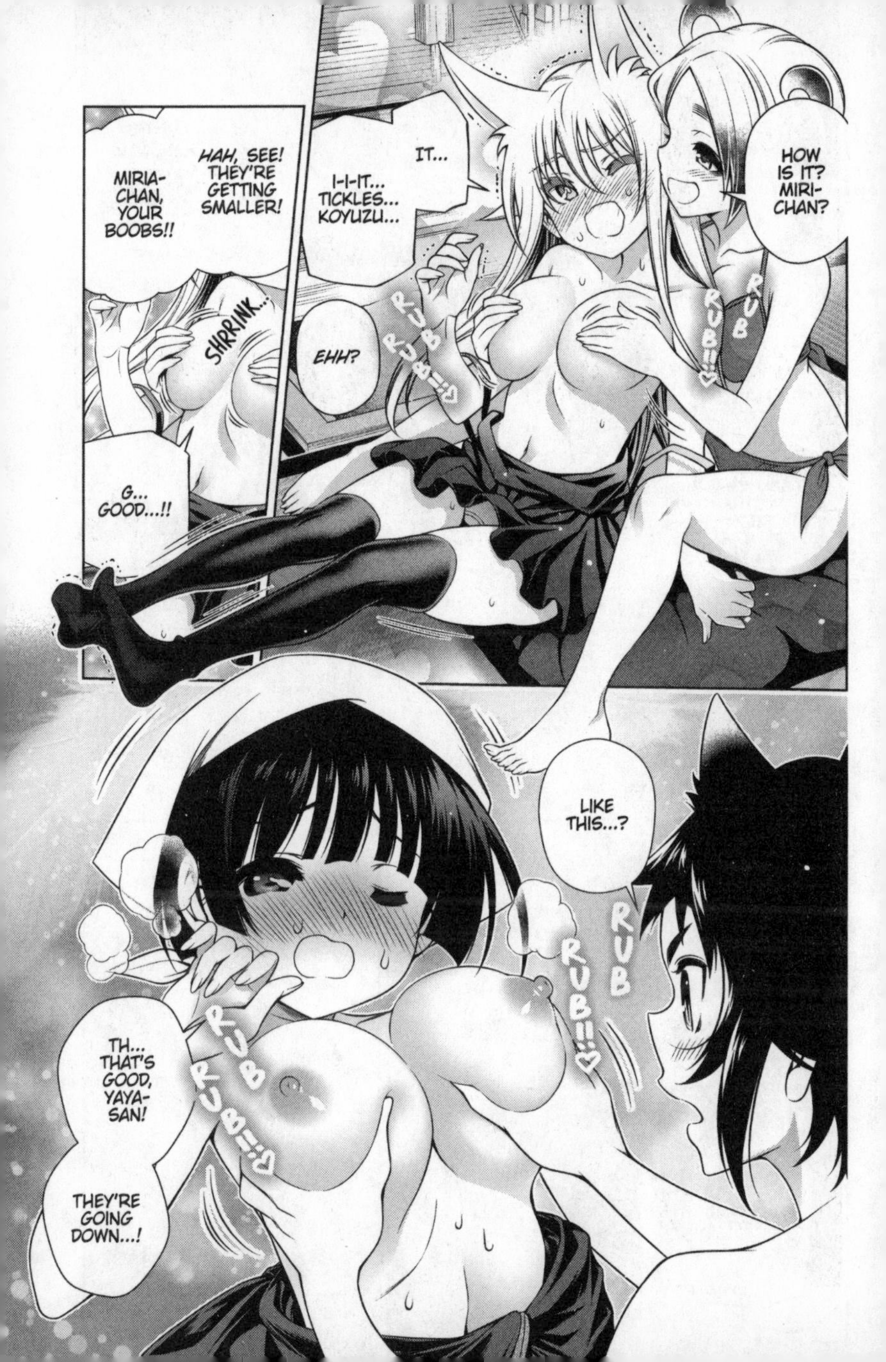
HOW IS IT? MIRI-CHAN?
RUB RUB!!♡
IT...
I-I-IT... TICKLES... KOYUZU...
RUB RUB!!♡
EHH?
HAH, SEE! THEY'RE GETTING SMALLER!
MIRIA-CHAN, YOUR BOOBS!!
SHRRINK...
G... GOOD...!!
LIKE THIS...?
RUB RUB!!♡
TH... THAT'S GOOD, YAYA-SAN!
RUB RUB!!♡
THEY'RE GOING DOWN...!

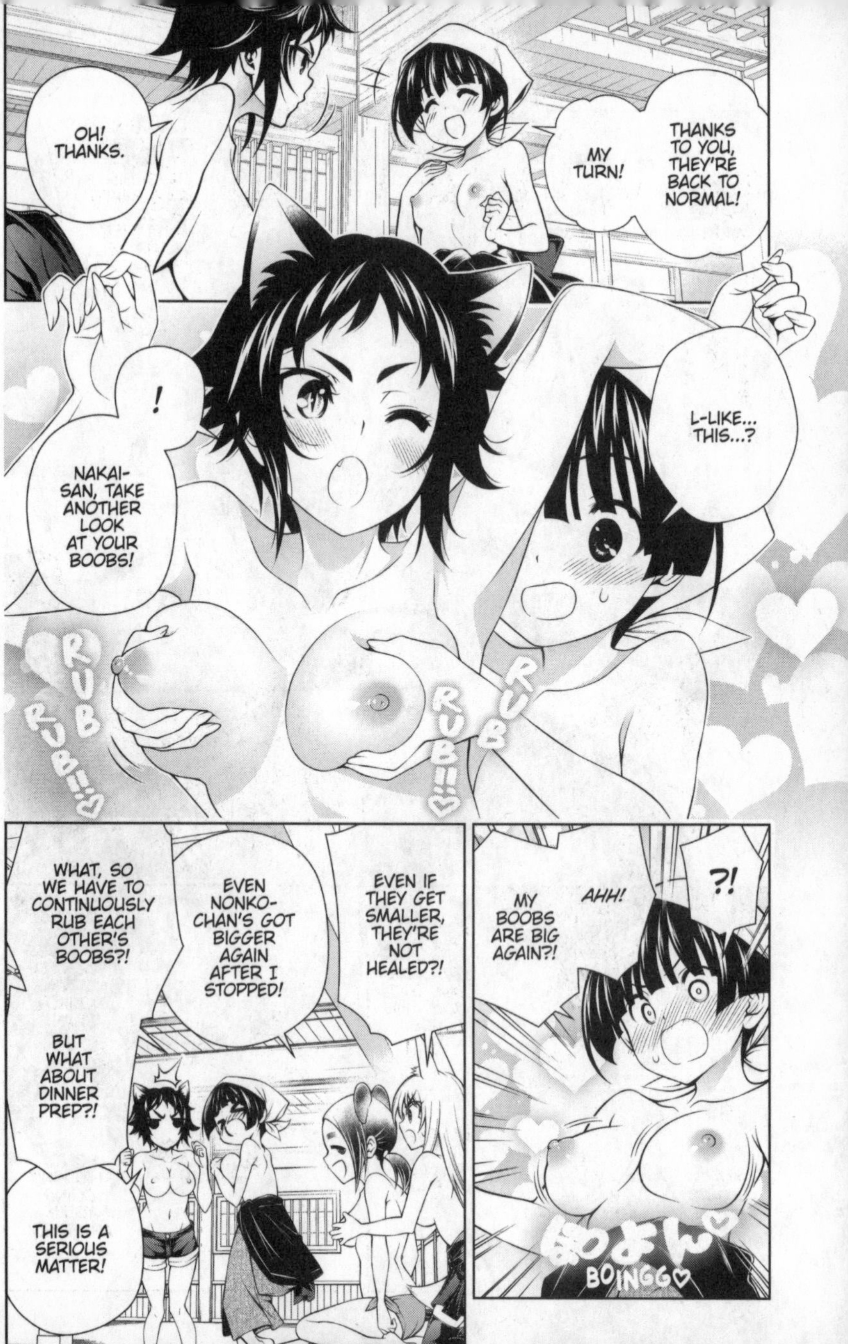
THANKS TO YOU, THEY'RE BACK TO NORMAL!
MY TURN!
OH! THANKS.
L-LIKE... THIS...?
!
NAKAI-SAN, TAKE ANOTHER LOOK AT YOUR BOOBS!
RUB RUB!!♡
RUB RUB!!♡
?!
AHH!
MY BOOBS ARE BIG AGAIN?!
ぽよん♡
BOINGG♡
EVEN IF THEY GET SMALLER, THEY'RE NOT HEALED?!
EVEN NONKO-CHAN'S GOT BIGGER AGAIN AFTER I STOPPED!
WHAT, SO WE HAVE TO CONTINUOUSLY RUB EACH OTHER'S BOOBS?!
BUT WHAT ABOUT DINNER PREP?!
THIS IS A SERIOUS MATTER!

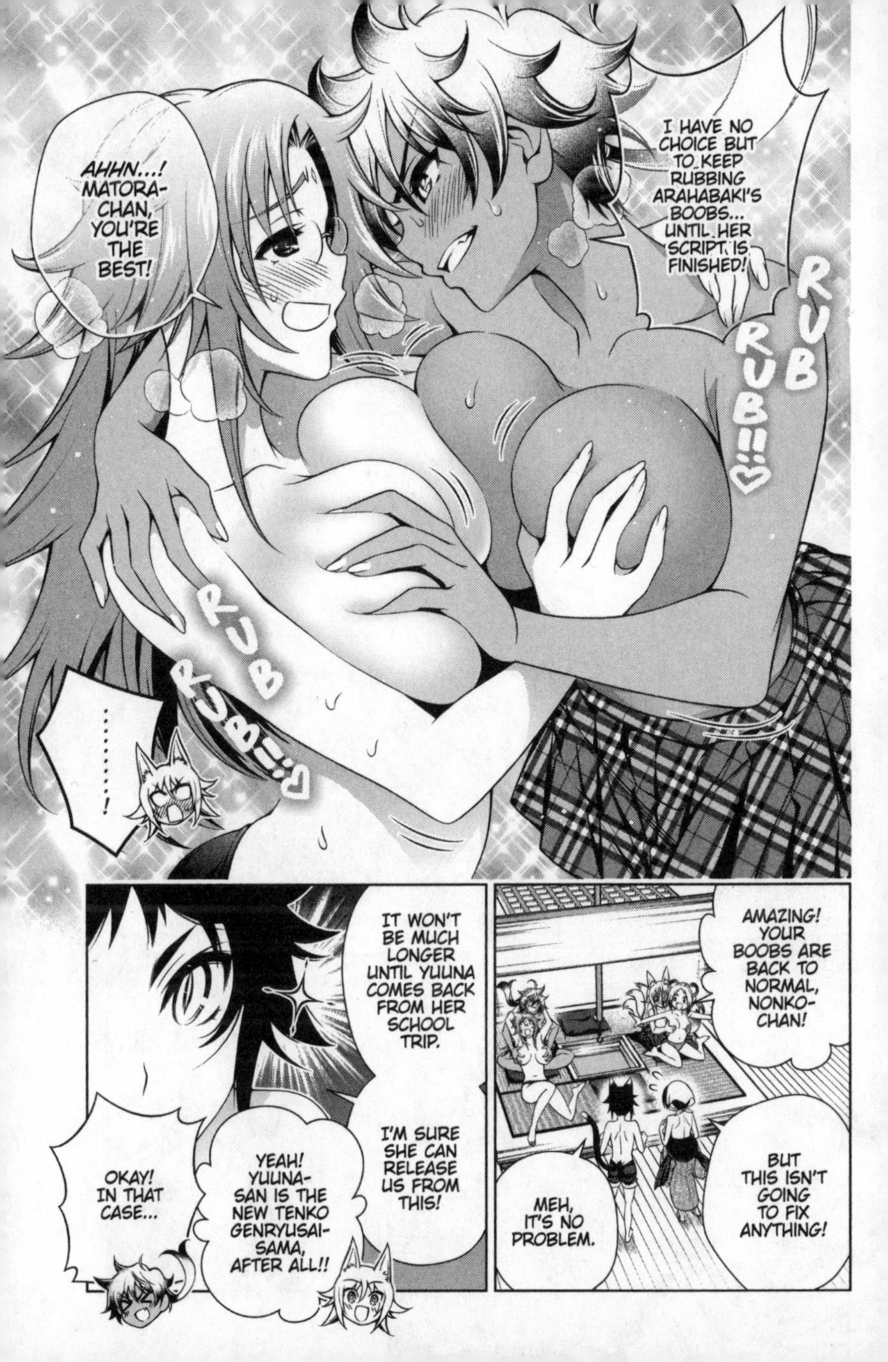
I HAVE NO CHOICE BUT TO KEEP RUBBING ARAHABAKI'S BOOBS... UNTIL HER SCRIPT IS FINISHED!
RUB RUB!!♥
AHHN...! MATORA-CHAN, YOU'RE THE BEST!
RUB RUB!!♥
......!
AMAZING! YOUR BOOBS ARE BACK TO NORMAL, NONKO-CHAN!
BUT THIS ISN'T GOING TO FIX ANYTHING!
MEH, IT'S NO PROBLEM.
IT WON'T BE MUCH LONGER UNTIL YUUNA COMES BACK FROM HER SCHOOL TRIP.
I'M SURE SHE CAN RELEASE US FROM THIS!
YEAH! YUUNA-SAN IS THE NEW TENKO GENRYUSAI-SAMA, AFTER ALL!!
OKAY! IN THAT CASE...

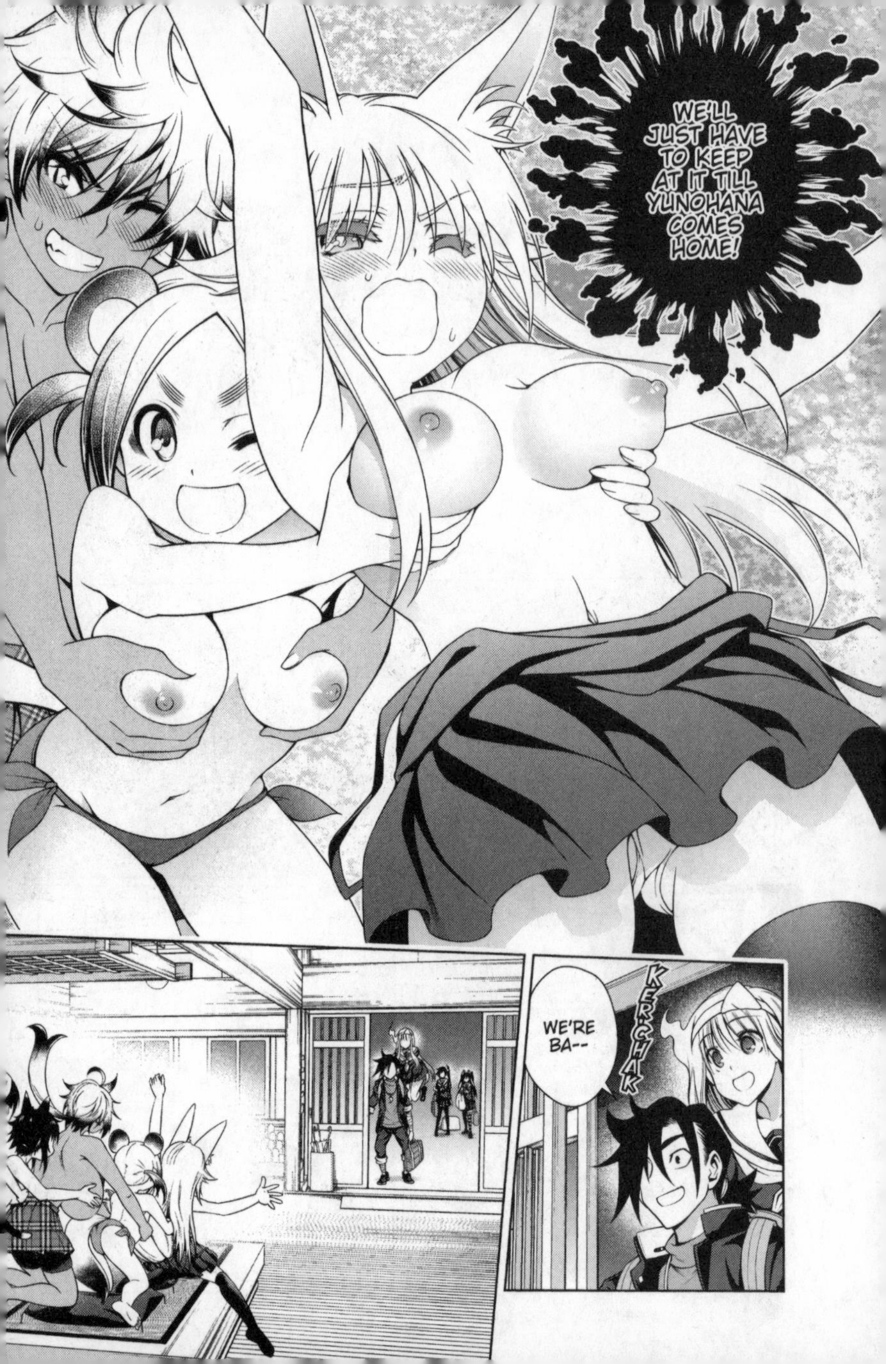
WE'LL JUST HAVE TO KEEP AT IT TILL YUNOHANA COMES HOME!
WE'RE BA--
KERCHAK

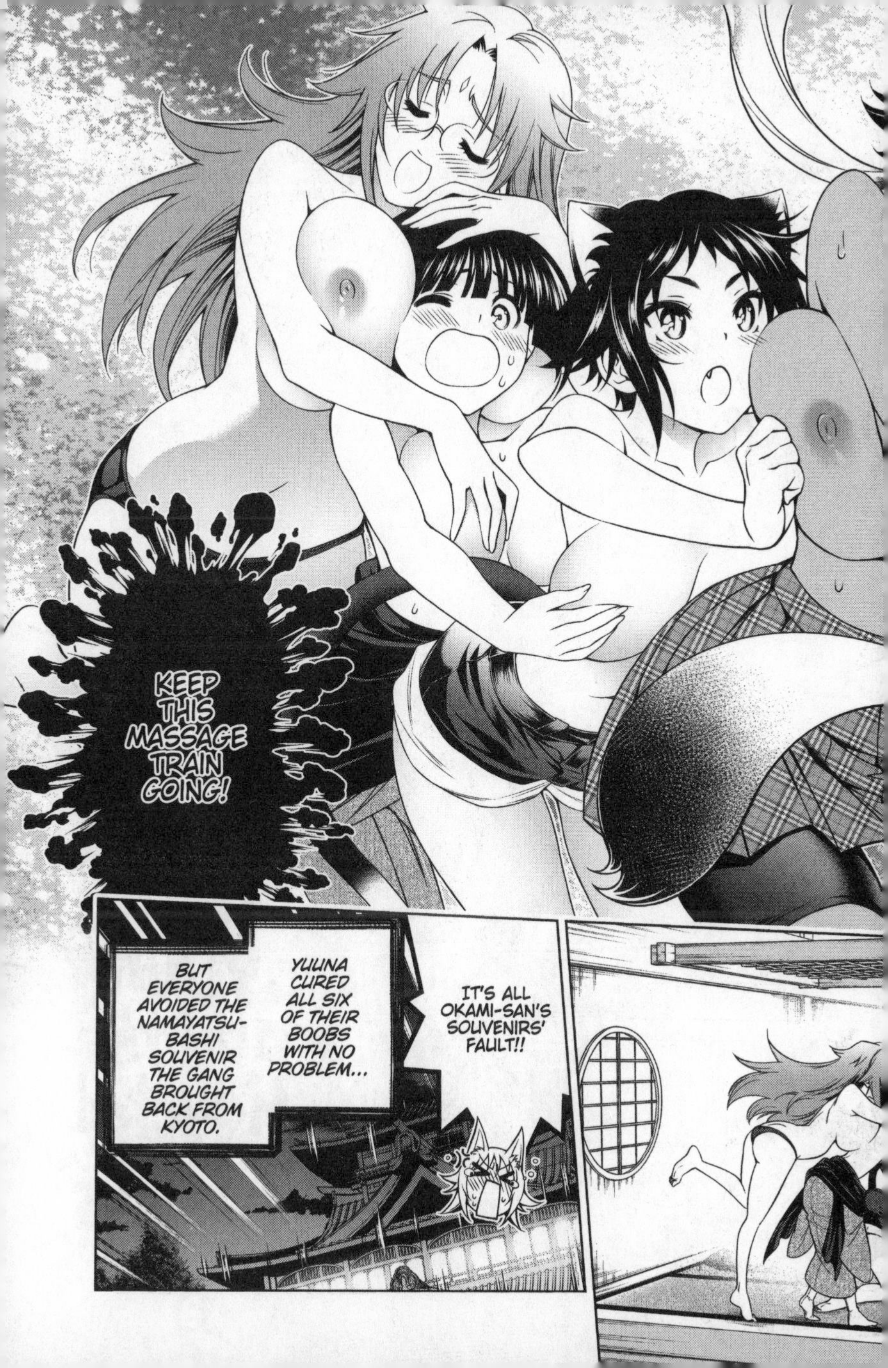
KEEP THIS MASSAGE TRAIN GOING!
IT'S ALL OKAMI-SAN'S SOUVENIRS' FAULT!!
YUUNA CURED ALL SIX OF THEIR BOOBS WITH NO PROBLEM...
BUT EVERYONE AVOIDED THE NAMAYATSU-BASHI SOUVENIR THE GANG BROUGHT BACK FROM KYOTO.

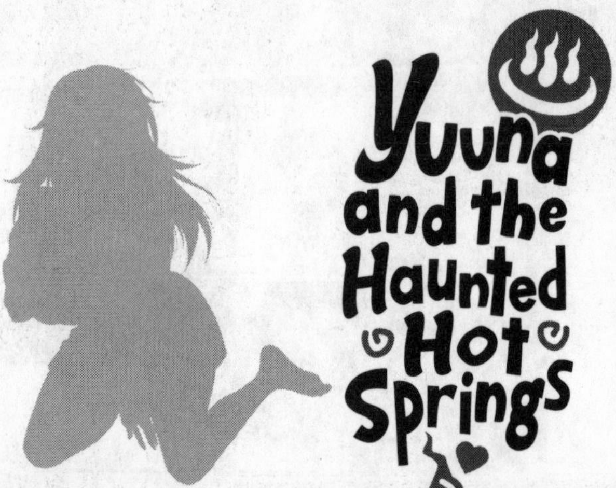

Yuuna and the Haunted Hot Springs

151 The Seven Wonders of Yukemuri High School: Report Part 2

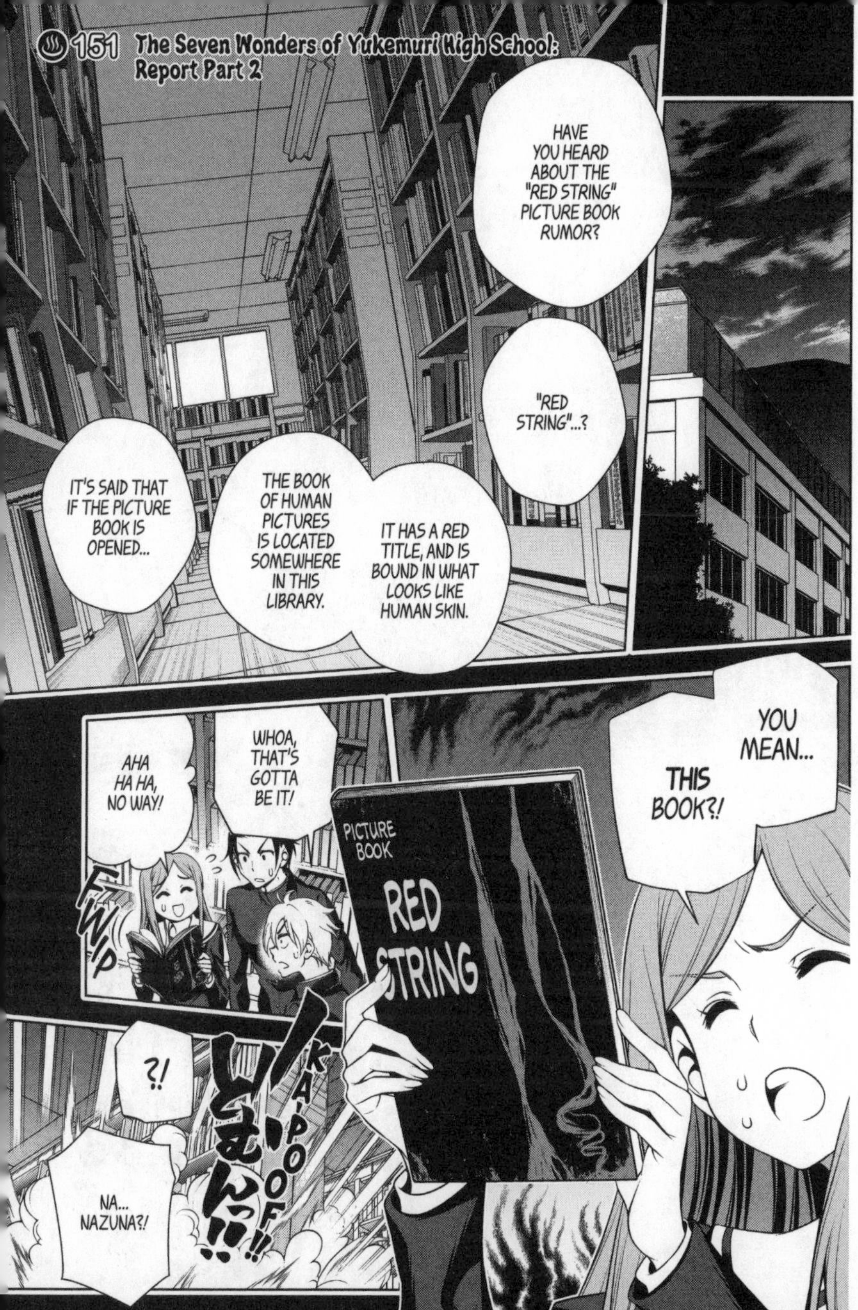
HAVE YOU HEARD ABOUT THE "RED STRING" PICTURE BOOK RUMOR?
"RED STRING"...?
IT HAS A RED TITLE, AND IS BOUND IN WHAT LOOKS LIKE HUMAN SKIN.
THE BOOK OF HUMAN PICTURES IS LOCATED SOMEWHERE IN THIS LIBRARY.
IT'S SAID THAT IF THE PICTURE BOOK IS OPENED...
YOU MEAN... THIS BOOK?!
PICTURE BOOK
RED STRING
WHOA, THAT'S GOTTA BE IT!
AHA HA HA, NO WAY!
FWIP
KA-POOF!!
どむんっ!!
?!
NA... NAZUNA?!

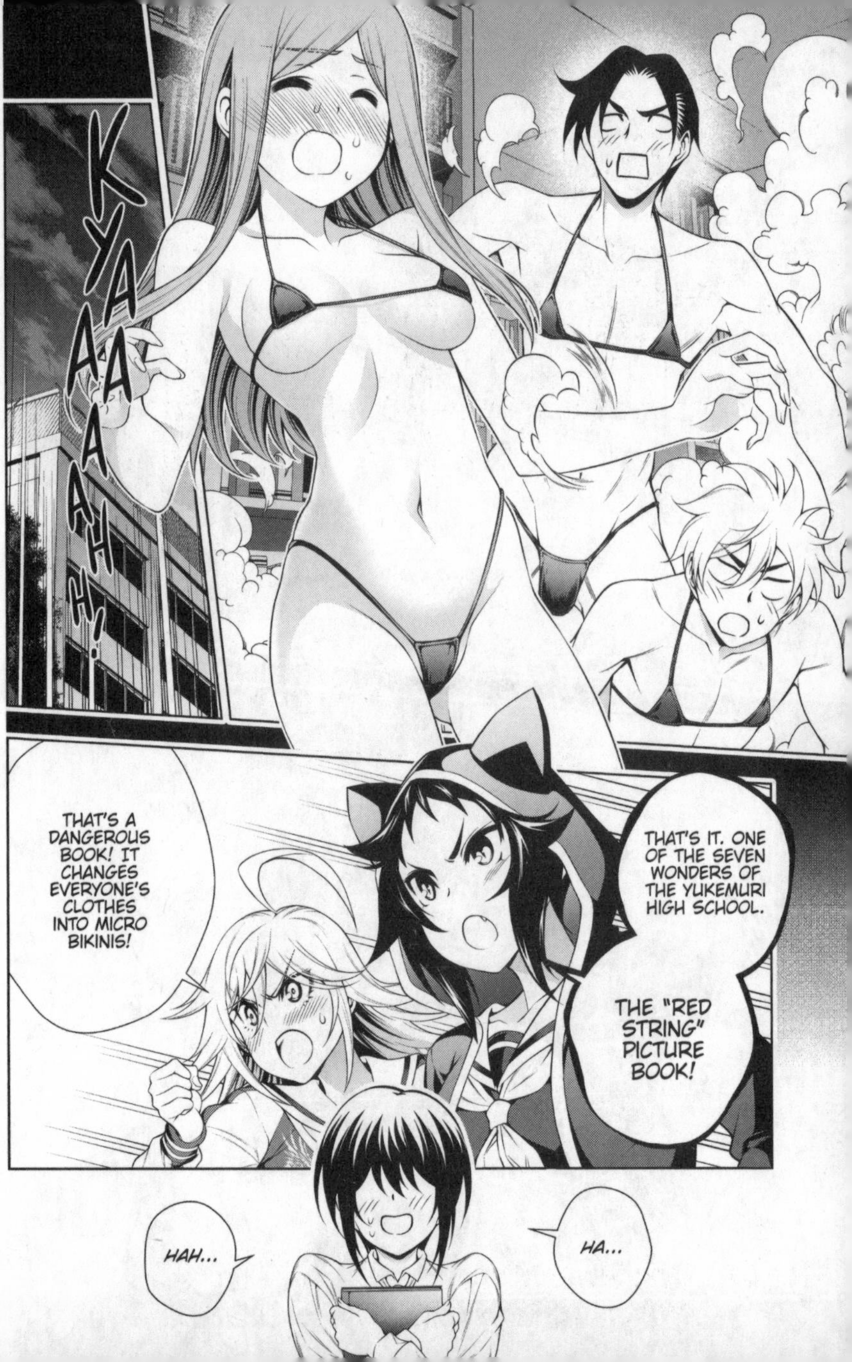
KYAAAAAAHH!
THAT'S IT. ONE OF THE SEVEN WONDERS OF THE YUKEMURI HIGH SCHOOL.
THE "RED STRING" PICTURE BOOK!
THAT'S A DANGEROUS BOOK! IT CHANGES EVERYONE'S CLOTHES INTO MICRO BIKINIS!
HA...
HAH...

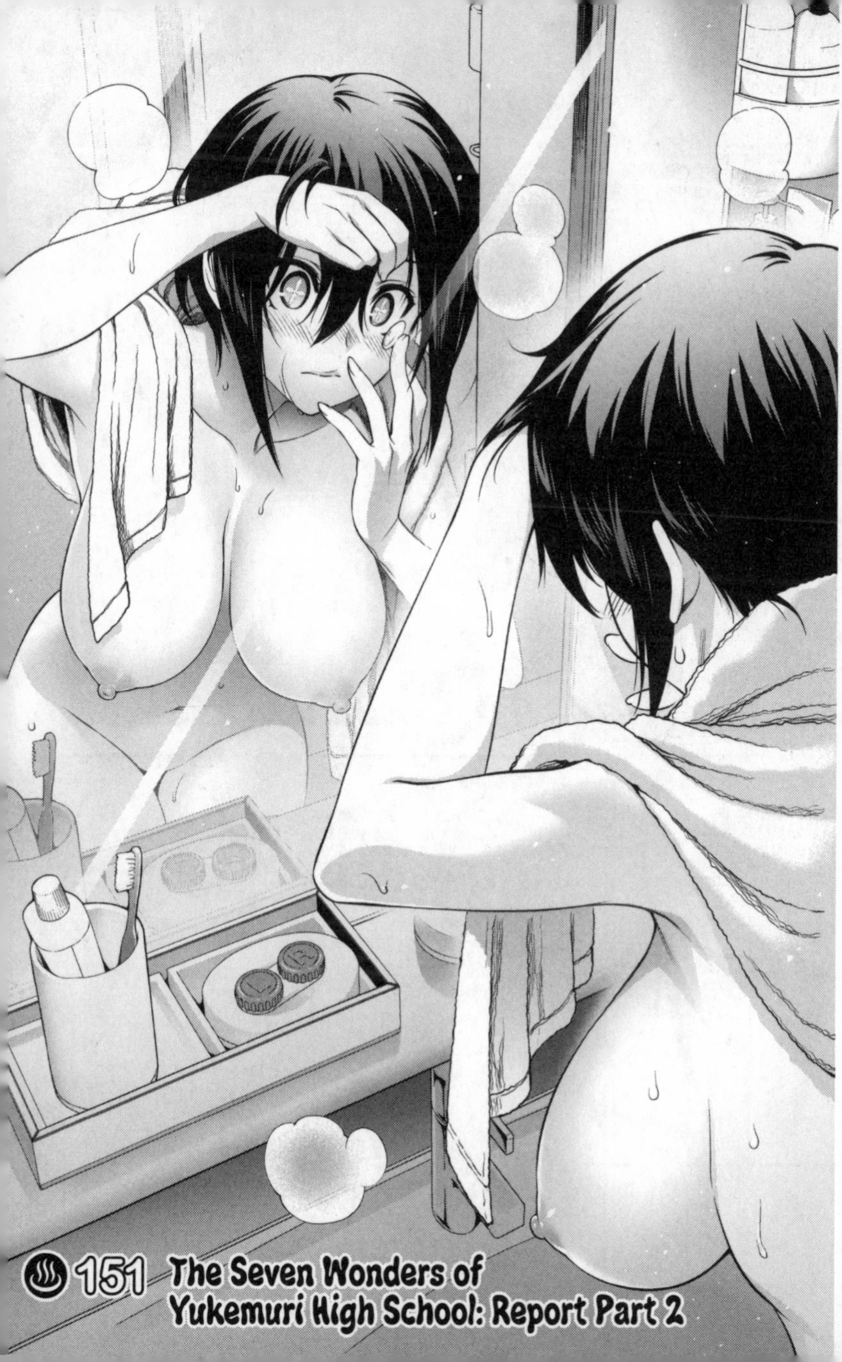

151 The Seven Wonders of Yukemuri High School: Report Part 2

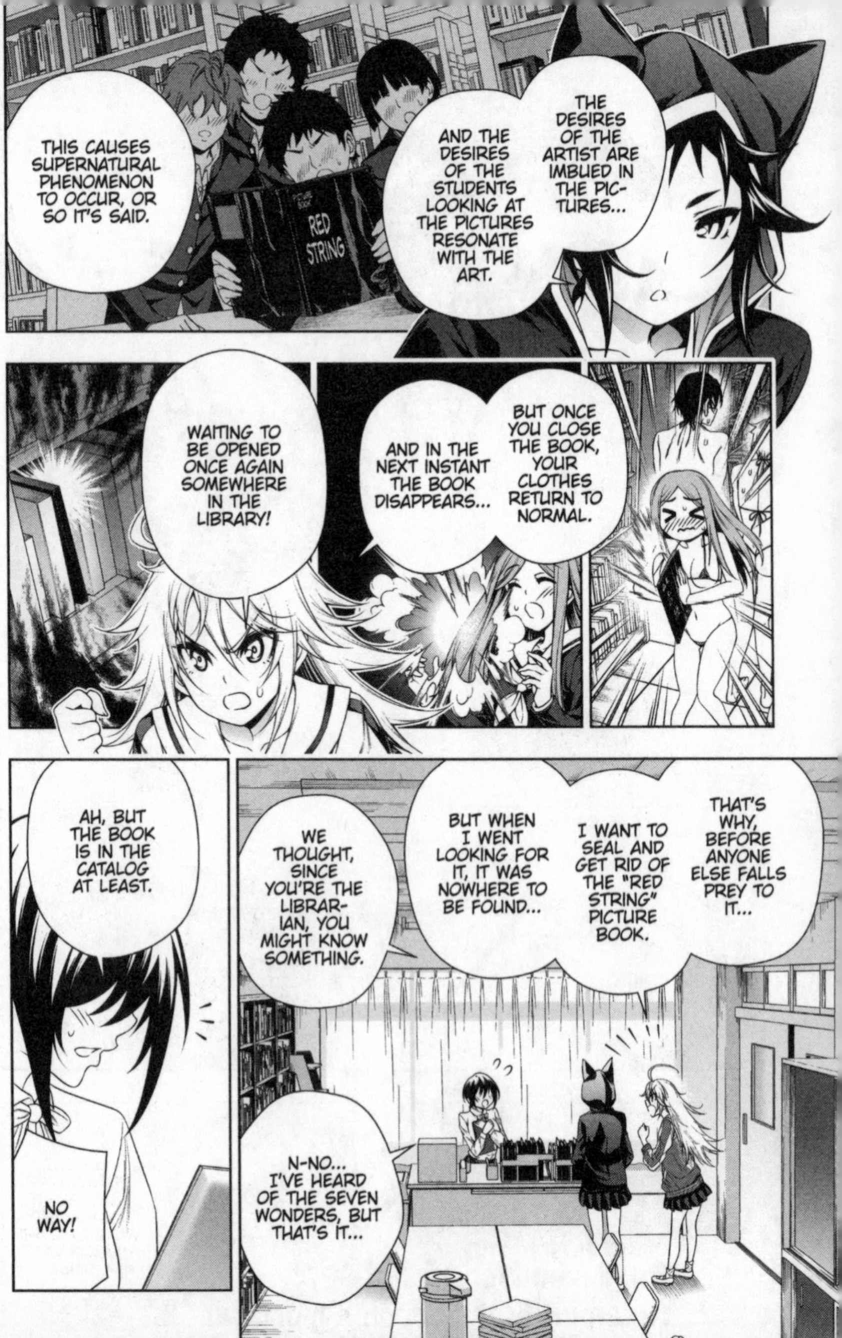
THE DESIRES OF THE ARTIST ARE IMBUED IN THE PICTURES...
AND THE DESIRES OF THE STUDENTS LOOKING AT THE PICTURES RESONATE WITH THE ART.
PICTURE BOOK
RED STRING
THIS CAUSES SUPERNATURAL PHENOMENON TO OCCUR, OR SO IT'S SAID.
BUT ONCE YOU CLOSE THE BOOK, YOUR CLOTHES RETURN TO NORMAL.
AND IN THE NEXT INSTANT THE BOOK DISAPPEARS...
WAITING TO BE OPENED ONCE AGAIN SOMEWHERE IN THE LIBRARY!
THAT'S WHY, BEFORE ANYONE ELSE FALLS PREY TO IT...
I WANT TO SEAL AND GET RID OF THE "RED STRING" PICTURE BOOK.
BUT WHEN I WENT LOOKING FOR IT, IT WAS NOWHERE TO BE FOUND...
WE THOUGHT, SINCE YOU'RE THE LIBRARIAN, YOU MIGHT KNOW SOMETHING.
N-NO... I'VE HEARD OF THE SEVEN WONDERS, BUT THAT'S IT...
AH, BUT THE BOOK IS IN THE CATALOG AT LEAST.
NO WAY!

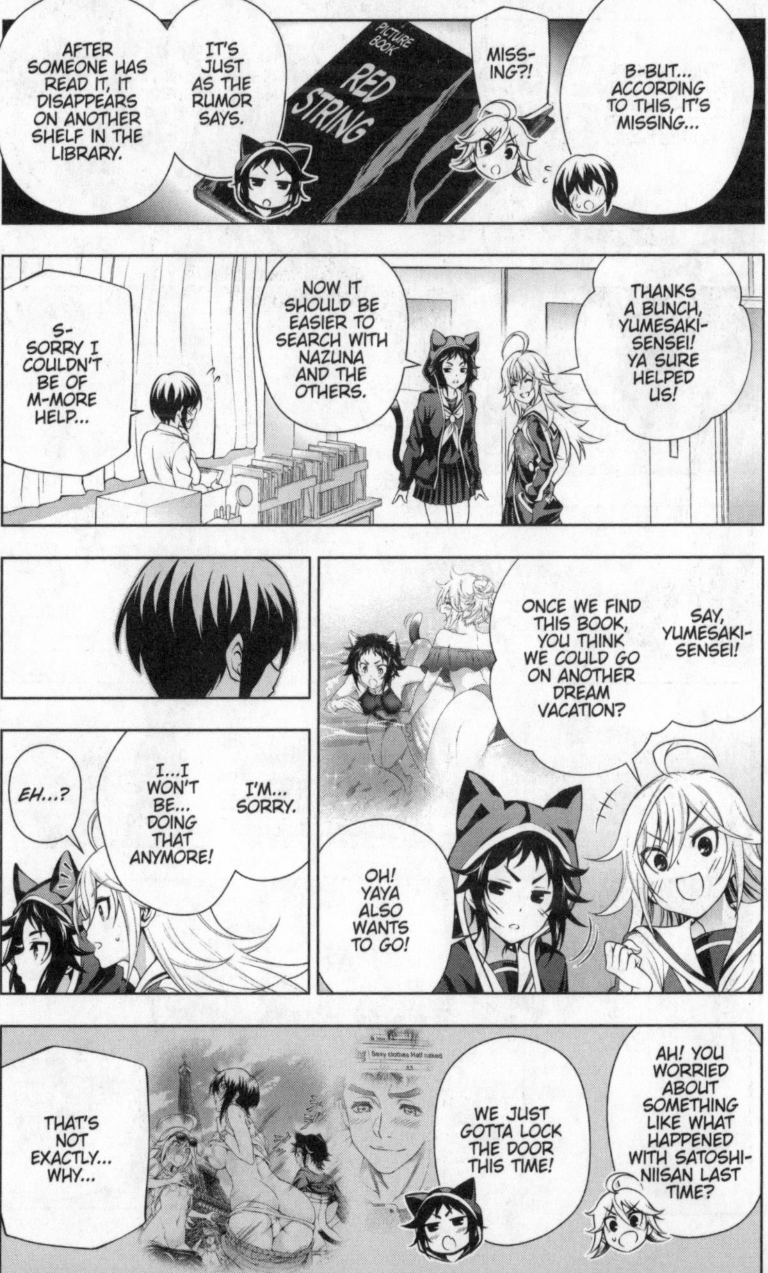
B-BUT... ACCORDING TO THIS, IT'S MISSING...
MISS-ING?!
PICTURE BOOK
RED STRING
IT'S JUST AS THE RUMOR SAYS.
AFTER SOMEONE HAS READ IT, IT DISAPPEARS ON ANOTHER SHELF IN THE LIBRARY.
THANKS A BUNCH, YUMESAKI-SENSEI! YA SURE HELPED US!
NOW IT SHOULD BE EASIER TO SEARCH WITH NAZUNA AND THE OTHERS.
S-SORRY I COULDN'T BE OF M-MORE HELP...
SAY, YUMESAKI-SENSEI!
ONCE WE FIND THIS BOOK, YOU THINK WE COULD GO ON ANOTHER DREAM VACATION?
OH! YAYA ALSO WANTS TO GO!
I'M... SORRY.
I...I WON'T BE... DOING THAT ANYMORE!
EH...?
AH! YOU WORRIED ABOUT SOMETHING LIKE WHAT HAPPENED WITH SATOSHI-NIISAN LAST TIME?
WE JUST GOTTA LOCK THE DOOR THIS TIME!
Sexy clothes Half naked
THAT'S NOT EXACTLY... WHY...

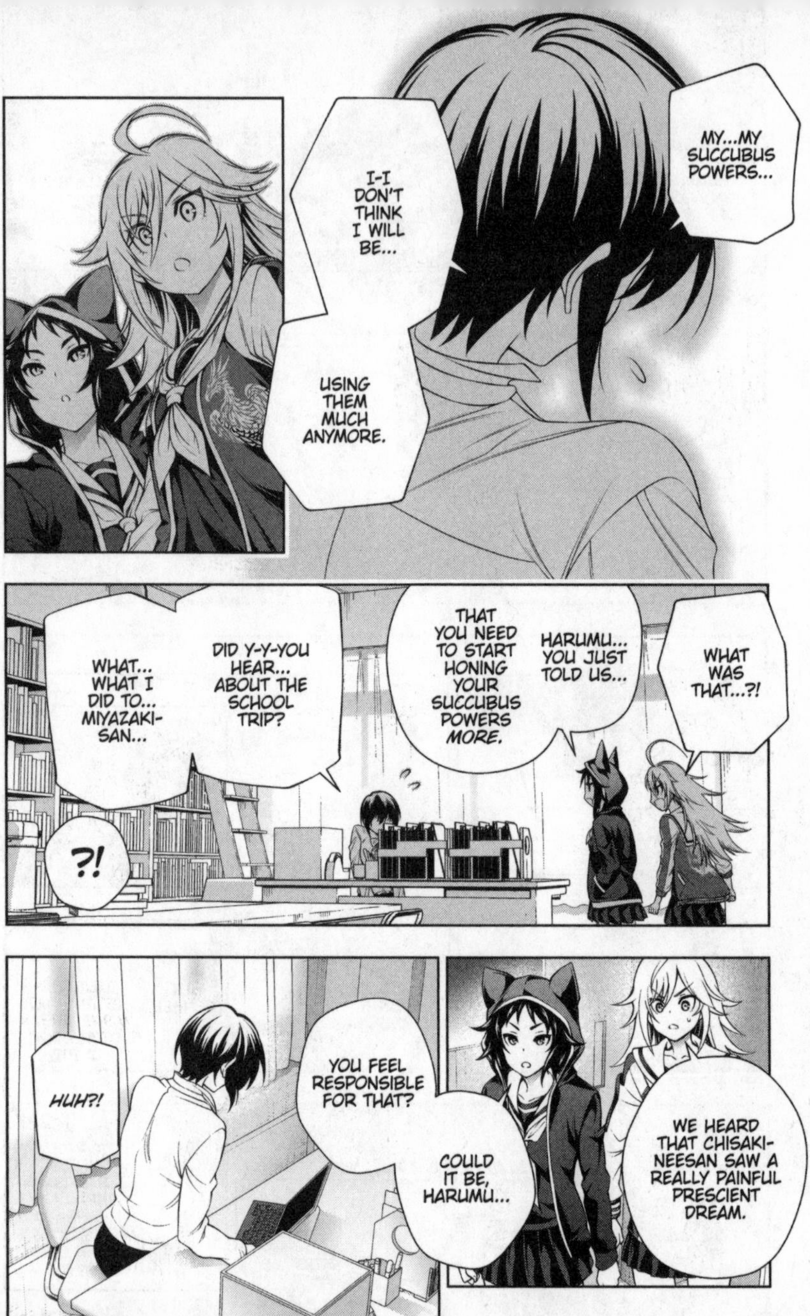
MY...MY SUCCUBUS POWERS...
I-I DON'T THINK I WILL BE...
USING THEM MUCH ANYMORE.
WHAT WAS THAT...?!
HARUMU... YOU JUST TOLD US...
THAT YOU NEED TO START HONING YOUR SUCCUBUS POWERS MORE.
DID Y-Y-YOU HEAR... ABOUT THE SCHOOL TRIP?
WHAT... WHAT I DID TO... MIYAZAKI-SAN...
?!
WE HEARD THAT CHISAKI-NEESAN SAW A REALLY PAINFUL PRESCIENT DREAM.
COULD IT BE, HARUMU...
YOU FEEL RESPONSIBLE FOR THAT?
HUH?!

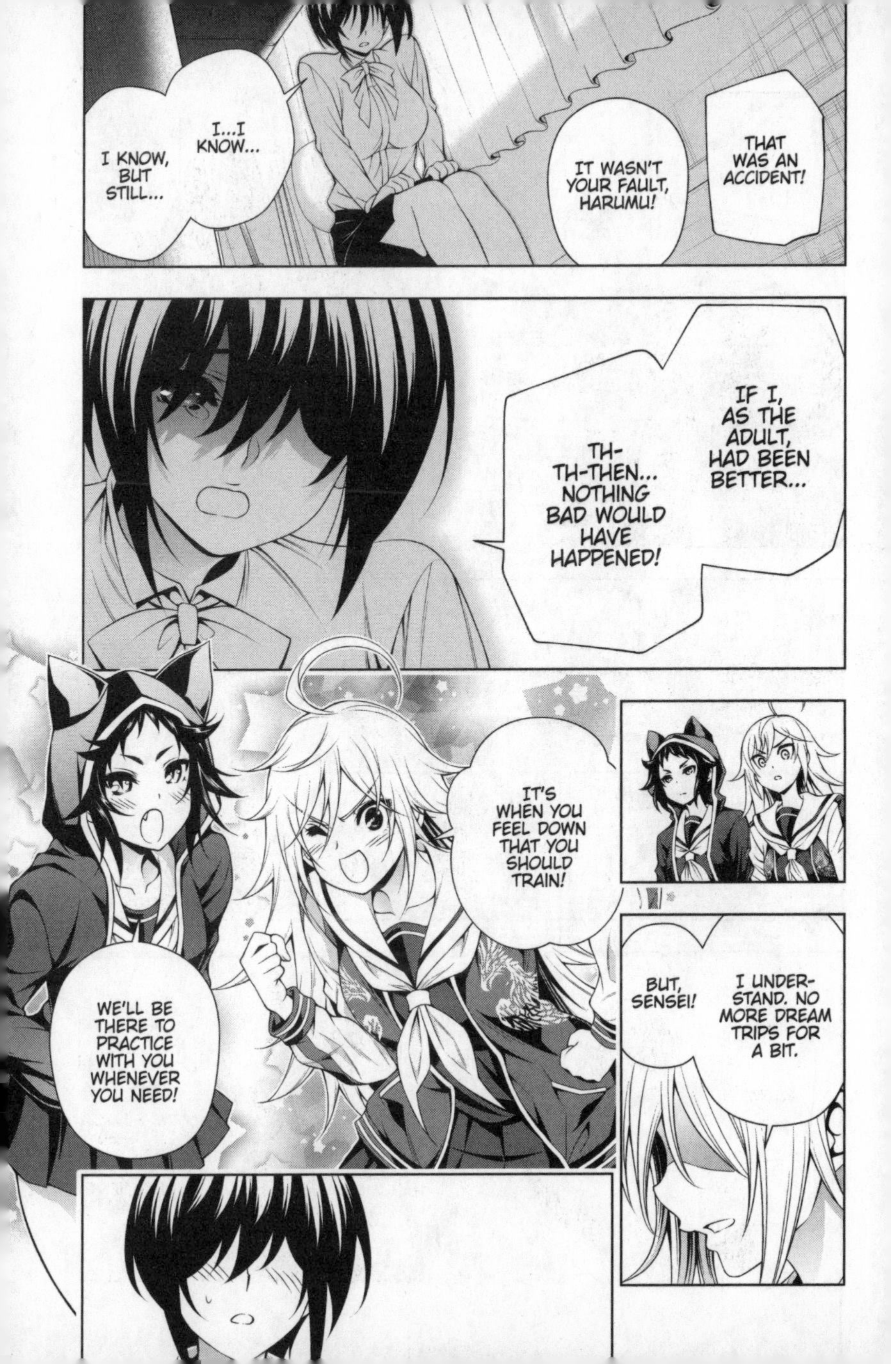
THAT WAS AN ACCIDENT!
IT WASN'T YOUR FAULT, HARUMU!
I...I KNOW...
I KNOW, BUT STILL...
IF I, AS THE ADULT, HAD BEEN BETTER...
TH-TH-THEN... NOTHING BAD WOULD HAVE HAPPENED!
I UNDER-STAND. NO MORE DREAM TRIPS FOR A BIT.
BUT, SENSEI!
IT'S WHEN YOU FEEL DOWN THAT YOU SHOULD TRAIN!
WE'LL BE THERE TO PRACTICE WITH YOU WHENEVER YOU NEED!

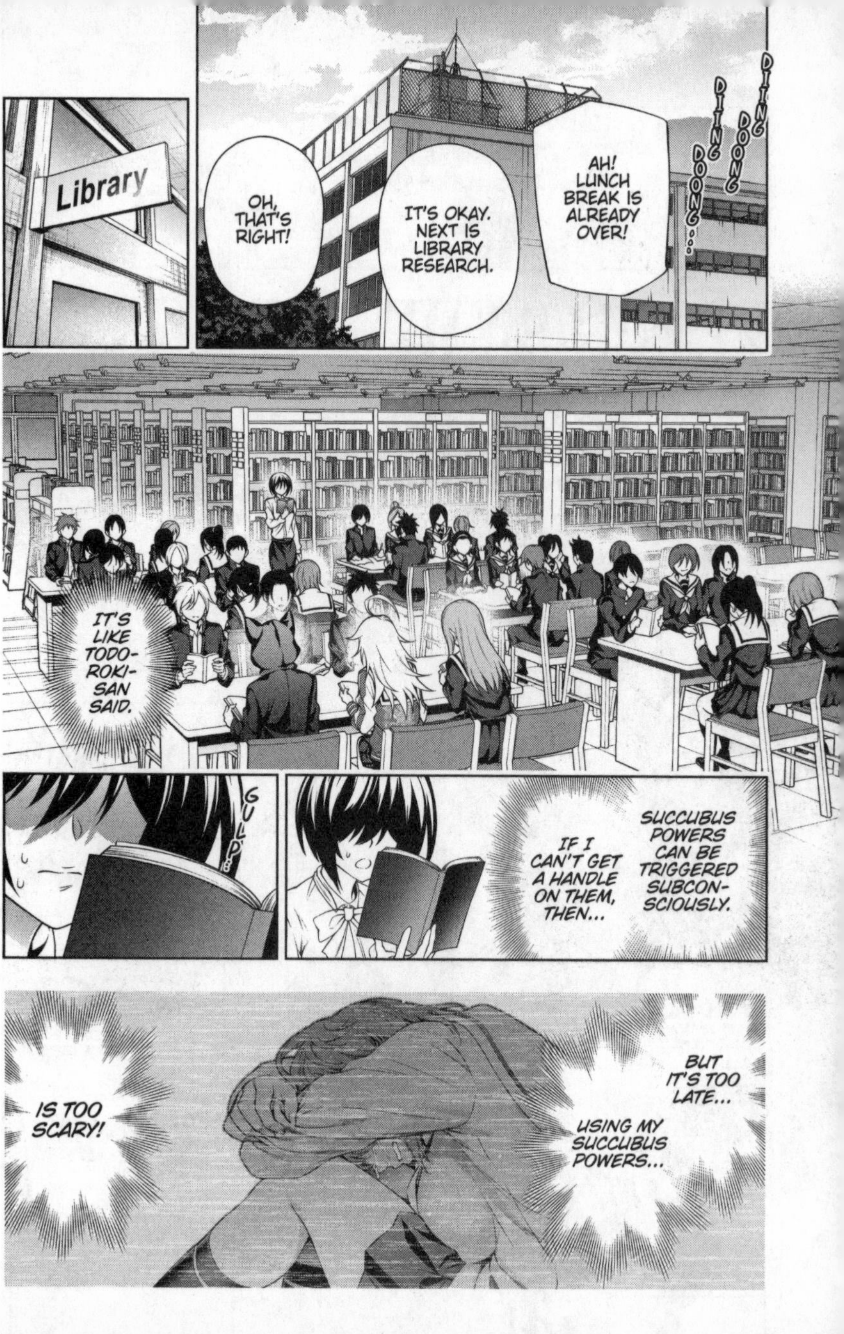
DITING DOONG
DITING DOONG...
AH! LUNCH BREAK IS ALREADY OVER!
IT'S OKAY. NEXT IS LIBRARY RESEARCH.
OH, THAT'S RIGHT!
Library
IT'S LIKE TODOROKI-SAN SAID.
SUCCUBUS POWERS CAN BE TRIGGERED SUBCONSCIOUSLY.
IF I CAN'T GET A HANDLE ON THEM, THEN...
GULP...
BUT IT'S TOO LATE...
USING MY SUCCUBUS POWERS...
IS TOO SCARY!

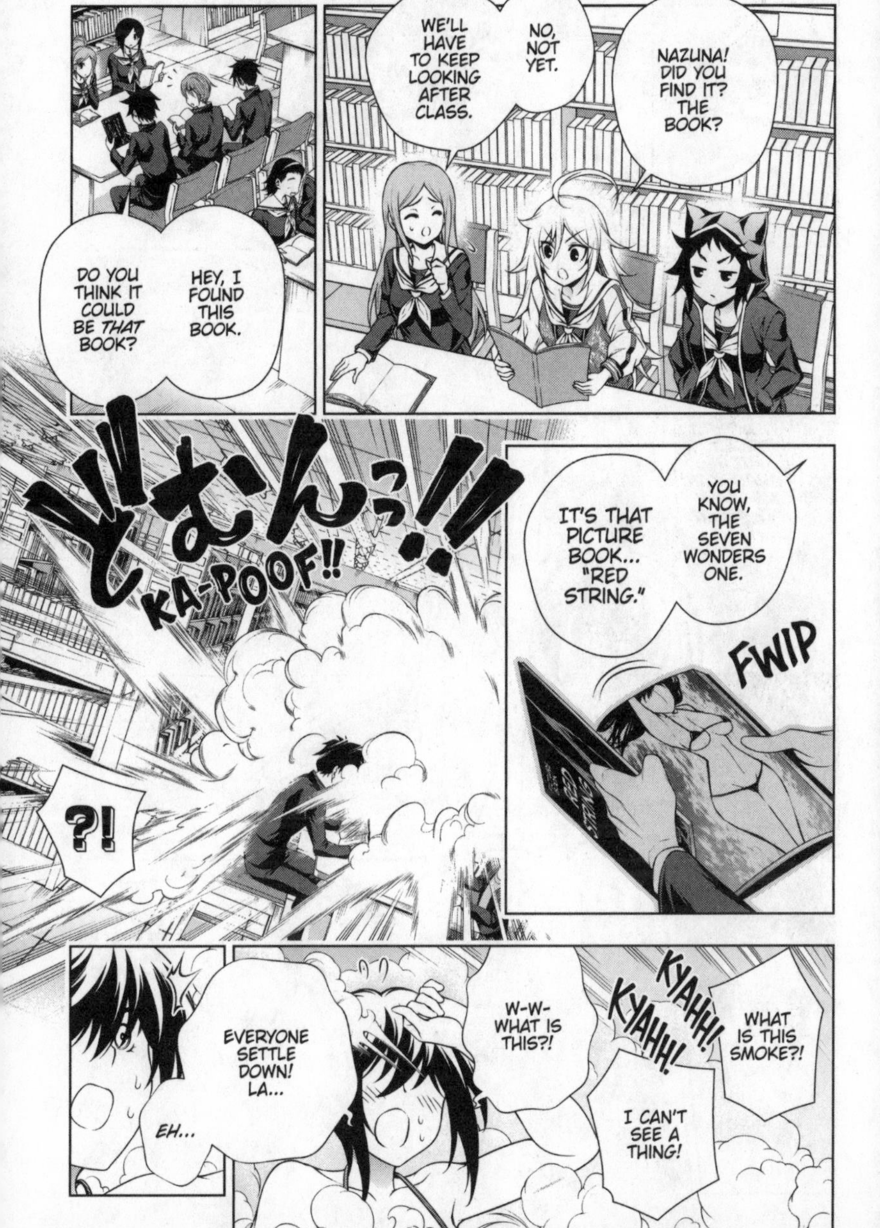
NAZUNA! DID YOU FIND IT? THE BOOK?
NO, NOT YET.
WE'LL HAVE TO KEEP LOOKING AFTER CLASS.
HEY, I FOUND THIS BOOK.
DO YOU THINK IT COULD BE *THAT* BOOK?
YOU KNOW, THE SEVEN WONDERS ONE.
IT'S THAT PICTURE BOOK... "RED STRING."
FWIP
どおんっ!!
KA-POOF!!
?!
WHAT IS THIS SMOKE?!
KYAHH! KYAHH!
I CAN'T SEE A THING!
W-W-WHAT IS THIS?!
EVERYONE SETTLE DOWN! LA...
EH...

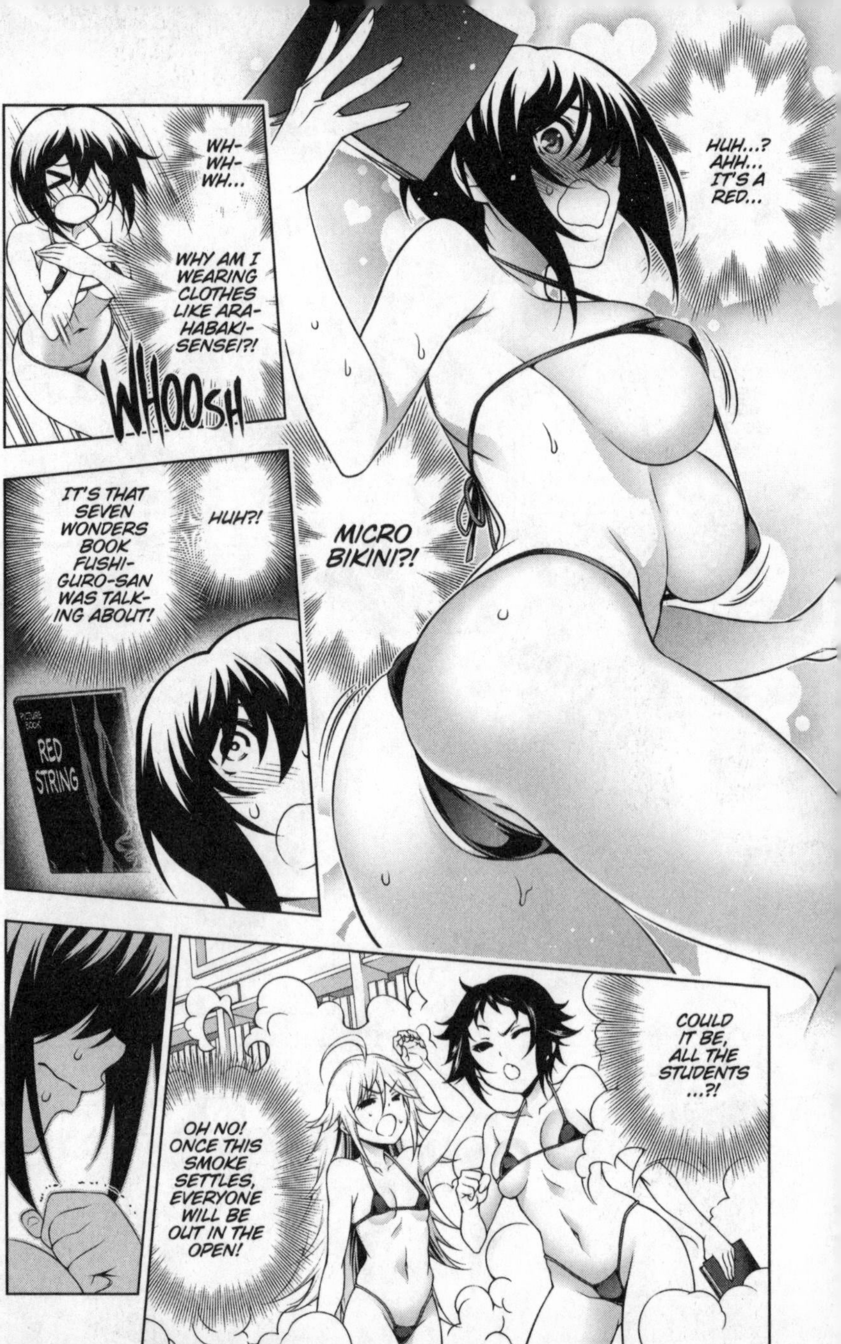
HUH...? AHH... IT'S A RED...
MICRO BIKINI?!
WH-WH-WH...
WHY AM I WEARING CLOTHES LIKE ARAHABAKI-SENSEI?!
WHOOSH
HUH?!
IT'S THAT SEVEN WONDERS BOOK FUSHIGURO-SAN WAS TALKING ABOUT!
PICTURE BOOK
RED STRING
COULD IT BE, ALL THE STUDENTS...?!
OH NO! ONCE THIS SMOKE SETTLES, EVERYONE WILL BE OUT IN THE OPEN!

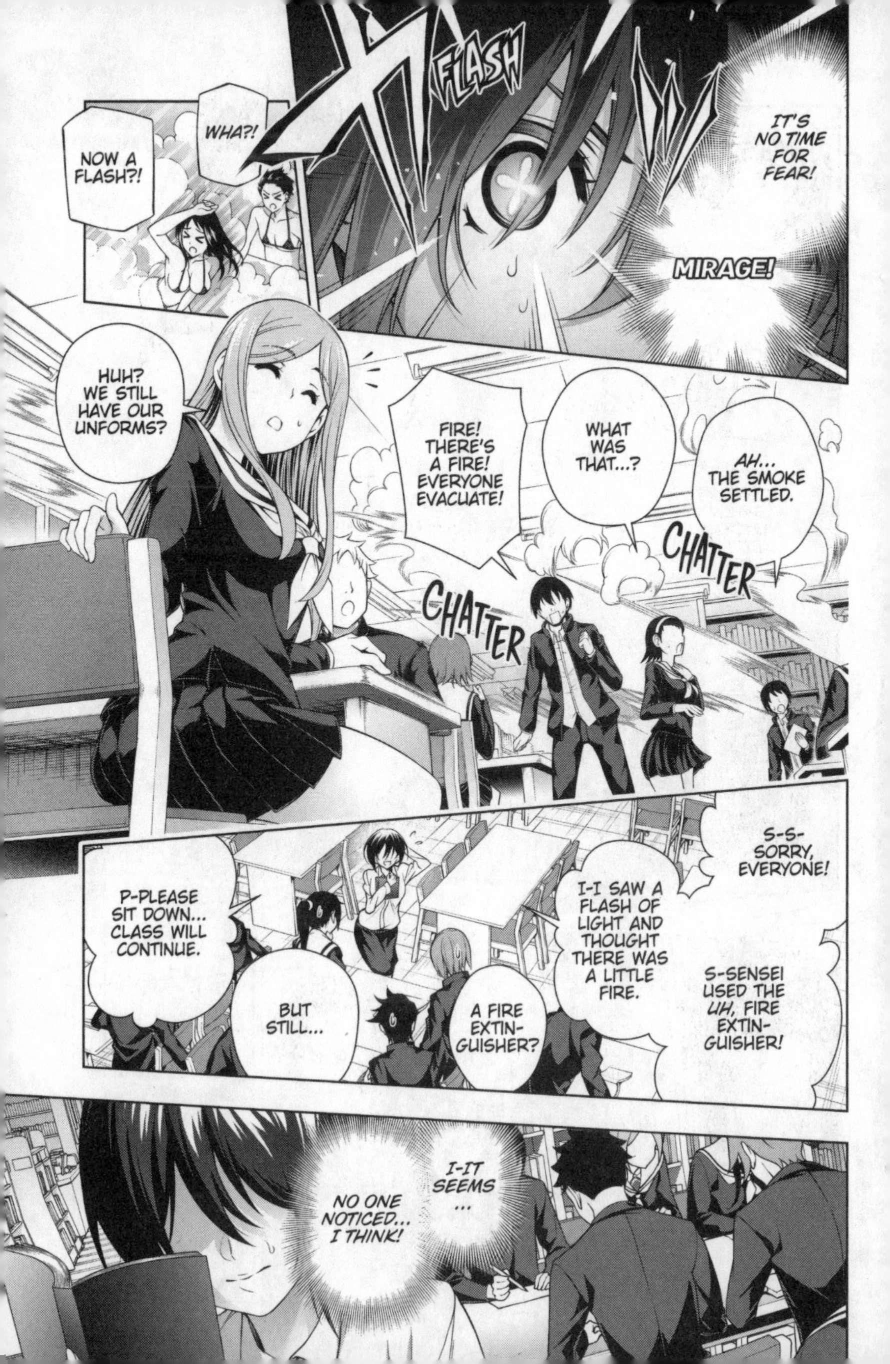
FLASH
IT'S NO TIME FOR FEAR!
MIRAGE!
WHA?!
NOW A FLASH?!
AH... THE SMOKE SETTLED.
CHATTER
WHAT WAS THAT...?
FIRE! THERE'S A FIRE! EVERYONE EVACUATE!
CHATTER
HUH? WE STILL HAVE OUR UNFORMS?
S-S-SORRY, EVERYONE!
I-I SAW A FLASH OF LIGHT AND THOUGHT THERE WAS A LITTLE FIRE.
S-SENSEI USED THE UH, FIRE EXTIN-GUISHER!
A FIRE EXTIN-GUISHER?
BUT STILL...
P-PLEASE SIT DOWN... CLASS WILL CONTINUE.
I-IT SEEMS...
NO ONE NOTICED... I THINK!

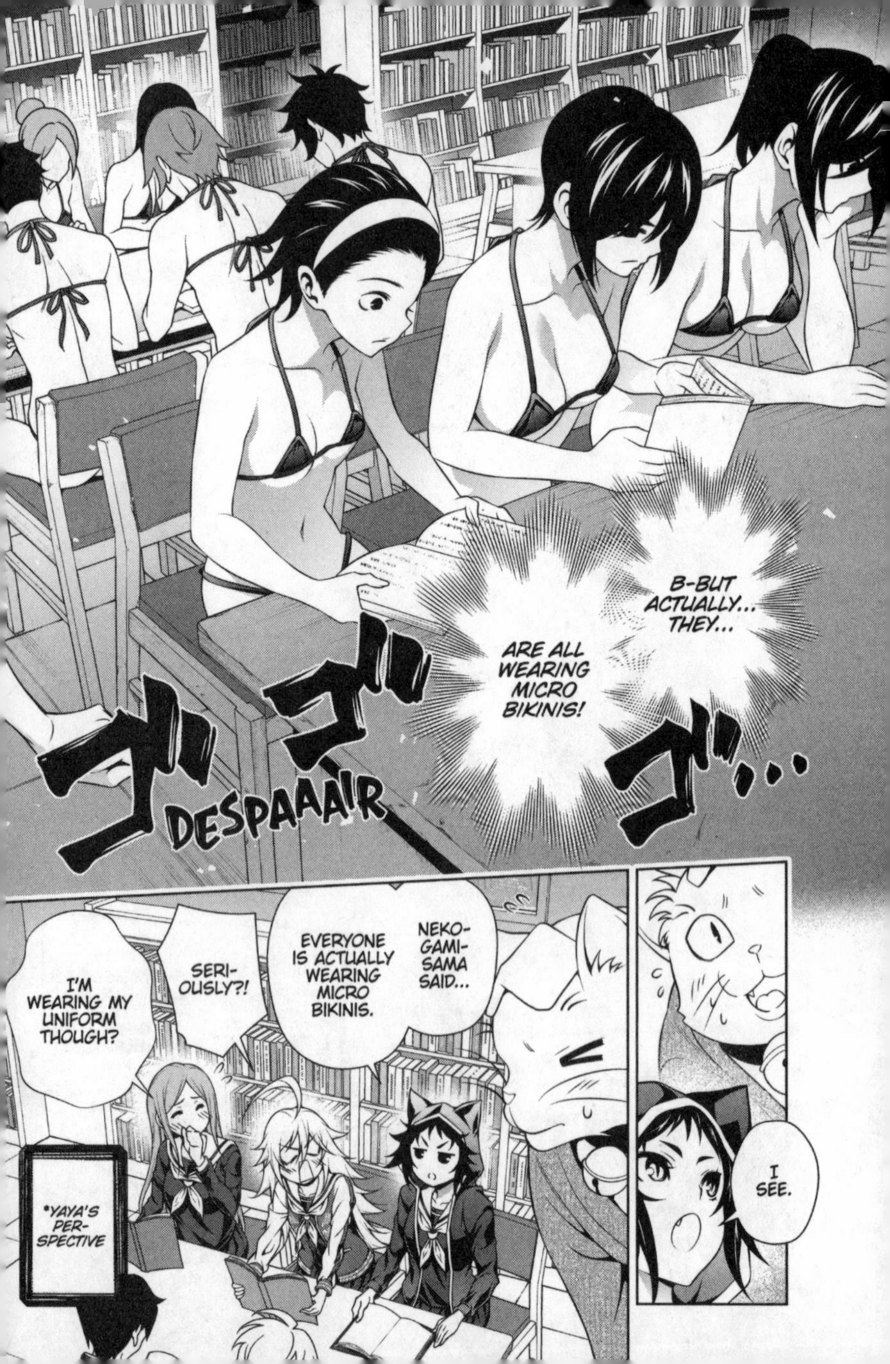
B-BUT ACTUALLY... THEY...
ARE ALL WEARING MICRO BIKINIS!
DESPAAAIR
I SEE.
NEKO-GAMI-SAMA SAID...
EVERYONE IS ACTUALLY WEARING MICRO BIKINIS.
SERI-OUSLY?!
I'M WEARING MY UNIFORM THOUGH?
*YAYA'S PER-SPECTIVE

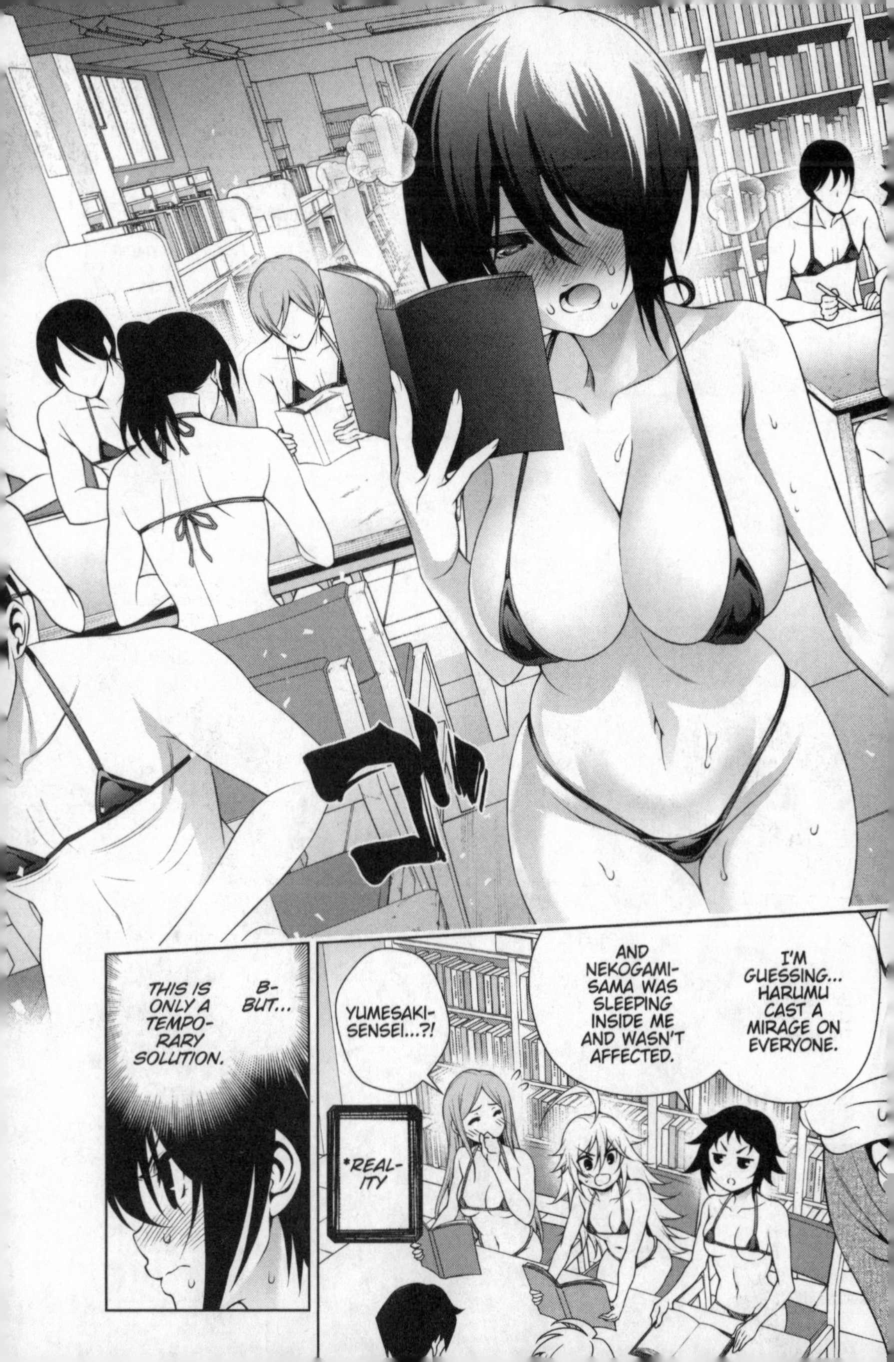
I'M GUESSING... HARUMU CAST A MIRAGE ON EVERYONE.
AND NEKOGAMI-SAMA WAS SLEEPING INSIDE ME AND WASN'T AFFECTED.
YUMESAKI-SENSEI...?!
*REALITY
B-BUT...
THIS IS ONLY A TEMPORARY SOLUTION.

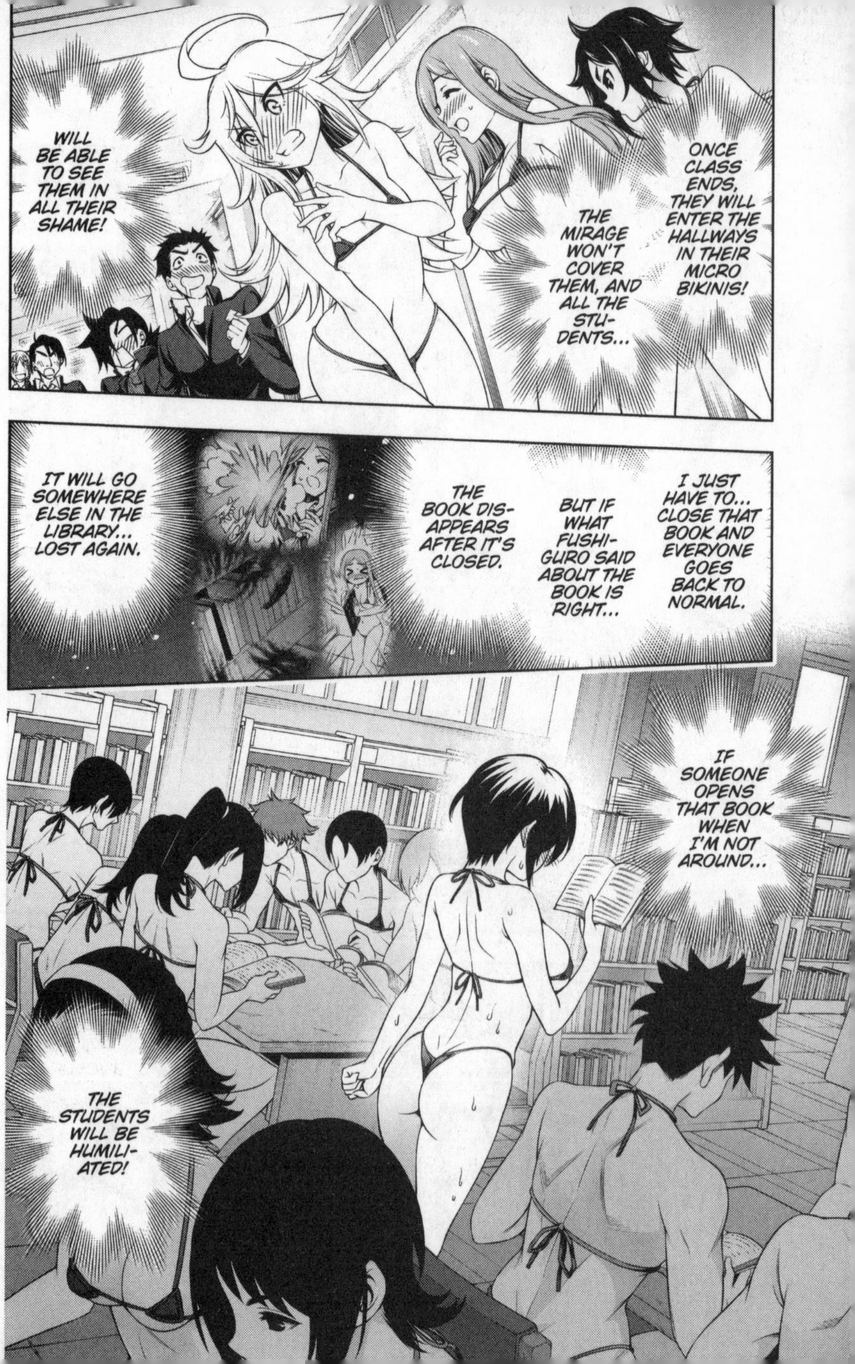
ONCE CLASS ENDS, THEY WILL ENTER THE HALLWAYS IN THEIR MICRO BIKINIS!
THE MIRAGE WON'T COVER THEM, AND ALL THE STUDENTS...
WILL BE ABLE TO SEE THEM IN ALL THEIR SHAME!
I JUST HAVE TO... CLOSE THAT BOOK AND EVERYONE GOES BACK TO NORMAL.
BUT IF WHAT FUSHIGURO SAID ABOUT THE BOOK IS RIGHT...
THE BOOK DISAPPEARS AFTER IT'S CLOSED.
IT WILL GO SOMEWHERE ELSE IN THE LIBRARY... LOST AGAIN.
IF SOMEONE OPENS THAT BOOK WHEN I'M NOT AROUND...
THE STUDENTS WILL BE HUMILIATED!

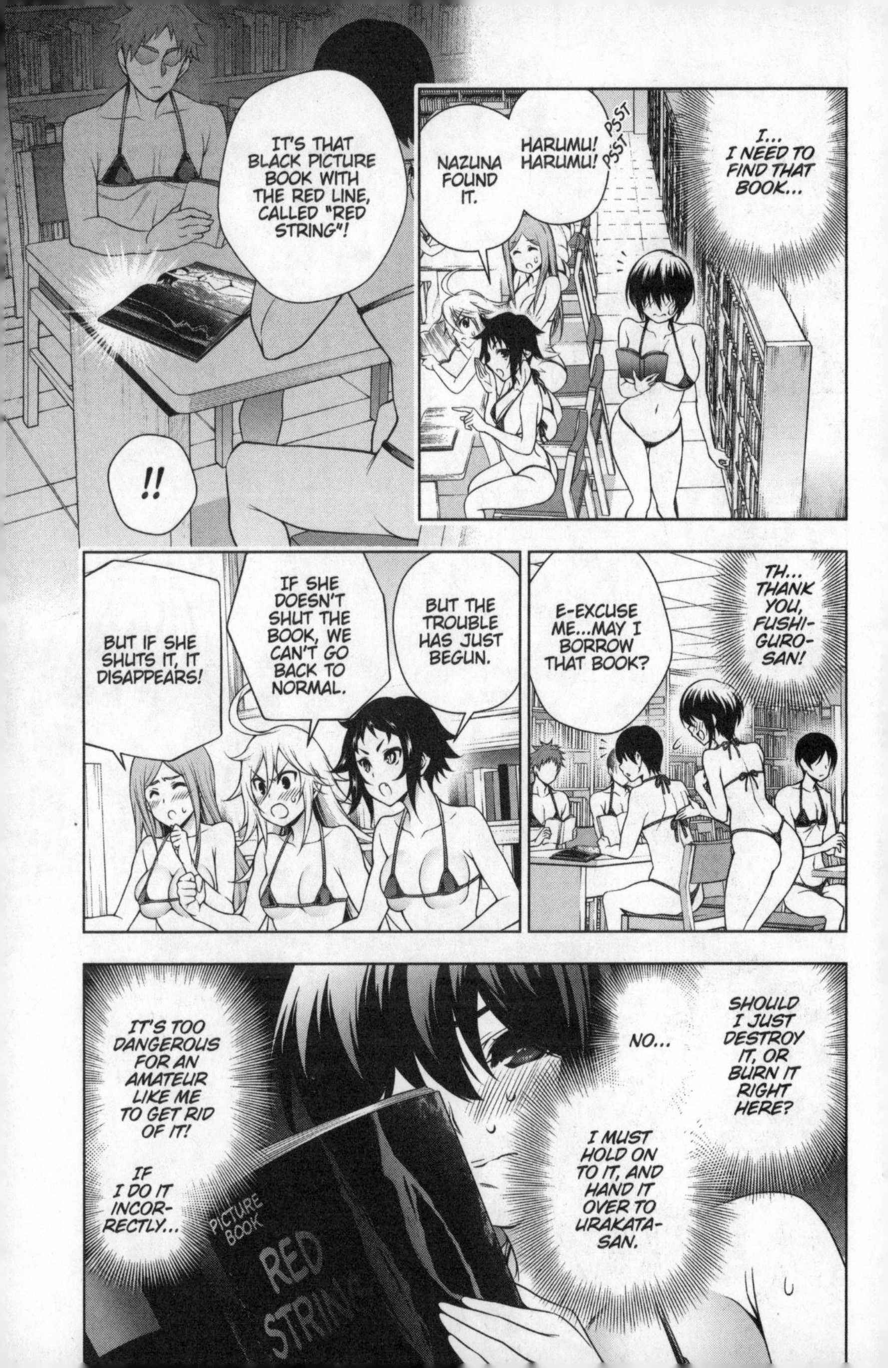
I... I NEED TO FIND THAT BOOK...
HARUMU! HARUMU!
PSST PSST
NAZUNA FOUND IT.
IT'S THAT BLACK PICTURE BOOK WITH THE RED LINE, CALLED "RED STRING"!
!!
TH... THANK YOU, FUSHIGURO-SAN!
E-EXCUSE ME...MAY I BORROW THAT BOOK?
BUT THE TROUBLE HAS JUST BEGUN.
IF SHE DOESN'T SHUT THE BOOK, WE CAN'T GO BACK TO NORMAL.
BUT IF SHE SHUTS IT, IT DISAPPEARS!
SHOULD I JUST DESTROY IT, OR BURN IT RIGHT HERE?
NO...
I MUST HOLD ON TO IT, AND HAND IT OVER TO URAKATA-SAN.
IT'S TOO DANGEROUS FOR AN AMATEUR LIKE ME TO GET RID OF IT!
IF I DO IT INCORRECTLY...
PICTURE BOOK
RED

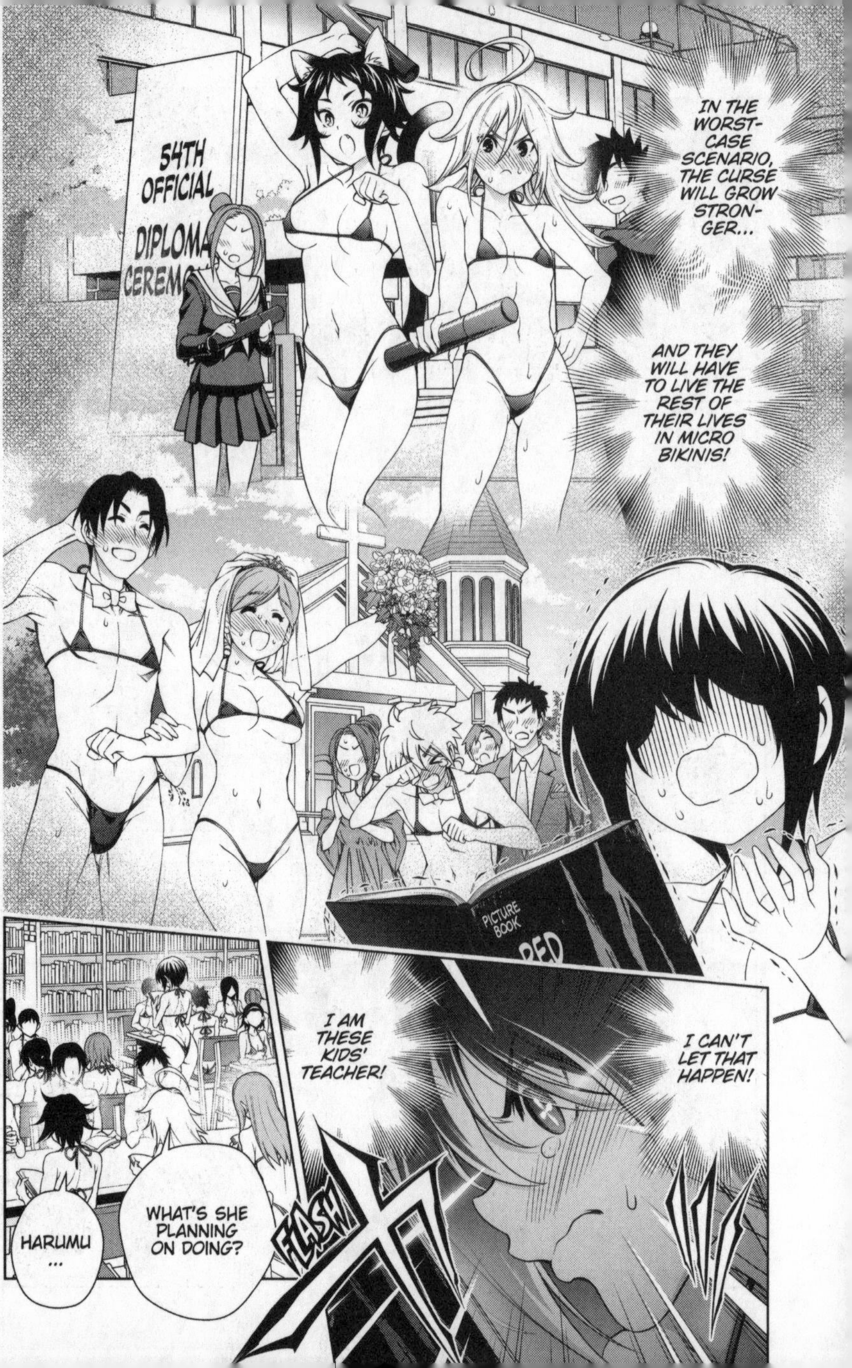
IN THE WORST-CASE SCENARIO, THE CURSE WILL GROW STRONGER...
AND THEY WILL HAVE TO LIVE THE REST OF THEIR LIVES IN MICRO BIKINIS!
54TH OFFICIAL DIPLOMA
PICTURE BOOK
RED
I CAN'T LET THAT HAPPEN!
I AM THESE KIDS' TEACHER!
FLASH
WHAT'S SHE PLANNING ON DOING?
HARUMU ...

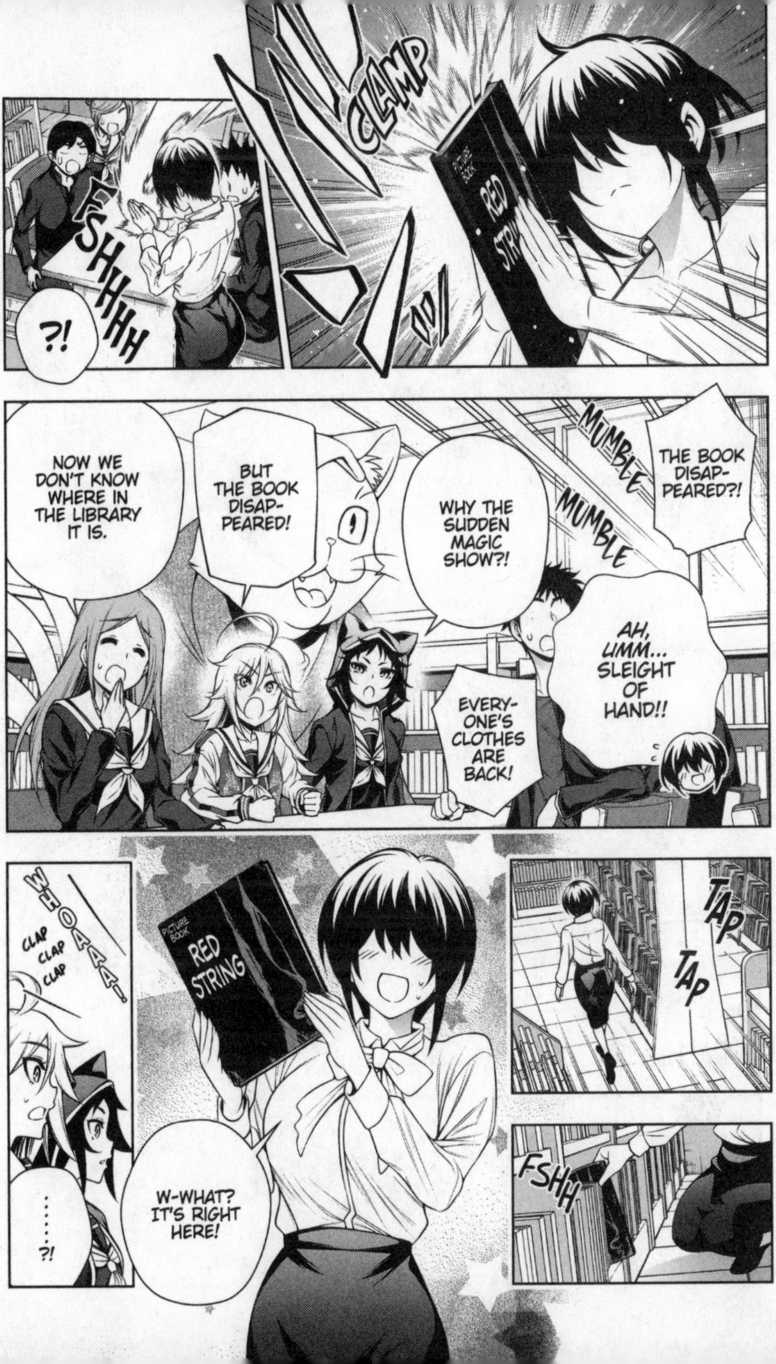
CLAMP
PICTURE BOOK
RED STRI
DD!
FSHHHH
?!
THE BOOK DISAP-PEARED?!
MUMBLE
MUMBLE
WHY THE SUDDEN MAGIC SHOW?!
BUT THE BOOK DISAP-PEARED!
NOW WE DON'T KNOW WHERE IN THE LIBRARY IT IS.
AH, UMM... SLEIGHT OF HAND!!
EVERY-ONE'S CLOTHES ARE BACK!
TAP
TAP
FSHH
PICTURE BOOK
RED STRING
W-WHAT? IT'S RIGHT HERE!
WHOAAAA!
CLAP CLAP CLAP
......?!

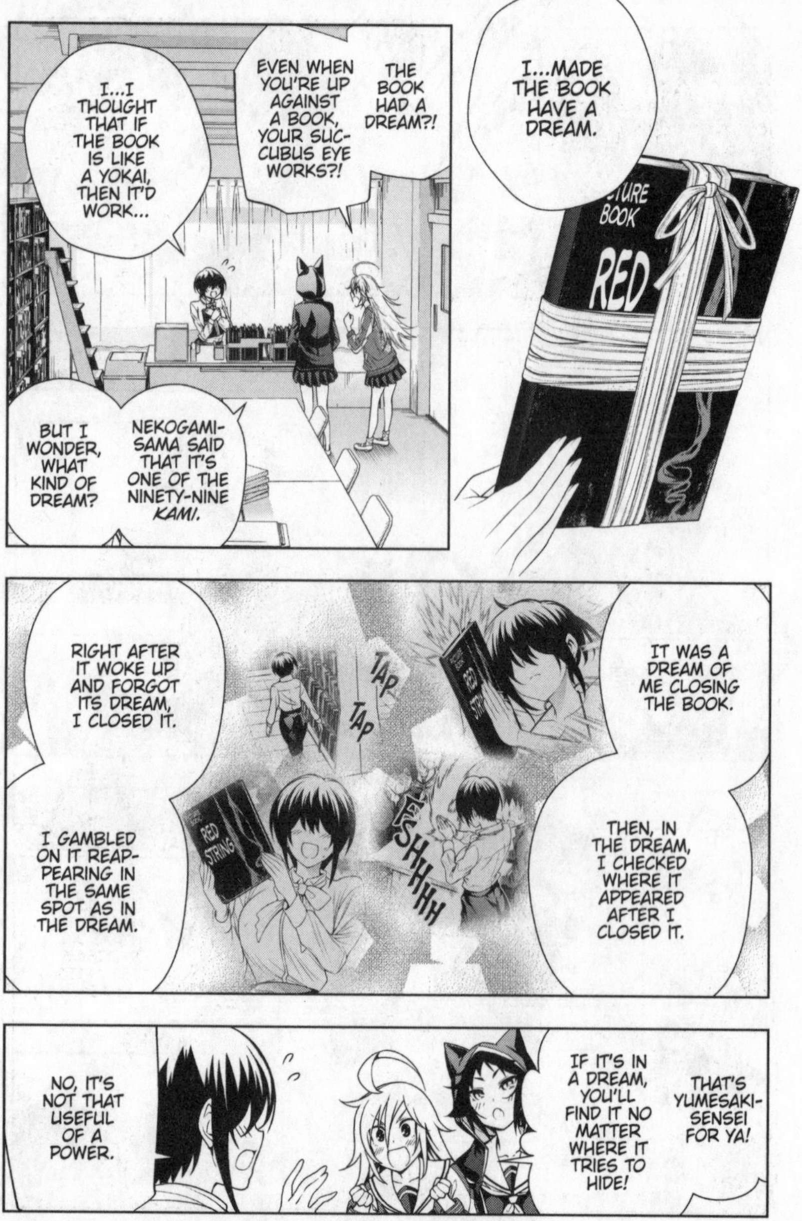
I...MADE THE BOOK HAVE A DREAM.
RED
THE BOOK HAD A DREAM?!
EVEN WHEN YOU'RE UP AGAINST A BOOK, YOUR SUCCUBUS EYE WORKS?!
I...I THOUGHT THAT IF THE BOOK IS LIKE A YOKAI, THEN IT'D WORK...
NEKOGAMI-SAMA SAID THAT IT'S ONE OF THE NINETY-NINE *KAMI*.
BUT I WONDER, WHAT KIND OF DREAM?
IT WAS A DREAM OF ME CLOSING THE BOOK.
TAP
TAP
RIGHT AFTER IT WOKE UP AND FORGOT ITS DREAM, I CLOSED IT.
THEN, IN THE DREAM, I CHECKED WHERE IT APPEARED AFTER I CLOSED IT.
FSHHHH
RED STRING
I GAMBLED ON IT REAPPEARING IN THE SAME SPOT AS IN THE DREAM.
THAT'S YUMESAKI-SENSEI FOR YA!
IF IT'S IN A DREAM, YOU'LL FIND IT NO MATTER WHERE IT TRIES TO HIDE!
NO, IT'S NOT THAT USEFUL OF A POWER.

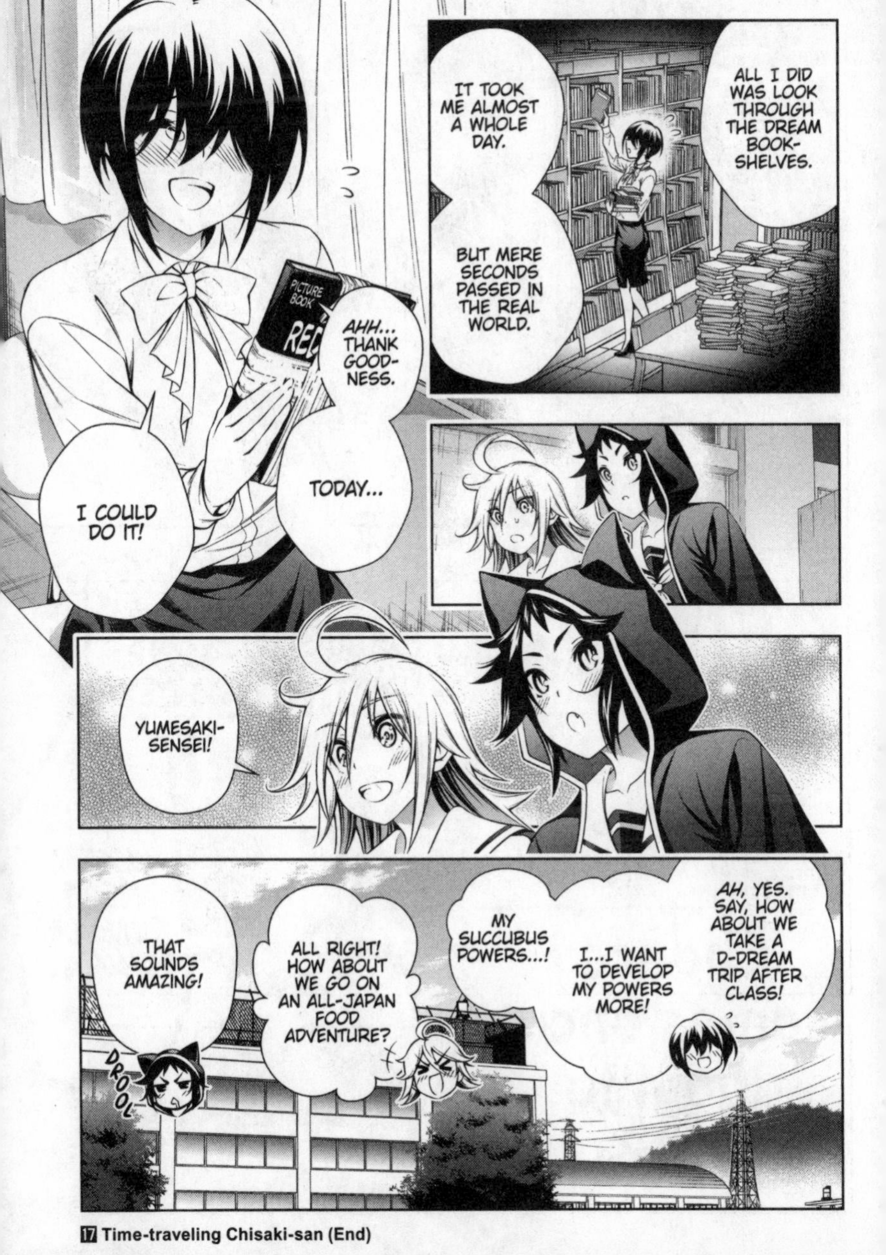
ALL I DID WAS LOOK THROUGH THE DREAM BOOK-SHELVES.
IT TOOK ME ALMOST A WHOLE DAY.
BUT MERE SECONDS PASSED IN THE REAL WORLD.
PICTURE BOOK
AHH... THANK GOODNESS.
TODAY...
I COULD DO IT!
YUMESAKI-SENSEI!
AH, YES. SAY, HOW ABOUT WE TAKE A D-DREAM TRIP AFTER CLASS!
I...I WANT TO DEVELOP MY POWERS MORE!
MY SUCCUBUS POWERS...!
ALL RIGHT! HOW ABOUT WE GO ON AN ALL-JAPAN FOOD ADVENTURE?
THAT SOUNDS AMAZING!
DROOL

17 Time-traveling Chisaki-san (End)

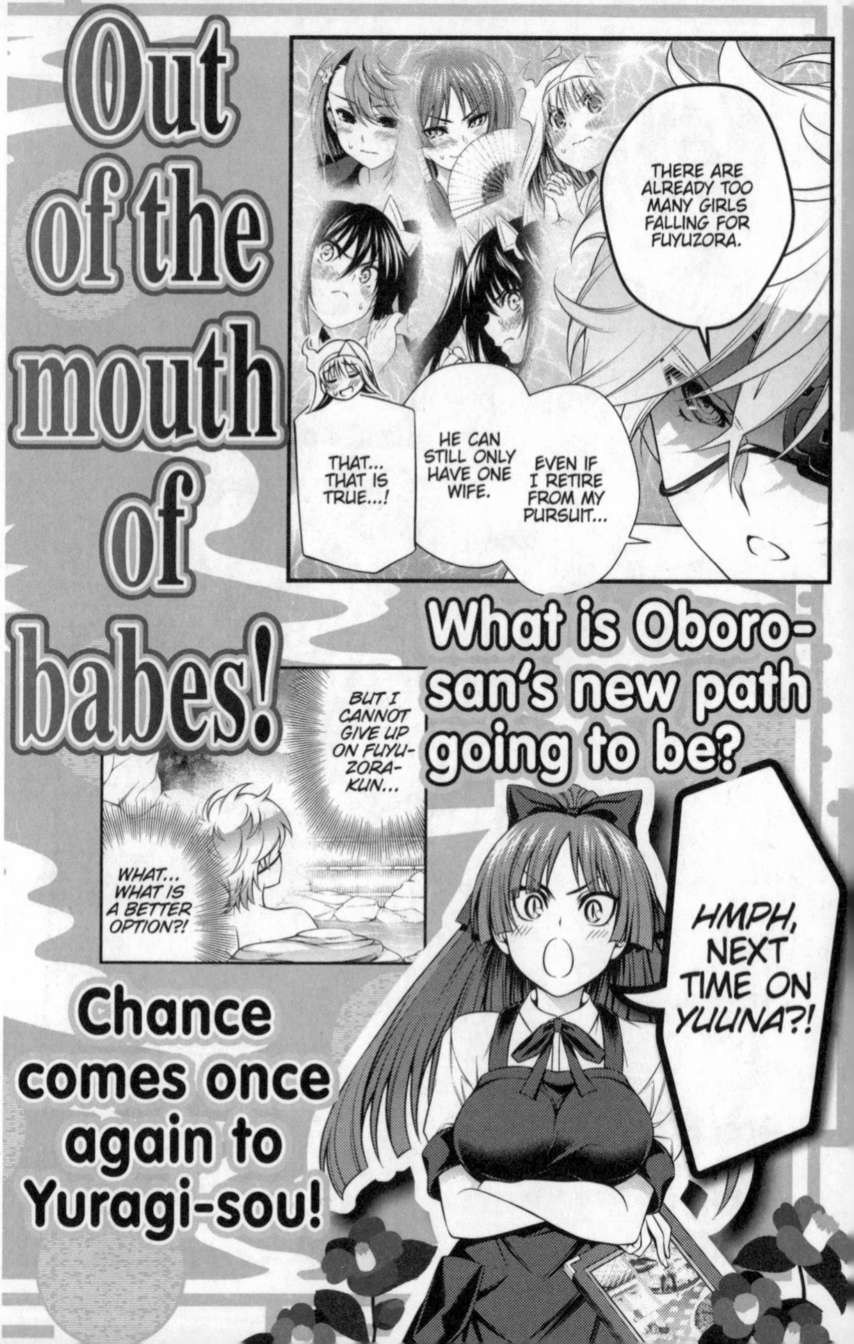
Out of the mouth of babes!
THERE ARE ALREADY TOO MANY GIRLS FALLING FOR FUYUZORA.
EVEN IF I RETIRE FROM MY PURSUIT...
HE CAN STILL ONLY HAVE ONE WIFE.
THAT... THAT IS TRUE...!
What is Oboro-san's new path going to be?
BUT I CANNOT GIVE UP ON FUYUZORA-KUN...
WHAT... WHAT IS A BETTER OPTION?!
HMPH, NEXT TIME ON YUUNA?!
Chance comes once again to Yuragi-sou!

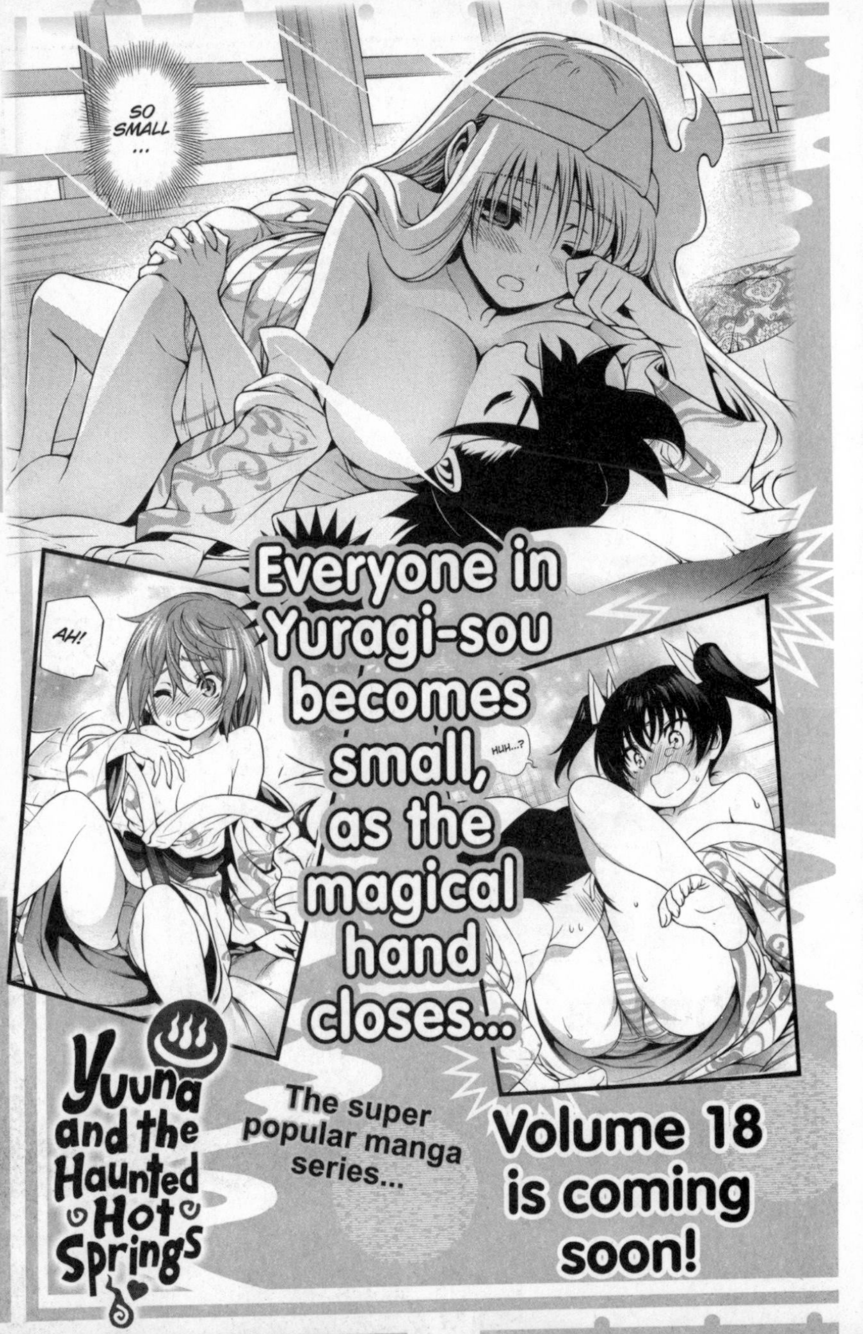
SO SMALL ...
Everyone in Yuragi-sou becomes small, as the magical hand closes...
HUH...?
AH!
Yuuna and the Haunted Hot Springs
The super popular manga series...
Volume 18 is coming soon!

Desire Pandora

story & art by
Akira Hizuki

story and art by
MEGURU UENO

1

Does a
Hot Elf
Live NEXT
DOOR to You

MASAHIRO MORIO'S
CALL GIRL in ANOTHER WORLD

1

WARNING
PARENTAL ADVISORY
EXPLICIT CONTENT

Ghost Ship

Find us online at: GhostShipManga.com

STORY AND ART BY
HARUKI

1

Cat IN A HOT GIRLS' DORM

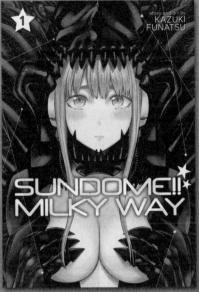

story and art by
KAZUKI FUNATSU

1

SUNDOME!! MILKY WAY

1-2

Story & Art by
Rui Takato

Booty Royale
Never Go Down Without a Fight!

DO YOU LIKE BIG GIRLS?

story & art by
Goro Aizome

1

HOKUEI

Dedicated to **SEXY** manga for **MATURE** readers!

SEVEN SEAS' GHOST SHIP PRESENTS

Yuuna and the Haunted Hot Springs VOL.17

story and art by TADAHIRO MIURA

TRANSLATION
Thomas Zimmerman

LETTERING AND RETOUCH
Phil Christie

COVER DESIGN
Nicky Lim
(LOGO) **Hanase Qi**

PROOFREADER
Kurestin Armada, Dawn Davis

EDITOR
Nick Mamatas

PREPRESS TECHNICIAN
Melanie Ujimori

PRINT MANAGER
Rhiannon Rasmussen-Silverstein

PRODUCTION MANAGER
Lissa Pattillo, George Panella (GHOST SHIP)

MANAGING EDITOR
Julie Davis

ASSOCIATE PUBLISHER
Adam Arnold

PUBLISHER
Jason DeAngelis

YUUNA AND THE HAUNTED HOT SPRINGS
YURAGISO NO YUUNA-SAN © 2016 by Tadahiro Miura
All rights reserved.
First published in Japan in 2016 by SHUEISHA Inc., Tokyo.
English translation rights arranged by SHUEISHA Inc.
through TOHAN CORPORATION, Tokyo.

Seven Seas press and purchase enquiries can be sent to Marketing Manager
Lianne Sentar at press@gomanga.com. Information regarding the distribution
and purchase of digital editions is available from Digital Manager CK Russell
at digital@gomanga.com.

Seven Seas, Ghost Ship, and their accompanying logos are trademarks of
Seven Seas Entertainment. All rights reserved.

ISBN: 978-1-64827-498-5

Printed in Canada

First Printing: January 2022

10 9 8 7 6 5 4 3 2 1

FOLLOW US ONLINE: *www.ghostshipmanga.com*

READING DIRECTIONS

This book reads from *right to left*, Japanese style.
If this is your first time reading manga, you start
reading from the top right panel on each page and
take it from there. If you get lost, just follow the
numbered diagram here. It may seem backwards at
first, but you'll get the hang of it! Have fun!!

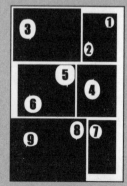